THE ART OF VERIFICATION WITH VERA

FAISAL I. HAQUE • KHIZAR A. KHAN • JONATHAN MICHELSON

Verification Central
Fremont, California
2001

Printed in the United States of America

A C.I.P. Catalog record for this book is available from the Library of Congress.

ISBN 0-9711994-0-X

To contact the publisher:

    5178 Mowry Ave, #2137
    Fremont, CA 94538
    Tel: 408-850-5860
    Fax: 408-850-5860

    sales@verificationcentral.com

For information on all Verification Central products, please visit our Web page at **www.verificationcentral.com**.

Acknowledgments

Although only the authors' names appear on the cover, this book is the culmination of a lot of hard work by many people: first and foremost, Renae Cunningham, without whose help it would not have been possible. Equally important were the patience and support of our families. Thank you, Shazia and Rachel, for putting up with our late nights and busy weekends.

Our thanks to Thomas Neuburger, who put in many painful hours in the final editing process and who was also responsible for the design and format of this book.

Our thanks go also to Eva Langfeldt, who did the first two edits on all chapters.

Special thanks to Mica Merce for the outstanding design of the front and back covers.

We would also like to thank the wonderful team at Synopsys—Shahid Khan, Diane Davis, and Mehdi Mohtashemi—without whose help this book would not have become a reality.

In addition, we owe thanks to our tremendous team of technical reviewers—Janick Beregeron, Arif Samad, Berend Ozceri, Eugene Feinberg, Salman Ahmed, Andy Peebles, Ahmed Shahid, and Yasser Khan—whose time and feedback contributed greatly to the book's accuracy.

And finally, we thank our printer, CPI, and Rick Rasmussen, whose suggestions were extremely helpful.

Preface

The exponential increase in the complexity of ASICs has made verification a critical part of the ASIC design process. In fact, by some estimates, 70 percent of the ASIC design schedule is spent in verification. This is because every bug found during simulation saves a substantial amount of time and money that would otherwise be needed to respin the chip or retrofit products in the field if a bug is found in the silicon.

As ASICs move beyond million-gate designs into multi-million gate designs, the traditional rudimentary approaches, which rely on tedious manual tests, are no longer adequate. Trade-offs need to be made between performance, efficiency, and extensibility when building testbenches. This book helps the engineer understand these trade-offs. It explains the strategies that can be used in the verification of complex ASICs. It explains strategies used to identify test cases, to generate stimulus, to check responses, and to determine coverage.

The book illustrates the implementation of these strategies using Vera and real world examples. It describes the OpenVera language and illustrates the implementation of testbenches with Vera. The Vera language is used because of the features it provides to facilitate testbench creation, concurrency, random stimulus generation and automatic response checking. Those features, along with its support of object-oriented programming and a structured RTL interface, make Vera a very attractive choice for most verification users.

We use an Ethernet MAC as an example throughout the book to demonstrate the concepts and principals being discussed.

What's in This Book? This text can be divided into three major parts:

- Verification strategies

- Vera language

- Sample testbench implementation with Vera

Chapters 1 though 3 and chapters 13 to 14 cover verification strategies:

Chapter 1 provides an introduction to verification by discussing the evolution of verification from using breadboards and silicon, to verifying hand-drawn schematics, to today's hardware verification languages.

Chapter 2 discusses the different verification strategies from identifying test cases to various mechanisms for automatic response checking.

Chapter 3 illustrates the application of these strategies to the Ethernet MAC.

Chapter 13 discusses methods for measuring the amount of the design that has been tested, which include test plan coverage, functional coverage, and code coverage. It also provides an overview of regression.

Chapter 14 focuses on an important topic: debugging. It discusses techniques and tools for debugging and provides some insights and guidelines for debugging complex designs and testbenches.

Chapters 4 through 9 cover the Vera language:

Chapter 4 discusses the basic programming constructs of Vera and takes the reader through a simple Vera program.

Chapter 5 discusses the RTL interface and explains how data is transferred between the design under test and the Vera testbench.

Chapter 6 discusses concurrency (parallelism) in Vera. It takes the reader through process spawning, process synchronization, and message passing.

Chapter 7 discusses the basic concepts of object-oriented programming and the basic object-oriented constructs in Vera.

Chapter 8 discusses object-oriented random generation features in Vera.

Chapter 9 discusses some of the more abstract object-oriented concepts such as inheritance and polymorphism.

Chapters 10 through 12 illustrate the implementation of the components of a testbench for an Ethernet MAC:

Chapter 10 discusses the stimulus generator for the MAC, and the trade-offs, and class design and use of constraints for random generation.

Chapter 11 discusses the transactors and illustrates those concepts with a transactor implementation.

Chapter 12 discusses in detail the result checking strategies the user can implement, and then illustrates the checkers and monitors used for the MAC.

Interesting Areas of the Book. The book is structured to cover the needs of a wide range of people, and although we recommend reading the entire book, it might be useful for some people to start off by reading just a few chapters.

For engineers who are new to verification, we suggest starting with chapters 1 through 3 and chapters 13 to 14.

For verification engineers who are familiar with Verilog testbenches, we recommend chapters 4 though 9 to ramp up quickly on the Vera language.

For design engineers who just want to understand verification, we recommend chapters 1, 2, and 14.

For software engineers who are familiar with C/C++ and want to get into verification, we recommend chapters 1 through 3 and chapters 4 through 9.

For engineers who are familiar with Vera but want to understand some different techniques, we recommend chapters 8, 10, 11, and 12.

For hardware and ASIC managers who want to understand and manage the verification process, we recommend chapters 1, 2, 13, and 14.

We recommend that all readers go through chapters 10, 11 and 12 once they have gained some experience in Vera, because they tie the concepts of Vera together with the concepts of verification by showing a real world testbench implementation.

Notation Used in this Book. In syntax displays throughout this book, the following conventions are used:

< >   Indicates values which must be supplied by the user

[ ]   Indicates optional arguments or fields

Contents

Figures

CHAPTER 4   Vera Programming Constructs

CHAPTER 5   RTL Ports & Interfaces in Vera

CHAPTER 6   Creating Concurrency in Vera

CHAPTER 7   Objects in Vera: Modeling Higher Levels of Abstraction

CHAPTER 12   Result Checking

CHAPTER 13   How Do I Know I Am Done?

CHAPTER 14   Debugging

Tables

CHAPTER 1

Introduction to Verification

This chapter introduces verification and reviews the chip design process and the role of verification in that process. It answers three basic questions:

- What is verification?

- What is the role of a testbench in verification?

- What is the need for high-level verification languages?

Introduction to ASIC Design

The exponential increase in the complexity of ASIC designs has made verification the most critical bottleneck in the chip design flow. Roughly 70 to 80 percent of the design cycle is spent in functional verification. It is estimated that by the year 2002, ASIC designs will reach 8 to 10 million gates. This explosion in complexity requires new approaches and new thinking in functional verification.

Testbenches need to provide more automation to maximize the functional coverage from each test case and reduce the time needed to create a test case. However, there is a tradeoff between the sophistication of the testbench and the time spent developing it. Testbench development should not be in the critical path of ASIC development; at the same time, a little sophistication in the testbench can reduce the creation time of many test cases. Thus, it's a difficult tradeoff.

Many other tradeoffs need to be made during the verification of an ASIC. In this book, we try to address these tradeoffs, as well as the implementation of the components of a testbench. This book starts with the fundamentals of functional verification. It discusses strategies and options for building an optimal verification environment tuned to the requirements of the DUT. It also covers practical approaches to building testbenches with Vera and discusses important tradeoffs.

All approaches are elaborated with practical examples to clarify the concepts. An Ethernet media access controller (Ethernet MAC) is used as a case study to illustrate the application of the verification concepts and the construction of a Vera testbench on a design. While the Ethernet (MAC) is not as complex as a multimillion-gate system-on-a-chip (SoC) design, it offers valuable insights into the verification tradeoffs and practical strategies for building the components of the testbench. The MAC testbench also provides some practical implementation examples for building testbenches in Vera.

The ASIC Design Flow

Figure 1-1 illustrates a high-level view of the ASIC design flow from specification to silicon.

Currently, the critical component in the flow is functional verification. Although functional verification is shown as a single box in Figure 1-1, it includes a complex set of activities—specifying test cases, creating a test environment, creating the actual tests, and making sure all the *interesting* cases are covered.

Functional tests are also run at the gate level to check gates-to-RTL equivalence, reset conditions, clocks, race conditions, and poor coding styles. In some flows, formal verification techniques may be used instead of or in addition to functional tests at the gate level. For large designs such as system-on-chip (SoC) designs, formal techniques are the primary means of equivalence checking. Gate-level simulations are only used for sanity testing. For smaller designs either formal or gate-level simulations may be used. Timing, usually verified with a static tool, is no longer done in simulation.

FIGURE 1-1   Basic ASIC Design Flow

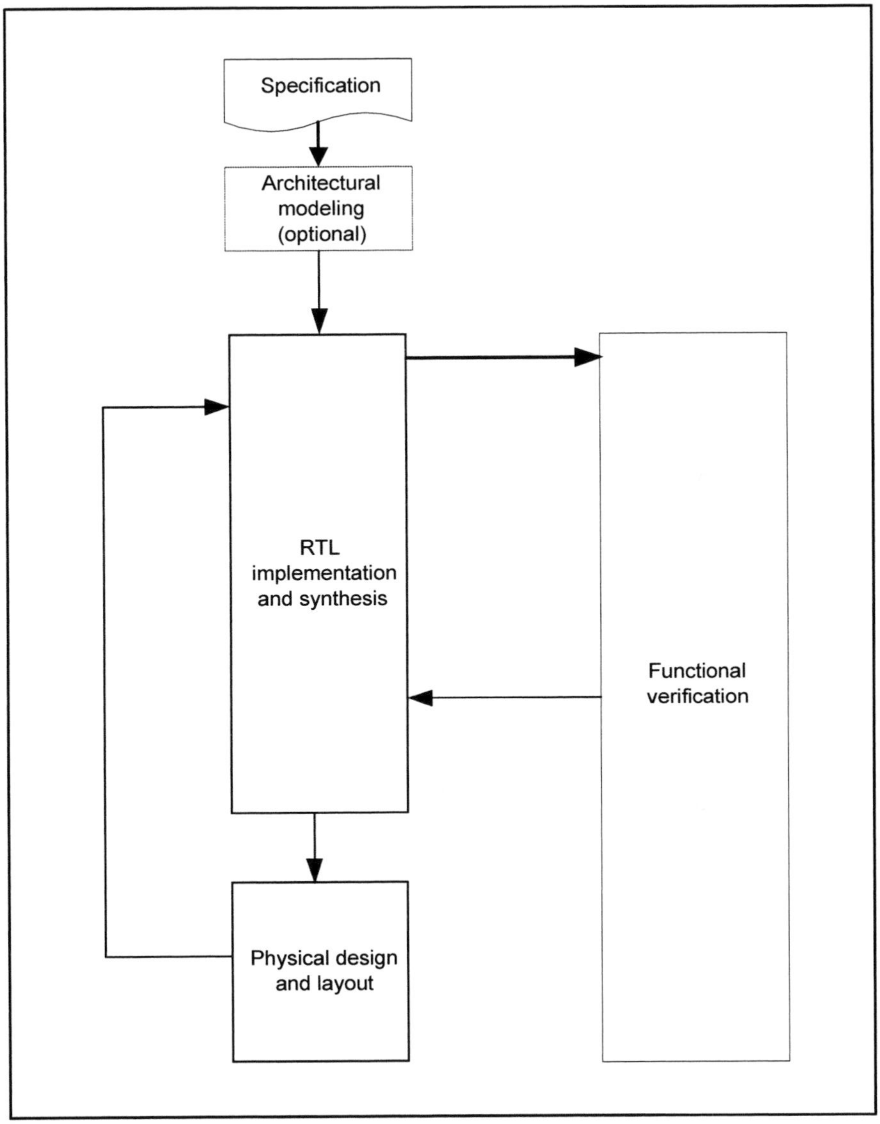

Verification activities start once the specification is almost complete and continue at least until the layout is complete. In some cases, verification may continue beyond the layout phase. The next section goes into more detail about functional verification and the verification flow.

What Is Verification?

Verification is a process for ensuring conformance of a design to some predefined set of expectations. The expectations are usually defined by one or more specifications. For ASICs, there are many forms of verification:

- Functional verification of RTL

- Gate-level simulation, to verify that the synthesized netlist matches the expected functionality

- Formal verification (equivalence checking) to make sure that the gate-level netlist is equivalent to the RTL

- Timing verification, to verify that the design can run at speed—this usually involves a static timing tool

For the purposes of this book, the term "verification" means "functional verification of RTL." The other forms of verification are outside the scope of this discussion.

Functional verification in ASIC flows focuses on the behavioral aspects of the design, and almost all of the functionality is verified at the RTL level. The test environment and the test cases are developed and the design is debugged with the RTL.

FIGURE 1-2   Role of the Testbench in Functional Verification

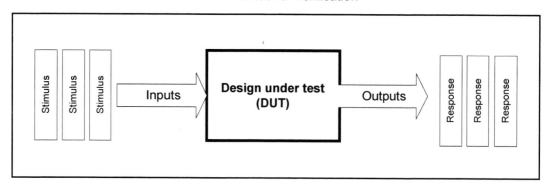

Figure 1-2 shows a high-level view of functional verification. An ASIC design can be viewed as having a set of inputs and a set of outputs. The outputs of the design are based on the inputs and the state of the design. In functional verification the engineer creates a test environment (testbench) around the DUT. The testbench is used to apply one or more sets of stimulus to the input. The stimulus may be generated by the testbench or created manually. The output is then checked for the proper response. The checking may be done by the testbench, by a script, or manually.

In the late 1970s and early 1980s, most designs were not simulated. Instead, the designer traced the flow of 0s and 1s across the logic paths by hand. This process, of course, was neither very reliable nor very comprehensive and led to frequent mistakes and bugs in the design. Ultimately, the design was verified when the actual silicon was available and run in a real board or system.

The concept of a logic simulator, which could compute the propagation of binary values across logic paths, significantly improved pre-silicon verification. The designer created binary values, which were used to *simulate* the design. The simulator computed the binary values that would appear on the output of the design, and the designer could manually check them for correctness.

The introduction of hardware description languages (HDLs), such as Verilog and VHDL, in the early 1990s brought about the use of bus models, which read stimulus from files or procedurally created the stimulus and applied it to the DUT. These bus models and the environment around the DUT came to be known as the testbench.

Functional Verification Flow

Figure 1-3 shows the functional verification flow. The verification activities can be broken down into the three major phases: determining strategy; creating, running, and debugging the tests; and regression and coverage.

Although Figure 1-3 shows a specific order of activities in the strategy phase, the process is iterative and can be done in different order. Chapter 2 and Chapter 3 use different orders of activities to illustrate the options available to the verification person.

Strategy Phase

The strategy phase deals with three major issues:

1. Interesting test cases

   The test space of today's complex designs is very large. A typical million-plus-gate design has millions—maybe billions—of possible test cases. Narrowing that test space down to a manageable and practical set without compromising the functionality is the first step.

2. Level of abstraction of the testbench

   The level of abstraction of the testbench determines whether it deals primarily with bytes, packets, or a higher-level data structure. A higher level of abstraction enables automation of the lower-level functions in the testbench.

   For example, an Ethernet testbench running at a bit level of abstraction would require the verification engineer to craft each test case by hand by individually creating each packet. However, if the same testbench deals at a higher level of abstraction, for example, the packet level, it can automatically generate and inject packets rather than requiring the verification person to create packets manually. This approach tremendously reduces test case creation time and allows better test coverage. It frees up the verification engineer to focus on hard-to-find corner cases. It also raises the abstraction of the testbench to a level similar to that of the DUT and makes it easier to create test cases and check results.

   However, there is a tradeoff in control. With lower-level testbenches, the verification person has far more control over the stimulus and the test case and can create very specific scenarios. However, at a higher level of abstraction the verification engineer does not have that control. To hit specific scenarios, he or she may have to create special code, which leads to some inefficiencies. Nonetheless, a well-constructed testbench can minimize those inefficiencies.

FIGURE 1-3   Verification Flow

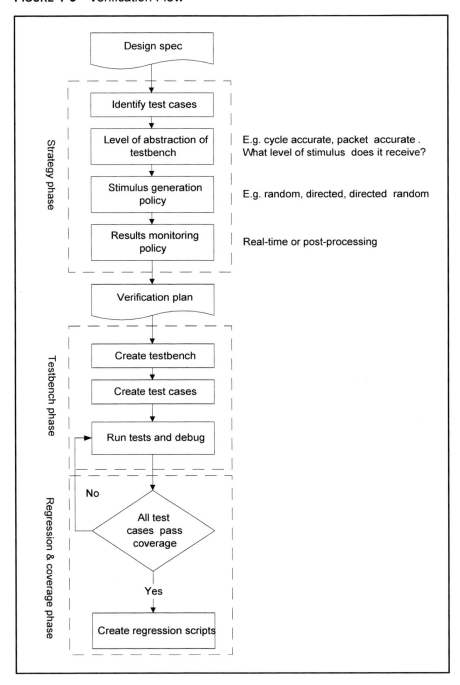

For example, in a PCMCIA interface, the level of abstraction can be at the byte or the word level. In an Ethernet MAC, if the testbench operates at the byte or word level, the packets have to be created by hand. If, however, the level of abstraction is the packet, the user can specify a range of values for the packet headers and the number of packets. The testbench can then generate the packet and check the output of the MAC to verify that the packets are received properly.

At an even higher level of abstraction, that of the network switch, the engineer could construct a test that would generate various traffic patterns, in order to create congestion scenarios. In this case, the headers and payload of the packet could be randomly generated by the testbench and the user would indicate the level of congestion—that is, the arrival rate.

In an ASIC that interfaces to a disk drive, the ideal level of abstraction would probably be a sector (512-byte blocks of data).

3. Stimulus generation and results checking policies

These policies define how the input to the testbench is provided and how the results are checked to see if the test passed or failed.

The Testbench Phase

The second phase is the testbench creation, test creation, and debug phase. In this phase, the testbench is coded and the test cases are created. The testbench is continuously extended as test cases are added in this process.

The Regression & Coverage Phase

Once almost all test cases are run successfully, verification moves into the regression and coverage phase. Regression requires the ability to run tests periodically in batches, so the stimulus must be easily reproducible and pass/fail be automatically detected. Coverage shows how much of the design has been tested. This is discussed in detail in Chapter 13.

At this point, all tests should be regressible and are run periodically, daily or weekly for instance, on the DUT. The DV engineer may look at coverage to modify or add more test cases. The object is to get 100 percent coverage, or as close to 100 percent coverage as possible.

Different Verification Flows for Different Designs

Strategies must be adopted for each design

There is no best verification flow for all designs. Each design is different and has its own verification flow. For simpler designs, the stimulus generation and results checking strategies may not be explicitly defined. They would normally operate on bus-level transactions. The testbench typically uses directed stimulus, but it might not do checking. For a complex design such as a switch or router, all the stimulus generation policies and results checking policies are defined. Typically, testbenches for these designs operate at a much higher level of abstraction; for example, a switch testbench might deal not just with packets, but also with a variety of packet arrival patterns. It might create a uniformly distributed traffic pattern, or it might create congestion scenarios.

Scope of testbenches: unit, chip and multichip

The verification flow also depends somewhat upon the scope of the testbench, meaning the amount of the RTL it covers. For example, a chip can be broken down into several blocks. Therefore, you could have a separate, unit-level testbench for each block. You could also have a testbench that operates only at the chip level. Some designs, where the chips are designed to work as a system, can even have multichip or system-level testbenches.

The primary objective of unit-level testbenches is to help debug the various blocks being implemented within the chip to make the block-level integration of the chip much easier, whereas chip-level testbenches test primarily the interaction between the blocks.

What Does the Testbench Do?

The main purpose of a testbench is to

- Generate the stimulus

- Apply stimulus to the DUT

- Check results to verify that the test was successful—that is, the output of the DUT conformed to expectations

Generating Stimulus

Distinction between binary stimulus and user stimulus

It is important to make a distinction between binary stimulus and user stimulus. Binary stimulus is a sequence of 1s and 0s driven into the inputs of the DUT. User stimulus, on the other hand, is a directive from the user to the testbench to perform some operation. In very primitive testbenches, binary stimulus and user stimulus can be the same.

Approaches to generating user stimulus

There are many approaches to generating user stimulus, varying from directed to fully random. If the binary stimulus is derived from user-provided input, it is known as directed testing. If the binary stimulus is generated randomly with a seed, it is known as random testing. There is a big spectrum in testbenches, ranging from completely directed to completely random. These are covered in more detail in later chapters.

FIGURE 1-4   Manually Created Binary Stimulus

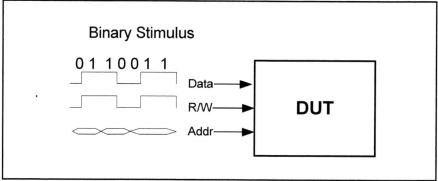

Stimulus generation in simple testbenches

In the most primitive testbenches, the stimulus is created as binary vectors on a cycle-by-cycle basis by the user. In testbenches with a little more sophistication—for example, PCMCIA or PCI testbenches—the stimulus may be created by the user, but at a higher level—for example, "Read a byte from address XXh and generate interrupt." (See Figure 1-5.) The testbench takes this user directive and generates the bus transactions. For the above case, it will initiate a read cycle on the host side and an interrupt cycle on the card side.

FIGURE 1-5   Verilog Tasks to Generate Binary Stimulus

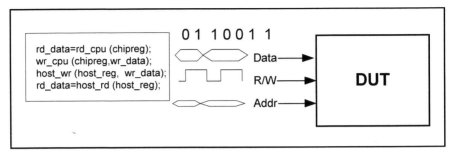

In a much more sophisticated testbench, the stimulus is completely generated by the testbench, based on user-specified constraints (see Figure 1-6). For example, the user could constrain the packet size to between 64 bytes and 1,522 bytes and set a distribution pattern for minimum-size and maximum-size packets. The user could also set up a distribution pattern for the packet arrival rate. The testbench would then generate and inject the packets.

FIGURE 1-6   Complex Testbenches Use a Generator to Generate Stimulus

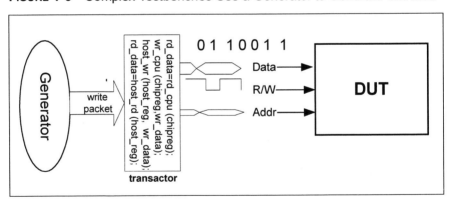

Applying Binary Stimulus

Ultimately, the testbench must inject one or more sequences of binary vectors into the DUT. Testbenches that operate at higher levels of abstraction take higher-level user stimulus. Binary stimulus is generated by the testbench and then applied with the appropriate interface to the DUT. The part of the testbench that performs this function is generally referred to as the transactor, the bus functional model (BFM), or the stub. In this book, the term transactor will be used. In a device that has many interfaces, there can be many transactors. One of the first tasks is to identify the number of transactors that a particular testbench will need.

Figure 1-7 shows a PCMCIA testbench block diagram.

FIGURE 1-7 PCMCIA Interface Testbench

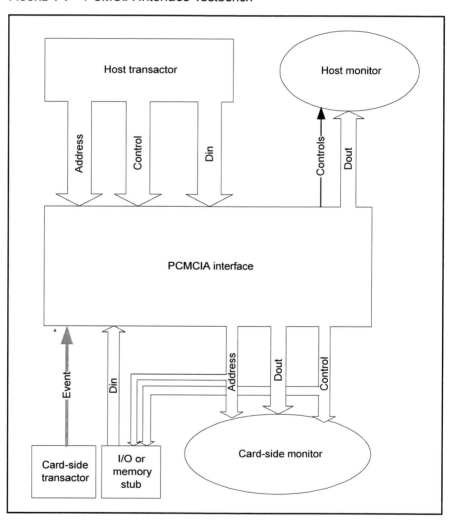

PCMCIA implements an expansion bus protocol which primarily deals with 16-bit and 8-bit transfer across the interface as well as some system events.In the PCMCIA interface, the transactor can take commands to generate certain types of cycles or events.

In this environment, there are two transactors, the host side and the card side. The card-side transactor is used only to generate events such as ring, interrupt, status_change, and power_up.

The host-side transactor is used to read and write to the I/O and memory stubs on the card side. The other element this figure shows is monitors, which brings up the next topic: checking results.

Both transactors are synchronous and driven by the same user directives.

Checking Results

Generating and applying binary stimulus to the DUT is one aspect of verifying a feature. The other is to make sure the output of the DUT is what was expected—that is, to check the results. You can check results in many ways:

- Do visual checking

- Do automatic postprocessing: log the output of the DUT and run scripts to process them

- Implement real-time monitors that check results on the fly

Some tradeoffs are associated with each of these approaches.

Regressibility requires self-checking testbenches

Visual checking works only for very simple designs. No development is needed, but it is prone to human error and not very accurate. If regressions are used for these designs, some kind of automation is required for results checking.

Postprocessing of results is good, because it does not add more code and thus does not impact the simulation performance unless there is excessive logging, in which case the file I/O slows down simulation. In complex designs, you must carefully think through output logging. If all outputs are logged at every clock, the log file can become huge, even for small tests, in designs with many outputs and multiple interfaces. However, outputs can be logged at various levels of abstraction to reduce the log file size.

An added benefit of postprocessing, in purely HDL-based testbenches, is that it can be done with powerful languages such as Perl. The main problem in post-processing is that bugs are detected only after the entire test is complete, which results in wasted simulation cycles. Debugging is also more difficult, since the necessary state information may not also be logged.

Real-time monitors require additional development and, in most cases, slow simulation down somewhat. However, they are useful for debugging because they can flag an error as soon as it happens, so the state of the simulator and the testbench is completely visible to the user at that time. It also saves CPU cycles by stopping the simulation at the time the error occurs.

In most complex designs, testbenches use a combination of postprocessing and real-time checking, depending on the complexity of the design, the number of interfaces, and the scope of the testbench.

Problems of Verification

Today, with design complexity growing rapidly, the level of abstraction for system modeling has also increased tremendously. Verilog and VHDL can not easily model the complex data structures needed for complex testbenches. This gives rise to other approaches, such as linking Perl or C with Verilog, where Perl or C routines interface to the simulator through the PLI. Both approaches use a second language to model the high-level data structures and algorithms implemented in complex designs.

Along with the complexity of the design, the test space has also expanded. The number of I/Os and interfaces has grown so much that covering the entire test space with specific tests could take years. This increase in the test space requires automatic stimulus generation, which forces the testbench to create data randomly and use a higher level of abstraction.

Building testbenches for complex designs

In Verilog/Perl environments, Perl is used to create the stimulus and check the response, while Verilog is used to apply the stimulus to the DUT. Verilog still has to model some of the system behaviors, which can be quite complex.

In Verilog/C environments, C routines interface to Verilog bus models through the PLI interface. C is used to model the higher-level data structures and algorithms of the system, while Verilog implements lower-level functionality. However, neither Perl nor C have very powerful concurrency constructs, nor do they have the concept of other hardware constructs—such as clocks, ports, wires, and "x" or "z" values—that are needed for hardware emulation. These constructs must be created by the user and thus require some development effort.

Hardware Verification Languages (HVLs)

To address some of the problems in functional verification, special hardware verification languages such as Vera and *e* have been defined. These languages provide the high-level data structures available only in object-oriented languages, such as C++ and Java. These data structures enable a higher level of abstraction and modeling of complex data types, such as linked lists, queues, and hashes in testbenches. They also provide randomization capabilities to automate the generation of stimulus.

In addition to data structures, the HVLs also provide constructs necessary for modeling hardware concepts such as time, cycles, tri-state values, wires, buses, and concurrency. Vera also provides a well-defined, structural RTL interface, and string processing and file I/O capabilities useful in processing user inputs. In addition, Vera provides the Vera Stream Generator, used to generate stimulus sequences.

The Vera language consists of these capabilities:

- Basic programming constructs

- RTL interface and hardware constructs

- Object-oriented programming concepts

- Random stimulus generation

- Temporal checking

This book describes the Vera language in detail, starting in Chapter 3 with basic programming constructs. It then talks about the Vera RTL interface, hardware constructs, object-oriented programming, and random stimulus generation. The last section brings the entire language together by illustrating the construction of the major pieces of an actual testbench using Vera. Since temporal expressions were introduced into the Vera language as this book was being published, these will be covered in the next edition.

CHAPTER 2

Developing Verification Strategies

This chapter discusses many of the important high-level strategy decisions that should precede the implementation of verification. These decisions include creating the test plan and deciding on stimulus generation and error checking methodologies. Before the chapter delves into the details of these subjects, it introduces a simple Ethernet switch, which will be used as an example.

Ethernet Switch Example

Externally, an Ethernet switch is made up of some number of Ethernet ports. It receives Ethernet packets from any of its ports and forwards them to their destination ports. Common Ethernet switches have from four to dozens of ports. The typical example is a simplified four-port Ethernet switch, such as the one shown in Figure 2-1.

FIGURE 2-1   A Four-Port Ethernet Switch

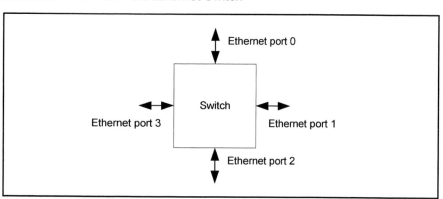

The Primary Blocks of an Ethernet Switch

As shown in Figure 2-2, Ethernet switches contain five primary blocks: an input data path (IPD), an output data path (ODP), a forwarding engine, a switch fabric, and an Ethernet interface block.

FIGURE 2-2   The Five Primary Blocks of an Ethernet Switch

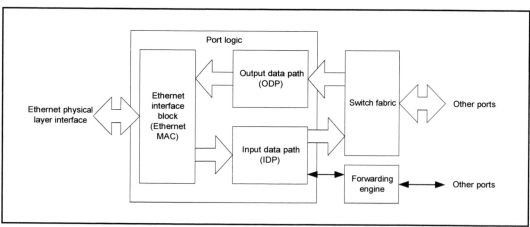

The forwarding engine decides where each packet should go, and the switch fabric routes packets from the input data paths to the output data paths. The Ethernet interface block, commonly called the Ethernet MAC, connects the

input and output data paths to the Ethernet physical layer interface. The input and output data paths have rate-matching FIFOs, because the switch fabric may not send and receive packets at the same rate as the Ethernet MAC.

The combination of the input data path, output data path, and Ethernet MAC is called the port logic. While the port logic is replicated for all ports regardless of system size, there is usually only a single forwarding engine and a single switch fabric in switches with eight or fewer ports. Figure 2-3 shows the typical configuration of a four-port switch.

FIGURE 2-3 The Blocks Within a Four-Port Ethernet Switch

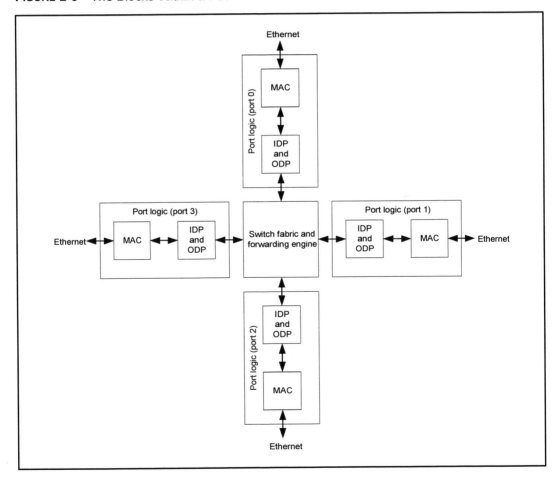

Packets in the Ethernet Switch

As Figure 2-4 shows, the packets traveling through the Ethernet switch have three components: a header, a data payload, and an error detection field. The packet header specifies the source Ethernet address, the destination Ethernet address, and the payload length. The data payload needs to be transferred from the input data path on the source port to the output data path on the destination port. The error detection field contains a cyclic redundancy check (CRC) code.

FIGURE 2-4   Packets in the Ethernet Switch

Header	Source address	Destination address	Payload length
Payload	Data		
Error detection	CRC		

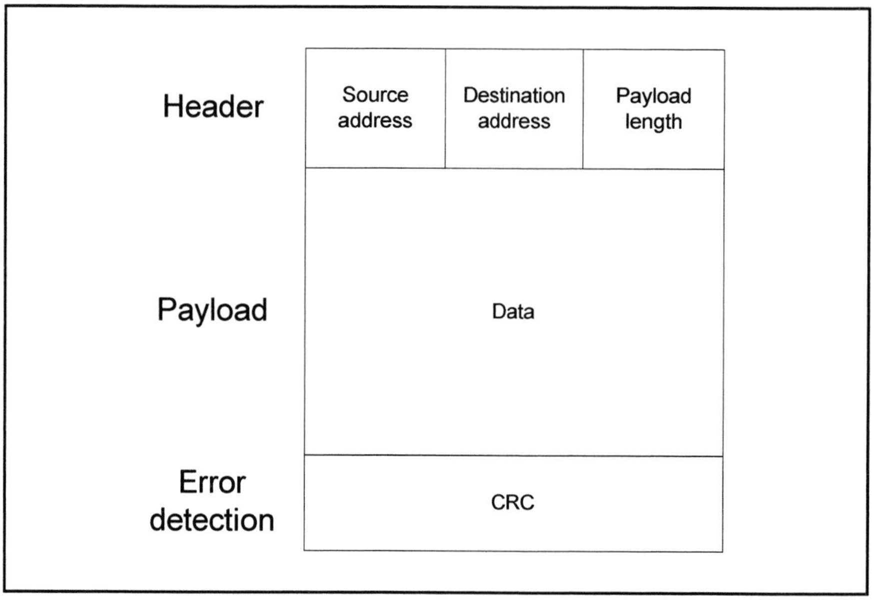

Forwarding Algorithm

The Ethernet switch figures out the proper destination port by keeping an internal table that maps Ethernet addresses to ports in the switch. Whenever an input port receives a packet, the switch does two lookups in its table. First, it looks up the port of the source Ethernet address, in case that source address is not in the address mapping table already. If the switch does not find an entry, it creates one and adds the port that received the packet to the table as the translation for the packet's source address. After this, the switch can properly forward packets to the source device.

The switch next looks up the destination port. If the destination port does not have an entry in the port mapping table, the switch does not know where to forward the packet. Although there are many ways to handle this situation, the Ethernet switch in these examples broadcasts the packet to all destination ports. If the switch finds the destination address in the port mapping table, the input port forwards the packet to the destination port returned by the lookup table.

Crossbar Architecture

Although there are many switch fabric architectures, this chapter discusses a simple crossbar architecture. Generally speaking, crossbars are fancy multiplexers with multiple data paths that can transmit data between more than one source/destination pair at the same time.

Figure 2-5 shows a single port of a crossbar. Each port can send a packet to other ports while simultaneously receiving a packet from any single port. For example, a crossbar can transmit a packet from port 0 to port 1 while simultaneously transmitting a packet from port 2 to port 0. In this example, port 0 is both sending and receiving a packet whereas ports 1 and 2 are only sending or receiving a packet.

The crossbar scheduler makes the arbitration decision about which input ports are sending to which output ports. The crossbar receives destination port requests from the input data paths and returns destination port grants. When the input data path receives a grant, it sends the appropriate packet to the crossbar.

FIGURE 2-5   A Single Port of a Crossbar

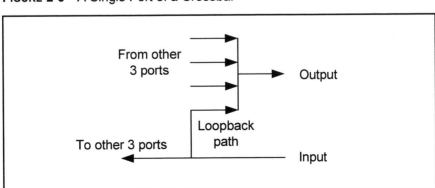

Verifying an Ethernet Switch

The switch architecture poses many interesting verification challenges, starting with its forwarding capabilities. Each input packet needs to exit the correct destination port uncorrupted. Within this broad statement, there are three axes of testing: packet contents, packet location, and packet timing:

- Packets can contain many combinations of payloads and payload lengths (packet contents).

- Any packet can be received by any input port and be destined for any output port (packet location).

- Finally, each input port can simultaneously receive and forward a unique sequence of these packets (packet timing).

The switch needs to function properly in every possible combination of these situations.

After the switch's forwarding capabilities are verified, higher level properties, such as fairness and starvation, need to be verified. Although many definitions of fairness are possible, one definition is that each input port forwards an equal number of packets per unit time.

While the switch should be fair, it should never starve an input port, which occurs when an input port is never allowed to forward a packet. If your computer were connected to a starved port, your Web surfing would not be very satisfying.

Although it is important to verify fairness and starvation in such an arbiter, it is difficult to do so, and it is usually done after the basics of the DUT have been verified. A discussion of fairness appears later in this chapter. The more basic verification tasks are discussed first, starting with the creation of the test plan.

Creating the Test Plan

With today's large, complex ASICs and full custom designs, design verification is on the critical path of the design flow. Although design and verification can overlap, verification is not complete until all features in the final design have been successfully tested.

As this chapter demonstrates, successful verification involves many steps over a long period of time. The test plan is a tool to help organize the efforts of the verification engineer by listing the time and resources necessary for adequate verification of all features of the DUT. Specifically, it lists

- All of the test cases, or functionality checks, required to adequately verify the DUT. Because each test case verifies the correct operation of a specific subset of design functionality, typical designs require anywhere from dozens to thousands of test cases for complete verification.

- All of the testbenches, or verification infrastructures, needed to implement these test cases. Because each testbench implements many test cases, complete verification of a typical design is usually accomplished with a few dozen or fewer testbenches. Testbenches are commonly named after the portion of the design to which they apply test cases.

- All of the time estimates needed to complete the test cases and testbenches.

- An educated guess about how much time will be spent diagnosing and fixing bugs in the DUT.

Figure 2-6 shows an example test plan for the Ethernet switch described above. The time estimates shown in Figure 2-6 include the time required to build and debug the relevant testbenches and test cases. They also include estimates for the amount of time to be spent debugging the DUT.

Accurate test plans are nearly impossible

Unfortunately, creating a complete and accurate test plan before any testing has begun is nearly impossible. New test cases and missing corner cases are always discovered throughout verification, as designers and verification engineers think through the operation of a design. New feature requests commonly add new test cases after verification has begun. Additionally, time estimates on first-pass test plans tend to be optimistic, because the verification engineers haven't fully realized the complexity of implementing the tests they have outlined and the effort required to debug the testbench and DUT.

Test plans help verification engineers

The list of tests in a test plan is extremely useful for verification engineers. Not only does the test plan help organize their efforts, but it also helps them decide on the higher-level verification policies up front. These policies, such as the type of testbench to be used, are discussed later in this chapter.

FIGURE 2-6 The Test Plan for the Ethernet Switch

Ethernet Switch Test Plan		
Testbench	Test Case (Features)	Time Estimate (Days)
Input data path (IDP)		5
	Packets of all lengths to 1 destination	2
	Packets of all lengths to all destinations	2
	With random gaps between received packets	2
	With random gaps between XB grants	2
	FIFO underflow (extra XB grant)	1
	FIFO overflow (too many packets filling IDP)	1
Output data path (ODP)		2
	Packets of all lengths from 1 IDP	2
	Packets of all lengths from all IDPs	2
	With random gaps between packets	
	FIFO overflow (too many packets filling ODP)	1
Cross bar (XB)		5
	One IDP to one ODP	2
	One IDP to all ODPs	2
	All IDPs to all ODPs	2
	With random gaps	2
	Fairness/starvation	5
Forwarding engine (FE)		5
	Neither source nor destination mapped	0.5
	Source not mapped but destination mapped	0.5
	Source mapped but destination not mapped	0.5
	Max rate, all mapped	0.5
	Max rate, nothing mapped	0.5
	Max rate, mapping random	0.5
	Neither mapped and mapping table full	0.5
	Source not mapped and mapping table full	0.5
	Destination not mapped and mapping table full	0.5
Ethernet switch		5
	One source port to one destination port, mapping random	2
	One source port to all destination ports, mapping random	2
	All source ports to all destination ports, mapping random	2
	With random gaps	1
	Maximum rate: everything mapped	1
	Maximum rate: nothing mapped	1

Additionally, the test plan helps verification engineers determine the progress made on the overall verification job. This progress is called test plan coverage, or simply test coverage. As features are tested, test cases in the test plan are completed and coverage rises. Verification is not complete until the test plan shows 100 percent test coverage.

Breaking Down the Test Space: Testbenches

The first job when creating a test plan is to decide on the required testbenches. In general, there are three types of testbenches, used in the following order:

1. Unit or subunit

2. Full-chip

3. Multichip

As shown in Figure 2-7, unit testbenches test a portion of a chip, and full-chip testbenches include all of the units in a chip. Multichip testbenches incorporate two or more chips.

FIGURE 2-7   Unit, Full-Chip, and Multichip Testbenches

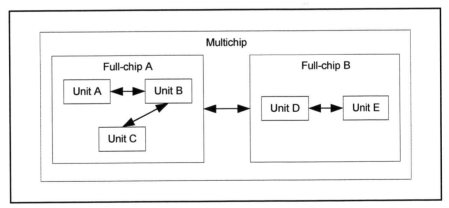

Unit Testbenches

As the name implies, unit testbenches break chips into units, or blocks, for individual testing.

Advantages of Unit Testbenches. Although it may seem more efficient to begin with a full-chip testbench, there are many advantages to unit testbenches:

- Simulation speed

- Controllability

- Bug isolation

- Verification of the basic blocks first

- Division of the verification tasks

- Earlier start

Simulation speed   Unfortunately, simulation speed is an important consideration. Even with today's fast compiled simulators, system-on-a-chip (SoC) designs are so large that it takes at least 10 times longer to simulate them as a chip than it does to simulate their blocks individually. A 10x factor may not seem like a lot, but when the number of test cases is very large, it makes a huge difference.

Controllability   At the full-chip level, it is very difficult to control the input stimulus applied to inner blocks. For example, some arbitration algorithms have a random component for breaking ties. If a verification engineer wants to control the random choices in order to control the inputs applied to the connected block or blocks, either the random function has to be perfectly modeled or it has to be overridden. Although both methods are possible, it is much easier to replace the random algorithm of the DUT with a portion of the testbench. The tests can then create the desired randomness or lack of randomness.

Bug isolation   At the full-chip level, it can be very hard to isolate bugs. Large SoC designs can have very complex interactions of large state machines, and this produces bugs. Debugging these situations is time-consuming and confusing. If state machines are tested individually, the environment creates inputs to the state machine directly, and the input combinations that cause the state machine to go awry are then known. Although there can still be bugs in the interactions of state machines after state machines are verified individually, keeping the environment simpler by eliminating other variables eases the initial debugging of each state machine substantially.

*Verification of the
basic blocks first* Breaking a design into smaller pieces also aids debugging a more fundamental way. A large, complex design will never work if its basic components do not work, and so it helps to prove that the building blocks work before trying to figure out if the entire design works. If the basic components do work but the full design does not, at least the bugs can be isolated to the interactions between working modules. As designs get larger, it is more important to be able to debug using a process of elimination.

*Division of the
verification tasks* Because today's SoC designs have thousands of lines of RTL code that must be verified in the shortest time possible, it is necessary to split the verification tasks among a few (or many) verification engineers. Although there are many ways to split the tasks, unit verification environments are helpful for doing so. The engineers responsible for each unit testbench can focus on the functionality of their units and get them done as efficiently as possible.

Earlier start From a practical point of view, unit testbenches have one more advantage. Designs with millions of gates are typically designed in parallel. Inevitably, some units will be ready before others. If each unit has its own testbench, verification can begin on those units as soon as they are designed. If only a full-chip environment is used, verification has to wait for the entire design to be finished.

Disadvantage of Unit Testbenches. The primary disadvantage of unit level testbenches is the number of testbenches which must be created, used, and maintained. Because the overhead of many testbenches can become substantial, the number of testbenches should be kept small, but not so small that the advantages of having them are eliminated.

Unit Testbench Candidates. Major design blocks provide convenient boundaries for unit testbenches, because they tend to be well documented and because they tend to be split along easier interfaces than the inner portions of units. Of course, major units are also usually sectioned for the ease of the designers, which makes them easy for verification engineers to work on as well. In Figure 2-6, the major blocks named in the functionality description of the switch have been sectioned into individual testbenches.

Full-Chip Testbenches

Unfortunately, testing is not complete after the unit testbenches and unit tests have shown their units to be bug-free. There can still be bugs in the connectivity and interaction of the units. Because different engineers design various units, they can make different assumptions about the timing or polarity of interface wires. Although these bugs might be found before the units are connected, verification cannot be considered complete until a full-chip testbench verifies that nothing has been overlooked.

Additionally, some algorithms and protocols might be distributed across multiple units. Although a unit testbench can verify that its unit implements its specification correctly, it cannot verify that the multiunit algorithm or protocol was designed properly. Only a multiunit or full-chip testbench can do that. Commonly, multiunit testbenches are created for testing the interactions of tightly coupled units, once the units have been verified individually. Sometimes, those intermediate testbenches are skipped and a full-chip test environment is used.

For these reasons, full-chip testbenches are required. It would be wonderful if the unit testbenches found all of the bugs in the connectivity and interaction of the units. Unfortunately, it rarely works this way in practice.

Multichip Testbenches

Although multichip testbenches are only applicable when the final design consists of two or more chips, the same reasoning that argues for full-chip testbenches applies as well to multichip testbenches. Setting up multichip environments is not trivial, because these testbenches sometimes test the limits of simulators, both in memory utilization and in simulation speed. Overcoming these problems can involve parallelizing the simulation across multiple processors and virtual memory spaces. A discussion of parallelization techniques is beyond the scope of this book.

Breaking Down the Test Space: Test Cases

Once the testbench decisions have been made, the next step is to break down the test space of each testbench into appropriately sized tasks. On the one hand, a test plan that states, "Test the DUT," will not suffice for accurate verification planning. On the other hand, if the test plan is too detailed, it will take too long to create.

Once each task is identified, it receives its own entry in the test plan and its own time estimate. For example, each row in Figure 2-6 is a task in the test plan. Some of the tasks in the test plan are to create testbenches.

There are three main ways to break down the test space into individual tasks:

- Test by features

- Test by interfaces

- Test by corner cases

Each of these test plan generation schemes is discussed in detail below.

Testing by Features

The easiest way to break down the test space is to list all of the design features specified in the documentation for the DUT. The resulting list, called the test-by-features test plan, must be the complete functionality list for the DUT and not the feature list that has been shortened for marketing purposes. For example, an Ethernet switch would contain the number and type of Ethernet ports; the possible combinations of packets flowing between the ports; the interaction of the forwarding engine with the flow of packets; and the worst-case operating conditions, given the implementation details of the switch. These features — including the packet lengths and possible error conditions — can be seen in the sample test plan in Figure 2-6.

Eliminating redundancy

It's important to eliminate redundancy in the test-by-features test plan. If an Ethernet switch has 1,000 ports, for example, it would be impossible to test every packet length on every port. Hopefully, the designers of the port input and output logic designed a single-port module and instantiated it 1,000 times. If they did so, testing all packet lengths on one port yields just as much verification coverage as testing all packet lengths on every port. The packet length testing could also be distributed to all 1,000 ports without compromising verification coverage. As long as every packet length has been tested on at least one port in the system, full packet length coverage is achieved.

When eliminating redundant packet length test cases, two constraints need to be kept in mind. First, there may be certain sequences of packet lengths that stress the port logic. Second, the crossbar scheduler may take into account the packet lengths of the packets available at all ports when making its arbitration decision. It is important to ensure that all of these sequences and combinations of packet lengths are tested as well. Be careful, therefore, when eliminating redundant test cases, to make sure other necessary test cases are not removed as well.

Limitations

Test by features can easily miss interesting test cases, because the internal implementation of externally visible features may be hard to infer from the external specification alone. For example, processor caches have multiple write-back policies, including write-through and write-back. The write-back policy selected will affect the logic of the design, and therefore the necessary test cases, but it should not change the result obtained by running a sequence of arithmetic operations over a given space in memory. In other words, the write-back policy selected would not change the processor's external specification but does change the test cases required for complete verification of the processor.

The differences in the design and testing of write-through and write-back caches can be summarized as follows. A write-through cache writes changes to the underlying memory every time an entry in the cache is modified. A write-back cache propagates changes to the underlying memory only when a modified entry is removed from the cache's memory. To stress the maximum write bandwidth of a write-through cache, the same entry is continually written. For a write-back cache, evicting modified entries in rapid succession tests the maximum write bandwidth. It is important to uncover which write-back policy is selected so that the proper test cases can be added to the test-by-features test plan.

In summary, there are two challenges in creating test-by-features test plans. The first is to ensure that the specification used to generate the test-by-features test plan is complete and accurate. Usually, the verification engineer needs additional information in order to generate test cases that properly verify the implementation of the high-level features described in the documentation. The second challenge, of course, is to invent the test cases that best verify the features being tested.

Testing by Interfaces

A DUT typically has multiple external interfaces. Each interface contains its own set of legal transactions or stimuli. For example, our Ethernet switch has multiple Ethernet ports. Each Ethernet port is composed of two interfaces: an interface for packets traveling from the switch to the Ethernet connector, and an interface for packets traveling from the Ethernet connector to the switch. A production-quality switch may also have a CPU interface (absent in our simplified example) to implement more complicated routing decisions, statistics gathering, and maintenance. The test cases for the test-by-interfaces test plan therefore test all packets and interface requests used to implement all features available at all the interfaces. Additional test cases explore the possible combinations of these requests.

*Designs where
testing by
interfaces excels*
The Ethernet switch described above is actually not a good example of the power of test-by-interface test plans. Test-by-interface test plans work especially well with buses with complex protocols, such as PCI or cache coherent processor buses. On these buses, many common sequences are specified by the protocols. Those sequences form the start of a test-by-interfaces test plan. Many lower-probability sequences are also possible on the buses, and studying the protocols can reveal them. Those lower-probability sequences reveal interesting test cases that can easily be missed by other types of test plans, and those test cases have high probabilities of finding bugs.

*Eliminating
redundancy*
Much like test-by-features test case deconstructions, identifying patterns that test the same logic can similarly eliminate redundant test-by-interfaces test cases. For example, in the Ethernet switch, a packet of length 100 followed by a packet of length 200, both destined for port 0, tests almost exactly the same logic as the same sequence of packets destined for port 1. The only differences between those two cases are the destination decoder and the connectivity of the destination request into the crossbar. Those are certainly features that needed to be tested, but packets of other lengths destined for those ports also test them. In general, the packet lengths do not affect the destination request made to the crossbar. Of course, a good verification engineer will find any cases in which the seemingly unconnected features do interact to create a bug.

Limitations
The primary limitation of testing by interfaces is that for simple interfaces, it does not add many test cases beyond what a test-by-features test plan reveals. However, there are two additional limitations. First, testing by interfaces can easily miss features in the DUT that require more than a legal sequence of transactions on an interface. For example, the same legal sequence of transactions can have different results, depending on the internal state of the design. Unless the test-by-interfaces test plan includes methods for modifying the internal state of the design and then replaying the same legal sequence of transactions, thus stimulating all of the possible outcomes, it will miss test cases. Second, the test-by-interfaces test plan might have found all the sequences necessary to stimulate a bug without injecting them in the correct order.

Both of these test-by-interfaces limitations can be overcome by combining a test-by-interfaces test plan with a test-by-features test plan. Combining these plans reveals which interface sequences have multiple results and which sequences need to be combined to stimulate a feature.

Testing by Corner Cases

There are two types of corner cases: (1) the boundary conditions of a DUT feature and (2) the boundary conditions of the DUT implementation of a feature. In the Ethernet switch, the smallest and largest legal Ethernet packets are the boundary conditions and, therefore, corner cases of packet reception and transmission. These boundary conditions are not necessarily corner cases of the DUT implementation of packet handling, however; they are merely the boundary conditions of Ethernet packets. The smallest and largest legal packet sizes are examples of the first type of corner case. This type of boundary condition is usually specified by or easily inferred from the externally published feature set of the design.

The boundary conditions of an implementation are different corner cases than those discussed above and are harder to find. For example, receiving continuous sequences of short packets is more difficult for an Ethernet switch than receiving continuous sequences of long packets, because of the increased rate at which forwarding decisions need to be processed in order to keep up with the arriving packets. Continuous reception of the smallest legal packet is therefore a corner case of the forwarding engine's implementation and an example of the second type of corner case.

Test-by-corner-cases test plans list all the test cases required to stimulate both corner case types. However, the corner cases of a particular feature (the first type of corner case) are usually listed in the test-by-features test plan; therefore a test-by-corner-cases test plan usually focuses on second type of corner case, that implied by the implementation of features. In the examples above, the smallest and largest Ethernet packets are specified in the test-by-features test plan, but the problem presented by a continuous stream of small packets is not.

Because test by corner cases usually focuses on the corner cases of the implementation of the DUT, it is the hardest test plan to write without detailed knowledge of that implementation. Sometimes, studying the external specification and external interfaces reveals corner cases, but it is usually the study of internal implementation that reveals them.

Pipelines contain plenty of corner cases

Pipelines are sources of plentiful test cases for test-by-corner-cases test plans, because their implementations can be complex. They nearly always have bypass logic that needs to be stimulated for complete verification of the DUT. Sometimes the designer thinks bypass logic is necessary, but the verification engineer can prove through testing that the bypass conditions never arise. More important, however, the verification engineer can detect incorrect operation resulting from missing bypass cases. In a random environment, missing bypass cases may come up; however, they may be so improbable that they need to be brought out specifically in a test-by-corner-cases test plan. (See "Random & Directed Random Testing Schemes" on page 38 for a discussion of random testing environments.) Clearly, it is the verification engineer's job to uncover missing but required bypass logic.

Limitations Although test-by-corner-cases test plans normally uncover the harder-to-find test cases and therefore the harder-to-find bugs, they easily miss important and usually basic test cases. It doesn't matter if the continuous streams of small packets mentioned above work if the Ethernet switch does not handle the first packet properly.

Summary—Test Plan Methodologies

The advantages and disadvantages of the three test plan generation schemes discussed above are summarized in Table 2-1.

TABLE 2-1   Summary of Test Plan Methodologies

	Testing by Features	Testing by Interfaces	Testing by Corner Cases
To Generate the Test Plan	List the documented features of the DUT.	List all combinations of transactions on all interfaces.	Study the implementation of DUT features.
Advantages of the Test Plan	Guarantees that advertised features are tested. Testing is not complete without full test-by-features coverage.	Exposes transactions implied by protocols supported at interfaces but not explicitly named in the DUT feature list. Exposes corner cases in complex protocols.	Finds the most complicated bugs by uncovering test cases not easily inferred from specifications or protocols.
Disadvantages of the Test Plan	Can easily miss corner cases, both from the interaction of features and from the implementation chosen.	Works best with complex protocols. Misses DUT features that require more than a sequence of transactions on an interface.	Requires detailed knowledge of DUT implementation. Misses the easy test cases.

Using all three methods is best Because each of the methodologies discussed have disadvantages, it is best to utilize all three methods to come up with a single, complete test plan. Redundancy can be eliminated, but each method normally uncovers tests undiscovered by the other methods. Therefore, utilizing all three methods helps create a complete test plan. Of course, a complete test plan helps achieve the ultimate goal for the verification engineer: a fully tested, bug-free design.

Test Generation Schemes

Once test cases are enumerated in the test plan, their stimulus needs to be generated and applied to the DUT. Test generation schemes are the general methodologies used to generate this stimulus.

This section first discusses reproducibility, a characteristic common to all test generation schemes, and also provides an overview of the schemes discussed. Then it considers the following types of test generation schemes:

- Exhaustive

- Directed

- Random and directed random

- Sliding window (sweep)

Reproducibility in Test Generation Schemes

All successful test generation schemes can be characterized in one important way: their reproducibility. For both passing and failing tests, the generation scheme must be reproducible.

Passing tests need to be reproducible — Passing tests should be added to regression lists so that the health of the design can be continually monitored throughout the design and verification process. If tests are not reproducible, regressions are impossible. See "Regressions" on page 400 for more information about regressions.

Failing tests need to be reproducible — Failing tests need to be reproduced even more quickly. If the stimulus of a failing test is legal and the problem is a design bug, a failing test should be rerun as soon as a fix is made to the design. If the same test case cannot be retried after a bug fix, the quality of that bug fix will be unknown. Of course, tests can also fail because their stimulus is illegal. In such a case, the test will not be reproduced exactly, but must be modified to provide correct input behavior and then retried.

Random tests are really pseudorandom Random testing is discussed below, but keep in mind that the random component of a random test is really pseudorandom. Random generators are initialized with well-known seeds so that the pseudorandom sequence can be replayed when needed. Fortunately, most random number generators in computer systems are actually seeded pseudorandom number generators, and therefore are not truly random number generators at all. The Vera random facilities are not an exception; they are pseudorandom as well.

Overview of Test Generation Schemes

If the complete, or exhaustive, test space is thought of as a circle as shown in Figure 2-8, complete test coverage occurs when tests completely fill the circle. Test generation methods differ in how they fill the circle.

FIGURE 2-8   Test Generation Schemes

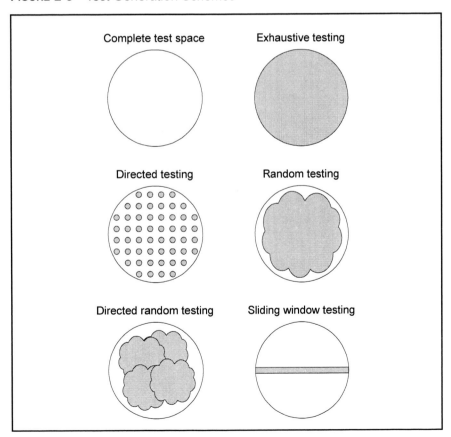

Exhaustive tests are commonly algorithmic tests that fill the circle with every possible test case. Directed tests fill points of the circle and are written until all points in the circle are covered. Random tests randomly fill the circle. Directed random tests constrain the randomness to smaller circles, and different constraints are then used until the entire circle is filled.

A sliding window scheme, or a sweep, can be thought of as a specific type of directed test, or as a highly constrained directed random test. Because it exhaustively tests combinations of two or more features, events, or transactions, a sliding window covers a line or an arc through the circle.

Exhaustive Testing Schemes

There are many styles of test generation for simulation-based functional design verification, but a few are not appropriate for SoC verification. For example, the most primitive test generation scheme is exhaustive testing. As the name implies, exhaustive testing attempts to stimulate the DUT with every possible combination of input stimuli.

Exhaustive tests are commonly written algorithmically. For example, when verifying an adder, all possible input combinations are computed and then tested.

Limitations of exhaustive testing — Exhaustive testing works well for small DUTs but breaks down quickly for large and complex ones. For example, it is impossible to list all possible streams of input packets for an Ethernet switch with a sufficiently large number of ports. An exhaustive test would have to take into account all combinations of every possible packet size arriving in all possible timing patterns at all ports. Even if it were possible to list all those cases, it would be impossible to simulate them all with limited simulation resources.

Exhaustive testing is no longer adequate for complete verification once test cases can no longer be easily stated, computed, or simulated. The solution is to break down the test space into the important tests, as described beginning on page 28, and then implementing those test cases with the most appropriate test generation scheme.

Directed Testing Schemes

Directed tests inject user-written stimulus into the DUT. Similarly, directed tests check for user-specified resulting conditions. Although directed tests can test multiple features simultaneously, complete coverage of a DUT requires many tests, or test cases, because each directed test is targeted specifically to a certain feature or set of features within the DUT.

For example, for an Ethernet switch, one directed test would be written to verify that a packet from every input port could reach every destination port. Clearly, this test verifies portions of the lookup engine and crossbar scheduler as well. However, a separate directed test or set of tests would be needed to exercise and stress the forwarding engine and crossbar scheduler.

In directed tests, the test writer must keep all input constraints in mind when generating tests. For complex designs, input constraints get tricky. For example, if the DUT is a four-bank synchronous dynamic random-access memory (SDRAM), timing constraints must be honored for each bank individually. Certainly, more sophisticated testing environments can help the writer of a directed test by automatically fixing illegal stimulus. In the SDRAM example, the testbench would keep track of all the independent timing requirements and adjust any illegal transactions the test requests. Unfortunately, these more sophisticated testbenches can also change the case tested by the directed test, since the test writer may forget exactly how the runtime environment resolves illegal input stimulus.

Where directed tests excel
Directed tests work extremely well with DUTs that have simple and completely unrelated features. In these cases, it is not hard for the test writer to keep the proper input constraints and expected results in mind. Furthermore, because the features are unrelated, tests do not have to be written to verify possible combinations of these features or possible sequences of their application. Unfortunately, most of today's SoC designs do not fit this mold.

Directed testing also excels when tests are easily implemented with regular patterns. For example, directed tests can verify that each bit in a register is properly connected, by individually inverting each register bit and reading back the results. A similar process can be used to verify that every address and data bit of a memory is working correctly.

Limitations of directed tests
Even with smart application of directed tests, it is easy to miss important test cases. For example, the crossbar scheduler may starve an input port with a complex set of recurring conditions. The logic to handle this set of conditions

might be present but malfunctioning. It is also possible that the designer never considered this set of conditions and therefore never added the proper logic to handle it. In the first case, it may be difficult to generate the exact conditions necessary in a directed test, because of the long sequence of simultaneous events required. In the latter case, where nobody has thought about those specific input conditions, the verification engineer will have a hard time writing the correct directed test to expose the bug.

Random & Directed Random Testing Schemes

A random testing environment can help uncover hidden test cases. In a random environment, the testbench knows how to apply every type of transaction and randomizes continuous streams, or sequences, of those transactions. For the Ethernet switch, a random environment would know how to generate packets of all lengths headed for all destination ports. This implies that it also knows how to initialize the forwarding engine and understands how the switch maintains the forwarding engine. The random environment then generates random, legal sequences of packets of various sizes heading for various output ports, hopefully finding additional bugs because of test cases the designers and verification engineers never thought to implement. For complex DUTs, a random testbench always finds unexpected bugs.

Random environments need to implement the test plan as well

It is extremely important for the random environment to be able to hit all test cases the designers and verification engineers can think of. In other words, a random environment must implement the test plan. Using a random environment is not a license to stop thinking about the possible or important test cases. In fact, in a fully random environment, some features in the DUT are so unlikely to be hit that they may never be tested in a finite simulation time.

For example, a corner case of the Ethernet switch may be a long stream of minimum-size packets, each destined for a port not initialized in the forwarding engine. If a random environment randomly picks between many initialized destinations and one uninitialized destination with an even probability distribution, a stream of uninitialized destinations is extremely unlikely. Because it is necessary to test this unlikely event, the randomness needs to be directed, or constrained, so that the unlikely events are tested.

Directed Random Testing

A variant of random testing is directed random testing. In this scheme, the random testbench is enhanced to include variable probability weights that steer the random choices. To generate the long stream of uninitialized destinations case mentioned above, the environment is run with uninitialized destinations having a higher probability than all initialized destinations combined. Similarly, to generate tests that stress the handling of initialized destinations by the forwarding engine, the same environment is run with initialized destinations having a higher probability than uninitialized destinations. The challenge for the verification engineer is to hit all known test cases by directing the randomness where necessary, while also allowing sufficient freedom for the environment to hit as many other cases as possible.

Benefits of Random Testing

Random environments are worth the effort

Clearly, the random testbench is the most sophisticated test generation scheme discussed so far, because it requires the greatest amount of automation. In directed testing, the test writer usually knows the input constraints and output behavior and transfers them to tests on a test-by-test basis. In random testing, the test writer must program that knowledge into an automatic test generator and an automatic results checker. (There is more information on results checking in the section "Logging & Error Checking" on page 44.)

For complex designs, however, this effort pays for itself when the first bug appears from a test case that the designers and verification engineers never thought about. With complex designs, random test environments will discover many of these bugs. A properly constructed random environment will also detect all bugs that directed testing would find.

Random Tests: How Long & How Many

Because the random generators in random tests never run out of stimulus choices, they can theoretically run forever. However, it is a bad idea to run them forever, for two reasons—for bug fix verification (since the same test needs to be rerun), and because reseeding moves them more efficiently to different operating regions.

Tests need to be rerun

After a design bug is found by a random test and the bug has been fixed, it is necessary to verify the bug fix by rerunning the same test case. If it took two days to hit the bug, it will take another two days to verify the fix. If the second two-day run determines that the bug was not fixed, it will take another two days to verify the second fix. Although this process cannot be repeated infinitely, it can be repeated enough times to make the verification engineer swear off long-running random tests forever.

Reseeding random tests moves them to different operating regions

Restarting random tests with a different seed is productive, because it tends to move their random walk to a different operating region. After a random simulation has been run for a very long time, it tends to provide the same input sequences repeatedly. Restarting a random test with a different seed not only interrupts the continuous application of the same input sequences, but it also helps the test move to different input sequences, thus testing different operating regions of the DUT.

In directed random environments, the effectiveness of the reseeding process is greatly enhanced if the input parameters, or directives, as well as the random seed, are changed. If the probability distributions of various parameters are changed, each directed random test verifies the implementation of a different operating region. Continually changing the operating region expedites finding bugs, because it helps bring out improbable sequences and therefore accelerates the testing of corner cases.

For example, in our Ethernet switch, a directed random environment could pick packet destinations with variable probability distributions. Some invocations of the random test could favor initialized destinations, some invocations could stress uninitialized destinations, and some invocations could favor a balance of destinations. All three tests will stress the forwarding engine in different ways, and therefore, each test will accelerate the discovery of bugs in the operating regions of the forwarding engine.

Some long tests are still required

Unfortunately, uncovering some bugs requires long test cases and therefore long simulations. For example, the overflow of a large FIFO cannot occur until the FIFO has had enough time to fill. For this reason, some random tests need to be run longer than most. It is usually easy to infer these longer tests from the test plan by noting the number of transactions required for a test case, such as the number of elements that need to be added to a FIFO before it overflows.

Careful initialization of random tests finds bugs more quickly

The number of tests that need lengthy runs can be minimized by manually placing the design in a specific operating region before a simulation is started. If the design has FIFOs of packets, for example, the FIFOs can be initialized with known packets instead of initialized empty. As long as this process is done carefully, the design will not know the difference and the simulation will begin as if it has been running for hours. This initialization process can be done by the test in zero simulation time and seconds or less of wall time.

Sliding Window

A commonly used testing strategy, which can be used in a directed environment or layered on top of a random environment, is the sliding window test, or sweep. In a sliding window setup, transactions that have different results depending upon their ordering are swept across each other, thus stimulating all the possible outcomes. This process stresses the design in important ways, because the designer may not have considered all possible event timings.

For example, in a two-port RAM, a read returns different data depending on when the same memory word is written. If the read takes place after the write, the read returns the new memory contents. If the read takes place before the write, the read returns the previous memory contents. If the read is simultaneous with the write, the read returns either the previous or the new memory contents, depending on the implementation of the RAM. A sliding window tests all of these cases by sweeping the read across the write.

Sweeps can be successfully used in both directed and random environments. As discussed above, fully random environments easily miss interesting test cases because of the low probability of those cases showing up in a finite simulation time. Sliding windows are commonly used to generate directed random tests to bring out those low-probability events.

Unfortunately, sweeps cannot be used for all parameters in large, complex SoC designs. Taken to its extreme, sweeping all parameters in the input stimulus is equivalent to exhaustive testing of the DUT. For SoC designs, exhaustive testing will not finish before tape-out.

Summary—Test Generation Schemes

The five test generation schemes are summarized in Table 2-2. Because each test generation scheme has advantages and disadvantages, it is usually best to use more than one scheme. The trick is to harness the advantages of a methodology while avoiding its disadvantages.

The test generation scheme best employed for each test case is usually dictated by the precision of control required by the test case. Note, however, that all test cases must be reproducible, regardless of the scheme used.

TABLE 2-2 Summary of Test Generation Schemes

	Exhaustive Testing	Directed Testing	Random Testing	Directed Random Testing	Sliding Window Testing
Test Generation	All possible input conditions	User-specified	Completely random	Constrained random	Parameters swept through their legal ranges
Advantages	Guarantees complete test space coverage	Simple and orthogonal test cases are easier to specify one at a time	Uncovers hidden test cases and bugs	Builds on random environments by stimulating low-probability test cases and bugs	Exhaustively tests swept parameters
Disadvantages	Impossible with SoC designs	Easy to miss interesting test cases and therefore bugs. Test writer must specify legal input stimulus and expected results for each test case	Can miss low-probability test cases. Must hit all test cases in the test plan as well	Must hit all test cases in the test plan as well as all test cases generated by unconstrained random environments	Cannot be done with all parameters in a limited simulation time

Transactors

Whether a testbench is random or directed, the components that stimulate the DUT are called transactors, stubs, or bus functional models. There are two types of transactors, directed transactors and automatic transactors.

Directed Transactors

In a directed environment, directed transactors are told what stimulus to inject by the test. In a random environment, directed transactors also inject the stimulus, but an additional, autonomous section of code, called the generator, controls the transactor. A diagram of each environment is shown in Figure 2-9.

For example, for the Ethernet switch, a packet transactor is connected to each Ethernet port. In a directed environment, user stimulus controls the transactors. In a random environment, the generator controls the transactors. In the case of the Ethernet switch, the generator is probably monitoring the status of all the ports, the crossbar, and potentially all the other units in the switch so that it can generate all interesting test cases.

FIGURE 2-9   Transactor Environments

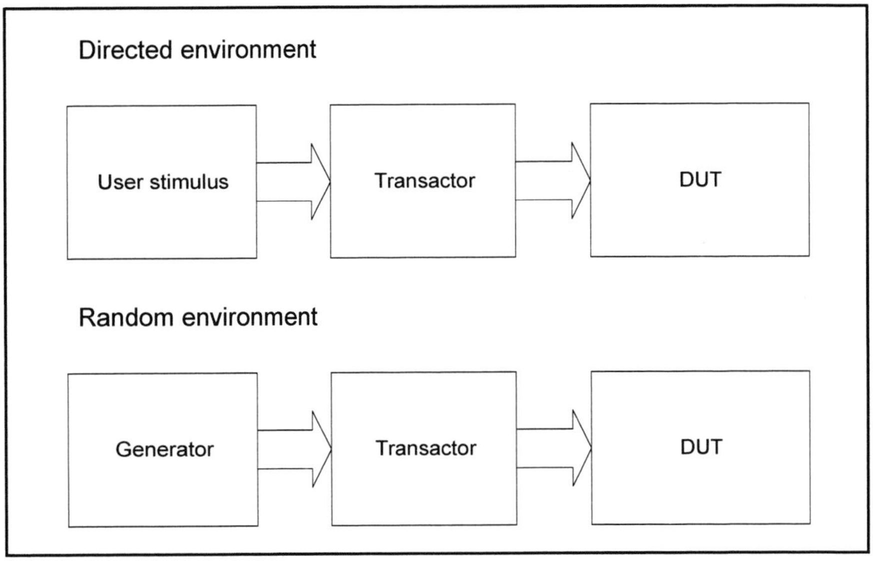

Automatic Transactors

Automatic transactors watch the stimulus on an interface or multiple interfaces and respond appropriately. An example of an automatic transactor is a memory model. A memory model accepts read and write requests and responds by updating its state or returning a portion of its state.

Background traffic

Automatic transactors may include generators so they can both generate and respond to stimulus. Combining transactors and generators allows the engineer to run random tests at the same time as other test types. This technique can be used to inject background traffic while another test is running.

For example, for the Ethernet switch, some ports could be automatically sending valid packets and checking the packets they receive while the verification engineer writes a directed test using the other ports. This background traffic should not affect the directed test, with the possible exception of the arrival timing of packets at destination ports. By keeping the crossbar busy with additional traffic and exposing it to a larger set of input combinations and state transitions, the presence of background traffic may uncover additional bugs. Note that the case described combines a directed environment with a random environment.

Logging & Error Checking

What good is a test if it is impossible to determine if the DUT behaved correctly? The most simplistic error checking strategy is human examination of log files or waveform dumps. The testbench applies stimulus and logs the results. The verification engineer then sorts through the data and verifies that everything worked properly. Although human verification is acceptable for simple environments, it is unacceptable for complex random ones. Because complex environments take a long time to hand-check and because hand-checking complex environments is extremely error-prone, there will never be sufficient time to test all necessary test cases.

Advantages of automated checking

The solution is automated checking, which has additional advantages as well. Generally, it is much better to be limited by CPU time than by human time, because CPU time is much less costly than engineering time. Additionally, CPUs are less error-prone and can work all hours of the day and night. Finally, human intervention is not regressable in an automatic regression environment. See Chapter 13 for a more detailed discussion of regressions.

Monitors & Assertion Checks

Monitors and assertion checks are the devices in a testbench that automatically check the behavior of the DUT. The position of monitors and assertion checks in the test environment is shown in Figure 2-10.

FIGURE 2-10 Position of Monitors and Assertion Checks

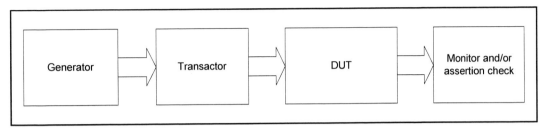

Monitors

There are two types of monitors: checking monitors and logging monitors. Each type watches part of the RTL and the inputs of that section of RTL. Checking monitors know how the RTL should behave, given an input stimulus, and flag errors appropriately. In other words, checking monitors verify the properties of the design, in a process called *property checking*. For example, a checking monitor for a divider would watch the numerator and denominator and compare the outcome to its own division computation.

Whereas some monitors watch the RTL inputs to determine the current stimulus, other monitors are told the current stimulus by the generators in the test environment. Generators in a test environment may provide monitors with a copy of the input stimulus or tell them what to expect. A separate, higher-level representation of the design may also tell monitors what to expect. No matter how the checking monitors determine the correct behavior of the DUT, their job is to flag errors.

Logging monitors log the activity in the RTL without checking it. Other monitors or transactors can use the output of this type of monitor. Sometimes, logging monitor output is just for debugging purposes.

Assertion Checks

Assertion checks are checking monitors that watch the DUT for invariants, or conditions that should always be present in the DUT regardless of the input stimulus. For example, in a one-hot-encoded state machine, an assertion check verifies that the state vector is one-hot on every clock cycle and flags errors when appropriate. In contrast, monitors check whether correct state transitions were made given an input stimulus.

Summarizing the Differences

Clearly, there is a fine line between a monitor and an assertion or invariant check. The difference is mostly semantic. Monitors can be used solely for logging purposes or for checking the behavior of the RTL under certain operating conditions. Invariants check for conditions that should always be true regardless of the operating conditions. Fortunately, it really doesn't matter what the checker is called, as long as errors are flagged and bugs are fixed. Remember, in both cases, the checker is only as good as the input stimulus provided.

Runtime Versus Postprocessing Monitors & Assertion Checks

There are two common strategies for implementing monitors and assertion checks: runtime checking and postprocessing. As the name implies, runtime checking is done by the testbench while a simulation runs. Both runtime checkers and stimulus generators are connected to the simulation engine. In postprocessing, all interesting events in the DUT are logged to files, and separate tools verify that the behavior stored in the log files is correct.

Each strategy has its pros and cons. The most commonly cited advantages of runtime checking are these:

- The ability to feed information back into the stimulus generators

- The ability to pinpoint errors and stop the simulation immediately

- The fact that only a single environment is needed

- The ease with which they can peek into more information in the DUT

The most commonly cited advantages of postprocessing are these:

- The flexibility inherent in postprocessors, in that any language or combination of languages can be used to implement them

- The speed with which test cases can be rechecked once a bug in the checking code is fixed

- License-free execution of postprocessors if they are written in a license-free language such as Perl. (License-free runtime checkers are also available, such as your own C/PLI code.)

*Quickly
rerunning a
postprocessor*
At first glance, the ability to rerun a simulation quickly after a bug in the checking code has been fixed seems like a minimal advantage, but with sufficiently complicated random environments, the checking code is at least as complicated as the DUT. Therefore, there will be many bugs in the checking code, and it is a limitation to have to rerun the entire simulation to verify a fix to the checking code. Running the entire testbench is much slower than just running the postprocessor.

*Connectivity of
checkers and
generators*
On the other hand, the ability to pass information between checkers and the stimulus code should not be underestimated. In order to hit various corner cases in the crossbar scheduler in an Ethernet switch, for example, it is normally easier for the stimulus generators to react to the current state of the scheduler than to try to predict it. Therefore, from the point of view of the stimulus generators, it is much easier to have the scheduler checker in the runtime environment than to have that code inaccessible in a postprocessor.

*Harness the
advantages of
each*
Because each strategy has advantages, it is common to use both postprocessing and runtime checking in the same environment. Checkers with useful information to feed to the stimulus generators can be run with the simulation, while checkers that are more easily implemented and debugged in another language can to be written as postprocessors.

Cycle Accuracy Versus Transaction Accuracy

Whether runtime checking or postprocessed checking is used, the checkers themselves can be programmed for various levels of granularity. They might predict the cycle-by-cycle behavior of the DUT, or they might predict only the order in which the DUT should execute transactions. A transaction, of course, can be the transfer of a entire packet or the complete execution of an instruction.

For many designs, transaction accuracy is much easier to implement. For example, in a cycle-accurate checker, variable delays need to be predicted exactly, which is difficult to do. Checkers can more easily determine and verify what the next transaction should be and what the allowable delay is before that transaction occurs.

Commonly, transaction-accurate checks are all that matter, and cycle-accurate checks are unnecessary extra details. For example, if two input ports of an idle Ethernet switch simultaneously receive a packet destined for the same output port, the order in which the packets emerge from the output port does not matter. In a cycle-accurate checker, the internals of the switch would have to be perfectly modeled so that the exit order of the packets could be predicted. A transaction-accurate checker, on the other hand, would check that the two packets emerged in any order, which is all that matters.

In general, complex DUTs imply complex verification environments. Keeping complex verification environments tractable means increasing the level of abstraction and eliminating extraneous detail wherever possible. Transaction accuracy is one level of abstraction that helps tremendously. It is much easier to think about a packet-switching system in terms of packets alone than in terms of the cycle-by-cycle generation and reception of those packets, and in fact, packets are all that matter in a packet-switching system.

Reference Models

Reference models are commonly used to check the behavior of the DUT. Any automatic behavior checker is, by definition, a reference model of the DUT in some degree. However, the term *reference model* is normally reserved for models that can accurately replace the RTL they are intended to model without neighboring blocks noticing the difference. This type of reference model is also known as a *black box model*, because it can be distinguished from the DUT only by looking at its internal implementation.

Reference models come in two granularities: cycle-accurate and transaction-accurate. The interfaces of a cycle-accurate reference model are completely indistinguishable from the interfaces of the RTL it replaces. Transaction-accurate reference models, on the other hand, are indistinguishable except for timing differences.

Verification with reference models   Whether a reference model is cycle-accurate or transaction-accurate, it can be used to verify the behavior of the DUT. Reference models are run concurrently with the RTL and given the same inputs as the RTL. The output of the DUT is then compared with the output of the reference model, and differences are flagged as errors. To enable this comparison, transaction-accurate reference models may require more sophisticated glue logic than cycle-accurate reference models.

Reference models are commonly written algorithmically, while RTL is written in the manner required by synthesis tools. For this reason, reference models are normally written in higher-level languages such as Vera or C++, but they still contain the necessary interface into the RTL world so that the reference model and RTL can be selectively used. Because Vera and C++ normally run faster than Verilog or VHDL synthesizable models, reference models can also be used to speed up simulation during verification of other blocks.

Of course, reference models can be used as part of a postprocessing results checker as well. In this case, the necessary RTL interface is not required, but some glue is still needed to connect the logs generated by the simulation environment to the reference model. Note that since this kind of reference model cannot be substituted into the simulation environment, simulation can not be speeded up using them.

Formal Verification

At this point, astute verification engineers will be asking, "If it is hard to come up with all necessary input stimulus, and if verification environments are only as good as the input stimulus allows, why aren't there any tools for generating input stimulus?" There actually are such tools, called formal verification tools. A full discussion of these tools is beyond the scope of this book. However, a brief overview follows.

Model Checking Verification

There are two main types of formal verification: model checking and equivalence checking. In model checking, the verification engineer writes invariants for the DUT, and the formal verification tool tries to find counter examples to prove those invariants false. Careful construction of invariants can yield powerful results.

Verifying fairness with model checkers

For example, fairness in arbiters is extremely difficult to prove in simulation. The first question one has to ask when verifying fairness is, "What is fairness?" If the DUT is an Ethernet switch, is fairness defined as a maximum delay before an input port is allocated a turn to send a packet; or the number of packets per time unit each port is allowed to send; or the bytes of payload per time unit each port is allowed to send?

Clearly, neither functional verification nor formal verification can proceed without an appropriate definition. Once fairness is defined mathematically, model checking can prove it for all combinations of packet arrivals. Even if an engineer could define all possible combinations of packet arrivals, they could not all be simulated in the limited time available for functional design verification.

Model checking is difficult

Although great strides have been made in model checking in the past few years, model checking can still be quite difficult to implement. Because the state space of complex problems grows quickly, a lot of time is spent refining problems down to a tractable size. For large, complex state machines that span multiple SoC-size chips, this process takes a long time. Of course, model checking is powerful because it can find test cases in complex environments yielding bugs that no one would have thought of.

Another difficulty lies in the fact that the formal verification tool, rather than the verification engineer, generates the input stimulus, and thus a lot of time is spent constraining the stimulus the tool applies. This is an easy place to make errors. Of course, the legal input stimulus problem also exists in simulation-based verification.

Finally, some formal verification tools have their own assertion languages and model-building languages. Normally, these languages are difficult to learn and are mastered only by people dedicated to the art of formal verification. Some tools use industry standard languages, which eliminates this last problem.

Equivalence Checking Verification

Equivalence checking verifies that different models contain the same properties. One of the models is usually called a golden or reference model, and the other is called a test model. Equivalence checking is much more common than model checking, because invariants and input stimulus constraints need not be written. Of course, functional verification by equivalence checking requires a perfect golden model, which isn't usually available. Models can be written in the language of the verification tool, but again, that process is difficult and time-consuming.

Equivalence checking is commonly used at physical design phases, such as synthesis and routing. The post-physical-design netlist is compared against the presynthesis netlist to ensure that the physical design process has preserved the behavior of the RTL. In this case, the RTL is the golden model.

CHAPTER 3

Applying Verification Strategies to the Ethernet MAC

This chapter introduces an Ethernet media access controller (Ethernet MAC) design and then applies the basic verification concepts introduced in Chapter 2 to the MAC testbench described throughout this book.

This chapter provides enough information about the Ethernet MAC and its specification to allow the reader to grasp the concepts of verification, but it does not attempt to provide all the details necessary to design or fully verify this device. The purpose here is simply to reinforce the concepts presented in Chapter 2 and to provide a base that can be used to illustrate other verification concepts through the rest of the book.

Specifically, this chapter covers the following subjects:

- Ethernet MAC specification

- Identifying testbenches

- Identifying test cases

- Test generation policies

Ethernet MAC Specification

The Ethernet MAC is a device that implements the media access protocol for Ethernet. The Ethernet media access protocol specifies how multiple devices access the Ethernet physical medium in both half-duplex (shared Ethernet) and full-duplex (switched Ethernet) modes. Figure 3-1 shows the connectivity of the Ethernet MAC and its major functional blocks.

FIGURE 3-1   Ethernet MAC in Context

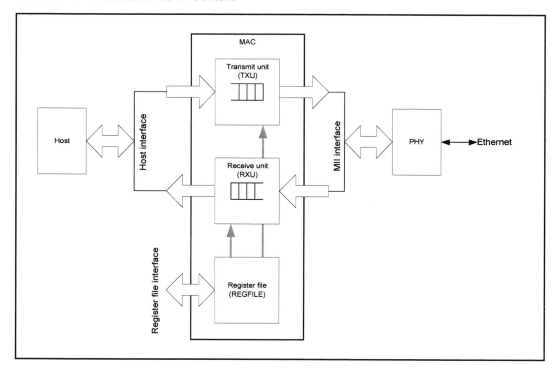

The MAC connects to the Ethernet medium via a physical layer device (PHY) that implements the Ethernet electrical specification. It communicates with the PHY via the medium-independent interface (MII), a standard interface used for this purpose.

The MAC connects to the host via the host interface. The host can be one of many devices, including a bus controller or a switch ASIC.

The MAC transmit unit transfers Ethernet packets from the host to the PHY, and the receive unit transfers Ethernet packets from the PHY to the host. The transmit and receive units have internal FIFOs to temporarily hold a maximum of 128 bytes of packets. The register file is connected to a CPU or I/O controller that configures and controls the transmit and receive units.

The host interface reads and writes packets in 32-bit words. The MII interface transmits and receives data from the PHY over a 4-bit-wide interface. The regfile is accessed via an 8-bit CPU interface. Figure 3-2 shows these interfaces in more detail.

The following lists the features of the Ethernet MAC:

- Support for 10-megabit-per-second and 100-megabit-per-second Ethernet

- Support for IEEE and Ethernet (bluebook) packet formats

- Unicast, multicast, and broadcast MAC addressing

- Support for half-duplex and full-duplex modes. In half-duplex mode, transmission is deferred when a carrier is present, indicating that the network is busy, and transmission is retried when a collision is detected.

- 128-byte receive (Rx) and transmit (Tx) FIFOs

- MII interface for Tx and Rx

- Statistics gathering

- Programmable interpacket gap (IPG)

- Programmable RxReady (Rx FIFO read strobe) assertion threshold

- Programmable TxReady (Tx FIFO write strobe) and assertion threshold

- Full-duplex host data transfer interface

Table 3-1 shows the format of the Ethernet packet.

TABLE 3-1   Format of the Ethernet Packet

Preamble (7 Bytes)	Start frame delimiter (SFD) (1 byte)	Destination address (DA) (6 bytes)	Source address (6 bytes)	Type or length (2 bytes)	Data (46–1500 bytes)	Cyclic redundancy check (CRC) (4 bytes)

FIGURE 3-2   Ethernet MAC

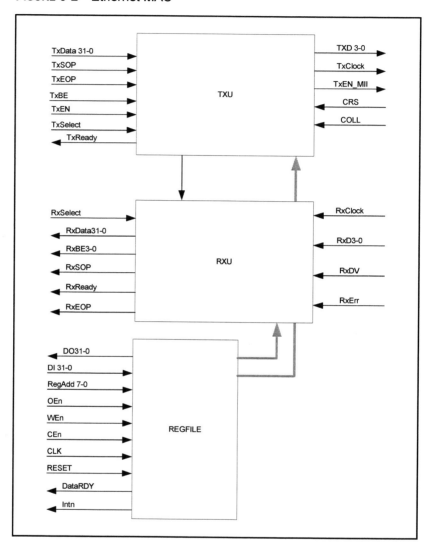

Transmit Operation

When transmit is enabled, the MAC transfers data from the host into its Tx FIFO. After the transmit FIFO is filled up to the programmed threshold level, the MAC may begin transmission. The actual transmission of the data onto the network is delayed until the network has been idle for a minimum interpacket gap (IPG) time. If there is activity on the network and the MAC is in half-duplex mode, transmission is deferred. The MAC calculates the packet CRC as it is being sent and appends the result to the end of the packet.

Concurrent transmission in half-duplex networks results in collisions. In full-duplex networks, transmissions can occur concurrently without collisions. During transmission in half-duplex mode, the PHY monitors network activity and asserts the MII collision signal when it detects a collision. If the MAC is transmitting when the MII collision signal is asserted, it backs off and retries transmission after a random interval. The packet transmission stops when either the packet has been transmitted successfully or an error condition occurs. The following errors can occur during transmission:

- Underrun—Transmit data is not ready when needed for transmission.

- Excessive collisions—A collision occurs 16 consecutive times during an attempt to transmit the same packet.

- Late collision—A collision occurs outside the collision window (after the transmission of the first 64 bytes of a packet).

Receive Operation

When reception is enabled, the MAC continuously monitors the network. It detects activity when the MII data valid signal is asserted and then starts to process the preamble bytes. If it receives a valid start-of-frame delimiter (SFD) followed by a destination address (DA) that matches its own Ethernet address, the MAC loads the packet into the Rx FIFO. Once the Rx FIFO reaches a certain threshold, it signals the host to start reading data out of it.

While the packet is being received, the MAC continues to monitor the network activity. It detects the end of the packet when the MII data valid signal is de-asserted. Reception terminates with a packet error if the packet is not a valid MAC packet or if an MII error is detected during packet reception. An MII error is detected when the receive error signal is asserted during packet reception. MII errors indicate that the PHY has detected an error.

The last four bytes received are the cyclic redundancy check (CRC), which the MAC uses to detect packet corruption. The MAC checks the CRC of all received packets and reports all errors. When reception terminates, the MAC loads the status of the received packet into the receive FIFO.

The following events, if they occur, are reported at the end of packet reception:

- Overflow—The MAC receive FIFO is full when packet data is received, causing packet data loss.

- CRC error—The 32-bit CRC received with the packet does not match the CRC calculated upon reception.

- Alignment error—The packet does not end on a byte boundary (i.e., has a spare nibble—4 bits), and a CRC error occurs.

- MII error—An MII error was detected during packet reception.

- Packet too short—A packet containing fewer than 64 bytes (including CRC) was received.

- Packet too long—A packet larger than the maximum size was received.

Identifying Testbenches

Once the specification for the design under test (DUT) is understood, the engineer needs to identify the testbenches needed to verify the specified functionality. All three types of testbenches introduced in Chapter 2—unit-level, full-chip, and multichip—are discussed below.

Unit-Level Testbenches

Recall that the Ethernet MAC contains three blocks—a transmit block that forwards packets from the host to the network, a receive block that forwards packets from the network to the host, and a register block that configures both the transmit and receive blocks. Each of these blocks is an obvious candidate for a unit-level testbench.

Register block testbench is not necessary   However, since the MAC register block does not contain complicated pipelines, algorithms, arbitration schemes, or anything else that should be tested in isolation before being integrated with a larger design, the effort required to build a separate register block testbench would be greater than the benefit.

Instead, the register file can be verified simultaneously with the transmit and receive blocks without the controllability or observability of any of the three blocks being compromised. Furthermore, the register block is simple enough that its presence does not significantly increase the debugging time of any of the other blocks, or significantly increase the simulation time of models including other blocks.

Independent transmit and receive testbenches are not necessary

In full-duplex mode, the transmit and receive blocks have their own dedicated interfaces and therefore run independently. Because they cannot interfere with each other, running them concurrently does not decrease the controllability or observability of either block.

In half-duplex mode, transmitters and receivers share access to the Ethernet medium by deferring transmissions when the network is active and retrying transmissions when a collision is detected. It's easy to add a test of this functionality to a single concurrent environment without the controllability or observability of either block being compromised.

Because the transmit and receive blocks are both small, simulating both bocks together will not be too slow. Although simulation would be faster with only a single block present, all of the required test cases for both blocks can be simulated in a short period of time with both blocks present.

For all of these reasons, the transmit and receive blocks do not need separate testbenches. A combined testbench is just as effective as two independent testbenches. Full-duplex mode tests the independent operation of the transmit and receive blocks; half-duplex mode tests the remaining functionality, the collision avoidance and detection mechanism.

Full-Chip Testbenches

Because all three blocks in the Ethernet MAC can be verified simultaneously without the verification of any individual block being compromised, and because the MAC full-chip testbench simulates quickly, only a full-chip testbench needs to be implemented. Unit testbenches are not required.

Figure 3-3 shows the full-chip Ethernet MAC testbench described in this book, including generators, monitors, and transactors. Overviews of these elements are presented below, and detailed descriptions are presented in the corresponding chapters.

FIGURE 3-3   The Ethernet MAC Testbench

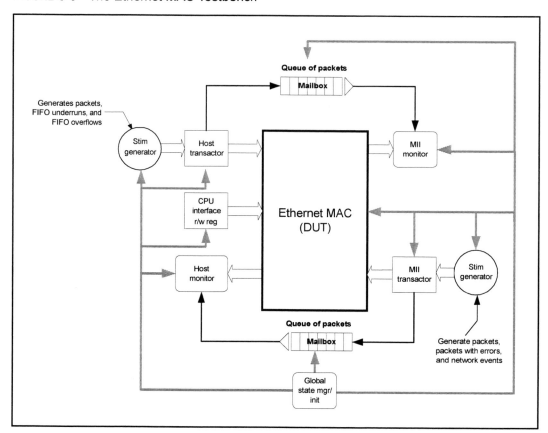

Multichip Testbenches

Some Ethernet MAC multichip testbenches can be useful for verifying the test environment. In the configuration in Figure 3-4, two Ethernet MACs are indirectly connected to each other, since their MII ports are connected to two Ethernet-connected PHYs.

This testbench simulates two Ethernet MACs communicating to each other via the Ethernet medium. It can be used to ensure that the MII transactors behave like real PHYs, and to verify that the MII packet generators and transactors have combined to model realistic traffic conditions, including realistic collision scenarios.

FIGURE 3-4 Multichip Testbench Including PHYs

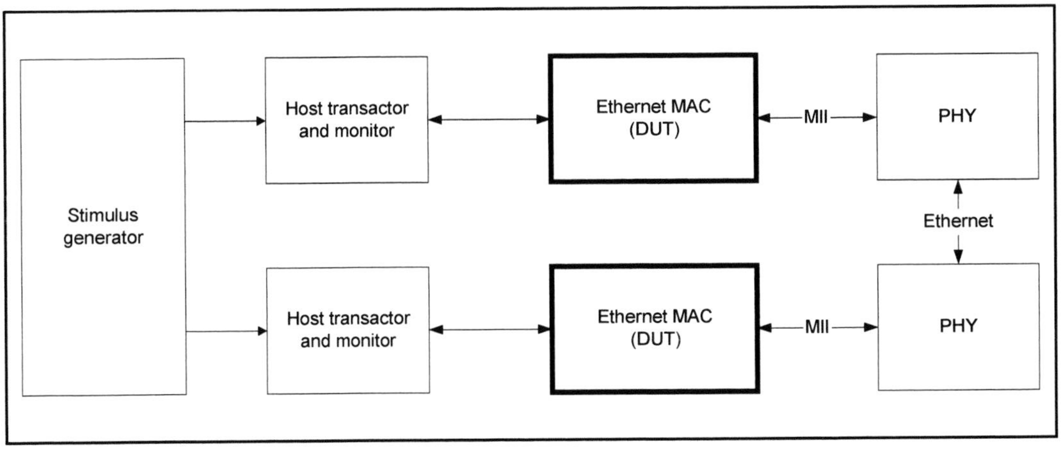

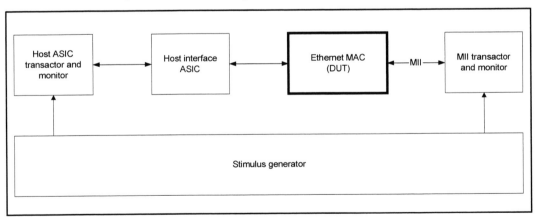

In a second multichip testbench, shown in Figure 3-5, the Ethernet MAC is connected to a host interface ASIC. In this case, the multichip environment verifies that the host transactor behaves like a real host.

FIGURE 3-5 Multichip Testbench Including Host Interface ASIC

These two environments can be combined so that two or more host interface ASICs communicate via Ethernet MACs and PHYs. Although this configuration is useful for a system-level test, the law of diminishing returns applies for the Ethernet MAC verification effort. It is possible that these bigger environments will find bugs not seen in smaller environments, but the probability of finding a bug is reduced once the transactors and generators are verified to be modeling the MAC operating environment completely and correctly.

Only full-chip environments described

Because the testbench in which two MACs communicate through two PHYs is a modification of the full-chip Ethernet MAC environment described in this book, this multichip environment is left as an exercise for the reader. The other multichip environments are also extensions of the environment presented, although they require additional transactors and monitors not shown in this book.

Identifying Test Cases

After the implemented testbench is understood, the engineer needs to create the test plan. Each test method described in Chapter 2—testing by features, testing by interfaces, and testing by corner cases—is discussed below.

Testing by Features

Recalling the functionality of the Ethernet MAC discussed above, you can create the test-by-features test cases easily. All the following features except initialization need to be tested with all legal packet sizes:

- Initialization (FIFO thresholds and so on)

- Full-duplex transmit

- Full-duplex receive

- Full-duplex transmit and receive

- Half-duplex transmit with and without deferral

- Half-duplex transmit with collisions

- Half-duplex transmit with max collision count exceeded

- Half-duplex receive

- Destination address (DA) match and mismatch

- Multicast

- Broadcast

- CRC error

- Alignment error

- Too short packets and too long packets

- FIFO overflow and underrun

- Deferral upon carrier sense

- Statistics

Testing by Interfaces

Examining the MII and host interfaces reveals the following test cases:

- Interpacket gap (IPG) sizing

- Collisions at various times during packet reception and transmission

- Presence of carrier sense at various times

Testing by Corner Cases

Because of the implementation of the MAC, the following corner cases need to be tested:

- Packets dropped by the MAC because of FIFO overflow

- Packets dropped by the MAC due to excessive collisions when two or more packets are present in the FIFO

Test Generation Policies

A scan of the test cases above reveals that many parameters need to be fully explored, such as the following:

- Packet size

- Destination address

- IPG timing

- Collision timing

Some of these parameters have combinations that also need to be explored. For example, a collision is normally detected during the reception of any of the first 64 bytes of a packet. However, collisions can also be detected anytime during the reception of a packet of any length. Therefore, the timing of collisions must vary so that they are received at every possible time during the reception of packets of all possible lengths.

Directed Random Environment

Because numerous parameters need to be varied, it is difficult to construct an exhaustive testbench. It is also difficult to convince yourself that a directed environment provides complete test space coverage. Therefore, the testbench needs to be a random environment. Every parameter, such as packet length, is picked randomly. Events, such as collisions, are generated randomly.

In addition, the testbench should have probability weights that change the distribution of the random selections. These programmable probability weights implement a directed random environment. For example, the distribution of packet lengths is programmable. This allows some tests to favor short packets whereas other tests favor long ones. Additionally, the delay between the injection of collisions is variable. All probability weights are flexible enough that most of the test cases described above can be implemented.

Some directed test cases are implemented as well

Occasionally, a specific sequence of events is required to implement a test case. Although it might be possible to configure the probability weights so that these sequences occur, the testbench can be programmed to ignore the probability weights and create these conditions. The number of these special circumstances is limited as much as possible, but they are implemented whenever the directed random environment cannot be relied on to hit a specific test case. These features are added to the testbench wherever they can be implemented most efficiently, which may mean replacing or modifying the generators, transactors, or monitors.

The bring-up phase of verification requires simpler test cases, since many simple bugs are found then. When simple test cases find bugs, debugging is correspondingly simple, which is desirable. For this reason, the probability weights in the testbench are flexible enough to implement simpler bring-up test cases. After the simpler test cases work correctly, the probability weights are changed to create more complicated test cases.

Specifically, the bring-up process begins by testing a single transmit packet and a single receive packet in full-duplex mode. Full-duplex mode is simpler than half-duplex mode, because full-duplex mode does not need to react to collisions. After a single packet can be transmitted and received, multiple packets in a single direction are tried; then multiple packets in both directions simultaneously; then half-duplex features; and so on until corner case testing commences.

Passing Arguments to the Testbench

For every configurable parameter, such as probability distribution weights, the testbench is preprogrammed with a default. Generally, these defaults constrain the parameter to correct operation. In other words, the defaults create completely random but always correct stimulus: Packets are always of legal length, the CRC is always generated correctly, and so on.

To modify the behavior of the directed random environment, either to enable other modes of operation, create corner cases, or test certain regions of operation more thoroughly, you can use one of two approaches. You can

- Pass arguments to the testbench with command line arguments (called *plusargs*) to modify the probability distribution weights, or

- Add additional plusargs to the testbench that create specific event orderings without relying on distribution probabilities

Since the testbench modification in the second situation is also enabled with plusargs, a configuration generator script can run randoms by launching simulations with random, legal plusargs. Running randoms automatically accelerates testing the design in different operating regions and therefore accelerates finding bugs.

Note that plusarg-configured test cases are both reproducible and regressible (see Chapter 13 for a detailed discussion of regressions). When a test case needs to be replayed, the simulation is launched with the same set of plusargs, including the plusarg that controls the random seed for the simulation. The plusargs are then stored in the regression list so that the same test case can be reproduced during regressions.

Transaction Accuracy

Because the Ethernet MAC sends and receives Ethernet packets, the testbench is naturally packet-accurate, which is a form of being transaction-accurate. The testbench cares only if the packets it sends are received correctly. Under certain circumstances, packets can be dropped, but partial packets should never be received with correct CRC.

The transactors and monitors have a cycle-accurate component that interfaces with the DUT on a cycle-by-cycle basis, but the transactors and monitors make the conversion from the cycle-accurate interface to the transaction-accurate testbench so that the rest of the testbench can use Ethernet packets as its basic building block.

Transactors

The MAC testbench has two transactors, a host transactor and an MII transactor. Each is responsible for properly formatting and transmitting packets across its interface to the MAC. The MII transactor also controls the interpacket gap on the packets it injects into the MAC. The transactors also inject error conditions and network events, such as collisions and presence of carrier sense, relevant to their interfaces.

The transactors do not create packets or automatically respond to them. They inject packets they receive from the stimulus generators; this makes them directed transactors, not automatic transactors.

Automatic transactors are useful for implementing memory models or other components that respond to stimulus but do not initiate it. Since the MAC is self-contained, no components of the testbench have these properties.

Automatic transactors are also useful for initiating background traffic that should not alter the behavior of the test case implemented by directed transactors. Since the MAC handles two independent packet streams, there are no extra ports with which to add such background traffic—another reason automatic transactors are not useful.

Monitors

As Figure 3-3 shows, the MAC testbench has two monitors, one to receive packets from the MII interface and one to receive packets from the host interface. When a monitor receives a packet, it compares the packet received with the next expected packet. Expected packets are added to a mailbox by each transactor after it has injected the packet into the MAC. Monitors load the next expected packet from the mailbox.

When a transactor creates error conditions that cause packet drop, it tells the monitors which packets in the mailbox should be dropped. The monitors then verify that those dropped packets are never received.

Logging & Error Checking

The MAC testbench verifies correct behavior at runtime. Because no postprocessors are used, only error messages and debugging information need to be logged.

All unexpected error conditions are logged, including the reception of a packet that does not match the next expected packet. For debugging purposes, all packets sent and received are logged. Additionally, all network events and injected error conditions are logged.

Pass/Fail Determination

The final task the testbench accomplishes is determining whether the design passes or fails the test cases. Clearly, the design fails whenever an unexpected error condition is detected. Therefore, all unexpected error messages are logged with a unique identifier. At the end of every test case simulation, this identifier is extracted from the simulation log file by the UNIX program grep. Built-in Vera error identifiers, such as those presented in its end-of-simulation status report, are also extracted from the log file. (The end-of-simulation status report is shown in Chapter 4.) If any of these identifiers are found, the design failed the test case. If none of these identifiers are found, the design passed the test case.

Summary

The MAC testbench is shown in Figure 3-3. A full-chip environment is sufficient because of the symmetry of the MAC and the limited functionality of the register block. The testbench is a directed random environment with some directed test case generation capabilities and is capable of creating all the required test cases.

CHAPTER 4

Vera Programming Constructs

This chapter provides an overview of the Vera programming language. It presents a series of basic examples and explains important elements. Readers not familiar with Vera should read all sections of this chapter; advanced readers can skip this chapter altogether.

The chapter starts with a simple program that serves as a foundation for the introduction of various data types, keywords, and control constructs. It also includes the basic environment setup, compilation, and execution procedures. More complex topics such as the interface with Verilog and object-oriented programming are covered in later chapters.

Vera Programming Syntax

Vera is a hybrid of conventional programming languages and hardware description languages. Syntactically, it resembles both C/C++ and Verilog. The regular programming constructs and more advanced techniques such as object-oriented programming are taken from C/C++, and the hardware-oriented constructs resemble Verilog. These similarities help users become comfortable with the syntax quickly. This chapter focuses on the procedural programming constructs of Vera.

Environment Setup

Before you start working in Vera, add the following lines to your .cshrc file (if you are using csh or tcsh). This makes the necessary tools available to you:

```
setenv LM_LICENSE_FILE path_to_license_file
setenv VERA_HOME path_to_installation_tree
setenv PATH "${PATH}:${VERA_HOME}/bin"
```

A Simple Program: hello

The first example is a program that prints the word "hello" to the screen. Enter the following code sample into a file named hello.vr.

```
// our first program
#include <vera_defines.vrh>
program hello {
    printf("hello\n");
}
```

To compile the program, enter the following at the command line:

```
vera -cmp hello.vr
```

If there are no errors, one Vera object file, hello.vro, is generated.

To run the program, enter the command

```
vera_cs hello.vro
```

When you do, the following output appears on the screen:

```
++------------------------------------------------------------------++
||                   VERA VERIFICATION SYSTEM                       ||
||   Copyright (c) 1995, 1996, 1997, 1998, 1999 by Synopsys, Inc.   ||
||                   All Rights Reserved                            ||
||            VERA is a trademark of Synopsys, Inc.                 ||
||     CONFIDENTIAL AND PROPRIETARY INFORMATION OF SYNOPSYS, INC.   ||
++------------------------------------------------------------------++

Version: 4.4_Beta2
hello
```

```
Vera: finish encountered at cycle        0
            total        mismatch: 0
                        vca_error: 0
                    fail(expected): 0
                            drive: 0
                           expect: 0
                           sample: 0
                             sync: 0
```

Notice the "hello" in the output.

Figure 4-1 illustrates the components of the hello program.

FIGURE 4-1 Anatomy of the hello Program

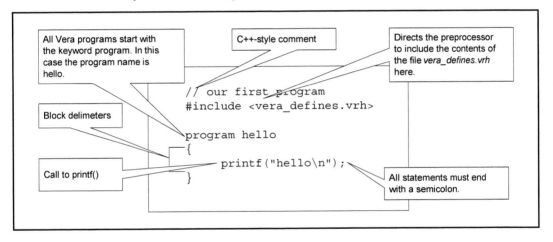

The following is a line-by-line explanation of Figure 4-1.

```
#include <vera_defines.vrh>
```

Vera has a built-in preprocessor that operates similarly to the preprocessor of both C and Verilog. Lines beginning with # and ' get the attention of the preprocessor. The preprocessor replaces #include statements with the text contained in the named files. The file vera_defines.vrh contains built-in Vera definitions; it should be included at the beginning of every Vera program.

```
program hello
```

The hierarchy of Vera programs begin with the keyword *program.*

```
printf("hello\n");
```

This is a statement. All statements terminate with a semicolon. This statement is a call to the task printf( ). The functionality of the Vera printf( ) is almost identical to printf( ) in C. The \n indicates a new line. The expression *hello* is enclosed in double quotes, so it is interpreted as a string.

Statements can be grouped into a block by enclosing one or more statements with curly braces. Note that a single statement block does not need to be enclosed with curly braces.

Program Structure

Notice the usage of the keyword *program* in the hello example. It denotes the top of a Vera program structure. The framework of a Vera program is shown in Figure 4-2.

FIGURE 4-2   Vera Program Framework

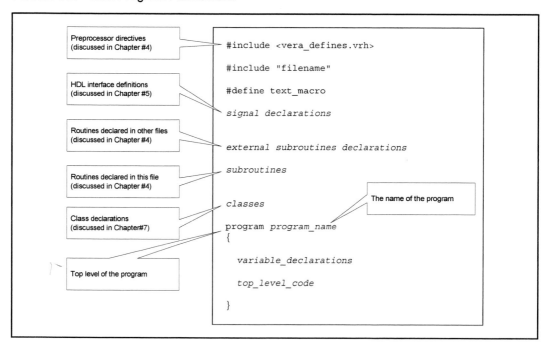

Numbers & Data Types

This section discusses the number and data types supported in Vera.

Numbers

Vera supports two forms of number specifications: sized and unsized. Both number formats are similar to Verilog's number formats.

Sized Numbers

Sized numbers are represented in *size-in-bits 'base number* format.

```
4'b1101  // This is a 4-bit binary number
16'hdead // This is a 16-bit hexadecimal number
```

Unsized Numbers

Numbers that have no size specification default to 32-bit signed integers.

```
4356     // 32-bit decimal number by default
'b0101   // 32-bit binary number by default
```

Replication

Number replication in Vera is the same as number replication in Verilog.

```
{32{1'b0}}
    // replicates 1'b0 32 times to form 32'b0
```

Variables & Data Types

Before you can write a useful program, you must know how to assign and store values. Vera supports the following data types:

Integer
Bit (reg)
Enumerated
Array
Associative array
Object

This chapter will discuss most of the data types supported in Vera. The exception is objects, which are discussed in Chapter 7.

One of the most commonly used data types is the integer. It can hold 32-bit integer values, which are signed nonfractional values. Thus, the numerical range of numbers that can be represented by integers is -2^{31} to $+2^{31}-1$.

All numbers in Vera can represent four states, 0 (logical low) and 1 (logical high), and the more hardware-oriented X (unknown) and Z (high impedance).

The following shows examples of integer declarations and assignments to integers:

```
integer new_variable;           // decalaration
integer another_new_variable = 3`h14c;
                                // declaration and initialization
new_variable = 332;             // a simple assignment
```

Vera supports the bit, reg, and enum data types. The bit and reg data types are synonymous. A variable of type bit can hold binary values up to the width declared. If no width declaration is present, the default width is 1 bit. This data type is useful when dealing with hardware signals, especially in conjunction with arrays.

The enumerated (enum) data type is useful for representing a finite set of named values, such as the state of a light switch. For example,

```
enum light_switch = on, off;
light_switch living_room_light;
living_room_light = on;
printf("living_room_light is %s\n", living_room_light);
// will print "living_room_light is on"
```

Operators & Expressions

Vera supports three operator types:

- Unary—An operator that precedes the operand

```
a = ~ b; // ~ is a unary operator
```

- Binary—An operator that appears between two operands

```
a = b || c; // || is a binary operator
```

- Ternary—An operator that separates three operands

```
a = b ? c : d; // ? : is a ternary operator
```

These operators behave like operators in C and Verilog. Table 4-1 provides a list of operators available in Vera. See the *VERA System Verifier User Manual* for more details.

TABLE 4-1 Vera Operators

Operator	Operation
{}	Concatenation
'{}	Concatenation left of assignment
+ - * /	Arithmetic
++ --	Autoincrement and autodecrement
%	Modulus
> >= < <=	Relational
!	Logical negation
&&	Logical AND
||	Logical OR
==	Logical equality
!=	Logical inequality
===	Case equality
!==	Case inequality
=?=	Wild equality
!?=	Wild inequality
~	Bitwise negation
&	Bitwise AND
&~	Bitwise NAND
|	Bitwise OR
|~	Bitwise NOR
^	Bitwise exclusive OR
^~	Bitwise exclusive NOR

TABLE 4-1   Vera Operators (Continued)

Operator	Operation
&	Unary AND
~&	Unary NAND
|	Unary OR
~|	Unary NOR
^	Unary exclusive OR
~^	Unary exclusive NOR
<<	Left shift
>>	Right shift
?:	Conditional

Expression evaluation

Expressions in the Vera programming paradigm are statements that evaluate to a true, false, or unknown value (1, 0, or X respectively).

Vera Equalities

Comparing values to find out whether certain conditions are true can be difficult, especially when there are many equality operators available. Table 4-2 shows the subtle differences between the equality operators available in Vera.

TABLE 4-2   Vera Equality Operators

	Equalities			Inequalities		
	Logical a==b	Case a===b	Wild a=?=b	Logical a!=b	Case a!==b	Wild a!?=b
a = 4'b0001; b = 4'b0001;	1	1	1	0	0	0
a = 4'b0101; b = 4'bxx0x;	X	0	1	X	1	0
a = 4'bxx0x; b = 4'bxx1x;	X	0	0	X	1	1

TABLE 4-2 Vera Equality Operators (Continued)

	Equalities			Inequalities		
	Logical **a==b**	**Case** **a===b**	**Wild** **a=?=b**	**Logical** **a!=b**	**Case** **a!==b**	**Wild** **a!?=b**
a = 4'bxx0x; b = 4'b1x0x;	X	0	1	X	1	0
a = 4'bxx0x; b = 4'b1xxx;	X	0	1	X	1	0
a = 4'b0000; b = 4'b000z;	X	0	1	X	1	0

Logical equality compares the operands bit by bit. It yields an x if either an x or a z is encountered in any of the operands.

Case equality compares the operands bit by bit, including X and Z values (all x and z bits must match).

Wild equality compares the operands bit by bit, including x and z values. If either an x or a z is encountered, it is treated as a don't care and matches any bit value.

Expression evaluation and unknown values

As mentioned above, an expression can evaluate to a true, false, or unknown value (1, 0, or X respectively). Handling X can be tricky, as it will not equate to a 1 in a logical equality. So make sure to use a case equality when such possibilities exist. For example,

```
#include <vera_defines.vrh>
program evaluate {
   bit a;
   a = 1'bx;
   if (a == 1) {
      printf ("Logical Equality: a is 1\n");
   }
   if (a == 1'bx) {
      printf ("Logical Equality: a is x\n");
   }
   if (a == 1'b0) {
      printf ("Logical Equality: a is 0\n");
   }
   if (a === 1'bx) { // case equality
      printf ("Case Equality: a is x\n");
   }
}
```

This program shows the following output:

```
Case Equality: a is x
```

Control Structures

The following program control structures are supported in Vera. Their behavior is similar to their counterparts in C and Verilog.

if-else statement

if-else statements allow you to execute different blocks of code based on a simple test. The syntax is

```
if (<expression>) {
    // if expression is true
}
else {
    // if expression is false
}
```

For example,

```
if (a > b) {
    printf("A is greater\n");
}
else {
    printf("B is greater or equal to A\n");
}
```

while statement

while statements are used for iterations. The syntax is

```
while (<expression>) {
    // body of loop
}
```

For example,

```
while (count != 5) {
    count++; // Loop terminates when count = 5;
}
```

for statement

for statements are also used for performing iterations. The syntax is

```
for ( <initializing_expression>;
    <terminating expression>;
    <loop_increment_expression>) {
    // body of loop
}
```

In the following example, the loop terminates when the value of count is equal to 100:

```
for (count = 0; count < 100; count++) {
    printf("Count is %d\n",count);
    // Prints "Count is 0" through "Count is  99";
    // loop terminates with count = 100
}
```

repeat statement

The repeat statement executes a loop for a specified number of iterations. The syntax is

```
repeat (<expression>) {
    // Loop code
}
```

For example,

```
integer number;
number = 5;
repeat(number) {
    number = 100;
    printf("Number is %d",number);
}
```

This loop executes only five times, not a hundred times, but the value printed will be 100. This is because the repeat statement evaluates and saves the value of the expression (in this example, the value of the variable number) before it enters the loop.

case statement

The case statement is useful for broad multiway branching. The syntax is

```
case (<case_expression>) {
    <constant_expression>: <statement_block>;
    <constant_expression>: <statement_block>;
    <constant_expression>: <statement_block>;
    default: <statement_block>;
}
```

For example,

```
case (number) {
    3'b001: printf("number is 001\n");
    3'b010: printf("number is 010\n");
    3'bxx1: printf("number is xx1\n"); // number must be xx1,
    default: printf("number is another value\n")
}
```

NOTE *case statements do a case match (===) and not a logical match (==). A statement block is executed only if its constant expression exactly matches the case expression.*

Vera supports two more variations of the case construct: casex and casez.

- casex treats all x values in the case expression as don't cares.

- casez treats all x and z values in the case expression as don't cares.

break & continue statements

The break and continue statements are used in conjunction with while, for, and repeat loops.

The break statement terminates the innermost loop. The syntax is

```
{  // loop body starts
   // loop body
   break;
   // loop body
}  // end of loop body
// break causes execution to jump to this line
```

The continue statement terminates execution of the current iteration of the loop. The syntax is

```
{  // loop body starts
   // loop body
   continue;
   // last line of loop body
}  // end of loop body; continue causes execution to
   // exit out of the current iteration
```

Functions & Tasks

Vera supports both functions and tasks. Each allows simulation time to advance. There are two differences between functions and tasks:

Tasks versus functions

- They have different name spaces, so there can be a task and a function that have exactly the same name but totally different functionality. Avoid doing this as it makes the code difficult to understand.

- Tasks do not have a return value, whereas functions do.

Vera versus Verilog functions

Unlike in Verilog, Vera functions and tasks can advance time. Of course, both functions and tasks can also execute in zero simulation time.

Vera tasks and Vera functions are exactly the same except for the two properties discussed. Later in the book, the terms functions and tasks will be used interchangeably when talking generally or abstractly.

Functions

Functions can be used for performing complex operations and computations. In Vera, a function can be called with any number of arguments, but has only one return value. The syntax for defining a function is

```
[scope] function <return_datatype> <function_name>
(<input_values>) {
   <function_name> = <value_to_be_returned>;
}
```

The value for the scope option may be extern or local. If no scope is specified, the function is presumed to be global.

For example,

```
// a function that returns the larger of two values
function integer get_larger_val (integer number1, integer number2) {
    integer temp;
    if (number1 >= number2)
        temp = number1;
    else
        temp = number2;
    get_larger_val = temp; // the value to be returned
}
```

The following explains the example code for get_larger_value( ):

```
function integer get_larger_value
    (integer number1, integer number2)
```

This is a function definition stating that get_larger_value( ) is a function with two integer arguments and an integer return type.

```
get_larger_value = temp; // the value to be returned
```

Here the return value of the function is assigned. In Vera, the return variable of a function is the name of the function itself. The type and size of the return variable is the type and size of the function itself. A function whose return value needs to be discarded must have its output voided, using the keyword void, as shown below.

Extern functions are not defined in the file in which they are called

In reasonably sized programs that span multiple files, if a call is made to a function not declared in the same file (or in an included file), an extern function definition is required in the caller file. This makes the compiler aware that the code for the program resides in some other file. A function declaration is merely the function definition line followed by a semicolon.

For example, the external function declaration for get_larger_value( ), the example above, looks like this:

```
extern function integer get_larger_value
    (integer number1, integer number2);
```

Tasks

Tasks are like functions, except that they do not return values. Otherwise, they can perform any operation a function can perform. The syntax is

```
[<scope>] task <task_name> (<input_values>) {
    // body of the task
}
```

The value for the scope option may be extern or local. If no scope is specified, the task is presumed to be global.

The following example shows how to declare a task and how to call it:

```
task print_integer (integer number1) {
    printf ("The integer to print is %d\n", number1);
}
program test {
    integer i;
    i=0;
    // call to print_integer()
    print_integer(i);
}
```

Call by Reference & the Keyword var

Typically, if a function or task is called with a set of values, Vera allocates space for the argument variables, copies the argument values into the allocated space, executes the function, and returns a copy of the return value to the caller. Any change the function makes to the value of an argument is not visible outside the function. This is known as "call by value."

When to use the keyword var

This feature becomes a limitation, however, when you want to change the value of the variable in the caller as well. For this, Vera provides the keyword var, which takes a handle to the variable in the caller and passes the handle to the called function or task instead of passing a copy of the variable. Thus, any change made to the variable in the called function is immediately reflected in the caller. This is known as "call by reference."

The Art of Verification with Vera

```
task swap_numbers (var integer number1, var integer number2) {
    integer temp;
    temp = number1;
    number1 = number2;
    number2 = temp;
}

// caller segment
integer a = 6, b = 9;  // a is 6 and b is 9
swap_numbers(a,b);     // a is 9 and b is 6
```

Task & Function Reentrance

Functions and tasks in Vera are reentrant. Each function call allocates new memory space for all variables declared in the function. Any number of callers can call the same function simultaneously without problem, because each instance of the function receives its own exclusive local variable storage space.

Static Variables

Variables in Vera are automatic variables, since Vera automatically allocates exclusive memory space for all the variables declared in a block when a block is entered, and deallocates the memory when the block is exited.

Static variables, denoted by keyword static, are an exception. Static variables are allocated only once, and are not dealloctted until the program terminates. The memory space allocated for them is shared, so when multiple instances of the same block execute concurrently, they reference the same memory location.

The value of a static variable is preserved in memory even after the block it is declared in exits. The preserved value is available every time the block is reentered.

The value of a static variable declared in functions is preserved and stored in memory between successive function calls. Thus, when a new call is made to a function, the value of the static variable is its value when the previous call to the function exited.

A variable should be declared as static when it is important to preserve the value of the variable between function calls. If it is not declared as static, then its value is lost when the code block in which it is declared exits.

The following code segment, which includes a task that uses a static variable, lets you find out how many instructions have been dispatched in a program.

```
task instructions_dispatched() {
    static integer num_dispatched = 0;
    printf("Number of instruction dispatched %d\n", ++num_dispatched);
}
```

Five successive calls to the above task print the following five messages:

```
Number of instruction dispatched 1
Number of instruction dispatched 2
Number of instruction dispatched 3
Number of instruction dispatched 4
Number of instruction dispatched 5
```

In contrast, had the variable number_dispatched not been declared as static (i.e. if the word static had been omitted), the value of the variable would not have been preserved between function calls, and the output observed would have been as follows.

```
Number of instruction dispatched 1
Number of instruction dispatched 1
Number of instruction dispatched 1
Number of instruction dispatched 1
Number of instruction dispatched 1
```

Another type of variable, called a *shadow* variable, also plays an important role in concurrent subroutines. It is discussed in Chapter 6.

Default Arguments

To handle common cases, Vera allows you to define default values for tasks and functions. The syntax for this is

```
task (<arg_datatype> <arg>=<default_value>, ...) {
    // task body
}
```

For example,

```
task my_task (integer j=0, integer k=3) {
    // task body
}

my_task(100,*);     // j = 100, k = 3
my_task(*,200);     // j = 0, k = 200
my_task(1,2);       // j = 1, k = 2
```

Optional Arguments

Vera also supports optional arguments for tasks and functions. This allows subroutines to evolve without your having to change all the existing calls to the subroutine. Optional arguments must be enclosed in parentheses and must have default values. The syntax is

```
task <task_name> ((<arg_datatype>
                <optional_arg>=<default_value>),...) {
    // task body
}
```

The arguments can be nested in parentheses to allow for non-order-dependent addition of arguments. For instance, you can make the first argument optional or the third argument optional by appropriately nesting the argument within parentheses. The lower nested arguments are filled first. For example,

```
task my_task (((integer j=1)),((integer k = 1)),(integer l = 2)) {
    // task body
}
my_task(2,3,4);     // j=2, k=3, l=4
my_task(39);        // j=1, k=1, l=39
my_task();          // j=1, k=1, l=2
```

Arrays & Associative Arrays

Vera arrays are an extension of basic data types. They are used to represent an ordered collection of identical data types, typically data that has a common purpose. Vera also supports one-dimensional arrays and associative arrays (more on associative arrays shortly). The syntax is

```
<datatype> <array_name>[<array_size>];
```

NOTE *array_size must be enclosed in square brackets—it is not an optional argument.*

In this syntax, type is the data type of each element stored in an array and array_size is the number of elements in the array.

Arrays must be declared and initialized in separate statements. For example,

```
integer my_integers[10];
    // my_integers is a ten-element array of integers
bit[7:0] bytes[8];
    // bytes is an eight-element array of eight-bit-wide bits
    // (eight bits make a byte, hence the name)
bytes[0] = 8'b0;
    //initialization of the first element
```

Accessing Arrays

The syntax for accessing arrays is

```
<array_name>[<index_expression>]
```

NOTE *index_expression must be enclosed in square brackets—it is not an optional argument.*

index_expression must evaluate to a positive integer. If it evaluates to an unknown (X), a simulation error occurs. If the location being accessed has not been initialized, X will be returned.

The bit fields of an element in the array cannot be referenced directly. The element value must first be retrieved and stored in a variable. For example,

```
reg[7:0] data_array[10];
reg[7:0] entry;
data_array[7] = 8'b00000000;
entry = data_array[7];    // get the 8th element of the array
if (entry[0] == 1`b0)     // check to see that the lsb is zero
```

Associative Arrays

In Vera, associative arrays are arrays whose dimensions have not been specified. Elements in the associative array are allocated dynamically. This makes the associative array the ideal data type for holding sparsely allocated data. The syntax is

```
<datatype> <array_name>[];
```

For example,

```
bit[31:0] ramdata[];
```

The elements in an associative array are accessed like those of a one-dimensional array.

Vera also provides the system function assoc_index( ) for modifying and analyzing associative array elements. The syntax is

```
<return_integer> = assoc_index(<OPERATION>,
    <associative_array_name>[,<index>]);
```

The functionality and return values of OPERATION are listed in Table 4-3.

TABLE 4-3   OPERATION Functionality

Operation	Description
CHECK	Checks whether the element exists at the index; returns 1 if true; otherwise returns 0. If the index field is omitted in the call, returns the number of allocated elements.
DELETE	Deletes the element if it exists at the index specified, and returns 1; otherwise returns 0. If the index field is omitted, all elements (but not the array itself) are deleted.
FIRST	Returns 1 if the first element is found, otherwise returns 0. The index is assigned the value of the first array element if it is found.
NEXT	Searches for the first element with an index greater than the index specified. If the function finds an element, the value of the index is assigned to the index argument and the function returns 1; otherwise, it returns 0 and leaves the index value unchanged.

The following example illustrates the use of the assoc_index( ) function, used to manipulate the contents of an associative array.

```
#include <vera_defines.vrh>

program assoc_array_test {
    integer index = 0;
    reg[7:0] my_assoc_array[];

    // initialize some entries
    my_assoc_array[0] = 8'b00000000;
    my_assoc_array[1] = 8'b00000001;
    my_assoc_array[2] = 8'b00000010;
    my_assoc_array[5] = 8'b00000101;
    my_assoc_array[7] = 8'b00000111;
    printf ("Total number of initialized entries %0d\n",
        assoc_index(CHECK, my_assoc_array));

    print_array (my_assoc_array);

    // let's find the first element and delete it
    void = assoc_index(FIRST,my_assoc_array,index);
    void = assoc_index(DELETE,my_assoc_array,index);
    printf ("First element has been deleted\n");
    printf ("Total number of initialized entries %0d\n",
        assoc_index(CHECK,my_assoc_array));

    print_array (my_assoc_array);

    // let's find the next element and delete it
    void = assoc_index(NEXT,my_assoc_array,index);
    void = assoc_index(DELETE,my_assoc_array,index);
    printf ("Next element found at index %0d has been deleted\n",
        index);
    printf("Total number of initialized entries %0d\n",
        assoc_index(CHECK,my_assoc_array));

    print_array (my_assoc_array);

    // let's delete all the elements
    void = assoc_index(DELETE,my_assoc_array);
    printf ("ALL elements has been deleted\n");
    printf ("Total number of initialized entries %0d\n",
        assoc_index(CHECK,my_assoc_array));

    print_array (my_assoc_array);
}
// define tasks/classes/functions here if necessary
task print_array (var reg[7:0] my_assoc_array[]) {
    integer index = 0;
    for (index = 0; index < 8; index++) {
        if (assoc_index(CHECK,my_assoc_array,index)) {
            printf("Entry %0d is valid, value is %b\n",
                index, my_assoc_array[index]);
        }
```

```
        else {
            printf ("Entry %0d is invalid\n", index);
        }
    }
}
```

Running the program produces the following output:

```
++----------------------------------------------------------------++
||                   VERA VERIFICATION SYSTEM                     ||
||    Copyright (c) 1995, 1996, 1997, 1998, 1999 by Synopsys, Inc. ||
||                    All Rights Reserved                         ||
||            VERA is a trademark of Synopsys, Inc.               ||
||     CONFIDENTIAL AND PROPRIETARY INFORMATION OF SYNOPSYS, INC. ||
++----------------------------------------------------------------++
Version: 4.4_Beta2.1
Total number of initialized entries 5
Entry 0 is valid, value is 00000000
Entry 1 is valid, value is 00000001
Entry 2 is valid, value is 00000010
Entry 3 is invalid
Entry 4 is invalid
Entry 5 is valid, value is 00000101
Entry 6 is invalid
Entry 7 is valid, value is 00000111
First element has been deleted
Total number of initialized entries 4
Entry 0 is invalid
Entry 1 is valid, value is 00000001
Entry 2 is valid, value is 00000010
Entry 3 is invalid
Entry 4 is invalid
Entry 5 is valid, value is 00000101
Entry 6 is invalid
Entry 7 is valid, value is 00000111
Next element found at index 1 has been deleted
Total number of initialized entries 3
Entry 0 is invalid
Entry 1 is invalid
Entry 2 is valid, value is 00000010
Entry 3 is invalid
Entry 4 is invalid
Entry 5 is valid, value is 00000101
Entry 6 is invalid
Entry 7 is valid, value is 00000111
ALL elements has been deleted
Total number of initialized entries 0
Entry 0 is invalid
Entry 1 is invalid
Entry 2 is invalid
Entry 3 is invalid
```

```
Entry 4 is invalid
Entry 5 is invalid
Entry 6 is invalid
Entry 7 is invalid
Vera: finish encountered at cycle          0
          total          mismatch: 0
                        vca_error: 0
               fail(expected): 0
                            drive: 0
                          expect: 0
                          sample: 0
                            sync: 0
```

Strings

Strings are arrays of characters terminated by a null character ("\0").

Declaring & Printing Strings

The syntax for declaring a string is

```
string <string_name> [=<initial_value>];
```

For example,

```
string identify = "I am a program";
```

Vera provides a C-style printf( ) task. The syntax is

```
printf("<text_and_arg_formats>",<arg_list>);
```

The argument format specifiers shown in Table 4-4 are predefined in Vera.

TABLE 4-4 printf( ) Argument Format Specifiers

Format Specifier	Description
%d	Decimal number
%h or %x	Hexadecimal number
%o	Octal number
%b	Binary number
%c	Single character

TABLE 4-4   printf( ) Argument Format Specifiers (Continued)

Format Specifier	Description
`%s`	String
`%p`	Program name
`%_`	Path separator for the current simulator
`%v`	Instance path of the Vera shell (vshell module in HDL)
`%0<format>`	Removes leading zeros

String Operators

Vera provides the operators in Table 4-5 for manipulating strings.

TABLE 4-5   Vera Operators for Manipulating Strings

Operator	Description
`==`	Checks equality of two strings
`!=`	Checks inequality of two strings
`{<str1>,<str2>...}`	Generates a concatenated string with str1, sr2, where str1 and str2 are either string variables or quoted strings
`{<n>{<str>}}`	Generates a string with str replicated n times, where str is either a string variable or a quoted string

Functions for Analyzing & Manipulating Strings

Vera also provides a number of functions for analyzing and manipulating string contents, the definitions of which are listed in Table 4-6.

TABLE 4-6   Functions and Tasks for Manipulating Strings

Function / Task	Description
`<length> = <string_name>.len();`	(Function) Returns the length of the string
`<integer_i> = <string_name>.getc(integer <i>);`	(Function) Returns the ASCII value of the ith character in the string
`<string_name>.putc(integer <i>, string <char>);`	(Task) Puts the first character of the string char at the ith position in string_name

TABLE 4-6 Functions and Tasks for Manipulating Strings (Continued)

Function / Task	Description
`<string> = <string_name>.substr (integer <i>, integer <j>);`	(Function) Returns the string segment between index i and index j inclusively
`<index> = <string_name>.search (string <pattern>);`	(Function) Searches for pattern in the string; returns the index location where the found pattern begins. pattern can be a Perl regular expression.
`<index> = <string_name>.match (string <pattern>);`	(Function) Searches the string for pattern; if a match is found, returns 1; otherwise, returns 0. The functions prematch, postmatch, thismatch, and backref can then be used to access the matched string. pattern can be a Perl regular expression.
`<string> = <string_name>.prematch();`	(Function) Returns the string segment before the matched pattern
`<string> = <string_name>.postmatch();`	(Function) Returns the string segment after the matched pattern
`<string> = <string_name>.thismatch();`	(Function) Returns the string segment containing the matched pattern
`<string> = <string_name>.backref (integer <index>);`	(Function) Returns string pattern based on the last match( ) call. Similar to using $n in Perl to reference the matched strings within parenthesis.
`<integer> = <string_name>.atoi();`	(Function) Converts a decimal number in a string into an integer; returns the integer
`<string_name>.itoa(integer <i>);`	(Task) Converts an integer into a string
`<hex> = <string_name>.atohex();`	(Function) Converts a hex number in a string into bits; returns the bits
`<octal> = <string_name>.atooct();`	(Function) Converts an octal number in a string into bits; returns the bits
`<binary> = <string_name>.atobin();`	(Function) Converts a binary number in a string into bits; returns the bits

TABLE 4-6 Functions and Tasks for Manipulating Strings (Continued)

Function / Task	Description
`<string_name>.bittostr (<bit_string>);`	(Task) Converts bit_string into a string, where bit_string is a variable declared as a bit type, but containing ASCII values of characters
`sprintf (<string_name>, <"<text_and_arg_formats>">, <arg_list>);`	(Task) Like printf() but sends the output to string_name, a string variable. arg_formats are listed in Table 4-4.
`sscanf (<string_name>, "<arg_formats>", <arg_list>)`	(Task) Reads input from string_name, searches for the patterns specified in arg_formats, and extracts the found pattern matches into the variables. arg_formats are listed in Table 4-4.

Table 4-4 contains a list of argument format specifiers for sprintf( ) and sscanf( ). For more details on these functions, see the *VERA System Verifier User Manual*.

The match( ), prematch( ), postmatch( ), thismatch( ), and backref( ) functions have a special uses. The match( ) function can accept a Perl style regular expression as an argument. The result of the match( ) query is saved and available to the functions prematch( ), postmatch( ), thismatch( ), and backref( ). If the matching expression returns several values, backref( ) can be used to extract those values, as illustrated by the following example.

```
integer i;
string str, patt, str1, str2;
str = "1234 ABCD";
patt = "([0-9]+) ([a-zA-Z.]+)";
i = str.match(patt);
str1 = str.backref(0);     // str1 is 1234
str2 = str.backref(1);     // str2 is ABCD
```

Most of the functions in Table 4-6 are in the string_name.function( ) format. This is because strings in Vera are implemented as an object class. Chapter 7 covers object-oriented programming in Vera in more detail.

File I/O

Vera provides several routines to read from and write to external files.

The fopen( ) function opens a file and returns an integer file descriptor (see below). fopen( ) has the following syntax:

```
<file_descriptor> =
fopen("<filename>","<access>"[,<mode>]);
```

where access is one of the following:

r   Open for reading
a   Append to existing contents or create for writing
w   Replace existing contents or create for writing

and mode is either VERBOSE (the default) or SILENT. VERBOSE prints warning messages if the file cannot be opened, while SILENT does not.

file_descriptor is an integer assigned to the open file. It is used by the other file manipulation functions in referencing the file; thus it can be helpful to assign file_descriptor to a named variable. file_descriptor is set to 0, if the file cannot be opened.

In addition to the descriptors assigned to open files, Vera provides three built-in file descriptors that resolve to reserved integers:

stdin   Standard input
stdout   Standard output
stderr   Standard error output

The fclose( ) task closes the file. The syntax is

```
fclose(<file_descriptor>);
```

where file_descriptor is an integer returned by fopen( ).

The freadb( ), freadh( ), and freadstr( ) functions read data in binary, hexadecimal, and string formats respectively from a specified file. These routines read one line per invocation and appropriately ignore "//" comments. Their syntaxes are shown below:

```
<bit_data> = function bit freadb(<file_descriptor>);
```

```
<bit_data> = function bit freadh(<file_descriptor>);

<bit_data> = function str freadstr(<file_descriptor>
[,<mode>)];
```

The function freadstr( ) supports VERBOSE, SILENT, and RAWIN modes. In RAWIN mode, comments in the file being read are not filtered out.

Task fprintf( ) behaves just like printf( ), except it prints to a file identified by a file descriptor. Task printf( ) always prints to stdout. The syntax is

```
fprintf (<file_descriptor>,"<text_and_arg_formats>",
argument_list);
```

See Table 4-4 for a list of argument format specifiers.

When data is written to a file, it is first kept in a write buffer. When the buffer is full, all the data is written to the file. The function fflush( ) flushes the buffer and forces any data in the write buffer to be written out to the file immediately. The syntax is

```
<success> = fflush (<file_descriptor>);
```

The task rewind( ) resets the file access pointer to the beginning of the file. The syntax is

```
rewind (<file_descriptor>)
```

Following are simple examples that illustrate the usage of some of the Vera file I/O operators. In the first example, the Vera code shown reads data from file input.dat and prints it to stdout.

The contents of input.dat are

```
// Beginning of data
00000000
00000001
00000010
00000011
00000100
00000101
00000110
00000111
// End of data
```

file_io.vr contains the following:

```
#include <vera_defines.vrh>

program file_io {
    integer fdi;
    integer index;
    bit[7:0] my_array[8];

    fdi = fopen("input.dat","r",VERBOSE);
    if (fdi == 0) {
        printf("Cannot open input.dat");
        return;
    }
    for (index = 0; index < 8; index ++) {
        my_array[index] = freadb(fdi);
        fprintf(stdout,"Just read %b\n", my_array[index]);
    }
    // go back to the beginning of the file
    rewind (fdi);
    for (index = 0; index < 8; index ++) {
        my_array[index] = freadb(fdi);
        fprintf(stdout,"Read again %b\n",my_array[index]);
    }
}
```

Running the above code produces the following output:

```
++------------------------------------------------------------------++
||                  VERA VERIFICATION SYSTEM                        ||
||    Copyright (c) 1995, 1996, 1997, 1998, 1999 by Synopsys, Inc.  ||
||                    All Rights Reserved                           ||
||              VERA is a trademark of Synopsys, Inc.               ||
||    CONFIDENTIAL AND PROPRIETARY INFORMATION OF SYNOPSYS, INC.    ||
++------------------------------------------------------------------++

Version: 4.4_Beta2.1

Just read 00000000
Just read 00000001
Just read 00000010
Just read 00000011
Just read 00000100
Just read 00000101
Just read 00000110
Just read 00000111
Read again 00000000
Read again 00000001
Read again 00000010
Read again 00000011
```

```
Read again 00000100
Read again 00000101
Read again 00000110
Read again 00000111

Vera: finish encountered at cycle        0
         total       mismatch: 0
                    vca_error: 0
              fail(expected): 0
                        drive: 0
                       expect: 0
                       sample: 0
                         sync: 0
```

The next sample program illustrates the use of sscanf( ) and freadstr( ).
Assume that the program test_file (referenced in the sample Vera program) is
in the current working directory. The contents of test_file are

```
collision_enable 1
min_sized_packet 40
max_sized_packet 1500
```

The Vera sample program, scanf.vr, follows:

```
#include <vera_defines.vrh>

program sscanf {
  // variables for reading lines from the file
  integer file;
  string file_name = "test_file";
  string line;
  string arg_name;
  integer arg_val;

  // variables to load from the file
  integer collision_enable;
  integer min_sized_packet;
  integer max_sized_packet;

  file = fopen (file_name, "r");
  if (file == 0) {
     printf ("Could not open file %s for reading\n", file_name);
     return;
  }

  line = freadstr(file, SILENT);

  while (line != null) {
```

```
      sscanf (line, "%s %d", arg_name, arg_val);

      if (arg_name.match ("collision_enable")) {
        collision_enable = arg_val;
        printf ("Setting collision enable to %0d\n", collision_enable);
      }

      if (arg_name.match ("min_sized_packet")) {
        min_sized_packet = arg_val;
        printf ("Setting min_sized_packet to %0d\n", min_sized_packet);
      }

      if (arg_name.match ("max_sized_packet")) {
        max_sized_packet = arg_val;
        printf ("Setting max_sized_packet to %0d\n", max_sized_packet);
      }

      // load next line before going through loop again
      line = freadstr(file, SILENT);
    }
}
```

The output of this program is

```
Setting collision enable to 1
Setting min_sized_packet to 40
Setting max_sized_packet to 1500
```

A Complex Program: A CPU

This section shows an instruction-accurate model of a CPU with the following architecture:

- 32-bit wide instructions

- 32-bit wide data

- 12-bit-wide memory addressing

- Eight general purpose registers (%r0– %r7); %r0 is hard-coded to 0x0

- Eight instructions (NOP BR LDX STX ADD SUB CMP HALT)

- Nonpipelined implementation

In the example, the CPU is programmed to execute the assembly code equivalent of the following C code snippet.

Program Code

```
int a = 0;
int b = 9;

do {
    a++;
    } while (!(a==b))
exit;
```

Equivalent Assembly Code

```
0000 nop
0001 add %r0 %r0 %r1    # %r1(a) gets 0
0002 add %r0 0x9 %r2    # %r2 (b) gets 9
0003 add %r0 0x1 %r1    # a gets a + 1
0004 cmp %r1 %r2        # compare a and b
0005 br,e 0x7           #branch to address 7 if equal
0006 br,a 0x2           #branch to address 2 always
0007 halt               #exit
```

Contents of cpu.vr

```
#include <vera_defines.vrh>

#define    NOP   4'b0000
#define    BR    4'b0001
#define    LDX   4'b0010
#define    STX   4'b0011
#define    ADD   4'b0100
#define    SUB   4'b0101
#define    CMP   4'b0111
#define    HALT  4'b1110

// stx/load  opcode[31:28], src_type[27], des_type[26],
// reg[25:23] | imm[23:12], address[11:0]
// add/sub/cmp
// opcode[31:28]
// src_type[27], reg1[26:24], reg2[23:21] | imm[23:12], regd[2:0]
```

```
// br opcode[31:28], type[27] (0=always 1=equal), branch_target[23:12]
// halt opcode[31:28]

program  cpu {
    reg[11:0] pc = {12{1'b0}};
    reg[31:0] instruction = {32{1'b0}};
    integer  program_finish = 0;
    integer  instr_exe = 0;

    printf("----  Initializing\n");
    instruction = 32'b00000000000000000000000000000000;pc={12{ 1'b0}};
        // nop
    memop(1, pc, instruction); printf("\n");
    instruction = 32'b01000000000000000000000000000001; pc++;
        // add %r0 %r0 %r1
    memop(1, pc, instruction); printf("\n");
    instruction = 32'b01001000000000001001000000000010; pc++;
        // add %r0 0x9 %r2
    memop(1, pc, instruction); printf("\n");
    instruction = 32'b01001001000000000001000000000001; pc++;
        // add %r0 0x1 %r1
    memop(1, pc, instruction); printf("\n");
    instruction = 32'b01110001010000000000000000000000; pc++;
        // cmp %r1 %r2
    memop(1, pc, instruction); printf("\n");
    instruction = 32'b00011000000000000111000000000000; pc++;
        // br,e 0x7 #equal
    memop(1, pc, instruction); printf("\n");
    instruction = 32'b00010000000000000011000000000000; pc++;
        // br,a 0x2 #always
    memop(1, pc, instruction); printf("\n");
    instruction = 32'b11100000000000000000000000000000; pc++;
        // halt
    memop(1, pc, instruction); printf("\n");

    printf("----  Finished initialization\n");
    pc = 12'b000000000000;
    printf("----  Program starting\n");

    while (! program_finish) {
        instr_exe ++;
        memop(0, pc, instruction); // fetch new instruction
        printf(" opcode ");
        program_finish = cpu_pipe(pc, instruction); // execute it
        if (instr_exe > 1000) {
            break;
        }
    }
    printf("----  Program end\n");
}

// function cpu_pipe
// This function models the decode and the execute function of the cpu.
```

```
//
// Agruments
// pc : program counter; the value of pc in the caller will be modified
// instruction : instruction to be executed
//
// return value : 1 terminate the simulation
//               0 get next instruction

function integer cpu_pipe (var reg[11:0] pc, reg[31:0] instruction) {
    integer temp_return_value = 0;
    reg[31:0]  temp1 = {32 {1'b0}};
    reg[31:0]  temp2 = {32 {1'b0}};
    static reg  cc;
    printf ("----- ");
    case (instruction[31:28]) {
        NOP  : {  // Executes nop instruction
            printf("nop");
            temp_return_value = 0;
            pc++;
        }
        BR : {      // Executes br instruction
            printf("br");
            temp_return_value = 0;
            if (instruction[27] == 1'b0) {
                printf(" a, 0x%h <   TAKEN>",instruction[23:12]);
                pc = instruction[23:12];
            }
            else {
                if (cc == 1'b1) {
                    printf(" e, 0x%h <TAKEN>",instruction[23:12]);
                    pc = instruction[23:12];
                }
                else {
                    printf(" e, 0x%h <NOT TAKEN>",instruction[23:12]);
                    pc++;
                }
            }
            cc = 1'b0;
        }
        LDX : {      // Executes load instruction
            printf("ldx");
            // read the memory and write it to register
            printf(" <\%%h>",instruction[25:23]);
            memop(0,instruction[11:0], temp1);
            regop(1, instruction[25:23], temp1);
            temp_return_value = 0;
            pc++;
        }
        STX : {      // Executes store instruction
            printf("stx");
            case (instruction[27]) {
                1'b0 : { // read the register and write it to memory
                    printf(" <\%%h>",instruction[25:23]);
```

```
                regop(0,instruction[25:23], temp1);
        }
        1'b1 : { // store immidiate to memory
            printf(" <imm>");
            temp1 = instruction[32:12] || {32 { 1'b0}};
        }
    }
    memop(1, instruction[11:0], temp1);
    temp_return_value = 0;
    pc++;
}
HALT :{        // Executes halt intruction
    printf("halt\n");
    temp_return_value = 1;
    pc++;
}
ADD :{         // Executes add instruction
    printf("add");
    case(instruction[27]) {
    1'b0 : { // all registers
            regop(0, instruction[26:24], temp1);
            regop(0, instruction[23:21], temp2);
            temp1 = temp1 + temp2;
            regop(1, instruction[2:0], temp1);
        }
    1'b1 : { // imm
            regop(0, instruction[26:24], temp1);
            temp2 = instruction[23:12] | {32 {1'b0}};
            printf("  i  : <%h> ",temp2);
            temp1 = temp1 + temp2;
            regop(1, instruction[2:0], temp1);
        }
    }
    temp_return_value = 0;
    pc++;
}
SUB : {        // Executes subtract instruction
    printf("sub");
    case(instruction[27]) {
    1'b0 : { // all registers
            regop(0, instruction[26:24], temp1);
            regop(0, instruction[23:21], temp2);
            temp1 = temp1 + (! temp2) + 1'b1;
            regop(1, instruction[2:0], temp1);
        }
    1'b1 : { // imm
            regop(0, instruction[26:24], temp1);
            temp2 = instruction[23:12] | {32 {1'b0}};
            printf("  i  : <%h> ",temp2);
            temp1 = temp1 + (!temp2) + 1'b1;
            regop(1, instruction[2:0], temp1);
        }
    }
```

```
                temp_return_value = 0;
                pc++;
        }
        CMP :{            // Executes compare instruction
            printf("cmp");
            case(instruction[27]) {
            1'b0 : { // all registers
                    regop(0, instruction[26:24], temp1);
                    regop(0, instruction[23:21], temp2);
                    if (temp1 == temp2)
                        cc = 1'b1;
                    else
                        cc = 1'b0;
                }
            1'b1 : { // imm
                    regop(0, instruction[26:24], temp1);
                    temp2 = instruction[23:12] | {32 {1'b0}};
                    printf("  i : <%h> ",temp2);
                    if (temp1 == temp2)
                        cc = 1'b1;
                    else
                        cc = 1'b0;
                }
            }
            printf(" \%cc %b", cc[0]);
            temp_return_value = 0;
            pc++;
        }
        default : {   // This detects illegal opcodes
            printf("Unknown opcode %b\n", instruction[31:28]);
            temp_return_value = 1;
            pc++;
        }
    }
    printf("\n");
    cpu_pipe = temp_return_value; // The return value of the function
}

// Task memop
// This task models the memory system of the cpu
// to read operation = 0
//    write operation = 1
task memop (integer operation,reg[11:0] address,var reg[31:0] data)
{
    static reg[31:0] memory[]; // Sparse memory
    if (operation == 1) // write {
        memory[address] = data;
        printf(" 0x%h :<w 0x%h>", address, data);
    }
    else {
        data = memory[address];
        printf(" 0x%h :<r 0x%h>", address, data);
    }
```

```
}

// Task regop
// This task models the register file system of the cpu
// to read   operation = 0
//    write operation = 1
task regop (integer operation, reg[2:0] regd, var reg[31:0] data)
{
    static reg[31:0] register_file[8]; // Eight 32-bit wide registers
    if (operation == 1) // write {
        register_file[regd] = data;
        printf(" \%r%h :[w %h]", regd, data);
    }
    else {
        if (regd == 0)
            register_file[regd] = {32{ 1'b0}};

            data = register_file[regd];
            printf(" \%r%h :[r %h]",regd, data);
    }
}
```

Output

Executing the above example produces the following output:

```
 ++------------------------------------------------------------------++
 ||                     VERA VERIFICATION SYSTEM                     ||
 ||      Copyright (c) 1995, 1996, 1997, 1998, 1999 by Synopsys, Inc.  ||
 ||                     All Rights Reserved                          ||
 ||            VERA is a trademark of Synopsys, Inc.                 ||
 ||        CONFIDENTIAL AND PROPRIETARY INFORMATION OF SYNOPSYS, INC.  ||
 ++------------------------------------------------------------------++
Version: 4.4_Beta2.1
----   Initializing
 0x000 :<w 0x00000000>
 0x001 :<w 0x40000001>
 0x002 :<w 0x48009002>
 0x003 :<w 0x49001001>
 0x004 :<w 0x71400000>
 0x005 :<w 0x18007000>
 0x006 :<w 0x10003000>
 0x007 :<w 0xe0000000>
----   Finished initialization
----   Program starting
0x000 :<r 0x00000000> opcode ----- nop
0x001 :<r 0x40000001> opcode ----- add %r0 :[r 00000000] %r0 :[r 00000000] %r1 :[w
00000000]
0x002 :<r 0x48009002> opcode ----- add %r0 :[r 00000000]  i  : <00000009>   %r2 :[w
```

```
00000009]
0x003 :<r 0x49001001> opcode ----- add %r1 :[r 00000000]  i  : <00000001>  %r1 :[w
00000001]
0x004 :<r 0x71400000> opcode ----- cmp %r1 :[r 00000001] %r2 :[r 00000009] %cc 0
0x005 :<r 0x18007000> opcode ----- br e, 0x007 <NOT TAKEN>
0x006 :<r 0x10003000> opcode ----- br a, 0x003 <   TAKEN>
0x003 :<r 0x49001001> opcode ----- add %r1 :[r 00000001]  i  : <00000001>  %r1 :[w
00000002]
0x004 :<r 0x71400000> opcode ----- cmp %r1 :[r 00000002] %r2 :[r 00000009] %cc 0
0x005 :<r 0x18007000> opcode ----- br e, 0x007 <NOT TAKEN>
0x006 :<r 0x10003000> opcode ----- br a, 0x003 <   TAKEN>
0x003 :<r 0x49001001> opcode ----- add %r1 :[r 00000002]  i  : <00000001>  %r1 :[w
00000003]
0x004 :<r 0x71400000> opcode ----- cmp %r1 :[r 00000003] %r2 :[r 00000009] %cc 0
0x005 :<r 0x18007000> opcode ----- br e, 0x007 <NOT TAKEN>
0x006 :<r 0x10003000> opcode ----- br a, 0x003 <   TAKEN>
0x003 :<r 0x49001001> opcode ----- add %r1 :[r 00000003]  i  : <00000001>  %r1 :[w
00000004]
0x004 :<r 0x71400000> opcode ----- cmp %r1 :[r 00000004] %r2 :[r 00000009] %cc 0
0x005 :<r 0x18007000> opcode ----- br e, 0x007 <NOT TAKEN>
0x006 :<r 0x10003000> opcode ----- br a, 0x003 <   TAKEN>
0x003 :<r 0x49001001> opcode ----- add %r1 :[r 00000004]  i  : <00000001>  %r1 :[w
00000005]
0x004 :<r 0x71400000> opcode ----- cmp %r1 :[r 00000005] %r2 :[r 00000009] %cc 0
0x005 :<r 0x18007000> opcode ----- br e, 0x007 <NOT TAKEN>
0x006 :<r 0x10003000> opcode ----- br a, 0x003 <   TAKEN>
0x003 :<r 0x49001001> opcode ----- add %r1 :[r 00000005]  i  : <00000001>  %r1 :[w
00000006]
0x004 :<r 0x71400000> opcode ----- cmp %r1 :[r 00000006] %r2 :[r 00000009] %cc 0
0x005 :<r 0x18007000> opcode ----- br e, 0x007 <NOT TAKEN>
0x006 :<r 0x10003000> opcode ----- br a, 0x003 <   TAKEN>
0x003 :<r 0x49001001> opcode ----- add %r1 :[r 00000006]  i  : <00000001>  %r1 :[w
00000007]
0x004 :<r 0x71400000> opcode ----- cmp %r1 :[r 00000007] %r2 :[r 00000009] %cc 0
0x005 :<r 0x18007000> opcode ----- br e, 0x007 <NOT TAKEN>
0x006 :<r 0x10003000> opcode ----- br a, 0x003 <   TAKEN>
0x003 :<r 0x49001001> opcode ----- add %r1 :[r 00000007]  i  : <00000001>  %r1 :[w
00000008]
0x004 :<r 0x71400000> opcode ----- cmp %r1 :[r 00000008] %r2 :[r 00000009] %cc 0
0x005 :<r 0x18007000> opcode ----- br e, 0x007 <NOT TAKEN>
0x006 :<r 0x10003000> opcode ----- br a, 0x003 <   TAKEN>
0x003 :<r 0x49001001> opcode ----- add %r1 :[r 00000008]  i  : <00000001>  %r1 :[w
00000009]
0x004 :<r 0x71400000> opcode ----- cmp %r1 :[r 00000009] %r2 :[r 00000009] %cc 1
0x005 :<r 0x18007000> opcode ----- br e, 0x007 <   TAKEN>
0x007 :<r 0xe0000000> opcode ----- halt
---- Program end

Vera: finish encountered at cycle      0
        total        mismatch: 0
                    vca_error: 0
                fail(expected): 0
```

```
    drive: 0
   expect: 0
   sample: 0
     sync: 0
```

Anatomy of the CPU Program

In this example, the assembly program to be executed is hard-coded. The model consists of three main blocks: the function cpu_pipe( ) and the tasks memop( ) and regop( ).

The function cpu_pipe( ) models the instruction execution unit, and the tasks memop( ) and regop( ) perform the memory and register operations.

```
#define  NOP 4'b0000
```

This preprocessor directive is the opcode definition of the nop instruction. A similar definition is included for all other instructions.

```
program cpu
```

This is the beginning of the program block.

```
reg[11:0] pc = {12{1'b0}};
reg[31:0] instruction = {32{1'b0}};
```

This code defines the width of the program counter and the instructions.

```
 integer program_finish = 0;
```

The variable program_finish is used to detect when to halt the simulation.

```
integer instr_exe = 0;
```

The instr_exe variable stops runaway simulations (infinite loops). If the CPU program is nonterminating, this variable halts the simulation.

```
instruction = 32'b00000000000000000000000000000000;
pc = {12{ 1'b0}}; // nop

memop(1, pc, instruction); printf("\n");
```

As mentioned, the code to be executed is hard-coded. Before you can
execute the program, it must be loaded into memory with a call to the
memop( ) task. In this instance, a nop is written into memory location
0.

```
memop(0, pc, instruction); //fetch new instruction
program_finish = cpu_pipe(pc, instruction);
                                //execute it
```

The instruction fetch and execution take place here. The memop( )
task fetches the instruction, and the CPU pipe executes it.

```
function integer cpu_pipe (var reg[11:0] pc,
reg[31:0] instruction)
```

This is the cpu_pipe( ) function declaration. The function cpu_pipe( )
accepts a 12-bit program counter and a 32-bit instruction.

Note the keyword var just before the pc definition. This is a call by
reference (see page 81). If cpu_pipe( ) alters the value of pc, that
change is reflected back in the caller, while a change made to the
instruction bits is local. The program counter is implemented with var
because instructions can modify it. For example, the branch
instruction contains the address that should be loaded into the program
counter before the next instruction is executed.

```
static reg cc;
```

The variable cc models the condition code register. Only two
instructions, cmp and br, use this register. Since there is no need to
pass it in as a function argument, cc can be static. This preserves the
value of the variable when the function finishes and makes it available
when the function is called again.

```
case (instruction[31:28])
```

The case statement reads the opcode field and figures out which instruction is being executed. This is the instruction decode operation. Note the nested case in the add branch. Multilevel branching sometimes comes in handy.

```
task memop (integer operation, reg[11:0] address, var
reg[31:0] data)
```

The memop( ) task models the memory read and memory write operations. In the write operation, the data variable is an input, but in the read operation, it is an output. Hence, the data argument is declared as a var.

```
static reg[31:0] memory[]; // Sparse memory
```

This variable is an associative array (because of the empty [ ] at the end). The advantage of modeling a memory in this way is that the entries are dynamically allocated, which means that instead of allocating space for the complete memory, space is allocated for only those locations which are used.

Additionally, you declare it as static because you do not want to lose the contents of the memory every time you exit the function. To access the memory, the task memop( ) is used.

```
task regop (integer operation, reg[2:0] regd, var
reg[31:0] data)
```

```
static reg[31:0] register_file[8];
    // Eight 32-bit-wide registers
```

This task is almost identical to the memop( ) task. The difference is the width of regd—it is 3 bits wide because only eight registers are modeled. Again, the data is declared as a var. register_file is declared static for the same reason that memory was declared static. It is an eight-element array of 32-bit-wide entries to model eight 32-bit registers. Since only eight elements are needed, a one-dimensional array is used instead of an associative array.

Summary

This chapter has served as an introduction to the Vera language. It covered its basic features, as well as more advanced topics, such as tasks, functions, and associative arrays, and finally presented an example of a CPU model. You should now be able to write reasonably complex programs in Vera.

CHAPTER 5

RTL Ports & Interfaces in Vera

This chapter introduces the verification constructs provided by Vera. Verification constructs are the hardware-oriented features used for interfacing with the DUT. The chapter illustrates the use of these constructs by developing a simple RAM testbench.

Event-Based Versus Cycle-Based Simulation

In the real world, events happen asynchronously. If an attempt is made to model the real world, all asynchronous events must be evaluated, for an accurate result. And there are way too many events. This makes real-world modeling a noncomputable task, since there are so many events to evaluate.

To make modeling possible, the concept of a *time step* is used. Basically, evaluations are done and consequences modeled (events are scheduled to occur in future) at every time step. Simulators have a built-in time step, and they reevaluate the data structure of the model being simulated at every time step. The computational load of the simulation is dependent on the number of evaluated time steps and the memory size of the data structure of the simulated model.

Time-step-based simulations generate very accurate results for a behavioral analysis, especially in synchronous designs. Theoretically, the time step can be stretched so that it is exactly equal to the clock cycle and nodes of interest (in a synchronous design, the inputs and outputs of all flops) evaluated every clock cycle. This is a cycle-based simulation, since evaluations are performed every clock cycle. With this approach, computational load is greatly reduced (although at the expense of timing accuracy, in that fewer events are evaluated) and the simulation advances at a much faster rate.

FIGURE 5-1   Cycle-Based Versus Event-Based Simulator Scheduling

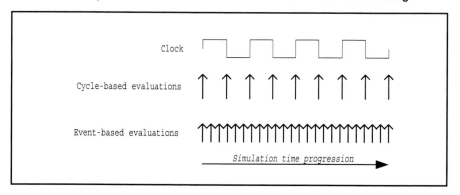

Verilog simulators are event-based. Since the majority of present-day digital designs have structures such as multiple clock domains, feedback loops, and timing checks, an accurate simulation demands computations more frequently than at every clock cycle.

Vera is cycle-based and has a cycle-based engine built in. Vera is designed to generate stimulus for synchronous interfaces of digital designs. If needed Vera does provide means of asynchronous evaluation of signals.

Designing Interfaces—Multiport RAM

Figure 5-2 shows how designers typically analyze a multiport RAM design.

FIGURE 5-2   How Designers Analyze a Multiport RAM

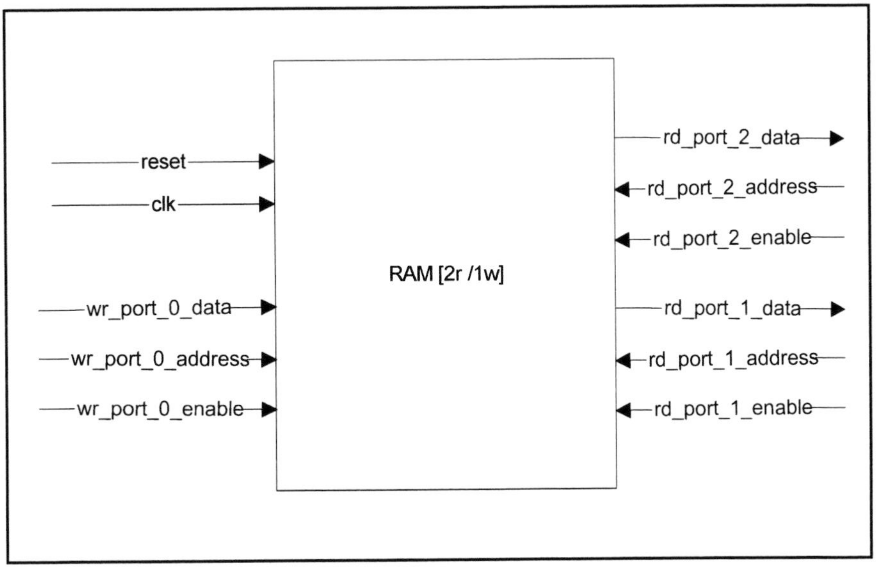

Vera sees designs differently, however, as shown in Figure 5-3. With the exception of the clock, all Verilog inputs are treated as Vera outputs and all Verilog outputs are treated as Vera inputs. Since signals of synchronous interfaces are driven relative to a clock, Vera interface signals are sampled and driven relative to the clock generated in Verilog.

The term *interface* as used here means a collection of signals related to one clock domain. The Vera-to-Verilog interface is defined by the built-in interface construct.

FIGURE 5-3   How Vera Analyzes a Multiport RAM

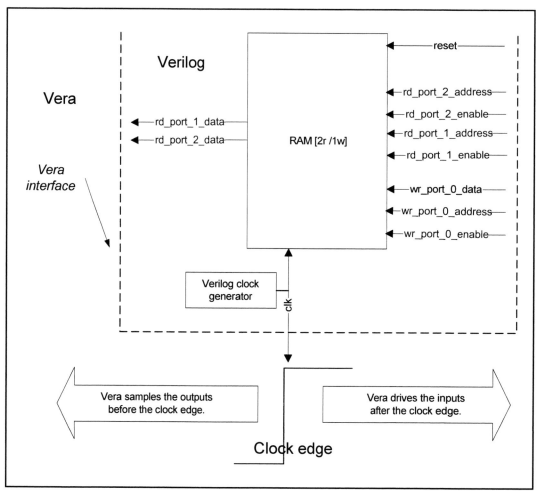

Interface Syntax

The syntax for defining a Vera interface is shown below. Note that interface definition(s) should precede the program block declaration.

```
interface <interface_name> {
   <direction>[<width>] <signame> <sigtype> [#<skew>];
   <direction>[<width>] <signame> <sigtype> [#<skew>];
   ...
}
```

where

interface_name is the name of the interface

direction is either input or output

width is the bit range in case of a bus, in Verilog style: [MSB:LSB]

signame is the signal name

sigtype is one of the signal types listed in Table 5-1

skew is an integer value offset from the clock edge

Vera provides the signal types listed in Table 5-1 for the interface structure, to interface to a wide array of synchronous design interface ports. Vera uses these to determine when to drive stimulus and when to read response relative to the interface clock.

TABLE 5-1   Interface Signal Types

Signal Type	Testbench Operation
NHOLD	Output will be driven on the negative edge of the interface clock.
PHOLD	Output will be driven on the positive edge of the interface clock.
NR <value>	Output will be driven on the falling edge of the interface clock for one cycle and then return to <value> (0,1,X,Z).
PR <value>	Output will be driven on the rising edge of the interface clock for one cycle and then return to <value> (0,1,X,Z).
NSAMPLE	Input will be sampled at the negative edge of the interface clock.
PSAMPLE	Input will be sampled at the positive edge of the interface clock.
CLOCK	Unique, required input specifies the clock used to synchronize the sampling and driving of the other signals in the interface.

Skew definition.   The skew needs to be defined for each signal so that the evaluation Vera interface inputs happen before the clock (and the signal) transitions, and drives of Vera interface output occurs after the clock has transitioned. To evaluate a signal before the clock transitions specifies a negative skew; to evaluate after the clock transition specifies a positive skew. Figure 5-4 illustrates this.

FIGURE 5-4   Skew Definition Relative to a Clock Edge

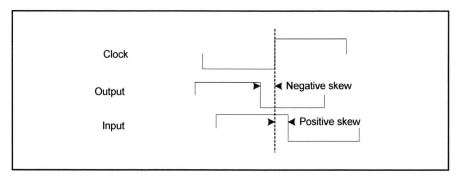

The example below shows the interface definition for the example RAM design.

```
interface ram {
    input           clk             CLOCK;
    input           reset           PHOLD #1;
    output[7:0]     rd_port_1_address PHOLD #1;
    output          rd_port_1_enable  PHOLD #1;
    output[31:0]    rd_port_1_data    PSAMPLE;
    output[7:0]     rd_port_2_address PHOLD #1;
    output          rd_port_2_enable  PHOLD #1;
    output[31:0]    rd_port_2_data    PSAMPLE;
    output[7:0]     wr_port_0_address PHOLD #1;
    output          wr_port_0_enable  PHOLD #1;
    output[31:0]    wr_port_0_data    PHOLD #1;
} // end of interface ram
```

Interface Architecture

Figure 5-5 shows the various components of a Vera/Verilog testbench and how they connect to each other. Vera generates the vshell automatically at compile time. The vshell will be discussed shortly.

FIGURE 5-5 Architecture of Vera Interface With Verilog

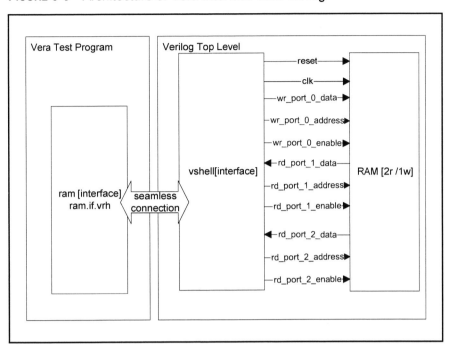

Automatic Interface Generation

Vera can automatically generate an interface definition for connecting to a simple design. This is helpful during the testbench development cycle. The Vera template generator can read the Verilog design module definition and generate a top-level testbench file and a Vera interface definition file.

The template generator works well with single-clock designs, but as yet cannot handle multiple-clock designs. A more detailed discussion of interfacing to a multiple-clock design is discussed later in the chapter.

The Verilog module definition for the example RAM design is as follows:

```
// 2r/1w port ram module
module ram (
        reset,
        clk,
        rd_port_1_address,
        rd_port_1_enable,
        rd_port_1_data,
```

```
                    rd_port_2_address,
                    rd_port_2_enable,
                    rd_port_2_data,
                    wr_port_0_address,
                    wr_port_0_enable,
                    wr_port_0_data
        );

        input reset;
        input clk;
        input [7:0]      wr_port_0_address;
        input [31:0]     wr_port_0_data;
        input [7:0]      wr_port_0_enable;
        input [7:0]      rd_port_1_address;
        input            rd_port_1_enable;
        output [31:0]    rd_port_1_data;
        input [7:0]      rd_port_2_address;
        input            rd_port_2_enable;
        output [31:0]    rd_port_2_data;
endmodule
```

The following command (shown in boldface below) invokes the Vera template generator, which automatically generates all the necessary interface files for the RAM design.

```
%vera -tem -c clk -t ram ram.v
Parsing ram.v..
Writing top_file to ram.test_top.v
Writing vera interface file to ram.if.vrh
Writing vera template file to ram.vr.tmp
Done.
```

The command line switch used above have the following results:

–tem places the Vera compiler in template mode.

–c identifies is the clock used in the template.

–t identifies the top of the Verilog hierarchy.

Refer to the *VERA System Verifier User Manual* for an explanation of the Vera command-line options.

When the command is run three files are generated:

ram.test_top.v—The top-level Verilog module for the testbench

ram.vrh—The interface definition that can be used with a Vera testbench ram.vr.tmp—A test template that can be used as a starting point in development of a new test

The example below, the ram.test_top.v generated file, shows how the design and the vshell module (discussed shortly) are instantiated.

NOTE *Outputs of Verilog design are inputs to Vera interfaces. The only exception is the clock, which is an input to both.*

```
module ram_test_top;
    parameter simulation_cycle = 100;

    reg             SystemClock;
    wire            reset;
    wire            clk;
    wire[7:0]       rd_port_1_address;
    wire            rd_port_1_enable;
    wire[31:0]      rd_port_1_data;
    wire[7:0]       rd_port_2_address;
    wire            rd_port_2_enable;
    wire[31:0]      rd_port_2_data;
    wire[7:0]       wr_port_0_address;
    wire            wr_port_0_enable;
    wire[31:0]      wr_port_0_data;
    assign          clk = SystemClock;

    vera_shell vshell(
        .SystemClock(SystemClock),
        .ram_reset(reset),
        .ram_clk(clk),
        .ram_rd_port_1_address(rd_port_1_address),
        .ram_rd_port_1_enable(rd_port_1_enable),
        .ram_rd_port_1_data(rd_port_1_data),
        .ram_rd_port_2_address(rd_port_2_address),
        .ram_rd_port_2_enable(rd_port_2_enable),
        .ram_rd_port_2_data(rd_port_2_data),
        .ram_wr_port_0_address(wr_port_0_address),
        .ram_wr_port_0_enable(wr_port_0_enable),
        .ram_wr_port_0_data(wr_port_0_data)
    );

`ifdef emu
/* DUT is in emulator, so not instantiated here */
`else
    ram dut(
        .reset(reset),
        .clk(clk),
        .rd_port_1_address(rd_port_1_address),
        .rd_port_1_enable(rd_port_1_enable),
        .rd_port_1_data(rd_port_1_data),
```

```
                    .rd_port_2_address(rd_port_2_address),
                    .rd_port_2_enable(rd_port_2_enable),
                    .rd_port_2_data(rd_port_2_data),
                    .wr_port_0_address(wr_port_0_address),
                    .wr_port_0_enable(wr_port_0_enable),
                    .wr_port_0_data(wr_port_0_data)
            );
    `endif // !`ifdef emu

        initial begin
            SystemClock = 0;
            forever begin
                #(simulation_cycle/2)
                    SystemClock = ~SystemClock;
            end
        end
    endmodule
```

Dealing With Multiple Clocks & Multiple Interfaces

Some designs have multiple clocks and multiple interfaces. How do you interface Vera with such a configuration? Answer: Simply define more interfaces, and make sure the names of the interfaces are unique and that only one clock drives a particular interface. So if the example design would have had two clocks, one for the read interfaces and another for the write interfaces, Vera interfaces would have been designed as follows:

```
interface ram {
    output          reset               PHOLD #1;
    input           clk                 CLOCK;
    output[7:0]     rd_port_1_address   PHOLD #1;
    output          rd_port_1_enable    PHOLD #1;
    input[31:0]     rd_port_1_data      PSETUP;
    output[7:0]     rd_port_2_address   PHOLD #1;
    output          rd_port_2_enable    PHOLD #1;
    input[31:0]     rd_port_2_data      PSETUP;
}   // end of interface ram

interface ram_wr {
    output          reset_wr            PHOLD #1;
    input           clk_wr              CLOCK;
    output[7:0]     wr_port_0_address   PHOLD #1;
    output          wr_port_0_enable    PHOLD #1;
    output[31:0]    wr_port_0_data      PHOLD #1;
}   // end of interface ram
```

As already mentioned, the automatic template generator cannot handle multiple clock design. In such cases it is best to do the following.

1. Run the template generator by treating the design a single interface/clock design, as shown in previous examples.

2. Update the generated interface definition to add additional interface definitions with different clocks, as shown in the code segment above.

3. Change port names of the vshell instantiation in the generated top level according to the port name convention, as shown in the next section.

The vshell Module

Note the vshell module in the file ram.test_top.v. Vera generates a vshell module when you compile a Vera program and writes it to a file with a .vshell extension. Most of the details of the vshell module are beyond the scope of this discussion, but the port list—specifically the naming convention of the ports—is important.

The port list comes in handy when connecting a design with multiple interfaces and multiple clocks to Vera. As discussed above, this must be done manually, since the automatic template generator cannot handle multiple clock designs.

The port names of the vshell module are derived directly from the interface definition in the Vera program. The syntax is

```
<vera_interface_name>_<signal_name>
```

Figure 5-6 shows the translation from Vera interface names to a vshell port list. Note how the name of the corresponding Vera interface is prepended to each signal name in the vshell port list. The only exception to this naming convention is the default system clock, which is referenced in Vera as "CLOCK" and in Verilog as "SystemClock".

FIGURE 5-6   Port Name Translation for the RAM Testbench

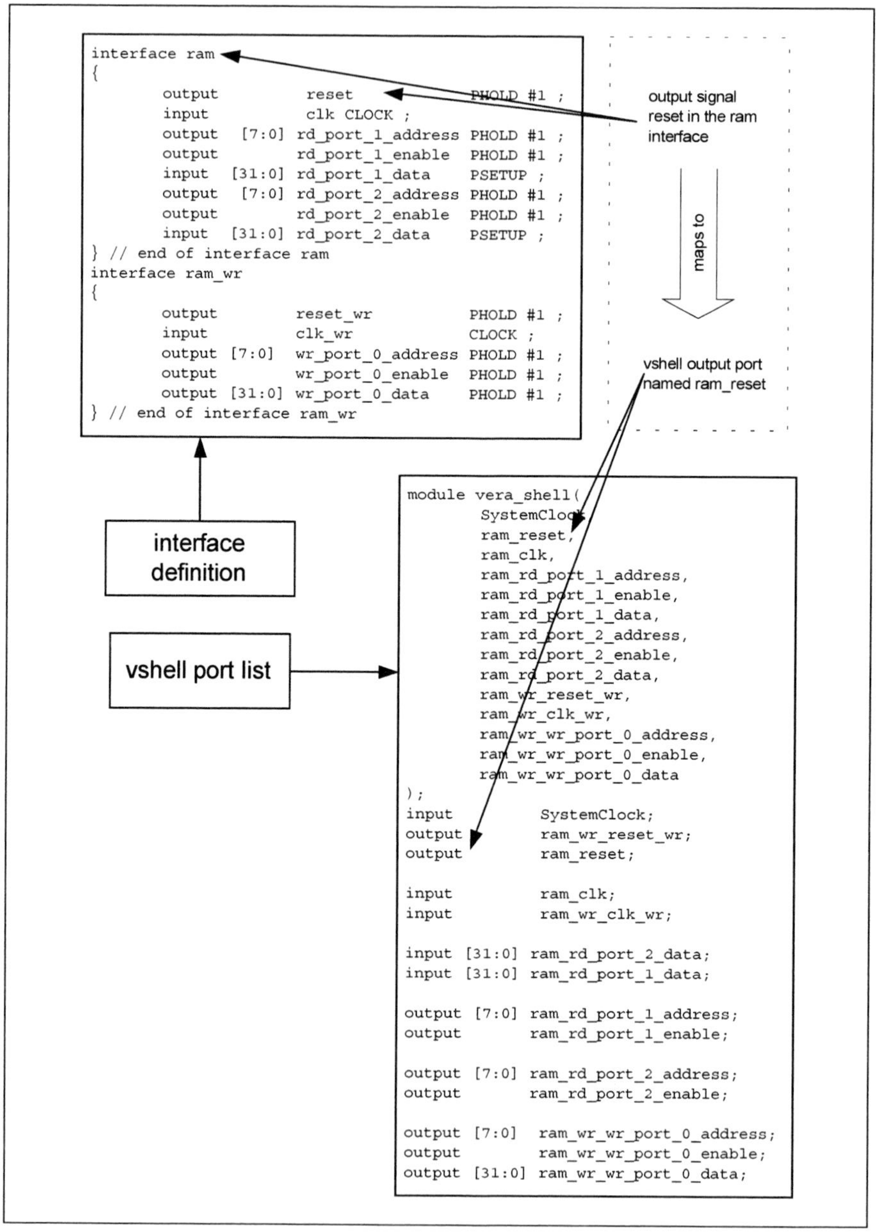

Directly Referencing Signals Embedded in the Hierarchy

When developing a testbench, you often have to force internal nodes of the design to particular values. To do this from Vera, add a signal to the Vera interface that represents internal node. For example, to include q_n, the inverted output of an internal flip-flop named DFF, make a direct connection to it by adding the following line to your list of interface signals.

```
input q_n PSAMPLE #1 verilog_node "top.DFF.q_n"
```

top.DFF.q_n is the full hierarchical path to the signal of interest. The Vera interface treats this as an internal wire, so you do not have to add it to the vshell instantiation.

The verilog_node argument can be used to instantiate interface wires as well, which eliminates needing to know the vshell port name mapping.

Stimulus & Response—Sending Traffic Across the Interface

So far, this chapter has covered how to connect Vera and Verilog—that is, it has defined the interface. This section covers how to send traffic across the interface.

Note that the point of view in this section is the testbench—"outputs" means outputs from the testbench; "inputs" means inputs to the testbench.

To verify a design, the user must know the following:

- Interface—Which signals must be driven (discussed in the previous section)

- Synchronization—When things should be evaluated

- Drives—Which values must be driven by the testbench

- Expects and samples—Which responses are expected by the testbench

Synchronization

Synchronization deals with the timing of the stimulus. Synchronization statements in Vera start with the @ operator and are used in the program body. The syntax is

```
@([<transition_edge>] <signal> [or <signal> ...])
```

where transition_edge is either posedge or negedge. Note that signal widths may be specified, as shown in the example below:

```
@(posedge clk)        // whenever clk has posedge transitions
@(data)               // whenever data changes
@(CLOCK)              // whenever the default system clock changes
@(negedge clk)        // negative edge of the clk
@(sig1 or sig2)       // whenever sig1 or sig2 changes
@(data[3:0])          // when any of the four least
                      // significant bits of data change
@(posedge data[1])    // at the posedge of data[1], must be 1 bit
```

If synchronization is performed relative to an edge (posedge or negedge), the signal must be one bit wide.

Drives

Drives set the values of testbench output or inout signals. Vera provides two methods for driving signals:

- Blocking drive

- Nonblocking drive

Blocking Drives

Blocking drives wait for the synchronization edge of the interface clock. Simulation waits for a specified cycle delay before driving the interface signal to the specified value. If no delay is specified, a default delay of 0 is used. The syntax is

```
[@<delay>] <interface>.<signal>[<bits>] = <data>;
```

At runtime, if a statement is encountered at a cycle boundary, the current cycle is counted as cycle 0. If a statement is encountered between cycles, the next cycle is counted as cycle 0.

If a delay of @0 is used and the drive statement is encountered at the correct driving edge of the signal, the drive happens right away. Otherwise, the drive happens at the next edge.

In the following example, execution waits for one cycle before driving bus.reset to 1'b1:

```
interface bus {
    clock  clk;
    output reset PHOLD;
    output value PHOLD;

}
    :
@1 bus.reset = 1'b1; bus.value = 1'b0;    // both driven in cycle 1
@1 nus.reset = 1'b0;                      // driven in cycle 2
    :
```

Nonblocking Drives

Nonblocking drives do not stall the execution, but schedule the drives to execute after the specified cycle delay. The syntax is

[@<delay>] <interface>.<signal>[<bits>] <= <data>;

In the following example, bus.reset is scheduled to be driven to 1'b1 after one cycle:

```
interface bus {
    clock  clk;
    output reset PHOLD;
    output value PHOLD;
}
@1 bus.reset <= 1'b1; // Both reset
   bus.value <= 1'b0; // and value will be driven at the same time.
```

Using Blocking Versus Nonblocking Drives

Blocking statements stall execution until the statement operation is finished. Nonblocking statements schedule execution of the desired event without waiting for the operation to finish, and the program proceeds to the next statement immediately.

```
{   // Blocking
    @1 reset = 0;          //reset is de-asserted  at cycle 1
    address = 8`h55;       //this will be executed at cycle 1
}


{   // Non-blocking
    @1 reset <= 0;         //reset is scheduled to be de-asserted in one
                           //cycle, and execution continues
    address = 8`h55;       //this is executed at cycle 0 [right away]
}
```

FIGURE 5-7   Comparison of Blocking and Nonblocking Drive Statements

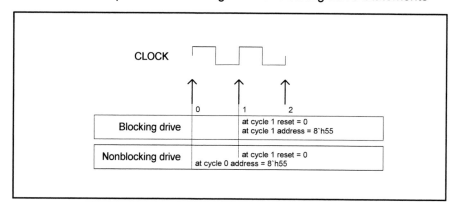

Void Drives

Drives can also be used as a mean of synchronizing the Vera program. For this use the keyword void to drive the signal, as shown in the following segment.

```
@1 bus.signal = void;
```

The above statement will block the execution till cycle 1 is encountered, and then continue execution, without actually driving any value into the testbench.

Drive Conflicts

To deal with conflict cases where a single signal might be driven by multiple sources, Vera provides strong and soft drives. See the *VERA System Verifier User Manual* to learn more about such cases.

Expects

In Vera, expects assert that given signals have given values at the given time. *All expects are blocking.* Any mismatch results in a simulation error and can cause simulation to abort. Thus, expects are useful only for checking the behavior of protocol handshake signals. For a more complex analysis of DUT response, use samples instead (discussed shortly).

The syntax for expects is

```
@<delay>[,<window>] <expect_expr> [,<expect_expr> ...];
```

Here, delay is either an integer cycle delay or an expect window indicated by two comma-separated integers. delay = 0 indicates the current clock cycle.

window specifies the number of cycles for which the check is performed. So the starting cycle for the delay is where the check starts and the ending cycle is delay + window. For example, a @4,5 delay window denotes that the check should start in cycle 4 and finish in cycle 9, for a total of 6 checks (a check per cycle at cycles 4, 5, 6, 7, 8, and 9).

expect_expr is a Vera expression of the form

```
<interface>.<signal> OPERATOR <value>
```

If multiple expressions (comma separated expect expressions) are used, then all expressions must be true when they are evaluated. In other words the "," behaves like an AND operator.

For example,

```
@1 bus.ack == 1, bus.req == 0;    // after 1 cycle bus.ack should be 1
                                  // and bus.req should be 0
@4,10 bus.data != 4'b0001;        // bus.data should be 4'b0001
                                  // within 4 to 10 cycles
```

Full Expects

Full expects, denoted by @@, make sure the equalities are true throughout the specified duration.

```
@@ 5,100 bus.data == 4'bxx11;
   // Data bits 1:0 remain 11 from cycle 5
   // onward for the next 100 cycles
@@ 100 bus.data[0] != 1'b0, bus.address == 2'b00;
   // Bit 0 of data is never zero for the next 100 cycles
   // and bus.address is 00 through the same interval.
```

In the first example above, the expression must hold true between cycles 5 and 105 inclusive.

Restricted Expects

Restricted expects, denoted by @@@, watch the first transition of the given signal to see if the signal value transitioned as expected.

```
@@@ 100 bus.data == 4'b0000;
   // If the data is not already 0000
   // make sure that it goes to 0000 on the next transition
@@@ 4,50 bus.addr == 2'b00, bus.data == 4'b0000;
   // At first transition of any of the signals or at the end
   // of the delay slot, both condition must hold true;
   // bus.addr should be 00 and bus.data should be 0000.
```

Void Expects

All expects block until the Vera thread that executes them encounters the appropriate clock edge. This feature can be used in conjunction with the void keyword to synchronize a Vera thread with Verilog.

```
@3 bus.data == void;
```

Sampling

Sampling assigns the value of a signal to a variable. The syntax may be either of the following:

```
<variable> = <signal_name>;
```

```
<variable> = <signal_name> OPERATOR <value>;
```

The signal must be an input or an inout in the interface definition.

Samples of the first type happen at the corresponding clock edge. If the statement is encountered at the cycle boundary, it happens right away. Otherwise, it waits for the next cycle boundary.

```
lsb_bus = data[0];              // happens at the corresponding edge
```

Samples of the second type (i.e., those with arithmetic expressions) happen immediately. In the following, cpu.ready is an output of the device cpu and count is an integer variable:

```
if (cpu.ready !=1'b1 && count==2048)
    printf (" Time Out Error\n");
```

The delay attribute @ cannot be used in sampling. To delay the sampling of a signal value, use an explicit delaying statement first. For example,

```
repeat(3) @(posedge CLOCK); // wait three positive edges of the clock
lsb_bus = data[0]; // then sample the signal
```

Virtual Ports, Binds & Generic Tasks

Designs often have multiple interfaces with essentially the same functionality or protocols. This is especially true in networking designs, where the most interfaces deal with packets. The RAM example discussed above also has several interfaces with essentially the same functionality.

It is redundant to write several sets of nearly identical functions, one for each port of the RAM, but it seemingly must be done, since port signals are embedded in the functions. To get around this, Vera provides virtual ports and binds, which enable the writing of generic tasks that operate on virtualized ports.

Virtual ports allow you to group signals, based on their functionality

Virtual ports allow you to group signals based on their functionality. Using virtual ports in conjunction with generic tasks isolates the testbench from design interface changes.

For example, if the name of a port in the design interface changes, you do not have to change all the tasks that drive the interface. Instead, you can simply update the port binding declaration and the interface declaration.

Virtual ports and generic tasks also make it easier to adapt existing testbenches to work with new versions of a design. Figure 5-8 shows the advantage of using virtual ports and generic tasks with a design that has many interfaces with the same functionality.

FIGURE 5-8 Direct Signal Reference Versus Virtual Ports

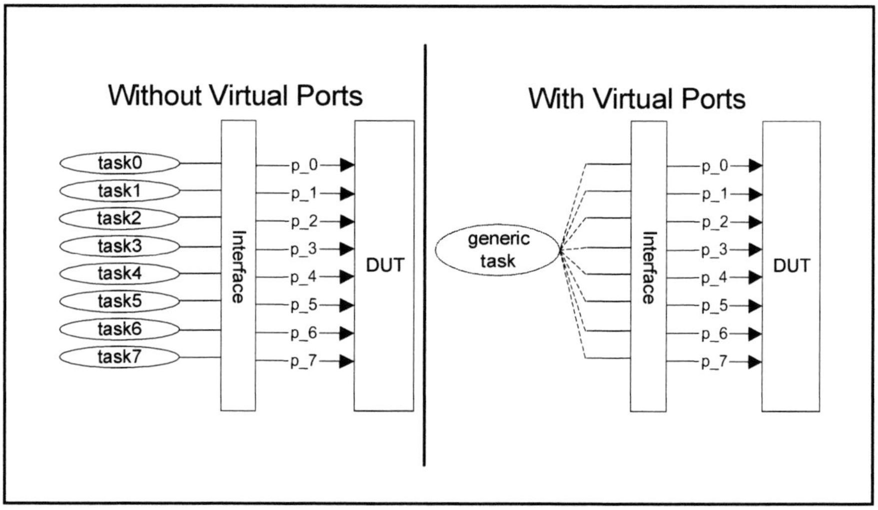

The example RAM testbench uses virtual ports as shown in Figure 5-9.

FIGURE 5-9   Virtual Port Connection to the RAM Design

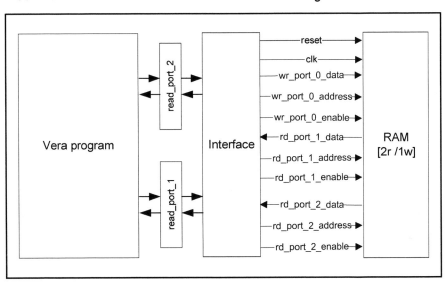

NOTE   *For the sake of brevity, the write port to the RAM is not shown in Figure 5-9.*

Defining Virtual Ports & Binds

Virtual port declarations, denoted by the keyword port, provide a new data type, virtual_port_name, which can be used as an argument in subroutines.

To use a virtual port, first define it using the keyword port, and then bind it to interface signals using the keyword bind. The bind name can then be passed as argument in call to the subroutines. The syntax is

```
port <virtual_port_name> {
   <virtual_port_signal>;
   <virtual_port_signal>;
   ...
}

bind <virtual_port_name> <bind_name> {
   <virtual_port_signal> <interface>.<signal>;
   <virtual_port_signal> <interface>.<signal>;
   ...
}
```

bind_name provides a new data type that is used in declaration of subroutines.

Virtual port name(s) are then passed in as argument when calling those subroutines (shown later).

All virtual port and bind definitions should be placed outside the program block definition.

The example below illustrates the usage.

```
// Port definition for read_port
port read_port {
    data;
    address;
    enable;
}

// Binding read ports
bind read_port read_port_1{
    data        ram.rd_port_1_data;
    address     ram.rd_port_1_address;
    enable      ram.rd_port_1_enable;
}

bind read_port read_port_2{
    data        ram.rd_port_2_data;
    address     ram.rd_port_2_address;
    enable      ram.rd_port_2_enable;
}
```

In this example, there is a new data type, read_port, that can be used to define subroutines. Additionally there are two instances of this data type, read_port_1 and read_port_2, that can be passed as arguments when calling routines that have read_port defined as an argument.

Writing Generic Tasks & Functions

As mentioned earlier, in Vera, a bind name can be defined as an argument in a task or a function definition. This allows the task or function to be written in a generic manner; when called, it performs the defined operation on the virtual port passed in as an argument.

The syntax for referencing virtual port signals is

<port_name>.$<signal_name>

For the RAM example, you can write one generic function for reading data from a read port of the RAM; then when calling the function, pass in a specific bind (either read_port_1 or read_port_2) as an argument. The function reads data from that interface of the RAM. The definition is

```
// Function for reading from read ports
// Read_address reads an address and returns the data read
// from that address using the port specified in the call.

function integer read_address (read_port this_port,bit[7:0] address) {
    bit[31:0] temp;
    @1
    this_port.$enable = 1;
    this_port.$address = address;

    // Wait for 3 clocks and then sample the data
    repeat(3) @(posedge CLOCK); temp = this_port.$data;

    // Show what you are reading, always a good practice
    printf("Read ... %h from %h \n",temp,address);

    // return the value read
    read_address = temp;
}
```

And this is the function call:

```
program {
    //function calls
    // read address 3'h0 using read_port_2
    data_read = read_address(read_port_2, 2'h0);

    // read address 3'h1 using read_port_1
    data_read = read_address(read_port_1, 2'h1);
}
```

Use of virtual ports eliminates the need to write a separate function for each interface. It also (almost) isolates your testbench from design changes, since routines are now dependent on only the port declaration and not on the signal names in the design.Thus if the design changes, only the net name in the port declaration and the interface definition need to be updated.

Running a Vera Program With a Simulator

To compile a Vera program, type

```
vera -cmp <program_name>.vr
```

This produces a program_name.vshell file and a program_name.vro file.

As already mentioned, the vshell file contains the vshell module that the design uses to interface with Vera. So the vshell file must be added to the list of design files used to compile the design.

To run the program, the following runtime switch must be passed to the simulator:

```
+vera_load=<program_name>.vro
```

This loads the compiled program and runs it with the simulator. The Vera PLIs should be linked into the simulator. Refer to the *VERA System Verifier Manual* for information on how to do this.

Guidelines & Techniques

The following guidelines can help you avoid basic pitfalls:

Do not sample signals in expressions

- Do not embed samples in expressions unless you want asynchronous values. As mentioned earlier, a signal is sampled immediately (asynchronously) if the sample is embedded in an expression. If the sample is not embedded in an expression, it happens at the next clock edge. Rarely will you need to sample something asynchronously; in general, sample separately and then use the sampled value in expressions.

Therefore, avoid the following:

```
data_received = dut.data[1] + 1'b1;
//asynchronous sample
```

Do this instead:

```
data_received = dut.data[1]; //synchronous sample
data_received = data_received + 1'b1;
```

Always use virtual ports

- *Always* use virtual ports and pass bind names as references into tasks. This is a very important guideline. It helps isolate the testbench from design changes and makes it a lot easier to port the existing testbench to work with new designs.

verilog_node versus interface port.

- Choosing between using an interface signal versus a verilog_node referencing an internal net of the design is difficult. The verilog_node allows you to add signals to an interface without altering the top level instantiation of the testbench. The disadvantage of referencing an internal node of the design is that typically the internal nets of the design (in development) change more frequently than the interface signals. So you can end up making more frequent changes to the interface, if the name of the internal net keeps changing. This is especially true when you go to a gate-level model of the design. First, the net is going to change for sure; second, the net name is not going to be consistent across versions of the netlist.

  This suggests the question, how about using the verilog_node to reference just the interface signal of the design, which does not change very frequently? Not using the verilog_node eases debugging, as the vshell ports are organized and can be seen clearly in any waveform viewer. In case of a verilog_node this becomes a little more difficult. For the original testbench developer this might not pose a problem, but if someone else has to debug this testbench, he or she will have to spend some time figuring this out how certain nets suddenly change values in the design.

Beware of alternating drives and expects

- Beware of how you use drives and expects, because they advance simulation time. If you drive at the posedge of clock and sample at the negedge and alternate drive and sample statements in the testbench, you might inadvertently advance simulation time. Try to drive all inputs first and then sample the outputs (or vice versa), rather than interleaving drives and samples.

Use a predefined number of global variables

- The vshell module generated by Vera changes every time the declaration of global variables used in a test changes. So if you are using a compile-one-time and run-many-times strategy, make sure the declarations of global variables used are identical across all tests, or else the vshell module used to compile the design will be outdated for some tests.

The generated vshell module changes whenever the declarations of global variables change in a test because it actually maintains a reference to all global variables used in the testbench (search for the keyword *global* in the vshell module file). This is great for debugging, because you can track global variables in the waveform viewer.

- Use blocking drives to make code more readable and avoid many pitfalls. In the following code sample, it isn't clear what is driven into the design, current_data or the incremented current_data:

```
@1 bus.data <= current_data;
current_data++;
```

When the same code is rewritten with a blocking drive, you can be certain that the value driven into the design is current_data, not the incremented current_data:

```
@1 bus.data = current_data;,
current_data++;
```

- If you need to find out the value of a signal being driven into the design by the Vera testbench, declare it as an inout and then sample it. You cannot sample Vera outputs, but you can sample inputs and inouts.

Alternately, you can drive a value and set a Vera variable simultaneously, and then sample the variable. However, sometimes this becomes difficult when the code that is driving is in a different scope from the code that needs to sample. These cases force you to declare global variables, which is not the best of programming practices.

- Avoid driving signals into the design while the design is sampling the signal. In other words, avoid driving a signal exactly at the positive edge or negative edge, because the stimulus might not make the setup/hold times of the flop.

Instead, either drive at the complementary edge or add enough skew in the interface definition (by setting PHOLD or NHOLD) to make the setup/hold times, so you end up sampling before the edge and driving after the edge.

- When analyzing the signal in a design, use expects only for checking the behavior of protocol handshake signals. For all data responses, use samples. Through sampling, you can do more complex response analysis.

- An inherent limitation of expects is that the compared value (the right side of the expression) must be calculated in advance. This is not always possible. Sometime you need to sample the response of the design and translate it to a higher level of abstraction before any analysis can be performed. Expects do not offer the flexibility to do this, whereas samples do.

The Complete Testbench Development Flow

Figure 5-10 shows the complete flow for developing a Vera testbench from scratch. Although the flow seems VCS-specific, it can easily be modified to work with other simulators.

FIGURE 5-10   Complete Testbench Development Flow

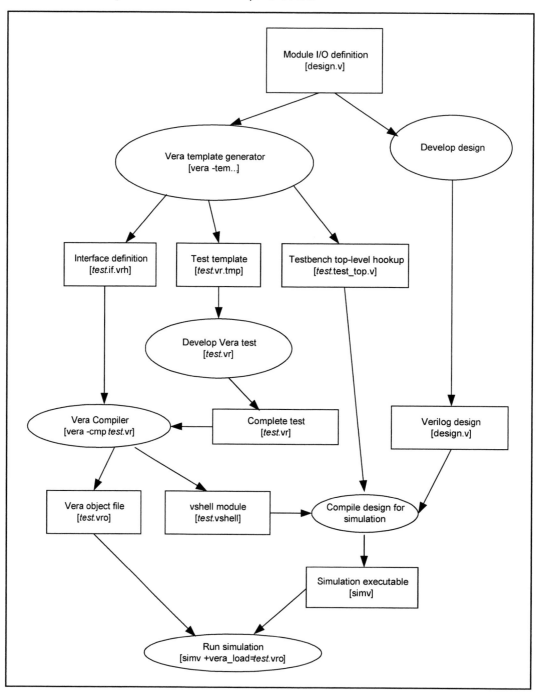

MAC Port Definition

This section shows the development of the Vera testbench interface for the MAC design. This design has several interfaces and multiple clock domains, as shown in Figure 5-11.

FIGURE 5-11 MAC Port List

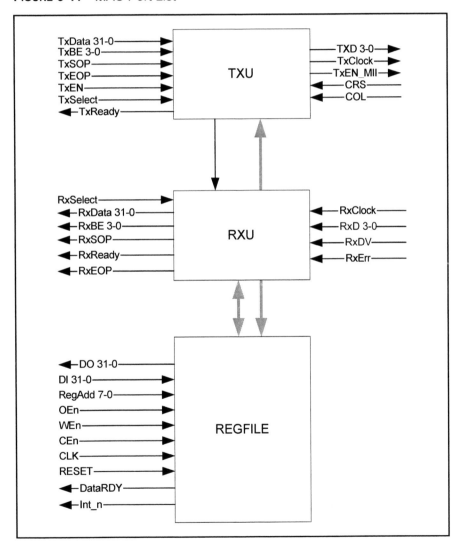

On the host side are

> Host transmit signals
> Host receive signals
> Register file signal

On the network side (MII side) are

> MII receive signals
> MII transmit signals

The interface definition groups all signals that synchronize to a common clock. So define the interfaces as follows:

```
#define OUTPUT_EDGE   PHOLD
#define OUTPUT_SKEW   #1
#define INPUT_EDGE    PSAMPLE

// Signals for the MAC - HOST interface
interface mac_host_intf {
    input         clk        CLOCK;
    output        reset      OUTPUT_EDGE OUTPUT_SKEW;
    output        CEn        OUTPUT_EDGE OUTPUT_SKEW;
    output        WEn        OUTPUT_EDGE OUTPUT_SKEW;
    output        OEn        OUTPUT_EDGE OUTPUT_SKEW;
    output[7:0]   RegAdd     OUTPUT_EDGE OUTPUT_SKEW;
    output[31:0]  DI         OUTPUT_EDGE OUTPUT_SKEW;
    output[3:0]   TxBE       OUTPUT_EDGE OUTPUT_SKEW;
    input[31:0]   DO         INPUT_EDGE;
    input[3:0]    RxBE       INPUT_EDGE;
    input         DataRDY    INPUT_EDGE;
    input         Int_n      INPUT_EDGE;
    output[31:0]  TxData     OUTPUT_EDGE OUTPUT_SKEW;
    output        TxSOP      OUTPUT_EDGE OUTPUT_SKEW;
    output        TxEOP      OUTPUT_EDGE OUTPUT_SKEW;
    output        TxEN       OUTPUT_EDGE OUTPUT_SKEW;
    input         TxERR      INPUT_EDGE;
    input         TxReady    INPUT_EDGE;
    output        TxSelect   OUTPUT_EDGE OUTPUT_SKEW;
    output        RxSelect   OUTPUT_EDGE OUTPUT_SKEW;
    input[31:0]   RxData     INPUT_EDGE;
    input         RxSOP      INPUT_EDGE;
    input         RxEOP      INPUT_EDGE;
    input         RxReady    INPUT_EDGE;
}  // end of interface mac_host_intf


// Signal for the MAC - MII interface
interface mac_mii_tx_intf {
```

```
    input               TxClock   CLOCK;
    input[3:0]          TXD       INPUT_EDGE;
    input               TxClock   CLOCK;
    input               TxEN_MII  INPUT_EDGE;
    output              CRS       OUTPUT_EDGE OUTPUT_SKEW;
    output              COLL      OUTPUT_EDGE OUTPUT_SKEW;
} // end of interface mac_mii_tx_intf

interface mac_mii_rx_intf {
    input               RxClock   CLOCK;
    output[3:0]         RxD       OUTPUT_EDGE OUTPUT_SKEW;
    output              RxDV      OUTPUT_EDGE OUTPUT_SKEW;
    output              RxErr     OUTPUT_EDGE OUTPUT_SKEW;
} // end of interface mac_mii_rx_intf
```

Then define virtual ports and bind them to interface signals based on the logical function of each signal.

```
port host_regfile_port {
    data_in;
    data_out;
    address;
    output_enable;
    write_enable;
    chip_enable;
    clock;
    reset;
    data_ready;
    interrupt;
}

port host_tx_port {
    transmit_enable;
    ready_to_transmit;
    transmit_data;
    transmit_byte_enable;
    transmit_select;
    transmit_sop;
    transmit_eop;
    clock;
}

port host_rx_port {
    receive_select;
    receive_ready;
    receive_data;
    receive_byte_enable;
    receive_sop;
    receive_eop;
    clock;
}
```

```
port mii_rx_port {
   receive_data;
   receive_data_valid;
   receive_error;
   clock;
}

port mii_tx_port {
   transmit_data;
   transmit_data_valid;
   carrier_sense;
   collision;
   clock;
}

bind host_regfile_port mac_host_regfile_port {
   data_in              mac_host_intf.DI;        // <-MAC
   data_out             mac_host_intf.DO;        // ->MAC
   address              mac_host_intf.RegAdd;    // ->MAC
   output_enable        mac_host_intf.OEn;       // ->MAC
   write_enable         mac_host_intf.WEn;       // ->MAC
   chip_enable          mac_host_intf.CEn;       // ->MAC
   reset                mac_host_intf.reset;     // ->MAC
   data_ready           mac_host_intf.DataRDY;   // <-MAC
   interrupt            mac_host_intf.Int_n;     // <-MAC
   clock                mac_host_intf.clk;
}

bind host_tx_port mac_host_tx_port {
   transmit_enable        mac_host_intf.TxEN;       // ->MAC
   ready_to_transmit      mac_host_intf.TxReady;    // <-MAC
   transmit_data          mac_host_intf.TxData;     // ->MAC
   transmit_byte_enable   mac_host_intf.TxBE;       // ->MAC
   transmit_select        mac_host_intf.TxSelect;   // ->MAC
   transmit_sop           mac_host_intf.TxSOP;      // ->MAC
   transmit_eop           mac_host_intf.TxEOP;      // ->MAC
   clock                  mac_host_intf.clk;
}

bind host_rx_port mac_host_rx_port {
   receive_select         mac_host_intf.RxSelect;   // ->MAC
   receive_ready          mac_host_intf.RxReady;    // <-MAC
   receive_data           mac_host_intf.RxData;     // <-MAC
   receive_byte_enable    mac_host_intf.RxBE;       // <-MAC
   receive_sop            mac_host_intf.RxSOP;      // <-MAC
   receive_eop            mac_host_intf.RxEOP;      // <-MAC
   clock                  mac_host_intf.clk;
}

bind mii_tx_port mac_mii_tx_port {
   transmit_data          mac_mii_tx_intf.TXD;      //->MAC
   transmit_data_valid    mac_mii_tx_intf.TxEN_MII;//->MAC
```

```
        carrier_sense              mac_mii_tx_intf.CRS;      //<-MAC
        collision                  mac_mii_tx_intf.COLL;     //<-MAC
        clock                      mac_mii_tx_intf.TxClock;
}

bind mii_rx_port mac_mii_rx_port {
        receive_data               mac_mii_rx_intf.RxD;      // ->MAC
        receive_data_valid         mac_mii_rx_intf.RxDV;     // ->MAC
        receive_error              mac_mii_rx_intf.RxErr;    // ->MAC
        clock                      mac_mii_rx_intf.RxClock;
}
```

Figure 5-12 shows the final hookup of the MAC ports.

FIGURE 5-12   MAC Port Hookup

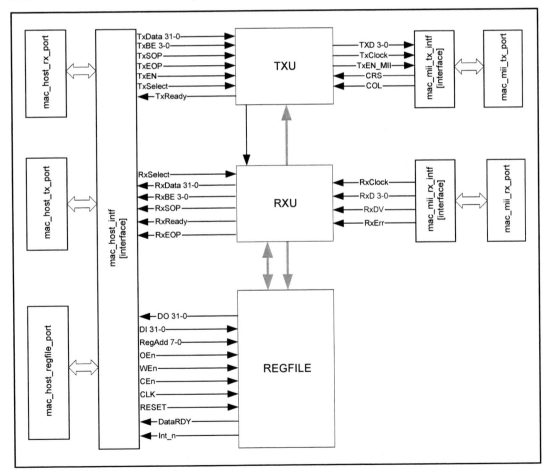

Defining virtual ports isolates the testbench from signal name changes in the design. You can also support more MACs in the testbench by adding more interface signals for the extra MACs and binding them to the existing virtual ports.

Conclusion

This chapter has covered how to connect a Vera testbench to a Verilog design and perform basic testing of the design using simple tasks and functions. The next chapter shows how to push the design further by utilizing some of the concurrency features of the language.

CHAPTER 6

Creating Concurrency in Vera

A hardware design can be thought of as many concurrent, or parallel, processes. For example, in a full-duplex Ethernet MAC, one block receives packets from the Ethernet medium while another block simultaneously sends packets to the Ethernet medium. As you examine the implementation of both the sending and receiving blocks, you see many simpler parallel processes: counters, decoders, comparators, and so on. Concurrency is obvious at any layer of abstraction, even at the transistor level.

Figure 6-1 shows the hardware implementation of two concurrent and independent processes. One process counts clock cycles, and the other process counts the number of valid packets with a specific destination address. Because the two processes do not share resources, they are guaranteed to be operating in parallel, even when operating in the same chip.

FIGURE 6-1   Two Concurrent & Independent Hardware Processes

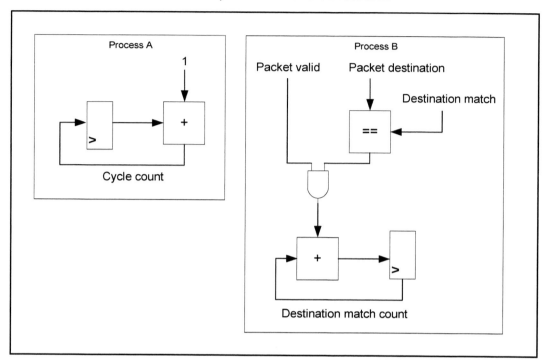

If the processes shown in Figure 6-1 were modeled in Vera as separate, concurrent code blocks, called threads, they would be programmed as follows. (Note that the mechanism for launching the code blocks as separate threads is not shown.)

```
// code block for process A
while (1) {
   @(posedge CLOCK);
   ++cycle_count;
}

// code block for process B
while (1) {
   @(posedge CLOCK);
   if (packet_valid &&
      (packet_destination == destination_match))
   ++destination_match_count;
}
```

You can model the same hardware nonconcurrently by combining both code blocks into a single process flow:

```
// code block for process A and process B
while (1) {
   @(posedge CLOCK);
   ++cycle_count;
   if (packet_valid &&
      (packet_destination == destination_match))
   ++destination_match_count;
}
```

Note that the independent threads in the concurrent version more closely resemble the parallel operation of the hardware than does the single-threaded implementation. The more closely the verification environment mimics the hardware, the easier it is to model and verify the hardware. For this reason, hardware verification languages support concurrency.

Concurrency in testbenches

Each logically separate and concurrent operation in the testbench is typically implemented with an independent thread. One thread is used per interface or per transaction. For example, in the Ethernet MAC testbench, a host transactor drives packets into the MAC while the MII monitor concurrently receives packets and verifies their correctness. Within the monitors and transactors, there may be additional parallel processes for modeling or verifying various aspects of the MAC. All of this testbench concurrency demands sophisticated concurrency features in the hardware verification language.

Concurrent Programming Model

The important features of concurrent programming are

- A method for launching code blocks as parallel threads

- Local variables unique to each thread invocation to provide thread isolation and reentrance

- Interthread communication mechanisms so that threads can work cooperatively

- Thread arbitration and mutual exclusion mechanisms so that access to shared resources can be controlled

- Synchronization mechanisms to control the execution order of threads

Vera provides the following concurrency features:

- Threading with the fork/join construct

- Local variables within threads

- Communication between threads with shared variables and mailboxes

- Arbitration among threads with semaphores, and data mutual exclusion with regions

- Synchronization between threads with events

Each of these concepts is discussed in detail in the following sections.

fork/join Construct

In Vera, the fork/join construct launches multiple threads. It takes an arbitrary number of code blocks and executes them in parallel. As shown in Figure 6-2, each code block within the fork/join construct becomes its own thread.

FIGURE 6-2   fork/join Launches Threads

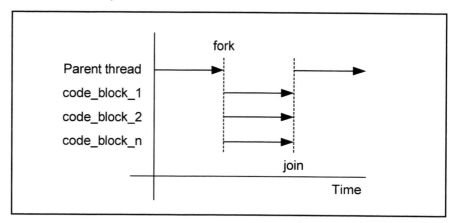

Syntax

The syntax of the fork/join construct is shown below. The join modifier is optional and is discussed in a following section.

```
fork
    { <code_block_1>; }
    { <code_block_2>; }
    . . .
    { <code_block_n>; }
join [<join_modifier>]
```

Parent and child threads

Threads spawned from fork/join constructs are called child threads. The code that contains and executes the fork statement remains in its own thread, which is called the parent thread. For example, when the following code is executed, three child threads are forked from the parent thread, for a total of four threads.

```
fork
    { @1 my_variable = 2'b0; } // child_1
    { @2 my_variable = 2'b1; } // child_2
    { @3 my_variable = 2'b2; } // child_3
join
```

Note that in this case, the curly braces are optional because each code block is a single line of code. Figure 6-3 shows the cycle-by-cycle execution of this example.

FIGURE 6-3 Execution of fork Example

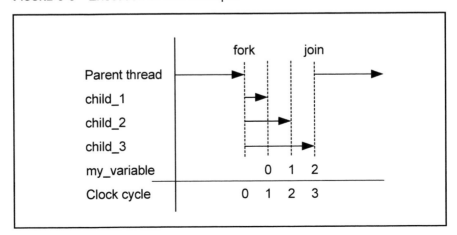

Child threads begin simultaneously and execute concurrently

All child threads start executing at exactly the same simulation time, when the fork operator is executed. Therefore, if the fork in the example is executed at clock cycle 0, the first thread spawned by the fork begins a one-cycle wait at clock cycle 0, the second thread begins a two-cycle wait at cycle 0, and the third thread begins a three-cycle wait at clock cycle 0. This results in the first thread assigning 0 to my_variable at clock cycle 1, the second thread assigning 1 to my_variable at clock cycle 2, and the third thread assigning 2 to my_variable at clock cycle 3. This whole process is shown in Figure 6-3.

Forking a single thread

The following simple modification of the code presented above behaves quite differently. In this case, there is only a single code block within the fork/join construct (note the braces), so only a single thread is spawned. As expected, the single thread executes in program statement order. In other words, if the fork is executed at clock cycle 0, my_variable becomes 0 at clock cycle 1, 1 at clock cycle 3, and 2 at clock cycle 6.

```
fork
    { @1 my_variable = 2'b0;
      @2 my_variable = 2'b1;
      @3 my_variable = 2'b2; }
join
```

fork/join Caveats

Threads must terminate or suspend themselves

There is one exception to the statement that all threads operate concurrently: Vera is not a preemptive multitasking environment, which means that threads must either or suspend themselves or self-terminate to allow other threads to execute. For example, the while loop in the following fork/join construct prevents all other threads from executing because it never terminates or relinquishes control:

```
fork
    { while (1) { my_var = 1; } }
    { @1 my_variable = 2'b0; }
join
```

Vera has the same problem with nonconcurrent programming constructs. An infinite while loop such as the one above always locks up Vera, no matter where the infinite loop is coded. Control never returns to any other portion of Vera code or the RTL simulator.

*Do not rely on the
order of execution
of threads* In addition, there are no guarantees about the order in which threads execute
when they execute at the same simulation time and do not explicitly
synchronize themselves with mailboxes, semaphores, regions, or events.
These synchronization mechanisms are discussed later in this chapter.

In general, it is a bad idea to rely on the order of execution of unsynchronized
threads. First, it makes debugging extremely difficult. In addition, the ordering
of unsynchronized threads may be different in different versions of Vera. It
would be a pity to have to continue using older versions of Vera or to have to
fix your Vera code when moving to a new version, just because of assumptions
made about the order of thread execution.

Resuming Execution of a Parent Thread: Ways to Join

Vera provides three ways for a parent thread to resume execution after its child
threads have been forked. This functionality is provided with three optional
modifiers to the join keyword:

- join all

- join any

- join none

In all cases, the parent thread resumes execution at the statement directly
following the join keyword and its optional modifier.

The join all construct is the default if no join modifier is present. As shown
in Figure 6-4, it causes the parent thread to resume execution after all child
threads have terminated. The join any construct causes the parent thread to
resume execution once the first child thread has completed; the remaining
child threads continue execution until finished. The join none construct allows
the parent thread to resume execution immediately after its child threads have
been forked; the parent thread effectively continues executing in parallel with
its children as soon as the fork keyword is executed.

FIGURE 6-4 join Modifiers

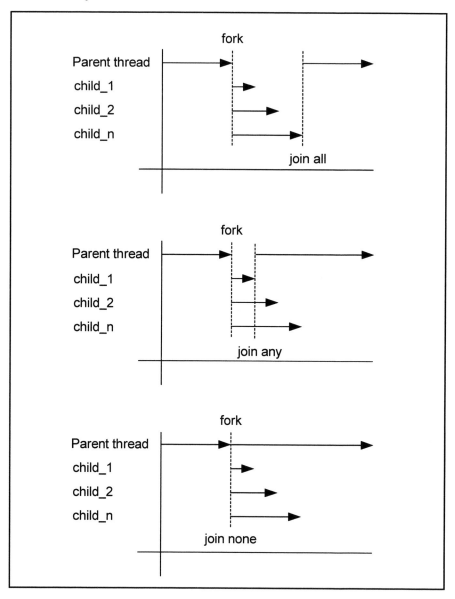

For example, the following fork/join block uses the join all construct. The packet destined for interface d is launched by the parent thread after all three packets launched by all three child threads have finished. If the join any construct were used instead, the packet destined for interface d would be launched after the first of the three child packets finished. Finally, if the join none construct were used, all four packets would be launched in parallel.

```
fork
    { launch_packet(interface_a); }
    { launch_packet(interface_b); }
    { launch_packet(interface_c); }
join all

launch_packet(interface_d);
```

Threads & Variables

Although threads can declare their own local variables, they also have access to the variables declared in the scope of the fork statement. By default, both parent and child threads can modify the variables the parent thread declares, and all threads see the modifications. These shared variables are commonly used for communication between threads.

Shadow Variables

Race conditions caused by shared variables

Communicating via shared variables is useful, but it can also be inconvenient, because race conditions can result. For example, the following code segment shows an easy way to fork off 10 parallel copies of the my_process( ) task, each with a unique ID as an argument.

```
integer i;

for (i=0; i<10; i++) {
    fork
        my_process(i);
    join none
}
```

Unfortunately, each parallel instance of my_process( ) races to get a changing value of i, because i changes as the loop iterates and each instance of my_process( ) has access to the same instance of the variable i.

Recall that you shouldn't rely on the order in which threads execute. In fact, in Vera, the for loop will have forked all 10 children before any of the child processes begins execution. The fork operator adds its child threads to the scheduler's process list, but it doesn't schedule its child threads for immediate execution. When the parent thread finishes or suspends itself, the scheduler will execute the next thread on its list. Therefore, when all 10 child processes are executed, the value passed in their argument is 10, because the parent thread has finished all iterations of its for loop.

Shadow variables resolve the race condition

To resolve the race condition described above, Vera provides shadow variables. Any variable declaration can include the extra keyword *shadow*, and shadow variables behave identically to nonshadow variables until they are passed into a newly forked child thread.

When a child thread containing a reference to a shadow variable is forked, a new instance of the shadow variable is created for the child and the current value of the variable in the parent's thread is copied into the new instance created for the child thread. The child thread can no longer communicate with any other thread through its instance of the shadow variable, and changes to the parent's copy of the variable are not reflected in its child threads either.

For example, the following small modification to the previous code sample instantiates 10 child instances of my_process( ), each one with a unique ID in the range of 0 through 9. Each my_process( ) child can modify its instance of the variable i, knowing that none of its sibling child threads or its parent thread can see its changes. Similarly, the parent thread can change its instance of the variable i, knowing that its child threads see its value of i only when each child thread is forked.

```
shadow bit[3:0] i;

for (i=0; i<10; i++)
    fork
        my_process(i);
    join none
```

Global variables cannot be shadow variables, nor can function and task arguments.

Mailboxes

Variables are not the only Vera mechanism for communication between threads. As shown in Figure 6-5, mailboxes behave as first-in-first-out (FIFO) storage arrays of any data type, including objects. Usually, one or more threads push data into a mailbox and one or more threads read data out of the mailbox. Consumer threads can suspend execution until data is available, which means that mailboxes can also be used for synchronization between producer and consumer threads.

FIGURE 6-5 Mailbox Behavior

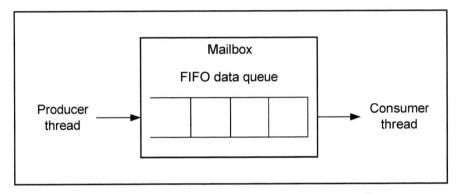

Mailboxes are useful in non-concurrent environments as well

Mailboxes are general and powerful enough that they have plenty of uses outside of concurrent environments. Anytime an arbitrarily sized FIFO storage element is helpful, a mailbox lets Vera writers avoid having to implement the FIFO and its associated memory allocation algorithms. In hardware designs, many queues can be implemented or modeled as FIFOs, which means that mailboxes have numerous uses in hardware verification and modeling environments.

Mailboxes are extremely useful in concurrent environments

Mailboxes provide extra features in concurrent environments. When data is pushed into a mailbox by one thread and pulled out of the same mailbox by another thread, the mailbox acts as a synchronizer between the two threads, thereby preventing race conditions between the two threads. It does not matter if one thread is running faster than the other, because the mailbox automatically grows if the producer is running faster than the consumer. Similarly, the mailbox can automatically block the consumer if the consumer is running faster than the producer. (The automatic block feature is optional; see below.)

Overview—Mailbox Usage

The process for using Vera's mailboxes is as follows:

- Initialize the mailbox with alloc( ), and either store the mailbox ID in a variable accessible in the scope of all users, or pass the mailbox ID to all users.

- Producers push data into the mailbox with a call to mailbox_put( ).

- Consumers pull data from the mailbox with a call to mailbox_get( ).

Mailbox Allocation

Mailboxes are allocated with a function call to alloc( ). The syntax is as follows:

```
<allocated_mailbox_id> = alloc(MAILBOX, <mailbox_id>,
    <mailbox_count>);
```

MAILBOX is a predefined constant that tells alloc( ) to allocate a mailbox or mailboxes.

mailbox_id is an integer representing the requested ID associated with the allocated mailbox. Although you can request mailbox IDs, it is best to pass in 0 and let Vera allocate the ID for you. Letting Vera automatically allocate the ID saves you from needing to keep track of which mailbox IDs are used. If 0 is used, the allocated ID is returned by alloc( ) upon successful allocation. Whether automatically allocated by Vera or specifically requested by the Vera code writer, the mailbox ID needs to be stored, because it is passed into mailbox_get( ) and mailbox_put( ) to uniquely identify each mailbox.

mailbox_count is an integer representing the number of mailboxes to allocate with a single call of alloc( ). If mailbox_count is greater than 1, the IDs are numbered sequentially, starting with the mailbox_id passed in. If 0 is passed into mailbox_id, Vera generates the IDs and they are numbered sequentially, starting with the ID returned. mailbox_count should never be less than 1.

The alloc( ) function returns an integer representing the mailbox ID of the first mailbox allocated if allocation succeeds. If allocation fails, 0 is returned.

Note that the allowable number of mailboxes is configured via the vera_mailbox_size property, which defaults to 256. See the *VERA System Verifier User Manual* for more information about increasing the default number of mailboxes.

Pushing Data into a Mailbox

Data is pushed into a mailbox with a call to the task mailbox_put( ). The syntax is as follows:

```
mailbox_put (<mailbox_id>, <data>);
```

mailbox_id is an integer that represents the ID of the mailbox that receives the data. It is the ID requested from or returned by alloc( ).

The data argument can be any scalar data type or any expression that results in a scalar data type. For example, integers, registers of any width, and objects are all scalar data types. Be careful with objects, however, because the object handle—not the object—is stored in the mailbox; see below, "Mailbox Caveats".

Values of different data types can be mixed in the same mailbox. This is also discussed in more detail in "Mailbox Caveats".

Pulling Data from a Mailbox

Data is retrieved from a mailbox with a function call to mailbox_get(). The syntax is

```
<number_of_entries> = mailbox_get (<wait_option>,
    <mailbox_id> [,<dest_variable>] [,<check_option>]);
```

mailbox_id is an integer that represents the ID of the mailbox whose oldest entry should be removed; it is the ID requested from or returned by alloc( ).

The functionality of mailbox_get( ), including its behavior with and without the optional dest_variable argument, is shown in Table 6-1. Note that wait_option must be one of the four predefined constants shown. Furthermore, the return values shown assume that if the scalar dest_variable is present, it is the same type as the oldest entry in the mailbox. If there is a type mismatch, the check_option argument comes into play. See below.

TABLE 6-1   mailbox_get() Assuming No Errors

wait_option	dest_variable present?	mailbox_get() suspends execution?	dest_variable gets oldest entry?	Oldest entry dequeued?	Return value
WAIT	Yes	Yes, until at least one entry is available in the mailbox	Yes	Yes	Number of entries, including dequeued entry
	No	No	N/A	No	Number of entries
COPY_WAIT	Yes	Yes, until at least one entry is available in the mailbox	Yes	No	Number of entries, including returned entry
	No	No	N/A	No	Number of entries
NO_WAIT	Yes	No	If available	If available	Number of entries, including dequeued entry
	No	No	N/A	No	Number of entries
COPY_NO_WAIT	Yes	No	Yes	No	Number of entries, including returned entry
	No	No	N/A	No	Number of entries

mailbox_get()
timeout

check_option is an optional argument that can take only one predefined constant value, CHECK, if present. It controls Vera's reaction to retrieving a value from a mailbox that is a different type than the provided dest_variable. When the type of the entry being loaded from the mailbox matches the type of dest_variable, check_option does not matter. If there is a mismatch, however, Vera behaves as follows: If check_option is not present, a runtime error results and the simulation terminates. If CHECK is used, then –1 is returned and no entry is removed from the mailbox.

By default, mailbox_get( ) never returns if the WAIT or COPY_WAIT option is used and the mailbox never receives an entry. However, a timeout can be set for the mailbox so that such a situation results in a runtime error. See "Timeouts" on page 183.

Mailbox Example

Mailboxes are extremely handy for decoupling a task that receives packets from the tasks or functions that consume those packets. As long as a mailbox is allocated, its ID is passed on to both the producer and consumer threads, and the threads all agree on the data type, they can be successfully decoupled. An example of this structure is shown below. The packets sent between the packet receiver thread and the packet processor thread are 64-bit vectors.

```
#include <vera_defines.vrh>

program mailbox_example {
    integer my_mailbox;

    // allocate mailbox, save the ID, and check success.
    my_mailbox = alloc(MAILBOX, 0, 1);
    if (!my_mailbox)
        error ("Mailbox could not be allocated\n");

    // start the packet receiver and the packet processor
    fork
        receive_packets();
        process_packets();
    join none

    // allow the threads to complete
    repeat (1000) @(posedge CLOCK);
}

task receive_packets() {
    integer i;
    bit[63:0] received_packet;

    // packet reception modeled by a for loop
    for (i=0; i<10; i++) {
        repeat (i) @(posedge CLOCK);
        received_packet = i;
        // put received packet in the mailbox
        mailbox_put (my_mailbox, received_packet);
    }
}
```

```
task process_packets() {
    integer ret;
    bit[63:0] packet;

    while (1) {
        // receive packet from mailbox and check success
        ret = mailbox_get (WAIT, my_mailbox, packet, CHECK);
        if (ret <= 0)
            error ("mailbox_get returned %0d\n", ret);

        // packet processing modeled by printf
        printf ("Got packet %0d at cycle %0d\n", packet, get_cycle());
    }
}
```

In this example, the program starts by allocating a mailbox and placing its ID in the global variable my_mailbox. The return code is then checked for success.

If the allocation fails, the returned ID is 0 and the built-in Vera function error( ) is called. The error( ) function attaches an error banner to the string provided and prints the result. Vera terminates the simulation after an error has occurred if the vera_exit_on_error property is set. See the *VERA System Verifier User Manual* for more information.

After the mailbox has been allocated, two parallel threads are forked. One thread simulates receiving 10 different packets from an interface, with increasing clock cycle delays between packet arrivals, while the other thread simulates processing the packets received.

The receive_packets( ) task simulates packet reception. In a for loop from 0 to 9, it waits the iteration number of clock cycles and then places the iteration number in the packet. Note that the integer is converted to a 64-bit value so that the packet is the proper data type. The packet is then added to the mailbox.

The process_packets( ) task removes a packet from the mailbox whenever at least one packet is waiting in the mailbox. Note that the CHECK option is used so that type errors do not generate a runtime error and that the return code is checked to make sure the Vera program catches all errors.

The output of the sample program is as follows:

```
Got packet 0 at cycle 0
Got packet 1 at cycle 1
Got packet 2 at cycle 3
Got packet 3 at cycle 6
Got packet 4 at cycle 10
Got packet 5 at cycle 15
Got packet 6 at cycle 21
Got packet 7 at cycle 28
Got packet 8 at cycle 36
Got packet 9 at cycle 45
```

As expected, the receive task waits until a valid packet is received and then prints out the sequentially incrementing packets. The cycle delays between packets also increment sequentially.

Mailbox Caveats

Be careful with multiple data types

Using a single mailbox to store multiple data types requires caution. In such cases, the CHECK option should always be used with mailbox_get( ) and the return code should always be checked. In general, it is better to use multiple mailboxes to store multiple data types or to use a single mailbox and group the multiple data types together in an object. Of course, it is also good programming practice to check for all possible errors, regardless of the intended use of the mailbox, because it makes debugging much easier.

Mailboxes store object handles, not objects

When mailboxes store objects, the object handle, not the object content, is copied into the mailbox. Therefore, changes made to the object between the time it is placed in the mailbox and the time the object is removed from the mailbox are visible by the consumer thread that dequeues the object from the mailbox. For this reason, it is generally a bad idea to modify objects after they have been queued in a mailbox. See Chapter 7 for more information about objects and object handles.

Multiple readers

If multiple threads read from the same mailbox by calling mailbox_get( ) with the same mailbox ID, they are served in the order they called mailbox_get( ). However, it is not recommended to rely on this ordering, because it is hard to guarantee that threads call mailbox_get( ) in the required order without explicit synchronization. See "Events" on page 174 for more details on thread synchronization and execution ordering.

For example, it is possible to turn a mailbox into a data broadcast mechanism by calling mailbox_get( ) with COPY_WAIT or COPY_NO_WAIT for all but the final copy of the data. The thread that dequeues the final copy of the data calls mailbox_get( ) with WAIT or NO_WAIT. It is extremely important that the threads calling mailbox_get( ) are synchronized so that only the final thread dequeues the data from the mailbox. Additionally, the dequeue call to mailbox_get( ) must occur before any other threads try to read the next entry.

Although this broadcast mechanism is possible, it is better to instantiate a mailbox per consumer and enqueue the data to every instantiation. In this setup, each consumer thread controls the dequeue of its own mailbox, which means that the order of execution of the calls to mailbox_get( ) is not important. Because the order of execution is not important, explicit synchronization between the threads is not necessary.

Semaphores

When communication is possible between multiple threads, race conditions can result. This chapter has already discussed how shadow variables can resolve race conditions between shared variables by creating unique instances of those variables. Additionally, it has shown how mailboxes can be used to resolve producer/consumer race conditions.

A similar problem exists when multiple threads compete to utilize a shared resource. Multiple threads might need to utilize a scarce resource, but only a limited number of threads are allowed access due to the physical constraints of that resource. For example, if multiple threads need to send a packet through a single interface, each thread has to wait its turn, because only one packet can be sent at a time.

Semaphores are used for arbitration

Whenever resource contention arises, access to the shared resource must be arbitrated. Vera provides arbitration functionality through semaphores. There is no automatic association between a semaphore and the resource it arbitrates, so users must explicitly maintain this association.

Any number of threads can request ownership of a semaphore, but only a configurable number of requestors are granted access at once. Either one or many threads can be granted access at the same time.

After a thread has been granted access to a semaphore and is finished with the shared resource, it must release its ownership of the semaphore. When ownership is released, the Vera scheduler is free to grant access to other threads.

Keys control the number of parallel accesses

The number of threads that can be granted access simultaneously is controlled via a key count. Each semaphore maintains a configurable number of keys and tracks the number of keys available at all times. When threads request access, they request a specific number of keys. If the requested number of keys is available, access is granted and the semaphore decrements its count of available keys appropriately. Of course, if the requested number of keys is not available, access is not granted, and the threads that have not received access can either suspend execution until they do receive access or resume execution, knowing they have not received access. Clearly, it is bad form for threads that have not received ownership of a semaphore to utilize the shared resource. After threads that have received access to the semaphore are finished with the shared resource, they need to release the number of keys they requested and therefore received.

Semaphore behavior example

Figure 6-6 shows one possible behavior of a semaphore with four total keys and two processes requesting keys simultaneously. Process A requests one key and receives one key. Process B already has access to a key and has not yet relinquished its control of its key. Process C requests three keys but is not granted access to any keys because the semaphore has only two keys available. Process C has to wait until the semaphore has three keys available.

The semaphore requests shown in Figure 6-6 have another possible outcome, because the process A request occurred simultaneously with the process C request. Had the semaphore granted process C all three available keys instead of granting process A one key, process A would have had to wait for a key to be returned to the semaphore instead of process C.

Semaphore implementation

Each semaphore is implemented as a special counter. The counter represents the number of available keys and is checked whenever a process requests keys. If the counter is less than the number of requested keys, the counter maintains its value and the process does not receive access to keys. If the counter is greater than or equal to the number of requested keys, the counter is decremented by the number of requested keys and the process receives access to them. When the process returns keys to the semaphore, the counter is incremented by the number of returned keys.

FIGURE 6-6 Semaphore Behavior

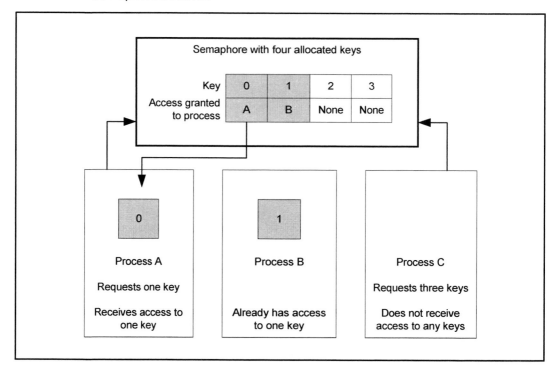

Overview—Semaphore Usage

The process for using Vera's semaphores is as follows:

- Instantiate the semaphore via alloc( ), and either store its ID in a variable in a scope accessible by all users or pass its ID to all users. While instantiating it, initialize its key count.

- When a thread wants access to the arbitrated resource, it requests a certain number of keys via semaphore_get( ).

- When access to the semaphore's keys has been granted to a particular requesting thread, that thread is free to utilize the shared resource.

- When the thread is finished with the shared resource, it releases its keys, giving the Vera scheduler freedom to grant those keys to another thread. The keys are released by a call to semaphore_put( ) with the number of keys originally requested.

Semaphore Allocation

Semaphores are instantiated with the alloc( ) function. The syntax is

```
<allocated_semaphore_id> = alloc(SEMAPHORE,
    <semaphore_id>, <semaphore_count>, <key_count>);
```

SEMAPHORE is a predefined constant that tells alloc( ) to allocate a semaphore or semaphores.

The behavior of the integers semaphore_id and semaphore_count is similar to that of mailbox_id and mailbox_count (see "Mailbox Allocation"). Semaphore IDs are in a separate name space from mailbox IDs.

The number of keys associated with the semaphore or semaphores being allocated is initialized by the integer key_count. This initialization can be used to control how many threads are granted simultaneous access to the resources the semaphore protects. If only one thread should be granted access to the semaphore, key_count is set to 1 and all threads request one key with semaphore_get( ). A value of 0 is legal, but semaphore_put( ) has to increase the number of keys available before any semaphore_get( ) has access to keys.

The alloc( ) function returns an integer representing the semaphore ID of the first semaphore allocated if allocation succeeds. If allocation fails, 0 is returned.

Note that the allowable number of semaphores is configured via the vera_semaphore_size property, which defaults to 256. See the *VERA System Verifier User Manual* for more information about increasing the default number of semaphores.

Requesting Access to a Semaphore

Access to semaphores is requested via the semaphore_get( ) function. The syntax is

```
<access_granted> = semaphore_get (<wait_option>,
    <semaphore_id>, <key_weight>);
```

The return value of the function is either 1, which indicates that access was granted to all requested semaphore keys, or 0, which indicates that access was not granted to any semaphore keys. The functionality of semaphore_get( ) is shown in Table 6-2.

TABLE 6-2   semaphore_get( )

wait_option	key_weight keys available?	semaphore_get( ) suspends execution?	Access granted?	Return value
WAIT	Yes	No	Yes	1
	No	Yes, until requested keys are available	Yes, when semaphore_get( ) returns	1
NO_WAIT	Yes	No	Yes	1
	No	No	No	0

wait_option must be one of two predefined constants: NO_WAIT or WAIT. With WAIT, semaphore_get( ) returns when the number of keys requested in key_weight is available. With NO_WAIT, the number of keys available is checked but control returns to the calling thread, regardless of whether access to the requested keys is granted. A 1 is returned if access was granted, and a 0 is returned if access was not granted.

semaphore_ID is an integer representing the ID of the semaphore whose keys should be taken. It is the ID requested from or returned by alloc( ).

key_weight is an integer representing the number of keys requested of the semaphore for access to be granted. Access will not be granted until all requested keys are available. When only a single thread should be granted access to a semaphore, key_weight should be 1 and the semaphore should be initialized with one key.

semaphore_get( )
timeout

By default, semaphore_get( ) never returns if the WAIT option is used, and the required number of keys is never returned to the semaphore. However, a timeout can be set for the semaphore such that this situation results in a runtime error. See "Timeouts" on page 183.

Releasing Access to a Semaphore

Once a thread has finished using a shared resource arbitrated by a semaphore, the thread must release the keys it was granted. This allows Vera to grant other threads access to the semaphore.

Keys are released via the semaphore_put( ) task. The syntax is

```
semaphore_put (<semaphore_id>, <key_weight>);
```

semaphore_id is an integer representing the ID of the semaphore whose keys are being returned. It is the ID requested from or returned by alloc( ).

key_weight is an integer representing the number of keys to be returned to the semaphore. It should be equal to the number of keys requested.

Dynamically increasing the number of available keys

The semaphore_put( ) task can also be used to dynamically increase the number of available keys for a semaphore. When semaphore_put( ) is called without a matching semaphore_get( ), the key_weight specified by semaphore_put( ) is added to the available key count for the semaphore.

Semaphore Example

The following short program illustrates the use of a semaphore to arbitrate access to a resource that can be used by only one thread at a time. In this example, multiple threads are trying to send packets through a single wire interface that takes as many clock cycles to complete as the length of the packet.

```
#include <vera_defines.vrh>

program semaphore_example {
    integer my_semaphore;

    // Allocate a semaphore with one key and store its ID.
    // Check for success.
    my_semaphore = alloc(SEMAPHORE, 0, 1, 1);
    if (!my_semaphore)
        error ("Semaphore could not be allocated\n");

    // start 30 threads that compete for access to the semaphore.
    repeat (10) {
        fork
            inject_packet (5);
```

```
            inject_packet (10);
            inject_packet (20);
        join none
    }

    // allow the threads to finish
    repeat (1000) @(posedge CLOCK);
}

task inject_packet (integer length) {
    // get access to the single key of the semaphore
    // and check success
    if (!semaphore_get (WAIT, my_semaphore, 1))
        error ("Semaphore_get returned 0\n");

    // model packet injection with print statements
    // and a variable clock cycle delay
    printf ("Injecting packet of length %0d...\n", length);
    repeat (length) @(posedge CLOCK);
    printf ("Done with packet of length %0d\n", length);

    // release the semaphore key
    semaphore_put (my_semaphore, 1);
}
```

The program starts by allocating a single semaphore with one available key and having Vera assign the semaphore ID. The semaphore ID that alloc( ) returns is stored in my_semaphore, a global variable, and compared with 0 to check the call to alloc( ) for success.

After the semaphore has been successfully allocated and its ID stored, 30 threads that need to inject packets through the same interface are forked off in parallel. Ten threads inject packets of length 5, 10 threads inject packets of length 10, and 10 threads inject packets of length 20. The program then waits for 1,000 clock cycles; this allows the threads to execute before the program terminates.

The arbitration happens in the inject_packet( ) task, which first requests access to one key of the semaphore with the WAIT option. This call to semaphore_get( ) returns when it is the turn of the calling thread to own the only key of the semaphore. Because it asks for one key when only one key is available, only one thread is able to run at a time. The return code is checked to make sure semaphore_get( ) successfully received access.

Once the thread has received access to the semaphore, it can enter its critical section, the section that utilizes the shared resource. In the example, packet injection is simplified to a clock cycle delay equal to the packet length. Once that delay is finished, the thread returns its ownership of the semaphore by calling semaphore_put( ) with the semaphore ID and the number of keys it requested. Vera can now grant semaphore access to another thread.

The sample program results in the following output:

```
Injecting packet of length 5...
Done with packet of length 5
Injecting packet of length 10...
Done with packet of length 10
Injecting packet of length 20...
Done with packet of length 20
Injecting packet of length 5...
Done with packet of length 5
Injecting packet of length 10...
Done with packet of length 10
...
```

Clearly, arbitration of the resource has succeeded. Despite the simultaneous invocation of multiple calls to inject_packet( ) and the variable length of time each invocation takes, only one thread executes at a time.

Semaphore Caveats

Semaphore function calls are not checked

Semaphores must be used carefully, because Vera does not check calls to alloc( ), semaphore_get( ), or semaphore_put( ). For example, if semaphore_get( ) requests more keys than initialized by alloc( ), the access to the semaphore will never be granted. Additionally, if the number of keys granted by semaphore_get( ) is not returned by semaphore_put( ), a phenomenon similar to a memory leak occurs. Keys are leaked from the semaphore until eventually none are left and no thread can obtain access to the semaphore. Finally, if more keys are returned by semaphore_put( ) than are granted by semaphore_get( ), a key generation error occurs and more threads obtain access to the semaphore than desired.

Do not rely on the order in which semaphores are granted

Although Vera grants access to semaphores on a first-requested, first-granted basis, it is generally a bad idea to rely on this order. It is hard to debug code structured in such a manner, and later versions of Vera might change this order, resulting in incompatible Vera code. Furthermore, the handshake mode of Vera's event variables provides this functionality in a more intuitive manner. (See "Events".)

Regions

Although semaphores can prevent multiple threads from executing simultaneously, sometimes it is useful to prevent multiple concurrent threads from using the same values.

For example, in a processor verification environment, multiple threads can read from and write to memory, but each thread should be guaranteed ownership of the memory it is modifying. It is not the execution of the threads that is being arbitrated, but rather the memory addresses the threads are using.

Semaphores can be used to implement this value-based mutual exclusion guarantee, but regions are built-in Vera constructs that provide this functionality.

Region reservations

Regions in Vera work by reservations. After a region is allocated, values can be reserved from the region. Similar to when a semaphore is requested, a thread requesting reservations for values can either suspend execution until it receives reservations or continue operating, knowing that it has not received them. When a thread is finished with its reservations, it returns its values to the region so that other threads can obtain reservations for the same values.

Region behavior example

Figure 6-7 shows the behavior of a sample region and the reservations of four of its values. Process A and process C simultaneously request a reservation of value 0. Process A receives the reservation for value 0, although either process could receive it first. Process B already has a reservation to value 3 and holds onto it.

FIGURE 6-7   Region Behavior

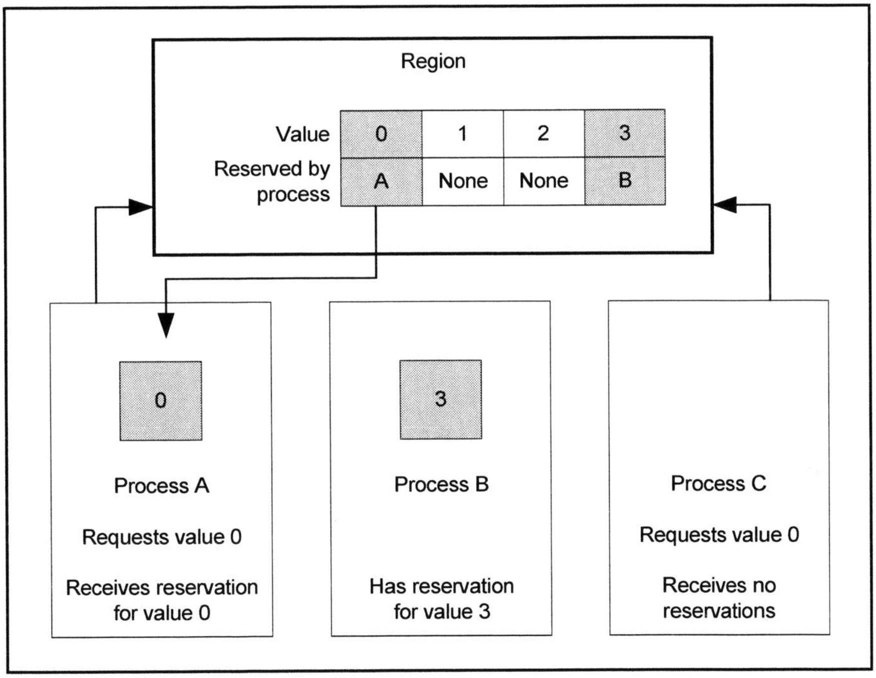

Overview—Using Regions for Exclusion

The process for using regions is as follows:

* Instantiate a region via alloc( ), and either store its ID in a variable in a scope accessible by all users, or pass its ID to all users.

* When a thread needs exclusive access to values the region controls, it requests reservations via region_enter( ).

* When the thread is finished with the values, it releases its reservations to them, giving the Vera scheduler freedom to grant those reservations to another thread. The reservations to the values are released by a call to region_exit( ) with the reserved values.

Allocating Regions

Regions are allocated with a call to alloc( ). The syntax is

```
<allocated_region_id> = alloc(REGION, <region_id>,
    <region_count>);
```

REGION is a predefined constant that tells alloc( ) to allocate a region or regions.

The behavior of the integers region_id and region_count are similar to that of mailbox_id and mailbox_count (see "Mailbox Allocation"). Region IDs are in a separate name space from mailbox IDs and semaphore IDs.

The alloc( ) function returns an integer representing the region ID of the first region allocated if allocation succeeds. If allocation fails, 0 is returned.

Note that the allowable number of regions is configured via the vera_region_size property, which defaults to 256. See the *VERA System Verifier User Manual* for more information about increasing the default number of regions.

Reserving Values

Values are reserved with a call to the region_enter( ) function. The syntax is

```
<reservation_granted> = region_enter (<wait_option>,
    <region_id>, <value1>, <value2>, ...);
```

wait_option must be one of two predefined constants: NO_WAIT or WAIT.

- With WAIT, region_enter( ) returns when reservations are available for all requested values.

- With NO_WAIT, the reservations for the requested values are checked but the call to region_enter( ) completes, regardless of whether reservations are made for all requested values.

No matter which wait_option is used, region_enter( ) returns 1 if reservations are successfully made for all requested values, and 0 otherwise. Reservations are made either for all requested values or for none of them.

region_id is an integer representing the ID of the region whose values should be checked. It is the ID requested from or returned by alloc( ).

The remaining arguments specify the requested values. They must either be integers or bit vectors up to 64 bits wide. Requested values cannot have Xs or Zs. Any number of values can be requested at once.

The functionality of region_enter( ) is described in Table 6-3.

TABLE 6-3   region_enter( )

wait_option	All requested values available?	region_enter( ) suspends execution?	Reserved values	Return value
WAIT	Yes	No	All	1
	No	Yes, until all values are available	All, when region_enter( ) returns	1
NO_WAIT	Yes	No	All	1
	No	No	None	0

region_enter( ) timeout

By default, region_enter( ) never returns if the WAIT option is used and requested values can never be reserved. However, a timeout can be set for the region so that such a situation results in a runtime error. See "Timeouts" on page 183.

Releasing Reservations

Reservations to values are released with a call to the region_exit( ) task. The syntax is as follows:

```
region_exit (<region_id>, <value1>, <value2>, ...);
```

region_id is an integer representing the ID of the region whose reservations are being returned. It is the ID requested from or returned by alloc( ).

Any number of values can be returned to a region with a single call to region_exit( ). Values must be either integers or bit vectors up to 64 bits wide. Values cannot contain Xs or Zs.

Although returning unreserved values to a region should be avoided, it does not cause errors or other side effects.

Region Example

The following program illustrates two threads vying for numbers between 0 and 3. Each thread tries to reserve a random value between 0 and 3. If it gets the reservation, it holds it for a random number of clock cycles. If the thread does not receive a reservation for its needed number, it prints out its inability to receive its reservation, waits a cycle, and tries again.

Note that the random( ) function returns a random integer (see Chapter 8 for more details).

```
#include <vera_defines.vrh>

program region_example {
    integer my_region;

    // allocate the region, store its ID,
    // and check success
    my_region = alloc(REGION, 0, 1);
    if (!my_region)
        error ("Region was not allocated\n");

    // start two threads that compete for numbers in the region
    fork
        grab_nums(0, my_region);
        grab_nums(1, my_region);
    join all
}

task grab_nums(integer id, integer region_id) {
    integer val, got_val;

    repeat (10) {
        // pick a random number to request ownership of
        val = (random() % 4);
        got_val = 0;
        // keep requesting ownership until it's granted
        while (got_val == 0) {
            // request ownership of val and place success
            // in got_val
            got_val = region_enter (NO_WAIT, region_id, val);
            // ownership not granted
            if (!got_val)
              printf("Thread %0d couldn't get val %0d at cycle %0d\n",
                    id, val, get_cycle());
```

```
        @(posedge CLOCK);
    }

    // ownership has been granted. Hold it for a
    // random delay from 0 to 4 cycles
    printf ("Thread %0d has val %0d at cycle %0d\n",
            id, val, get_cycle());
    repeat (random() % 5) @(posedge CLOCK);

    // release ownership of val
    region_exit(region_id, val);
  }
}
```

The output of this program appears below. The threads try to receive reservations for different values and proceed unbothered until cycle 8, when thread 1 tries to get a reservation for value 3 but thread 0 already has it. Thread 1 tries again every cycle until it finally gets its reservation to 3 in cycle 16.

Note that thread 0 released its reservation to 3 and then reserved it again while thread 1 continued to try to reserve it. Although unlikely, this process could theoretically repeat forever, resulting in the starvation of thread 1. This behavior illustrates the mantra reiterated many times throughout this chapter—never rely on the order of execution of unsynchronized threads.

```
Thread 0 has val 1 at cycle 1
Thread 1 has val 2 at cycle 1
Thread 0 has val 3 at cycle 4
Thread 1 has val 1 at cycle 4
Thread 0 has val 3 at cycle 5
Thread 0 has val 3 at cycle 6
Thread 1 has val 1 at cycle 7
Thread 1 could not get val 3 at cycle 8
Thread 1 could not get val 3 at cycle 9
Thread 1 could not get val 3 at cycle 10
Thread 0 has val 3 at cycle 11
Thread 1 could not get val 3 at cycle 11
Thread 1 could not get val 3 at cycle 12
Thread 1 could not get val 3 at cycle 13
Thread 1 could not get val 3 at cycle 14
Thread 1 has val 3 at cycle 16
Thread 1 has val 0 at cycle 17
```

Region Caveat

Once a reservation is made for a value, it should be returned. If it is not returned, other threads will not be able to reserve it.

Events

As previously described, mailboxes, semaphores, and regions can be used for thread synchronization. Events, however, are the most general form of thread synchronization in Vera.

Event terminology

Events are signaled through event variables. The signaling of an event is called a trigger. A code block that is waiting for an event or events to be triggered is called a sync.

Overview—Event Synchronization

The process for synchronizing threads via events follows:

- Declare event variables visible in the scope of all synchronizing threads.

- The thread that starts the synchronization, or the master thread, triggers an event by calling trigger( ).

- The threads that wait for the master thread, or the slave threads, wait for the event by calling sync( ).

Event Variables

Events are communicated through event variables. The syntax for declaring an event variable follows:

```
event <event_name>;
```

Event variables are usually used only in calls to trigger( ) and sync( ). However, they do show up in a few other contexts. Assigning NULL to events disables them, and assigning one event to another merges the two events. More details on disabling and merging events are presented in the following sections.

Event States

The user's code is normally unaware of the values of event variables because trigger( ) and sync( ) maintain the event variables on the user's behalf. However, the user can force event variables to be in one of three states: Disabled, On, and Off. The usage of these states is explored in the following sections.

Synchronizing to Events

Program execution is synchronized to triggered events by a call to sync( ), whose syntax takes two forms—one a task and the other a function.

The syntax of the task is:

```
sync (<sync_type>, <event1>, <event2>, ...);
```

The syntax of the function is:

```
<event_state> = sync (<sync_type>, <event1>);
```

sync_type can be one of four predefined constants, although three are valid only in task form and one is valid only in function form. The possible values of sync_type, the syntax used for each, and their actions are summarized in Table 6-4.

TABLE 6-4   Sync Types

sync_type	sync( ) form	Action
ALL	Task	Waits until all events are triggered
ANY	Task	Waits until any event is triggered
ORDER	Task	Waits until all events are triggered in the specified order
CHECK	Function	Checks to see if a single event is in the On state

event1, event2, and so on, are the event variables synchronized to. In task form, any number of event variables can be provided. In function form, when the CHECK keyword is used, only a single event variable can be provided.

Sync Types ALL and ANY

ALL and ANY behave similarly. ALL waits for all of the named events to be triggered. ANY waits for any single named event to be triggered. If named events are in the NULL (Disabled) state, they are treated as if they have been received immediately.

sync(ALL or ANY) timeout

By default, sync( ) never returns if the ALL or ANY options are used and the named events are never triggered. However, a timeout can be set for the event variables so that such a situation results in a runtime error. See "Timeouts" on page 183.

Sync Type ORDER

ORDER waits for all events specified to be triggered in the order they are presented to sync( ). If events are received out of order, sync( ) returns and a simulation error occurs. For example, the following code waits for the triggering of event1, then event2, and finally event3.

```
sync (ORDER, event1, event2, event3);
```

When ORDER is used, only the first specified event can be On. When events are in the NULL (Disabled) state, they are treated as if they arrived in the correct order.

sync(ORDER) timeout

By default, sync( ) never returns if the ORDER option is used and the named events are never received. However, a timeout can be set for the event variables so that such a situation results in a runtime error. See "Timeouts" on page 183.

Sync Type CHECK

When CHECK is used, sync( ) is called as a function and operates only on a single event variable. It can be used only with events in the On and Off states, and it never blocks the calling thread. It returns 1 if the supplied event is On and 0 if the event is Off.

Triggering Events

Events are emitted, or triggered, by a call to the task trigger( ). The syntax is:

```
trigger ([<trigger_type>,] <event_name>);
```

The triggered event is the event variable event_name. trigger_type can be one of five predefined constants, as shown in Table 6-5.

TABLE 6-5 Trigger Types

trigger_type	Action
ONE_SHOT	Triggers the event provided in event_name. All syncs waiting for the event will be unblocked, as long as they have already been blocked. This is the default if no trigger type is provided.
ONE_BLAST	Triggers the event provided in event_name. All syncs waiting for the event will be unblocked if they have already been blocked or if they are queued to block in the same simulation time.
HAND_SHAKE	Triggers the oldest pending sync, or queues a request if no sync is pending.
ON	Turns the event on.
OFF	Turns the event off.

Trigger Types ONE_SHOT and ONE_BLAST

Both ONE_SHOT and ONE_BLAST unblock all syncs waiting for the named event when trigger( ) is called. However, ONE_BLAST also unblocks syncs called in the same simulation time, even if the call to sync( ) occurs after the call to trigger( ).

In other words, ONE_BLAST eliminates a simulation race condition present with ONE_SHOT. If a ONE_SHOT call to sync( ) is made after trigger( ) has been called, that sync( ) will not receive the triggered event. ONE_BLAST removes this limitation and unblocks all syncs( ) queued in the same simulation time, even if sync( ) is called after the call to trigger( ).

For example, the following code results in an infinite loop, assuming that my_event is not triggered elsewhere:

```
trigger (ONE_SHOT, my_event);
sync (ALL, my_event);
```

However, the following code proceeds without delay:

```
trigger (ONE_BLAST, my_event);
sync (ALL, my_event);
```

ONE_SHOT discards the event trigger if no syncs are already waiting for the named event. Similarly, ONE_BLAST discards the event trigger if no syncs are waiting for the named event and no syncs to the named event are added in the same simulation time.

Trigger Type HAND_SHAKE

HAND_SHAKE either unblocks the oldest sync waiting for the named event or stores the trigger if no sync is waiting for the named event. If the trigger is stored, the next call to sync( ) with the named event returns immediately.

HAND_SHAKE can build mutual exclusion semaphores. To do this, replace the semaphore_get( ) call with a call to sync( ), and replace the semaphore_put( ) call with a call to trigger( ) using the HAND_SHAKE trigger type. Calls to sync( ) are dequeued by the call to trigger( ) one at a time in FIFO order. If no call to sync( ) is pending, the call to trigger( ) will allow the next call to sync( ) to proceed. The whole process starts with a single call to trigger( ) so that the first call to sync( ) is unblocked.

Even though HAND_SHAKE can be used to build mutual exclusion semaphores, it is best to use the built-in Vera semaphores instead. Using the most obvious mechanism makes the intent of the code much clearer; as a result, the code is much easier for the original code writer to deal with and for subsequent engineers to understand and debug.

Trigger Types ON and OFF

ON and OFF change the state of event variables to On and Off respectively. Events in the On and Off states cannot be used to synchronize concurrent threads automatically, since sync( ) can poll their status only with the CHECK sync option. The On state is the default state for events.

Events Example

The following program illustrates the use of a bidirectional event variable.

```
#include <vera_defines.vrh>

program events_example {
    // declare the event variable
    event my_event;
    // start the threads that need to communicate
    fork
```

```
        sync_then_trigger();
        trigger_then_sync();
    join all
}

task sync_then_trigger() {
    printf ("sync_then_trigger syncing at cycle %0d\n",get_cycle());
    sync (ALL, my_event);
    printf ("sync_then_trigger synced at cycle %0d\n",get_cycle());

    repeat (5) @(posedge CLOCK);
    printf ("sync_then_trigger triggering at cycle %0d\n",
            get_cycle());
    trigger (ONE_BLAST, my_event);
}

task trigger_then_sync() {
    repeat (5) @(posedge CLOCK);
    printf ("trigger_then_sync triggering at cycle %0d\n",
            get_cycle());
    trigger (ONE_SHOT, my_event);

    printf ("trigger_then_sync syncing at cycle %0d\n",get_cycle());
    sync (ALL, my_event);
    printf ("trigger_then_sync synced at cycle %0d\n",get_cycle());
}
```

The main program forks off two tasks, sync_then_trigger( ) and trigger_then_sync( ), and waits for both to finish. The sync_then_trigger( ) task waits for my_event to be triggered, delays for five clock cycles, and then triggers my_event. The trigger_then_sync( ) task does the opposite—it waits five clock cycles, triggers my_event, and then synchronizes to it. As the following output shows, sync_then_trigger( ) suspends execution until trigger_then_sync( ) triggers my_event, and then trigger_then_sync( ) suspends execution until sync_then_trigger( ) triggers my_event.

```
sync_then_trigger syncing at cycle 0
trigger_then_sync triggering at cycle 5
trigger_then_sync syncing at cycle 5
sync_then_trigger synced at cycle 5
sync_then_trigger triggering at cycle 10
trigger_then_sync synced at cycle 10
```

ONE_SHOT
versus
ONE_BLAST

The trigger_then_sync( ) task illustrates the subtle difference between ONE_SHOT and ONE_BLAST. It triggers my_event with ONE_SHOT and then syncs to my_event in the same simulation time. Because of this ordering and trigger type selection, the sync following the trigger does not return immediately. If ONE_BLAST were used, however, the sync would return immediately. The output of the program when ONE_SHOT in trigger_then_sync( ) is changed to ONE_BLAST follows. Note that trigger_then_sync( ) triggers and syncs in the same clock cycle, even though the sync happens after the trigger. Also note that sync_then_trigger( ) resumes execution concurrently with trigger_then_sync( ).

```
sync_then_trigger syncing at cycle 0
trigger_then_sync triggering at cycle 5
trigger_then_sync syncing at cycle 5
trigger_then_sync synced at cycle 5
sync_then_trigger synced at cycle 5
sync_then_trigger triggering at cycle 10
```

Merging Events

You can merge two events by assigning the event variable of one to the other. When one event variable is assigned to another event variable, subsequent triggers of either event variable unblock future syncs of both variables. However, syncs already waiting for those newly merged event variables are unchanged; they wait for triggers of the originally specified event or events only. Because the left hand side event in the event assignment effectively becomes an alias for the right hand side event when the assignment takes place, syncs already waiting for the left hand side event can no longer be triggered.

The following code illustrates event mergers. Note that the sync to e1 and e2 in the third thread is triggered by the merged e2. Also, the sync to e2 in the second thread can never be unblocked because e2 becomes an alias to e1 a clock cycle after the sync to e2 begins waiting. Therefore, the original e2, which thread 2 is waiting for, can no longer be triggered.

```
event e1, e2, e3;

fork
  {
     // thread 1
     sync (ALL, e1);
  }
  {
     // thread 2
     sync (ALL, e2);
     // never unblocks because old e2 is not triggered
  }
```

```
{
    // thread 3
    @(posedge CLOCK);
    e2 = e1;                    // e2 is now e1
    trigger (ONE_BLAST, e2);    // triggers new e2 and e1
    sync (ALL, e1, e2);
}
join all
```

More Thread Controls

Although the concurrency constructs presented thus far should be sufficient for most needs, Vera does have a few more methods for controlling threads. The wait_child( ) and wait_var( ) tasks are used to wait for other processes, and suspend_thread( ) is used to temporarily stop the active thread. Finally, the terminate command is used to halt child threads.

wait_child( )

The wait_child( ) task causes the parent thread to suspend execution until its child thread or threads have completed. It waits for the termination of child threads only in the scope of the caller. Because join all causes the parent thread to wait for all children, wait_child( ) is useful only when threads have been forked with join any or join none. The syntax is

```
wait_child();
```

For example, the following program forks off many parallel tasks and terminates once all have finished.

```
program test {
    fork
        my_task1();
        my_task2();
        ...
    join none
    wait_child();
}
```

This program would behave identically if the wait_child( ) call were eliminated and join all used instead of join none.

wait_child()
timeout

By default, wait_child( ) never returns if the child threads never complete. However, a timeout can be set for wait_child( ) so that this situation results in a runtime error. See "Timeouts" on page 183.

wait_var()

The wait_var( ) task blocks the calling thread until one of the variables in its argument list changes value. Effectively, wait_var( ) turns any nonobject variable into an event variable with an implicit trigger on any value change.

Only legitimate value changes unblock wait_var( ). In other words, reassigning a variable to its current value does not unblock wait_var( ).

The syntax for wait_var( ) is

```
wait_var (<variable1>, <variable2>, ...);
```

The variables passed into wait_var( ) must be integers, bit vectors, strings, or enumerated types. Objects cannot be used.

wait_var( )
timeout

By default, wait_var( ) never returns if the named variables never change value. However, a timeout can be set for wait_var( ) so that this a situation results in a runtime error. See "Timeouts" on page 183.

suspend_thread()

The suspend_thread( ) task causes the Vera scheduler to temporarily halt execution of the active thread and place the active thread at the end of the run list for the current simulation time. In other words, when suspend_thread( ) is encountered, all other ready threads are executed until they are finished for the current simulation time. After all other threads have been given a chance to run, the thread that called suspend_thread( ) is resumed. The syntax is

```
suspend_thread();
```

In general, suspend_thread( ) is used to resolve race conditions between threads. Before using suspend_thread( ) for this purpose, consider other mechanisms, such as semaphores, mailboxes, events, shadow variables, and regions. Code in which race conditions have been avoided with suspend_thread( ) is usually hard to debug, and it is also hard for other engineers to decipher.

terminate

The terminate command causes child processes to be terminated, regardless of their current state. The syntax is

```
terminate;
```

If terminated child processes have their own child threads, the descendant child threads are terminated as well.

For example, the following combination of fork/join and terminate causes child threads to run in parallel until the first child thread finishes. Upon the completion of the first child thread, the terminate command executes and all other child threads are stopped.

```
fork
    { block1; }
    { block2; }
    ...
join any
terminate;
```

Timeouts

Timeouts can be applied to mailboxes, semaphores, events, and regions so that mailbox_get( ), semaphore_get( ), sync( ), and region_enter( ) do not hang forever. Timeouts can be set for individual instances of these mechanisms or globally for all instances of the mechanisms. Timeouts can also be set globally for all instances of wait_child( ) and wait_var( ). Timeouts for individual instances override global timeouts for a mechanism.

Timeouts are set via the timeout( ) system call, which has two syntactical forms.

timeout( ) Syntax 1

The first syntactical form of the timeout( ) task is

```
timeout (<object_type>, <cycle_limit> [,<object_id>]);
```

object_type must be one of six predefined constants: MAILBOX, SEMAPHORE, EVENT, REGION, WAIT_VAR, or WAIT_CHILD.

cycle_limit is an integer that represents the timeout value to apply to the instance of object_type or to all instances of object_type. It is the number of SystemClock clock cycles to wait before triggering a timeout. (SystemClock is the default simulation clock; see Chapter 5 for more details.) Setting cycle_limit to 0 disables all specified timeouts.

object_id is an optional integer allowed only when object_type is set to MAILBOX, SEMAPHORE, or REGION. When object_id is absent, timeout( ) applies the cycle_limit to all instances of object_type globally. When present, object_id is the ID of the object_type to which cycle_limit applies. In the latter case, it is the ID requested from or returned by alloc( ).

timeout() Syntax 2

With the first syntax of timeout( ), timeouts can be applied to events only globally, because object_id cannot be an event variable. The second syntactical form of timeout( ), presented below, is used to set timeouts for individual event variables:

```
timeout (<event_name>, <cycle_limit>);
```

event_name is the event variable to which the timeout applies. It is similar to object_id above, except that it is an event variable and not an instance ID.

cycle_limit is an integer that represents the timeout value associated with the event variable. It has the same behavior as cycle_limit in the first syntax.

Conceptually, the second syntax of timeout( ) is equivalent to the syntax timeout(EVENT, cycle_limit, event_name). Unfortunately, this usage is illegal Vera code.

How Timeouts Work

Mailbox, semaphore, and region timeouts

In the case of a call to mailbox_get( ), semaphore_get( ), or region_enter( ), Vera checks to see if the relevant mailbox, semaphore, or region has been assigned an instance timeout. If an instance timeout does not exist, Vera checks to see if a timeout has been assigned globally to the mechanism type.

Whichever is found first becomes the timeout value for the blocking call. If neither timeout value is found, no timeout is active for the blocking call and it can suspend execution forever without causing a simulation error.

Event timeouts   In the case of a call to sync( ), Vera computes the minimum timeout value assigned to all included event variables. The globally assigned timeout for all events is used in the minimum calculation whenever instance timeouts cannot be found. The result of the minimum computation is the timeout associated with the call to sync( ). If no instance timeouts have been set and a global timeout has not been set for events, sync( ) will never time out; it can suspend execution forever without causing a simulation error.

wait_child( ) and wait_var( ) timeouts   Timeouts can be applied only globally to wait_child( ) and wait_var( ). When one of these calls executes, Vera checks to see if the global timeout has been assigned to the relevant call type. If no timeout value has been assigned, no timeout is active for the blocking call and it can suspend execution forever without causing a simulation error.

When a timeout is triggered, a verification error occurs. The simulation continues unless the vera_exit_on_error property is set. See the *VERA System Verifier User Manual* for more information.

Summary

Vera provides a rich set of primitives for implementing concurrent environments. The major mechanisms and their purposes are summarized in Table 6-6.

TABLE 6-6   Vera Concurrency Mechanisms

Concurrency Mechanism	Purpose
fork/join	Spawns threads
Join modifiers	Controls when the parent thread resumes execution
Variables and shadow variables	Allows or prevents communication
Mailboxes	Allows FIFO-based data communication
Semaphores	Arbitrates execution
Regions	Arbitrates data
Events	Synchronizes threads

CHAPTER 7

Objects in Vera: Modeling Higher Levels of Abstraction

So far, this book has covered the basic programming constructs of Vera as well as the implementation of concurrency to emulate the hardware implementation. This chapter initiates the discussion of another major feature of Vera: object-oriented programming. This chapter describes:

- The basic concepts behind objects

- Vera implementation of object-oriented programming

- Defining objects in Vera

It uses Ethernet packets as examples to illustrate some of these object-oriented programming concepts.

The next chapter covers use of objects to generate stimulus with Vera's randomization facilities.

What Is an Object?

An *object* encapsulates code and data into a single programming construct. It binds together a set of data commonly known as the *data structure* with its associated methods. A *method* is a task or function that operates on the data structures defined in the object.

Procedural Versus Object-Oriented Programming

In non-object-oriented languages, data structures and the functions or tasks that operate on them are kept separate. For example, in the C language, functions and data structures are defined independently and are not formally connected. A C function can operate on more than one structure, and more than one function can operate on the same structure. In object-oriented languages, code and data are bound together in a single indivisible object.

Figure 7-1 illustrates the difference between procedural and object-oriented approaches. In the procedural model, the three functions operate on the three different data variables and there is no central theme or approach. To repeat the same functionality elsewhere, multiple data variables or arrays of these variables would have to be defined, and the functions would have to be modified to deal with them.

FIGURE 7-1   *Procedural Versus Object-Oriented Languages*

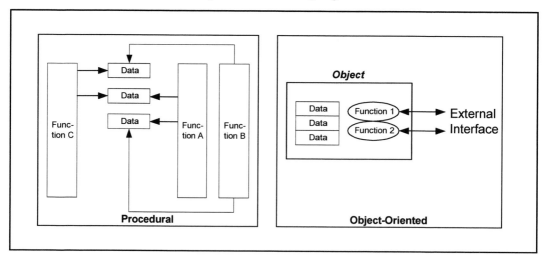

In object-oriented implementations, the functions and the data-structures that define a logical entity or operation are bound together into an object. The object interfaces to the external world through the functions. The object can be instantiated multiple times, if the same functionality is desired elsewhere. The internals do not change. Therefore, objects lend themselves to a hierarchical implementation in which you can bundle common operations and data into objects and reuse them easily.

Benefits of objects   Another strong motivation for object-oriented programming is that a user of an object *does not need to know about its internals*. Instead, the user interacts with the object only through its methods. This allows modification of the details of the object without affecting user code. In testbenches, this is useful for sharing code.

In verification, a strong motivation for using objects is the level of abstraction they allow in the testbench, which allows the developer to focus on the interaction between the testbench and the DUT.

Abstraction: a   In computing, abstraction allows the user to interact more easily with
definition   information. In a testbench, abstraction maps complex situations to simpler, higher-level concepts. For example, in digital logic, the levels of abstraction go from logic gates to comparators, to multiplexors, and then to ALUs or CPUs.

In verification, abstraction defines

- The way the testbench interacts with the DUT

- The way the testbench interacts with its user, the person creating the test cases

Once the level of abstraction has been determined, it can be mapped to user-defined types. In Vera, user-defined types are classes that define the data structure and the operations that can be performed on that data.

Classes

How are objects defined? An object is defined via its *class*, which determines everything about an object. A class is a template for an object; it defines the data and methods used in the object. Objects are individual instances of a class.

For example, you might create a "credit card" class. The credit card class defines what it is to be a credit card account object and also defines all the credit card account-related transactions that can happen to such an object.

You could then define an instance of this class called "Visa". Visa is now an object. You could instantiate more than one object of this class—called MasterCard, American Express, Discover, and so on—one for each account. The credit card class defines data associated with a generic credit card account, such as the name of the account holder, address, and account number. It also defines all the operations, such as "calculate interest," "add transaction," "calculate balance," and "make credit payment," that can happen in a credit card object.

A method is an operation that an object can carry out. For instance, the credit card class has methods for "calculate interest," "add transaction," "calculate balance," and the like.

Some Real-Life Examples

In verification, objects can represent almost any data structure or transaction in the system. You can easily move to a higher level of abstraction by building a new set of objects composed of the objects defined at a lower level.

For example, when creating testbenches, linked lists, queues, hashes, and trees can be defined as objects. When testing networking devices, the packet is commonly abstracted as an object while a higher level of abstraction might define a stream of packets to emulate network traffic.

When testing Peripheral Component Interconnect (PCI), a single transaction can be defined as an object, and packet transfers can be implemented at a higher level of abstraction. When testing CPUs, instructions can be abstracted into objects. When testing storage devices, sectors and tracks are easily abstracted into objects, while the next level of abstraction could be the file, conceptually sets of sectors.

Objects in Vera

In Vera, objects are defined by declaring classes, created by declaration in a *program*, *class*, *function* or *task*, and constructed (instantiated) by explicitly calling the constructor method *new*.

Figure 7-2 is an example of a class definition in Vera. The object is a simple first-in, first-out queue.

FIGURE 7-2   Queue Class Definition

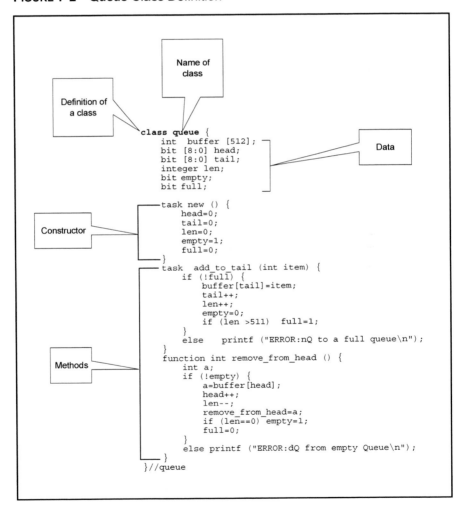

Basic Class with Methods

The syntax of a basic class with methods is

```
class <class_name> {
   <variable_declaration>;
   <variable_declaration>;
      .
      .
      .
   <task_or_function_declaration>;
   <task_or_function_declaration>;
      .
      .
      .
}
```

For example,

```
class packet {
   bit[7:0] destination;
   bit[7:0] source;
   bit[9:0] length;
   bit payload[];

   task new (bit[7:0] d, bit[7:0] s) {
      destination = d;
      source = s;
      ...
   }
   task set_da (bit[7:0] a) {
   ...
   }
}//end class packet
```

Both the variables (data) and the methods declared within a class are known as members of the class. Members can be *public* or *private* for encapsulation purposes. Vera uses the term *local* or *protected* to define private members. These are discussed in detail in a later section.

A public member can be accessed by any entity outside the class in which it is defined. A private member is available only to methods of the class in which the member is declared.

The methods are declared within a class in the same way tasks and functions are declared outside a class. Methods have two interesting characteristics:

- They can access all the private members in the class in which they are defined. External functions or tasks cannot access any of the private members of the class.

- All members of the class in which the method is declared are available to the method. That includes other data and method members.

For the sake of readability, a method prototype can be declared inside the class while the real method body is declared outside the class. A scope operator (::) can indicate the class to which a method belongs. Scope operators are typically used when class definitions balloon; function bodies are then specified externally to improve the readability of the class definitions.

Instantiation & Construction

To use objects, a designer has to take three basic steps:

1. Define the class. For example, the following provides a template for an object called packet:

```
class packet {...}
class queue  {...}
```

2. Declare objects in the main program, class, function or task.

The following declaration creates three identifiers—two (my_packet and packet_array) for the class packet and one (rxqueue) for the class queue:

```
packet my_packet;
packet packet_array[32];
queue rxqueue;
```

Identifiers hold the handle for an instance of the object. A valid handle is created when that instance is constructed:

3. Create an instance of the object by invoking the *new* constructor.

The following creates handles for the objects and assigns them to the identifiers my_packet and rxqueue, respectively. It also allocates memory for the objects and associates the handles with those memory locations.

```
my_packet=new (32,64);
rxqueue=new ()
```

The following sample program defines, declares, initializes, and then uses an object. Figure 7-3 shows the mappings in this example.

```
#include <vera_defines.h>
#include "my_defines.vrh"
#include "my.if.vrh"

//class declarations
class packet {
    bit[7:0] destination;
    bit[7:0] source;
    bit[9:0] length;
    bit[7:0] payload[];

    task integer new (bit[7:0] da, bit[7:0] sa, bit[9:0] len) {
        destination=da;
        source=sa;
        length=len;
        init_payld();
    }
    task init_payld() {
        integer i;
        for (i=0; i<length;i++) {
            payload[i] = 8'h55;
        }
    }
    task set_da (bit[7:0] a) {
        destination=a;
    }
    task set_src (bit[7:0] src_address) {
        source=src_address;
    }
    function bit[7:0] get_da() {
        get_da=destination;
    }
    function bit[7:0] get src() {
        get_src=source;
    }
    task print_packet_header() {
        printf("DA=%0d SA=%0d len=%0d\n",destination,source,length);
    }

//extern declarations
program gen {
    packet b_pkt, e_pkt;
    b_pkt=new (69,33,0);
    e_pkt=new (28,61,0);
    b_pkt.set_da (56);
    b_pkt.set_src (29);
    b_pkt.print_packet_header();
}
```

FIGURE 7-3   Mapping of Methods and Object Instances

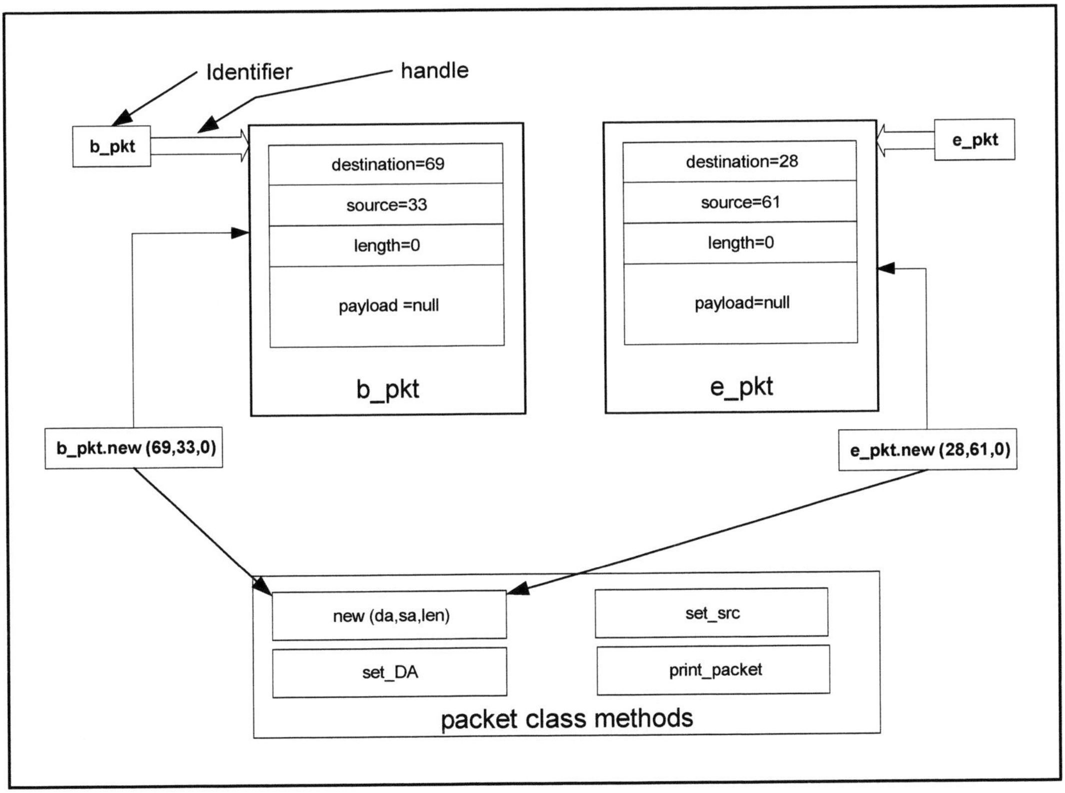

Defining a Class

Classes and objects are useful in testbenches for stimulus generation and whenever there is a need to model a higher-level data structure. Classes can also be useful if the same "operation" is performed in many different components of the testbench. For example, the Ethernet MAC has a stimulus generator on the host side as well as on the MII side. They both perform a similar function: packet generation. Therefore, you could have two packet generators (classes declared as packet_gen) running in parallel if you declared the same object twice and bound it in one case to the host bus and to the MII bus in the other.

```
packet_gen host_gen;
packet_gen MII_gen;
host_gen =new (USE_HOST);        //USE_HOST is #define macro
MII_gen = new (USE_MII);         //USE_MII is #define macro
```

In the above example there are two instances of packet_gen class. Each instance is directed to bind to a different port by using a flag. The flag is used instead of a virtual port because the port type for MII interface is different from that of the host interface.

As another example, take a four-port Ethernet switch. The testbench needs four transactors, all identical and running in parallel. A class xactor can be defined and then instantiated four times, one for each port. In this case, all four transactors run concurrently and independently.

```
switch_xactor port_xactor[4];
for (i=0; i<4; i++) {
    //eport is a declared virtual port that is bound
    //somewhere else to the switch ports
    port_xactor[i] = new (eport[i]);
}
```

Declaring Objects

Objects are declared just like any other data type. Single instances and arrays of objects are both supported, as are associative arrays of objects.

For example, you can create a packet list by simply declaring

```
packet pktQueue[];
```

This creates an identifier (or "handle") called pktQueue, which references a list of packets. At declaration, this handle contains a null value.

An instance of the object is created when it is constructed. The construction allocates memory and a valid value, which is assigned to the handle.

Object identifiers can also be declared inside a class definition:

```
class pktlist {
    packet pqueue[];
    integer len;
    task new() {
        ...
    }
    task insert_pkt();
    task get_pkt();
}
```

In this case, each packet in pqueue must be constructed explicitly. The constructor of pktlist will not call the constructors for the packet.

Self-reference in a class declaration A class can reference itself in its definition. In the following example, the declaration of the class packet also contains a definition of the member next, an object of type packet.

```
class packet {
    packet next;
    bit[9:0] destination;
    bit[9:0] source;
    payload payld;

    task new();
    task get_packet();
    task set_packet();
}
```

Self-referencing declarations can be used to declare some very complex data structures, such as doubly linked lists and search trees. This type of self-reference is different from the "this" operator, which is used by an instance of the object to reference itself.

Declaration does not mean the object is created, and declaration does not allocate memory. It simply creates an identifier, which is used as a handle for the object. The handle contains a null value at declaration; it is assigned a valid value when memory is allocated for that instance of the object.

To allocate memory for the object, the user must *construct* the object. The process of construction is explained in the next section.

Construction

Once a class is defined, objects based on that class can be declared. The declaration associates an identifier with each object. As you saw, however, no memory is allocated for the object and the identifier contains a null value. Most object-oriented languages do not allocate memory until a constructor is called for that object. When the constructor is invoked, memory is allocated for the data members of the object and a valid value (handle) is created that references the memory and methods associated with that object (instance). The constructor can also be used to initialize the data members of the object instance.

The memory handle is also referred to as an instance of the object. When there are multiple objects of the same class, each object gets a separate memory location for its data members. However, all object instances share the code for the methods.

If an object is not constructed—that is, if

```
object_name=new (...)
```

is not used—then the memory for that object is not allocated and the handle contains a null value. The object handle is treated as a null handle and, if referenced, will cause runtime errors. Null object handles can be detected by comparison of the object handle to a null value.

```
If (object_name == null) {
    exit();
}
```

Repeated invocation of new( )

Consider the following example. Each time through the loop, Vera creates another instance of the object and a new handle, which is assigned to myobject.

```
class myclass {
    ...
}
myclass myobject;
for (I=0; I < 31; I++) {
    myobject=new;
    ...
}
```

The memory referenced by the older handles is reclaimed if no other identifier references it. If another identifier references it, the memory location can be accessed only through that identifier.

Initializing Objects

Objects in Vera are initialized with the new( ) constructor. If a data member is not initialized in new( ), it takes a null value. In the constructor, data members can be assigned default values, as shown in the example below:

```
task new() {
    a =0;
    max_dist=10;
    min_dist=20;
}
```

You can also pass parameters to new( ) and use these parameters to assign values to the data members, as illustrated in the following example:

```
task new (int mx_dist,int mn_dist) {
    someint =0;
    max_dist=mx_dist;
    min_dist=mn_dist;
}
```

Note that in the above example, someint is also assigned a default value, even though it wasn't passed to new( ) as a parameter.

How Objects Are Reclaimed in Vera

Vera automatically reclaims an object instance (i.e., a memory location) when that memory is no longer referenced by an identifier. Therefore, the testbench does not need to do a dealloc to free the memory allocated for an object. It just needs to make sure that the instance is not referenced.

Take care, however, when copying or assigning objects. If not done properly, copying and assigning can leave behind references to instances. In these cases, testbench memory usage grows exponentially.

See Figure 7-4, in which two processes, pA and pB, both use an object based on the class message to exchange information. At startup, pA creates a new object by calling the constructor:

```
msg=new;
```

This allocates memory for the new object and assigns the handle for this memory location to pA.

FIGURE 7-4   Memory Reclamation Example

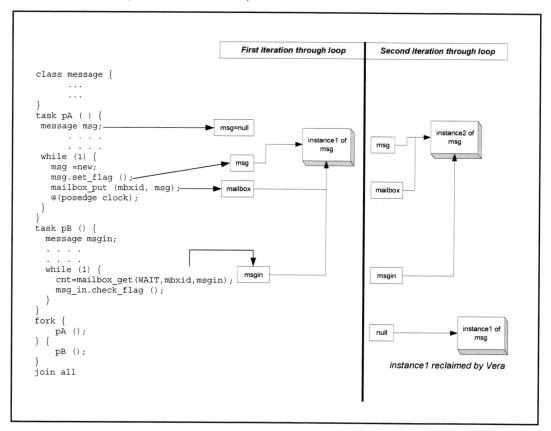

It then passes msg through a mailbox to process pB. pB does a mailbox_get( ) to receive the message. The handle for the instance is assigned to msg_in. After one clock cycle, pA does msg=new again, which creates a new instance of msg.

The object msg now references the new instance, so only pB references the old instance of msg. Vera keeps this instance of msg until pB gets a second message. When pB goes through the loop the second time, it does a mailbox_get( ) again and receives a new msg. This process assigns a new object handle to msg_in. Since there are now no references to the old instance of msg, Vera assumes that the first instance of the object is no longer in use and reclaims the memory associated with that instance.

Testbenches should not leave hanging references

Even though Vera automatically reclaims memory, it is very easy in a testbench to leave objects with references to them. This is especially true when one process passes objects it created though a mailbox to another process. It also is true when a process deals with linked objects, such as packet queues or packet lists. An example follows.

Creating memory leaks

Say you have an object sector and a doubly linked list of sectors. Sectors are added or removed from anywhere in the list. In the linked list implementation, each sector points to the next sector. A thread comes in; adds a sector to the list; and passes it to another thread, which removes the sector from the list.

```
class sector {
    sector previous;
    sector next;
    integer sector_id;
    Bit[7:0] data[512];
    task new();
    task setnext (sector nxt);
    task setprev (sector prev);
    function sector getnext();
    function sector getprev();

}
class sector_list {
    sector head;
    sector tail;
    int     list_size;

    task new();
    task insert_sector (sector isec){
        . . . .
        . . . .
        isec.setnext (next);
        isec.setprev (previous);
        . . . .
    }
    function sector remove_sector (int rsid) {
        . . . .
        . . . .
        sec_to_rem.setnext (null_sector);
```

```
                    sec_to_rem.setprev (null_sector);
                    . . . .
                    . . . .
              }
      }
      .
      .
      sector s, rs;
      integer I=0;
      sector_list slist;
      slist =new;
      fork {
          while (1) {
              s=new; //this creates a new instance of s
              slist.insert_sector (s);
          }
      } {
          while (1) {
              rs=slist.remove_sector (I);
          }
      }
```

In lists, explicitly set nested references to null

When a sector is inserted, it is set to point to the previous sector and the next sector in the list. Therefore, when it is removed by *slist.remove_sector (I)*, it must set the previous sector reference and the next sector reference to null. Otherwise, if any of these references is not cleared, Vera will not deallocate the memory or the handle associated with that instance of the sector. However, it will continue to allocate new memory, because *s=new* is being continuously executed. As a result, the testbench will grow in memory usage until it occupies the entire system memory.

Copying & Assigning Objects

Assigning does not copy data members

In Vera there is a difference between copying and assigning an object. Copying objects means copying the contents of the memory location of one object to another. Assigning refers to the assignment of an object identifier to another, as shown in the example below.

```
second_packet=first_packet;
```

In the above code, first_packet is assigned to second_packet. Let's take a look at it in more detail using the code snippet below:

```
packet first_packet, second_packet;
first_packet=new (23,45,64);
second_packet= first_packet;
```

The second_packet object does not copy the values from first_packet. Instead, second_packet has the same handle as first_packet. Figure 7-5 illustrates the assignment

```
second_packet= first_packet;
```

In assignment, second_packet does not have its own memory. It is just assigned to the same location as first_packet.

FIGURE 7-5 Assigning an Object

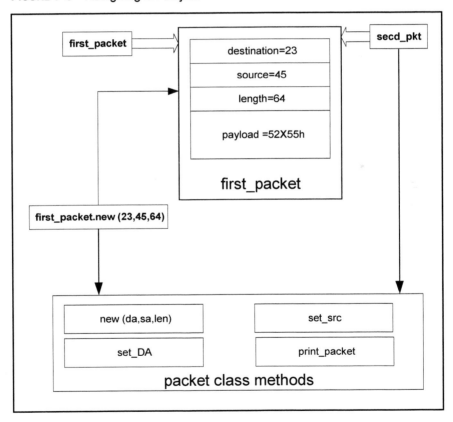

Copying objects in Vera requires the use of

```
second_packet = new first_packet;
```

Copying an object   In this case, all the data members of first_packet are copied over to a new location, which is created for second_packet. Vera will not copy other objects instantiated within the object, but it will copy the handle of the instantiated object. So if there are other objects declared within the class declaration, you need to create a custom method to copy objects.

FIGURE 7-6   Copying Data Members of an Object

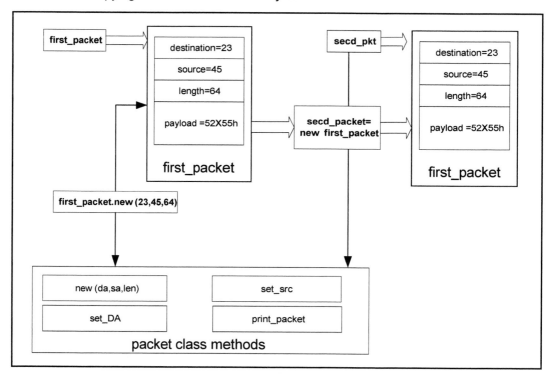

For example, if the packet class included an object IP_packet instead of payld, as in the following code:

```
class IP_packet {
    integer dest_IP;
    integer src_IP;
    integer TOS;
}
```

```
class packet {
    bit[7:0] destination;
    bit[7:0] source;
    bit[9:0] length;

    IP_packet payld;
    ...
}//class packet
```

second_packet= new first_packet would copy the values of all the data members except the payld member. It will copy the handle of first_packet.payld to second_packet.payld.

Private Versus Public Data

One of the motivations for object-oriented programming is the concept of data encapsulation or data hiding. Vera supports two encapsulation controls in classes:

- protected—Visible only to methods within the class and extended classes

- local—Visible only to methods within the class; not visible to extended classes

If no control is specified, the data is available to any function, internal or external to the class.

The syntax is

```
class class_name {
    [local]     datatype  identifier;
    [protected] datatype  identifier;
}
```

where datatype is the type declaration for the variable and identifier identifies the data variable. Valid data types include integer, bit, string, event, or a user-defined type.

Private is used in testbenches only for code sharing

In traditional software engineering, most of the data members would be protected or local. In testbenches, unless the class is being designed for reuse or sharing, data members don't have to be explicitly declared private. However, it is a good practice to follow when declaring objects. If data members are declared local, functions must be provided to allow these members to be read or written. If a member is declared as local in a class, then it also provides a hint of the ramifications of removing, renaming, or revising that member of the class. It indicates a strong recommendation from the creator of the class not to modify that member.

Take the packet class example:

```
class packet {
    protected bit[7:0] destination;
    protected bit[7:0] source;
    protected bit[9:0] length;
    //bit[] payload;
    IP_packet payld;

    task new (bit[7:0] dest, bit[7:0] src, bit[9:0] len) {
        destination=dest;
        source=src;
        length=len;
        payld=new;
    }
    function declaration
    function declaration
    ...
}//packet
```

The data members of the class—destination, source, and length—all are now declared as protected members. These members are now initialized through the constructor new.

If you still require access to the data members, define functions for reading and writing them:

```
function bit[7:0] get_dest();
function bit[7:0] set_dest();
function bit[7:0] get_src();
function bit[7:0] set_src();
function bit[7:0] get_len();
function bit[7:0] set_len();
```

You should identify other operations on the packet class and then define methods for each of the operations.

Additional Object-Oriented Constructs

In addition to the constructs defined already there are additional constructs related to use of objects and classes in Vera. These are

- *this* self-reference operator

- *extern* declaration

- *typedef* declaration

- *static* variable declaration

this Operator

The this operator is used to reference the instance from which it is invoked. The syntax is

```
this.<method_name>();
this.<data_member_name>;
```

For example,

```
//invokes calc_crc method of this instance.
this.calc_crc ();
this.crc; //refers to crc member of this instance
```

extern Declaration

extern references a variable or object that is declared somewhere outside the namescope of the current entity. The syntax is either of the following:

```
extern <object>;
extern <variable_name>;
```

For example,

```
extern ether_packet_gen;
```

typedef Declaration

typedef indicates a class that is declared further down. The syntax is

```
typedef class <class_name>;
```

For example,

```
typedef class packet;
```

static Declaration

If static is prepended to a data member, that data member is shared across all instances of that class. The syntax is

```
[static] <datatype> <variable_name>;
```

For example,

```
static integer sequence_number;
```

Guidelines for Working with Classes & Methods

One of the problems that beginning object-oriented programmers face is how to work with classes and methods for those classes. For people coming from a procedural background, learning these things can be difficult and time-consuming.

Working with Classes

Here are a few guidelines for creating classes:

Try to do everything through classes

- Although Vera allows you to do things either procedurally or through objects, try to do everything through classes and objects. This means sometimes creating classes with only methods as members.

Bind common data structures and operations into a class

- To identify possible classes, group common data structures or common operations into a class. Packets, cells, sectors, and queues are examples of data structures that can be created using classes. Other less intuitive examples are classes for PCI bus transactions, classes for reading/writing from registers or memory locations, and classes for implementing schedulers and arbiters.

Use methods to access data members

- Procedural programmers will instinctively try to provide direct access to the data members of an object. However, it is better to provide methods for reading or writing these members than to allow direct access, since methods improve opportunities for reuse. However, don't implement method-based access for all data members of a class; limit method access to only those members you anticipate will need to be accessed externally.

Keep class size
small
- Just as in procedural programming, it is important in object-oriented programming to keep tasks and functions, as well as classes and methods, to a reasonable size. If a class becomes too big, it is difficult to maintain, and this will result in bugs. Generally, keep the number of data members and methods in a single class to a manageable and readable size. If the class size is so large that it is difficult to comprehend, then create additional classes and nest them within the class.

Maintain balance
between public
and private
- In software engineering, it is usually recommended that all data members be declared as local (private). In verification, however, some data members remain public by default. Make this decision based on whether the class will be shared and also on how much schedule pressure there is to complete the testbench. If the class is not shared and there is schedule pressure, it may be acceptable not to use local.

Start simple and
then grow classes
- It is always best to begin by creating the simplest testbench and classes. Once the basic class is working, start adding functionality. Vera provides an extension mechanism for adding functionality to classes. This extension mechanism is covered in detail in Chapter 9.

Nest objects in
class definitions
- For complex operations and structures, you can use objects inside a class declaration. This makes a class more manageable. For example,

```
class packet {
    header_class header;
    payld_class payld;
    bit[31:0] crc;
    task new();
    task calc_crc();
}
```

Include utility
methods in
classes
- Generally, in verification, there are some useful utility methods, such as print values and consistency checks, that can be built for almost any class. When creating methods, keep the utility functions in mind.

Working with Methods

Once you have identified a class, identifying methods is simpler. Methods are operations you expect to perform on the data members of the class. For example, in the MAC testbench, there are two basic test cases:

- Write a packet to the host side of the MAC, receive it on the MII side, and make sure it is received correctly.

- Write a packet to the MII side of the MAC, and receive it on the host side.

These two test cases indicate that you need to support the following operations:

- Print data variables

- Generate packet

- Generate CRC

- Read from and write to the host side of the MAC

- Read from and write to the MII side of the MAC

- Check packet:

    Check dest
    Check CRC

Each of these operations can be defined as methods within the packet class, but this makes the packet class very large, with lots of methods. This makes maintenance of the class more difficult. In addition, as verification progresses, operations may need to be added, which requires further modification to the class definition and additional methods. In other cases, the data members may need to be changed, which can cause problems with existing test cases.

The need for inheritance

The solution lies in the use of inheritance, a property of Vera and other object-oriented languages that offers an easy way to extend the properties and capabilities of the class without affecting the current properties and members. This avoids introducing bugs into working test cases. Normally, inheritance is used to specialize a class, not to add generic capabilities. But if adding capabilities for new test cases requires significant modifications, consider using inheritance and extension instead of modifying the original class.

Extend a class by creating a derived class. When you do, the current class is used as a base, and is referred to as the super class or base class. The extended class is referred to as the subclass or the derived class. The derived class inherits the properties and methods of the base class but may also add some of its own properties and methods. These changes do not affect the operation of the base class, so the original test cases continues to function as before. See Chapter 9 for more information on inheritance.

Summary

Objects and classes are powerful concepts that can be used to create new data types or increase the level of abstraction in testbenches. Classes and objects can be instantiated and constructed, and are automatically reclaimed by Vera when no longer in use.

Object-Oriented Keywords

The following shows object-oriented keywords.

TABLE 7-1 Object-Oriented Keywords

Keyword	Usage	Example
class	Declaration of classes	```class queue { integer q[]; ... }```
new	Object constructor	```queue intQ; intQ =new; cell c; c= new (size,da,sa);```
this	Refers to the current instance of the object	`this.count +=1;`
local	Means data variable or method is accessible only to local methods	`local integer number;` `local task get_count();`
protected	Means data variable or method is available only to local methods and derived classes	**protected** `sector next;`

TABLE 7-1   Object-Oriented Keywords (Continued)

Keyword	Usage	Example
extern	External declaration for the class	```extern class burst_wr { bit[31:0] addr; bit[31:0] d1; bit[31:0] d2; task new(); task wr(); }```
typedef	Indicates that the class is defined elsewhere	```typedef class sector; class sector_list { sector next; ... }```
Static	Used to create a data member that is shared across all instances of the class. In this class, pktcnt will be shared by all instances of packet.	```class packet { int dest; int payld[64]; static int pktcnt; }```

CHAPTER 8

Automatic Stimulus Generation & Randomized Testing in Vera

This chapter explains the concept of random stimulus testing, how to generate random stimulus, and the methodology behind randoms. It also explains the issues in stimulus generation and the use of random stimulus generation to create test cases. It then looks at stimulus generation issues for the Ethernet MAC and describes the various features Vera has for building random stimulus generators. Finally, it closes with a discussion of test case creation issues.

Stimulus Generation

Stimulus generation options

Stimulus generation is one of the most important aspects of verification, since it actually creates the test. Chapter 2 discussed the three stimulus generation options:

- Directed testing

- Directed random testing

- Random testing

FIGURE 8-1   Test Space Coverage With Different Stimulus Generation
Strategies

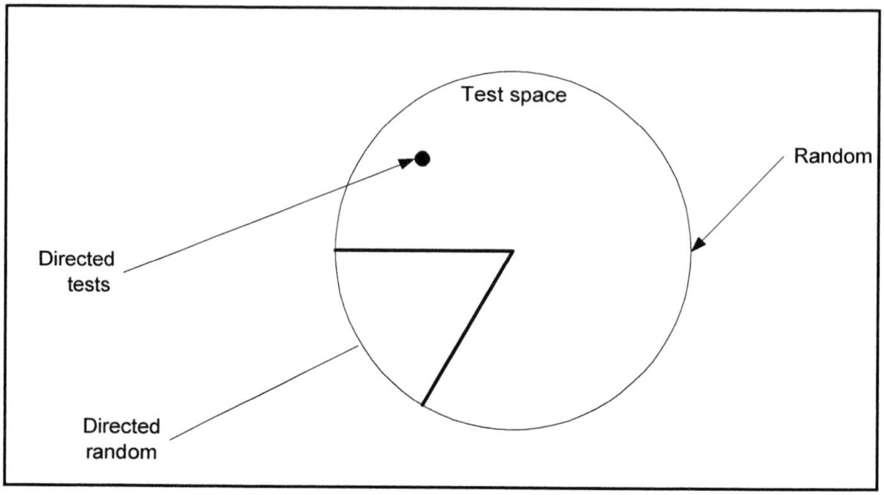

Each of these strategies addresses the test space differently. Figure 8-1 shows the test space as a circle in which each possible test is a point and axes (lines) through the circle represent testable parameters or functions of the DUT. In a complex design, the test space can have tens, if not hundreds, of axes. If a directed test is represented as a point in the test space placed at a specified location, and a random test is a point placed randomly in the test space, then a directed random test is a group of random tests that attempt to cover an area of the test space, or an axis through it, by constraining the randomness to a range of values.

Differences between directed, directed random and random tests

Directed tests are normally fully specified, but even they have some parameters that are not of interest in the test, and those parameters can be generated randomly, especially if the testbench is operating at a high level of abstraction. Directed random tests allow you to constrain the randomness of each parameter and thereby "direct" the test within a narrow slice of the test space. Random tests are not at all specific; the testbench randomly creates the parameters for the test and, therefore, can hit any point in the test space.

When to use directed versus random tests

Directed tests are suitable for simpler designs in which the test space is small enough to be covered by a reasonable number of tests. Directed tests are also appropriate for testing simple features in complex designs, where those features are unlikely to contain bugs, either in themselves or when interacting with other features. For example, parity error injection in a complex design can be tested by a directed tests, either alone or layered on top of a random test.

Random tests can be created for any type of design but are usually better suited for designs with huge test spaces or with numerous interesting interactions. It's the possibility of uncovering interesting interactions that makes random testing appealing, since it's usually impossible to conceive of all interesting interactions. A random test can create many unexpected simultaneous asynchronous events, which leads to complex and unique interactions.

Definition of Random

Gaming algorithms and cryptography have long driven the need for randomness in computer systems. A sequential execution machine, such as a processor, is a deterministic system; it blindly executes instructions. The deterministic nature of computers make their number sequences predictable. For true randomness the current number should not allow you to predict the next number. The determinism of computer systems makes it difficult to implement a random action.

Randomness is introduced into computer systems by pseudorandom number generators. As the name suggests, pseudorandom numbers are not truly random. Rather, they are computed from a mathematical formula or simply taken from a precalculated list. A lot of research has gone into pseudorandom number theory, and modern algorithms for generating these numbers are so good that the numbers closely approximate random values.

Pseudorandom numbers are predictable if you know where in the sequence the first number comes from. For some purposes, predictability is a good characteristic; for others, it is not. For verification, predictability is good, because it allows failing tests to be rerun with the same conditions that caused the failures. For simulations, it is convenient that a series of random numbers can be replayed for use in several tests, and pseudorandom numbers are well suited for this purpose.

The exponentially increasing complexity of ASIC designs requires automation of stimulus generation, which can be either deterministic or random. Deterministic tests are used to examine specific set of DUT parameters and functionality. Random stimulus can be used to explore different axes of a test space and reduce the overhead of test creation, but it increases the testbench complexity. Vera uses pseudorandom-number generators to allow generation of random variables, which can be used to create stimulus.

Issues in Random Testing

Random tests involve tradeoffs. The most common are

- In general, random tests are harder to debug than directed tests.

- Test space coverage needs to be measured with random tests.

- Constraints need to be specified and implemented so the randomly generated stimulus does not violate design parameters.

- The testbench for random testing is usually more complicated than a testbench for directed tests, requiring generators and runtime monitors.

Debugging

Debugging random tests can be harder than in directed tests, for many reasons:

- As noted before, the testbench is much more complex.

- The random tests typically hit bugs after long runtimes, so finding bugs and rerunning tests adds complexity and time to the debug cycle.

- At a certain level of complexity, the random stimulus generator appears to have a mind of its own. So to debug these test situations, you have to spend extra time understanding what interactions that took place, and why.

The typical debug process for random tests involves tracing the transactions through log files or monitors. It might also involve tracing the waveforms with the simulator or the Vera Debugger.

Test Case Coverage

Because random tests are automatically created, you must track how much of the test space random testing has covered. You can do this by logging and tracking statistics in the testbench using either your own statistics trackers or the event coverage facilities provided in Vera. However, there is no substitute for a verification engineer personally analyzing the test cases and the design to determine the test case coverage. Tools can provide metrics for coverage, but analysis of the coverage metrics must be done by a person.

Random Stimulus Requires Constraints

Since random stimulus is automatically generated, it may violate design parameters. To make sure stimulus is generated properly, most hardware verification languages provide constructs for constraining the random generation capability. The constraints define the valid limits for random values and are used to define the arcs for the directed random tests.

Complexity of Random Stimulus Testbenches

In general, a testbench used for random testing is more complex than a testbench used for directed testing. In addition to all of the other capabilities, testbenches for random tests require stimulus generators and runtime monitors and checkers.

Stimulus Generation for MAC

Consider the stimulus generation for the Ethernet MAC design example. Most of the tests can be divided into three categories:

- Normal transmit and receive

- Transmit and receive with errors

- Transmit and receive with multiple packets in the FIFO

Table 8-1 lists the test cases needed to ensure basic design functionality.

TABLE 8-1   MAC Basic Test Cases

Interface	Feature	Basic Test
Host	Full-duplex Tx	Send packets in full-duplex mode. Vary packet size from minimum to maximum.
	Half-duplex TX	Send packets in half-duplex mode. Vary size and inter-packet gap (IPG). Insert collisions, late collisions, max collisions, deferral.
	Tx errors	Force FIFO underflows.
	Stats	Check Tx and Rx stats. Check all relevant stats counters for appropriate events.
MII	Full-duplex receive	Receive packets in full-duplex mode. Vary receive packet size. Check IPG, destination address matches or fails. Check unicast, broadcast, and multicast addresses.
	Half-duplex receive	Receive packets in half-duplex mode. Vary all the parameters specified in full-duplex mode and inject collisions.

	Receive errors	Check packets received in full- and half-duplex mode for
		    CRC errors
		    Runt packets (less than min-size, 64 bytes)
		    Too-long packets
		    Alignment errors
		Check for other errors, such as
		    IPG violations
		    MII errors
		    FIFO overflows

Host and MII	Multiple packets in a FIFO	After one min-size, 64 bytes, packet has been received in Rx FIFO, create an error on receive of second packet. Transmit two minimum packets in FIFO and abort the first packet due to error.

Normal transmit and receive   For normal transmit and receive, you need to generate packets of various sizes, calculate the CRC, and inject the packets into the MAC on the host side for transmit and on the MII side for receive. These packets are expected in order on the other side.

The two things that should vary in these tests are packet size and interpacket gap (IPG). The IPG on Tx is maintained by the MAC. The monitor on the MII side needs to make sure the IPG of the received packets conforms to the programmed IPG. The IPG on the receive side is generated by the testbench and varied randomly. The interesting cases here are the back-to-back transmits and the back-to-back receives. Tests in this category are usually the first to be implemented and run, because they help with the debug of both the RTL and the testbench.

Transmit and receive error cases

Transmit and receive with errors also requires the creation of random events. These events include network errors and host-side errors, such as forced underrun and overrun on the FIFOs. Network errors are generated on the MII side. These include packet length errors, packet CRC errors, and MII errors.

Multipacket transmit and receive

Multipacket transmit and receive involves many specific corner cases. If enough randoms are created for the category 1 and 2 tests, the probability of hitting these corner cases is reasonably high. But to be certain, you can constrain the stimulus generators further, for example by limiting packet sizes to only minimum packets, or by increasing the distribution of minimum-size packets.

Testbench Implementation

Packet generator requirements

Figure 8-2 shows the architecture of the testbench. From the stimulus generation point of view, there are two packet generators—the host side and the MII side—with a network event generator on the MII side. The packet generators on the host and MII sides can be the same. The only difference is in the transactors, which take the packet, convert it to binary format, and then apply it to the DUT.

The transmit side of the host transactor receives a packet from the host packet generator through a mailbox and injects it into the DUT. A similar operation occurs on the MII-side transactor.

Event generator requirements

The event generator on the MII side randomly creates network events, such as collisions, carrier sense, runt packets, and MII errors. For normal transmit and receive, the event generator is turned off with an enable flag, at least for the initial tests, to allow proper bring-up of the environment and to bring up the basic functionality of the RTL.

On the MII side, the IPG is controlled by the packet arrival rate, which is randomly generated and implemented by the MII transactor. The transactor creates these gaps using the randomly generated IPG value as a gap timer.

FIGURE 8-2   Testbench Block Diagram

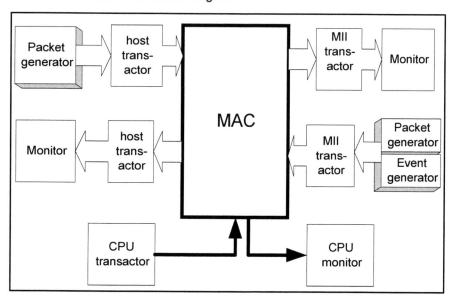

The handshaking between generator and transactor
The interface between the packet generator and transactors may be of interest. The transactor gets the next packet when it has finished injecting the current packet into the DUT. The packet request from the transactor can be implemented in many forms: events, semaphores, mailboxes, or just a queue of packets. A simple approach is to use mailboxes—the generator puts the packet into the mailbox, and the transactor gets the packet from the mailbox when it is ready. Figure 8-3 shows the interface between the packet generator and the transactor.

FIGURE 8-3   Interface Between Packet Generator and Transactor

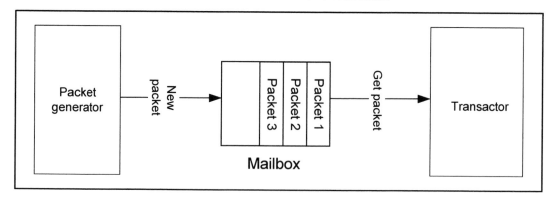

For the normal packet case, vary

- The packet size

- The MAC destination address (for the MII side)

For error cases, generate the following errors:

- Runt (too short) packets

- Alignment errors (extra nibbles)

- Too large packets

- CRC error packets

You can create packet of various sizes in directed tests by specifying the length of each packet, or more preferably, in random tests by allowing the length to be randomly selected. In random cases, be sure to control the distribution of the different packet lengths. In Ethernet, the packet length, including the header, can vary from 64 bytes to 1,522 bytes. Typical Ethernet traffic is strongly bipolar; that is, most of the packets are either 64 or 1,522 bytes in length. So if you wanted to emulate typical Ethernet traffic, implement weights for three byte-length ranges: 64, 65 to 1,521, and 1,522. The example code for this is shown in the section "Constraints—Directing the Chaos", later in this chapter.

On the MII side, the MAC destination address (DA) needs to be forced to the address of the MAC in order to test the DA-match logic of the MAC. The DA also needs to be forced not to match the MAC address in order to test the discard of packets whose DA does not match the MAC address. On the host side, the DA can be generated randomly, but the source address must be set to the Ethernet address of the MAC. DA generation can also include control over whether the destination address is unicast, multicast, or broadcast. Therefore, in random cases, a distribution has to be set for each of the three packet types.

For error cases, the testbench should maintain a packet state field for each packet, indicating the type of packet: good, runt, too large, CRC error, alignment error, and so on. This field can be part of the generator object but is never injected into the MAC. It can, however, be placed in the payload, where the testbench can read the field and use it as a consistency check to make sure the packet was interpreted correctly. The problem with placing packet state fields or other testbench-specific tags in the payload is that their delivery depends on the reliable delivery of the payload under all conditions. So you may need to implement some kind of reliable transport protocol or build monitors that can deal with missing tags. It is simpler in this case to use mailboxes.

Figure 8-4 shows the constraint decision tree needed to generate a packet for all stimulus generation scenarios.

FIGURE 8-4 Distribution Hierarchy for Packet Generation

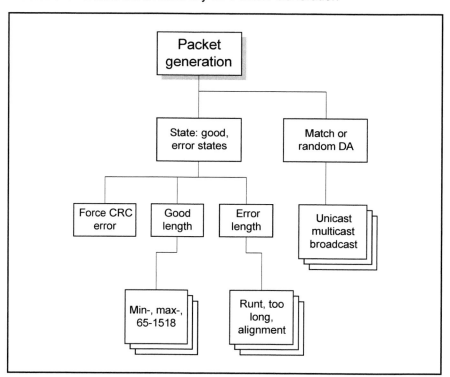

Creating events randomly   The MAC testbench also needs to generate network event states on the MII side and host-created errors on the host side. These can be either randomly created or user-directed.

For randomly created events, network-event and a host-event generators are needed. Since these events are independent of the packet transmission or reception, they should be treated as asynchronous processes. Network-event and host-event generators create states that are viewed by the transactors, which in turn signal the events to the MAC and the testbench.

Network events of interest include

- Collisions

- Excessive collisions

- Carrier sense

- MII errors

- Minimum IPG violations on the network side

Network events are generated periodically, at either user-specified or random intervals. Once generated, they set state bits in the MII transactor, which then forces appropriate signals to the MAC. The event-generation interval can also be varied using random numbers that determine the next firing of the generator, or by specifying distribution weights.

Host events of interest include

- Rx FIFO overflow

- Tx FIFO underrun

The overflow case requires the transactor to stop reading data out of the FIFO, and the underrun scenario requires the transactor to stop writing data to the Tx FIFO. So both of these presume some control over the transactor. If overflow is enabled, the idle periods are set to be very large values; otherwise, they are set to very small values. Similarly for the underflow on the transmit-side host transactor.

Other stimulus generation requirements

For bring-up, the MAC starts with specific tests, such as transmitting and receiving a single minimum-size packet under normal conditions, followed by a single maximum-size packet. Once those tests pass, fully randomized packets can be generated, during which the generator is constrained to single packets of a specific length. Because exception event and network event generation needs to be disabled, a disable control, in the form of an enable flag, is needed in those generators.

Vera Support for Randoms

Vera has three mechanisms for creating randomization:

- The utility random number generator functions random( ), urandom( ), rand48( ), and urand48( )

- The randcase construct, for randomly selecting a branch

- Object randomize functions, for randomly initializing the values of specific data members of objects

Each of these mechanisms can be used for randomization. Object based randomization is powerful if you want to use constraint solvers in Vera. The randcase and random number generator functions are useful if you just want to pick random values or to create your own constraint solver.

Utility Random Number Generator Functions

Vera provides four built-in random number utility functions, random( ), urandom( ), rand48( ), and urand48( ). The syntaxes are

```
<random_num> = random([<seed>]);

<random_num> = urandom([<seed>]);

<random_num> = rand48([<seed>]);

<random_num> = uran48([<seed>]);
```

The following are examples of usage:

```
random(my_seed);

dest = random();

source = random();

dest = urandom();

data = rand48();
```

random( ) and rand48( ) return a non-negative 32-bit vector in the range 0 to $2^{31}-1$. MSB is forced to 0.

urand( ) and urand48( ) return a 32-bit vector in the range 0 to $2^{31}-1$. MSB is randomly generated.

NOTE *Note: Current version of Vera return urandom( ) and urand48( ) values in the range $-2^{31}-1$ to $2^{31}-1$. This error and will be fixed in future versions of Vera.*

random( ) and urandom( ) use a large state table and therefore have a much longer period before the sequence of random numbers is repeated. rand48( ) and urand48( ) use 48-bit states, so their period is smaller. urand48( ) and rand48( ) are not faster than random( ) or urandom( ) implementation, so random( ) and urandom( ) are recommended.

Each of these functions can take an optional seed argument. As long as the seed stays the same, they provide deterministic output, since the random values are repeated every time the program is run. This repeatability of random values is important for regression purposes. If a seed is used, it becomes the seed for all other random functions.

randcase statement

The randcase statement is a case statement in which a branch is randomly picked, based on weights. The syntax is

```
randcase {
    <W1>  :  <statement>;
    <W2>  :  <statement>;
    . . .
    <Wn>  :  <statement>;
}
```

The weight, W1 and so on, can be an integer or any Vera expression that evaluates to an integer. All weights are evaluated every time randcase is invoked. The probability of hitting W_1 is $W_1/(W_1+W_2...+W_n)$. For example,

```
data = urand48();
randcase {
    30 :    packet_type=unicast;
    10 :    packet_type=multicast;
    10 :    packet_type=broadcast;
}
```

In this example, unicast packets will be selected 60 percent (30/50), of the time, while multicast and broadcast packets will each be selected 20 percent (10/50) of the time.

Applications

The randcase statement can be used to select a random distribution of values when weights are made constant. In addition, far more sophisticated real-world scenarios can be implemented with randcase if variables are used with feedback in the weights. For example, to support bursty operations in the above example, a continuous burst of unicast packets could be generated. The randcase statement could be used with variables to help create bursts of unicast packets.

In a burst scenario, once you hit a branch, you want to increase the probability of hitting that same branch on the next invocation of randcase. The code looks like this:

```
unicast_wt=0; mcast_wt=0; bcast_wt=0;
n=10;
burst_prob=70;
randcase {
    n+unicast_wt : packet_type=unicast;
        randcase {
            2: unicast_wt=0;
            8: unicast-wt=burst_prob;
        }
    n+mcast_wt : packet_type=multicast;
        randcase {
            2: mcast_wt=0;
            8: mcast_wt=burst_prob;
        }
    n+bcast_wt : packet_type=broadcast;
        randcase {
            2: bcast_wt=0;
            8: bcast_wt=burst_prob;
        }
}
```

At the beginning of the simulation, all packet types have an equal probability of being selected. But once a packet type has been selected, its probability of bursting will be about 80 percent—that is, burst_prob+10.

If you want a "reverse burst", in which the probability of the same packet type being repeatedly selected is lower rather than higher, subtract u, m, or b from n.

Objects With Random Variables

Vera also supports random generation of selected data members within an object by declaring those members as random variables. To do this, indicate the field as a random variable by placing a rand or randc keyword in front of the member.

rand and randc

The rand and randc keywords allow random creation of a variable. Note while rand simply selects a random value from the set, randc is cyclical. randc does not repeat a value until it has cycled through all the other values in the set.

randc keyword can only be applied to enum and bit types. The maximum size is 8 bits, which limits the randomization space for randc variables to 256 values. In this example,

```
randc bit[3:0] a_number;
```

the range from which a value can be picked is 0 to 15. randc causes the choices to cycle through all 16 possible values before repeating any of them.

In the MAC testbench, to generate a basic Ethernet packet, the class is first declared:

```
class ether_packet {
    bit[47:0]          dest_addr;
    bit[47:0]          src_addr;
    bit[15:0]          type_len;
    bit[7:0]           payld[];
    bit[31:0]          fcs;

    task new();
    task gen_payld();
    task calc_fcs();
}
```

Now if you need to generate a packet randomly, you could do this:

```
class ether_packet {
    rand        bit[47:0]      dest_addr;
    rand        bit[47:0]      src_addr;
    rand        bit[15:0]      type_len;
                bit[7:0]       payld[];
                bit[31:0]      fcs;
```

```
    task new();
    task gen_payld();
    task calc_fcs();
}
```

Prepending the dest_addr, src_addr, and type_len fields with rand identifies these members as random variables. The payld field is declared as an associative array, and if appended, rand or randc requires the declaration of a range defined by assoc_size, for example,

```
bit[7:0] payld[] assoc_size pay_len;
```

where pay_len is a user-specified variable of a randomly created value.

To generate these variables, objects of ether_packet class need to be declared and instantiated, and then the built-in randomize routine must be invoked.

The randomize( ) routine generates random values for that instance of the object. For example,

```
integer status;
ether_packet gen_packet;
gen_packet= new();
status=gen_packet.randomize();
```

Randomization Rules

Vera randomization routine observes the following rules:

- Only data members with an active rand or randc prefix are randomized.

- The randomize function may be called with or without a seed. The seed does affect the values generated. It also resets the seed for other random functions.

- If there are nested objects declared inside the class and they have a rand or randc prefix, randomize automatically invokes the randomize function of the nested object.

- Nested object members of a class are randomized after the nonobject data members of a class.

- The order of randomization of the nonobject data members of a class is determined by the constraints only.

- Nonobject data members are randomized first, followed by base class variables and the nested object variables are randomized last.

- If associative arrays are randomized, only the elements specified in the range declared by assoc_size are randomized.

- Random static variables are shared by all instances of a class. Each randomization changes the values in all the classes.

Constraints—Directing the Chaos

If a random number is created, it is normally in the value space of the random variable. However, sometimes a completely random value is not acceptable. For example, a legal Ethernet packet cannot be less than 64 bytes and more than 1,522 bytes in length. Vera supports constraints for limiting the value space of random variables.

Types of Constraints

Vera supports two types of constraints: limit-setting constraints and distribution constraints.

- Limit-setting constraints specify limits for random variables.

- Distribution constraints assign probabilities to certain values or ranges, or limit a random variable to a specific set of values.

Constraints are defined within constraint blocks. Constraint blocks are members of a class that define constraints on random variables of that class. For example, take the ether_packet class:

```
class ether_packet {
    rand    bit[47:0]      dest_addr;
    rand    bit[47:0]      src_addr;
    rand    bit[15:0]      type_len;
            bit[7:0]       payld[];
            bit[31:0]      fcs;
    constraint packet_size_limit {
        type_len >=64;
        type_len <=1518;
    }
```

```
    task new();
    task gen_payld();
    task calc_fcs();
}
```

The constraint packet_size_limit is a constraint block. It is a limit-setting constraint that limits the packet size (type_len) to between 64 and 1,518 bytes.

Limit-Setting Constraints

Limit-setting constraints are used to set limits on the actual value of a random variable. The syntax is

```
class <class_name> {
    rand <datatype> <random_variable>;
    <other data members>...
    constraint <constraint_name> {
        <random_variable> <operator> <expression1>;
        <random_variable> <operator> <expression2>;
        ...
    }
    task new();
    task other_tasks();
}
```

The expression can be any valid Vera expression except a task or function. The operator can be any of the following:

$<$, $<=$, $==$, $>=$, $>$, $!=$, $===$, $!==$, $=?=$, or $!?=$

Limit-setting constraints set upper and lower limits or an equality/inequality relationship on a random variable. For example,

```
constraint length_lim {
    length <= max_len;
    length > min_packet - err_length;
}
constraint da_lim {
    dest_addr != curr_dest_addr;
}
```

The values of min_packet and err_length can either be set by the user or randomly generated.

In general, if a randomly generated variable is used in a constraint for another random variable, Vera automatically generates the constraining random variable first. Having a random variable as limit in a constraint is a recommended approach because it allows better test coverage and better automation.

For example, if the Ethernet packet length is constrained by a constant value for the maximum packet size, then the packet length would always stay below the maximum. In this case, however, to test a too long packet, another test case would have to be created. But if the maximum packet length were constrained by a random variable, the too long packet case could easily be tested in the same test case.

Distribution Constraints

Distribution constraints control the distribution of a random variable. There are two types of distribution constraints:

dist Controls the distribution of a random variable within a specified value set

in or !in Specifies the set from which a random value can be selected (in) or a set of values that must be excluded from the random value (!in).

dist constraint

The syntax for dist is

```
constraint <constraint_name> {
    <random_var> dist {<val1> :=<w1>, ..., <valn> :=<wn>};
}
```

The values, val1 and so on, can be either single values or a ranges. Each can be a constant or a Vera expression.

The weights, w1 and so on, can be constants, variables, or Vera expressions. Each range can be specified by a Vera expression, in the form "low value:high value". Weight can be assigned with either a := or :/ operator:

If := is used for a range, then each value in the range gets the weight. For example, 2:3 := 25 assigns a weight of 25 to both 2 and 3.

If :/ is used, the weight is equally divided among values in the range. For example, 2:3 :/25 assigns a weight of 12.5 to 2 and 12.5 to 3.

If a range is specified with dist, each value in the range is assigned that distribution probability. In this example,

```
constraint pkt_len_dist {
   pkt_len dist {
      64:67 :=10, 512:515 :=5, 1518 :=40
   };
}
```

the weights are assigned as in Table 8-2.

TABLE 8-2   Example Distribution Probabilities With := Operator

Packet Length	Weight	Actual Probability With :=
64 bytes	10	10/100 (10%)
65 bytes	10	10%
66 bytes	10	10%
67 bytes	10	10%
512 bytes	5	5%
513 bytes	5	5%
514 bytes	5	5%
515 bytes	5	5%
1518 bytes	40	40%
Total weight	**100**	

The probability of each value is calculated by dividing its weight by the sum of all the weights. In this example, the weights add up to 100% to illustrate the concept, but that is not a requirement.

In contrast, if you use the constraint with the :/ operator,

```
constraint pkt_len_dist {
   pkt_len dist {
      64:67 :/10, 512:515 :/5, 1518 :/40
   };
}
```

then weight 10 is divided by the number of values in the range 64:67 and each value is assigned a weight of 2.5 (10/4). Likewise for the other ranges. Table 8-3 shows the complete probability calculations.

TABLE 8-3   Example Distribution Probabilities With :/ Operator

Packet Length	Weight	Actual Probability with :/
64 bytes	2.5	2.5/65 = 3.8%
65 bytes	2.5	3.8%
66 bytes	2.5	3.8%
67 bytes	2.5	3.8%
512 bytes	1.25	1.25/65 =1.9%
513 bytes	1.25	1.9%
514 bytes	1.25	1.9%
515 bytes	1.25	1.9%
1518 bytes	40	40/65 =61.5%
Total weight	**65**	

in and !in constraints

The syntax for in and !in is

```
constraint <constraint_name> {
    <random_variable> [!]in {<value1>, ..., <valuen>};
}
```

The value can be either a single value or a range. For example,

```
constraint pkt_cast_lim {
    pkt_cast in {UNICAST, MULTICAST, BROADCAST};
}

constraint bufp_exclusion {
    buffer_pointer !in {0:(chip_mode*20),(qlen):(qlen+64),
                        max_occupancy};
}
```

Ethernet Example

For the Ethernet packet class example, to set length distribution probabilities at 40 percent for minimum-size packets (64 bytes), 20 percent for packets in the 65-to-maximum-1 range, and 40 percent for maximum-size packets (1,518 bytes), use the following code:

```
constraint len_dist {
    len_type dist {min_pkt:=40, min_pkt+1:(max_pkt-1) :=20,
                   max_pkt:=40};
}
```

where min_pkt and max_pkt are variables or defined constants. Note that this produces probabilities of

$$40/(80+20*(max\_pkt\text{-}1 - (min\_pkt+1)))$$
$$= 40/(80+1452)$$
$$= 2.6\% \text{ for min\_pkt and max\_pkt}$$

For lengths between min_pkt and max_pkt, each of the lengths is assigned a probability of 20/(1532) = 1.3%. Figure 8-5 shows the distribution.

FIGURE 8-5   Example Packet Distributions With := Operator

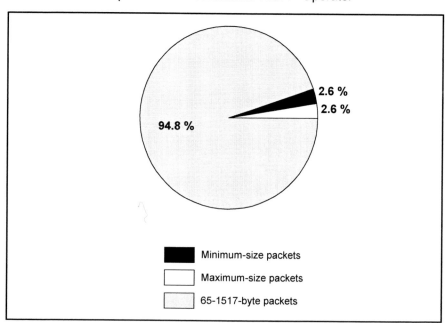

If, however, you want to force distribution to be 40 percent for min_pkt, 40 percent for max_pkt, and 20 percent for the total combination of packets between these lengths, use the :/ operator:

```
constraint len_dist {
    len_type dist {min_pkt :/40, min_pkt+1:(max_pkt-1) :/20,
                   max_pkt :/40};
}
```

Figure 8-6 shows the distribution of packet sizes over a sufficiently large number of packets.

FIGURE 8-6   Packet Distribution Using dist :/ Constraints

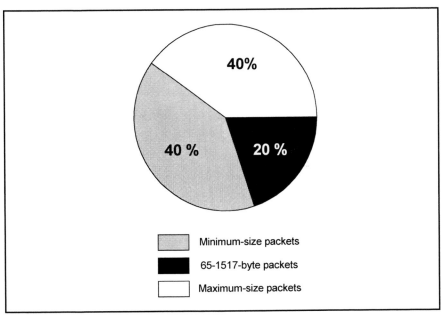

*When to use in
instead of dist* The dist constraint is best suited for stimulus where some of the value sets should have higher probability than others. If "in" is used, all members of the set are selected with equal probability. The probability of any single value being randomly selected is 1/(number of members in the set). The drawback of dist and in is that the value set cannot be changed dynamically. It can be overloaded or changed with derived classes, but it cannot be changed dynamically at runtime during object invocation. For example, if you wanted

to add another range to the len_dist constraint for packet lengths of 780-850 the constraint would have to be re-written and the testbench re-compiled and rerun.

To allow for some constraint selection at runtime, Vera provides conditional constraints, which are covered in the next section.

Dynamic Modification of Constraints

Creating new test cases often requires modifying existing constraints, either to change the limits, to change the distribution weights, or to add or remove ranges. For regressibility and efficiency, it is better to modify constraints at runtime than to rewrite constraints and recompile. Vera supports constructs to allow conditional selection of expressions in constraints, and allows variables or expressions to be used for limits or distribution weights. It also allows constraints to be turned off or on at runtime.

Vera supports several ways of dynamically modifying constraints:

- Using conditional constraints with the ternary ? operator

- Using variables instead of constants as constraint limits

- Using active and inactive constraints

This section discusses each of these constraint mechanisms, followed by an example of a completely dynamic distribution scheme.

Conditional Constraints

Frequently, constraints must be changed from one test case to another. For example, Ethernet packets might or might not contain virtual LAN ID (VLANs). If they contain VLAN ID, the length of the packet is limited to 1,522 bytes; otherwise, the length cannot exceed 1,518 bytes.

In the packet generator, constraint modification can be handled in one of three ways:

1. Write a custom routine to set the maximum length value.

2. Modify the constraints at runtime.

3. Use inheritance to create a VLAN-based class.

To modify the constraints at runtime, use the ternary operator ?, which works just like the Verilog ? operator as an if statement. The syntax is

```
<expression> ? <value_if_true> : <value_if_false>
```

where expression is any valid Vera expression.

Take the Ethernet packet example:

```
enum ptype = ieee, enet, ieee_vlan;
class ether_packet {
    rand        bit[47:0]        dest_addr;
    rand        bit[47:0]        src_addr;
    rand        bit[15:0]        type_len;
                bit[7:0]         payld[];
                bit[31:0]        fcs;
    protected rand integer max_pkt_len;
    protected rand ptype pkt_type;

    constraint packet_size_limit {
        type_len >=64;
        type_len <=max_pkt_len;
    }
    constraint max_limit {
        max_pkt_len <= (pkt_type == ieee_vlan) ?
        1522 : 1518;
    }
    task new();
    task gen_payld();
    task calc_fcs();
}//class ether_packet
```

Note the following: A user-defined type called ptype enumerates the different types of packets that can be expected by an Ethernet MAC. The ieee_vlan packet has a maximum size of 1,522 bytes in size. A random variable, max_pkt_len, is used as a value in the packet_size_limit constraint. Another random variable, ptype, is a member of the packet class pkt_type.

Upon randomization, the sequence is

1. Vera randomizes pkt_type first to select the packet type, because pkt_type is a constraint for max_limit.

2. packet_type is used by the max_limit constraint to constrain and generate max_pkt_len.

3. The max_pkt_len variable is then used during randomization to generate the type_len field of the packet.

This order is dictated by the needs of the constraints. Otherwise, the order is arbitrary.

The randomization order of the variables in the current instance is determined by the constraints. Circular constraints (for example, j < p+4; and p >j;) are not allowed.

NOTE   *The above circular constraint can be rewritten as j <p+4 and j>p.*

You could also set the max_pkt_len variable using a custom routine.

Using Variables for Limits

Variables can also be used in constraint limits. Returning to the Ethernet packet class:

```
enum ptype = ieee, enet, ieee_vlan;
class ether_packet {
    rand          bit[47:0]          dest_addr;
    rand          bit[47:0]          src_addr;
    rand          bit[15:0]          type_len;
                  bit[7:0]           payld[];
                  bit[31:0]          fcs;
    protected integer max_pkt_len;
    protected rand ptype pkt_type;
    constraint packet_size_limit {
        type_len >=64;
        type_len <=max_pkt_len;
    }
    task new() ;
    task gen_payld() ;
    task calc_fcs() ;
    task set_max_pkt_len (int max) {
        max_pkt_len =max;
    }
}
```

Note that the packet_size_limit constraint is itself limited to 64 bytes on the minimum size packets and max_pkt_len on the maximum size packets. In Ethernet, the packet size has to be less than 1,518 bytes (1,522 for VLAN packets), so you could make it a hard constraint:

```
type_len <= 1518;
```

But in order to generate error packets, the max_pkt_limit has been made a variable and a task provided so the limit can be changed at runtime.

Active & Inactive Constraints

Normally all defined constraints for a class are considered active, but at runtime some constraints can be turned off (made inactive) by use of the constraint_mode( ) function. The syntax is shown below:

```
<result> = <object_name>.<constraint_mode> (<mode>,
    "<constraint_name>");
```

result is either ON or OFF, and mode is also either as ON or OFF. constraint_name is the name of the constraint block being made inactive.

If a constraint is turned off, then it is not used during randomization. A constraint can be turned on or off any time after the object is constructed.

For example,

```
class xyz {
    rand integer a;
    rand integer b;
    constraint limit_a {
        a > 30;
    }
    constraint limit_b {
        b < 50;
    }
    task new() {
        statements;
    }
}//end class

program test {
    xyx sample_obj;
    integer result;

    sample_obj = new();
    result=sample_obj.constraint_mode (OFF, "limit_a");
    void=sample_obj.randomize();
    result=sample_obj.constraint_mode (ON, "limit_a");
    result=sample_obj.constraint_mode (OFF, "limit_b");
    void=sample_obj.randomize();
}
```

Here the constraint limit_a is turned off and the object is randomized. Next, limit_a is turned on and limit_b is turned off.

This technique is useful in

- Overriding invariants to test error cases

- Creating many constraints and selectively turning some constraints on and off to hit different points in the test space

Using dynamic constraints allows you to change the behavior of an instantiated object without creating an extended class, instantiating that class, and then using it in the main portion of the code.

All of the dynamic constraint modifiers supported in Vera let you quickly and efficiently create new stimulus and, by extension, new test cases to explore the functionality of the DUT.

Limitations of Vera Constraints

Vera constraints allow you to create a wide range of stimulus, but in some cases, you need to write a constraint solver. One instance is when you want to modify a distribution range at runtime to generate a different test case. In Vera, if limit-setting constraints use variables for limits, the limits can be modified at runtime. In distribution constraints, however, only the weights and value of the ranges can be modified at runtime; the number of ranges cannot be changed.

There are many ways to write constraint solvers that let you specify and modify the number of ranges dynamically. A specific implementation is shown in the following example. It demonstrates how a class can be used to add distribution ranges at runtime. Note that two classes are defined here:

    dyn_range
    dyn_constr

```
#define OUTPUT_EDGE PHOLD
#define OUTPUT_SKEW #1
#define INPUT_EDGE PSAMPLE
#define int integer
#include <vera_defines.vrh>

// define interfaces, and verilog_node here if necessary
```

```
// declare external tasks/classes/functions here if necessary

class dyn_range {
    int hival;
    int loval;
    int prob_wt;
    rand int val;
    constraint valimit {
        val < hival;
        val >= loval;
    }

    task new (int hv, int lv, int p) {
        hival =hv;
        loval=lv;
        prob_wt=p;
        val=0;
    }

    function int gen_value(){
        bit status;
        status=0;
        status=this.randomize();
        if (status)
            gen_value=val;
        else {
            printf ("range randomization error\n");
            printf ("high:&0d low:%0d prob_wt:%0d\n",
            hival, loval, prob_wt);
        }
    }//gen_value
}//class dyn_range
```

The dyn_range class provides a single range and a randomly generated value. The method gen_value function is used to generate the value, which is constrained by the high and low values defined for the range. prob_wt provides the probability weight for the range being used.

In the next example,

```
class dyn_constr {
    dyn_range ddist[];
    int num_of_ranges;
    int curr_range_indx;

    //This function selects a range randomly based on
    //probabilities and the number of ranges set
    function int sel_range() ;

    //sets of changes values of a given range
```

```
task set_range (int index, int hi, int lo, int prob_wt);

//calc sum of prob_wt of al th ranges present
function int sum_of_prob();

task new (int num_of_range, int def_hival, int def_loval,
          int def_prob) {
    int i;
    curr_range_indx=0;
    num_of_ranges=0;
    for (i=0; i < num_of_range; i++) {
        ddist[i]=new (def_hival, def_loval, def_prob);
        num_of_ranges++;
        curr_range_indx++;
    }
}//new

//adds a new range to curr_range_indx+1
task add_range (int hi,int lo, int prob_wt);

//deletes range at specified index
function bit del_range (int indx);

//generate value
function int gen_value ( );
}//class dyn_constr
```

---

the dyn_constr class uses an associative array of dyn_range. This allows the user to add or remove ranges dynamically. It supports the following operations:

- Sum probabilities of all ranges

- Add a range

- Remove a range

- Set values for a particular range

- Select a range

- Generate value for the selected range

The sel_range( ) function is important. It selects a range based on the probability weights assigned to each range. The code of the methods used for this class is provided below.

```
function int dyn_constr::sum_of_prob() {
    int i;
    int sum;
    sum=0;
    for (i=0; i < num_of_ranges; i++) {
        sum += ddist[i].prob_wt;
    }
    sum_of_prob=sum;
}//sum_of_prob

    task dyn_constr::add_range (int hi, int lo, int prob_wt) {
    num_of_ranges++;
    curr_range_indx++;
    ddist[curr_range_indx]=new (hi,lo,prob_wt);
}//add_range

function bit dyn_constr::del_range (int indx) {
    bit sts;
    sts=0;
    sts=assoc_index (DELETE,ddist,indx);
    del_range=sts;
}//del_range

task dyn_constr::set_range (int index,int hi,int lo,int prob_wt) {
    ddist[index].hival=hi;
    ddist[index].loval=lo;
    ddist[index].prob_wt=prob_wt;
}//set_range

function int dyn_constr::sel_range() {
    int sum_prob;
    int selindx;
    int sum;
    int i;
    bit found;
    int ret_val;
    sum_prob=sum_of_prob();
    selindx= random() % sum_prob;
    found=0; sum=0; i=0;
    while (!found) {
        sum += ddist[i++].prob_wt;
        if (selindx < sum) {
            found=1;
            ret_val=--i;
        }
    }//while
    sel_range=ret_val;
}//sel_range

function int dyn_constr::gen_value() {
```

```
    int rng_indx;
    rng_indx=sel_range();
    gen_value=ddist[rng_indx].gen_value();
}//dyn_constr
```

The sel_range function adds up the probabilities of all the ranges and calculates a selection index (selindx) by randomizing a number that is the remainder (modulo) after division by the sum of probability weights. It then finds the specific range by adding up the probably weights of each weight starting at element zero. The range whose probability weight added to the sum of weights exceeds the selindx value is the correct range.

The following code shows an application of the dyn_constr class.

```
program dynconstr_top_test {
    // start of top block
    // Start of emcc_top_test
    dyn_constr dyconstr;
    int genv;
    int cnt;
    int i;
    dyconstr=new (5,30,10,10);
    dyconstr.set_range (0,20,5,50);
    dyconstr.set_range (1,70,50,20);
    dyconstr.set_range (2,90,80,10);
    dyconstr.set_range (3,5,1,10);
    dyconstr.set_range (4,1518,512,30);
    for (i=0; i < 25; i++) {
        genv=dyconstr.gen_value();
        printf ("gen value=%0d \t ",genv);
        if ( ((i % 5) == 0) && i >0 )
            printf ("\n");
    }
} // end of program
```

The dyn_constr class shown above can be used for test cases where you need to change the distribution ranges dynamically. For example in the Ethernet packet class you can change the distributions of packet lengths dynamically starting with the bipolar distribution and then covering all the interesting packet ranges within the same test case.

Pre-Randomization & Post-Randomization

Vera provides support for automatic processing of pre- and post-randomization functions. If some things need to be done before randomization, create a task called pre-randomize( ). For operations that need to be performed immediately after randomization, create a task called post-randomize( ).

Figure 8-7 shows the pre- and post-randomize execution flow during randomization.

FIGURE 8-7   Pre- and Post-Randomize Invocation

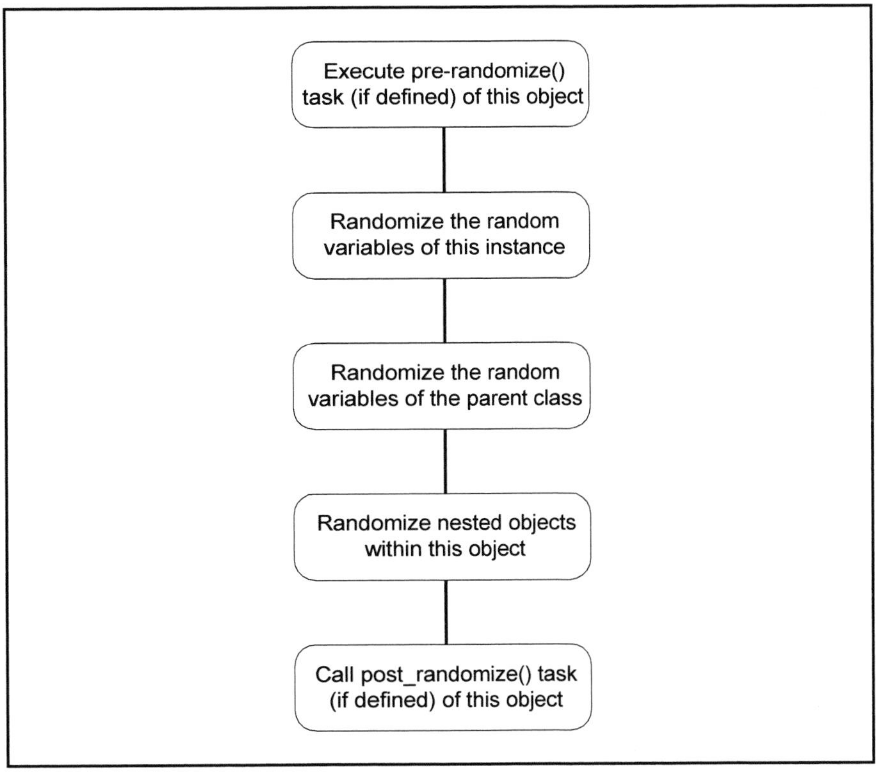

Again, note that the randomization order of the variables of the current instance is determined by the constraints.

You can use pre-randomize( ) in the packet generator to set the max_pkt_len value based on packet type. However, in such a case, the packet type has to be randomized separately within the pre-randomize( ) function.

Similarly, post-randomize( ) can be used to set some variables after the random variables have been set. In the packet generator case, this could be the CRC calculation, as in the example below:

```
enum ptype = ieee, enet, ieee_vlan;
class ether_packet {
    rand        bit[47:0]        dest_addr;
    rand        bit[47:0]        src_addr;
    rand        bit[15:0]        type_len;
                bit[7:0]         payld[];
                bit[31:0]        crc;
    protected rand integer max_pkt_len;
    protected rand ptype pkt_type;

    constraint packet_size_limit {
        type_len >=64;
        type_len <=max_pkt_len;
    }
    constraint max_limit {
        max_pkt_len <= (pkt_type == ieee_vlan) ?
        1522 :1518;
    }
    task new();
    task gen_payld();
    protected task calc_crc();
    task post_randomize() {
        calc_crc();
    }
}//ether_packet
```

Applying the Stimulus

The preceding section dealt with generating the stimulus, but once you have generated it, how do you apply it to the DUT?

In the Ethernet MAC example, the host side of the MAC has a 32-bit Tx interface. The generated host packet must be reformatted into an array of 32-bit words, which are written one per cycle to the MAC. The packets come out at the MII Tx side in a nibble stream.

The MII side of the MAC Rx block is a 4-bit-wide interface. On this side, the generated packet must be reformatted into an array of 4-bit nibbles and then written one nibble at a time to the MAC to simulate an Rx frame.

On the Rx host side, the data is received as a series of 32-bit words, which need to be reformatted into the Ethernet packet. (See Figure 8-8.)

FIGURE 8-8 Packing and Unpacking at the MAC

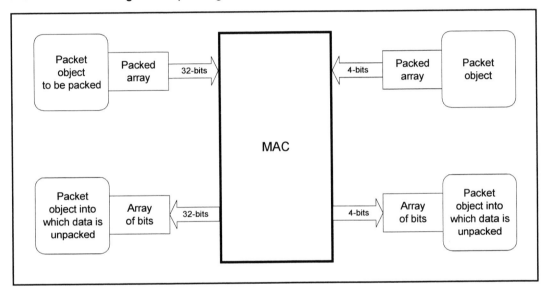

To facilitate the reformatting of data for injection into the DUT and for checking out of the DUT, Vera provides built-in pack and unpack routines.

Packing & Unpacking Variables

Each data variable in a class can be prepended with the attribute "packed", which identifies the variable as one to be packed or unpacked.

Once variables to be packed are identified, you can perform the actual packing by invoking the built-in pack routine for the instantiated object. The syntax is

```
<num_pack_bits> = <obj_inst_name>.pack (<arry_packd>,
    <start_indx>, <left>, <right>);
```

num_pack_bits indicates the total number of bits packed during the current invocation of the function.

start_indx, left, and right are variables declared as integers. They are updated by the pack routine to keep track of bits already packed. They are usually set to zero before invoking the pack routine.

arry_packd is an associative array of the required width. For instance, for single-bit-wide packing,

```
bit single_bit_arry[];
```

allows the packed object to be sent as a single bit stream, and

```
bit[3:0] nibble_wide_arry[];
```

allows the packed object to be sent as a 4-bit-wide stream.

The pack and unpack routines let you control whether packing should start with the least significant byte or the most significant byte. Do this by adding an attribute, little_endian or big_endian, after the pack or unpack prefix. The default, little_endian, specifies LSB first. The syntax is

```
packed <pack_attribute> <variable_type> <variable_name>;
```

For example,

```
packed big_endian bit[47:0] dest_addr;
packed bit_reverse bit[31:0] crc;
packed bit_normal bit[31:0] crc;
```

Consider the Ethernet packet class defined on page 238, and then look at the main program:

```
program sample_pack {
    ether_packet p;
    bit[31:0] host_pkt[];
    int o,l,r;
    int bit_count;
    o=0;l=0;r=0;
    p=new();
    p.randomize();
    bit_count=p.pack (host_pkt, o,l,r);
}
```

The unpack routine is similar to the pack routine, except the process is reversed. The syntax is

```
<void> = <obj_inst_name>.unpack (<arry_unpck>,
   <start_indx>, <left>, <right>);
```

Take the case of an Ethernet packet received at the 32-bit-wide Rx host interface into an associative array. The received data is then unpacked into an Ethernet packet (ether_packet object p) by the following:

```
program sample_pack {
    ether_packet p;
    bit[31:0] host_pkt[];
    int o,l,r;
    int qword_count;
    o=0;l=0;r=0;
    p=new();
    receive_packet (host_packet);
    qword_count=p.unpack (host_pkt, o,l,r);
}
```

The only fields affected by unpack are those declared as packed. The values in the array are unpacked into the data members declared as packed.

Vera also supports these built-in methods: pre-pack( ), post-pack( ), pre-unpack( ) and post-unpack( ). As the name suggests these are executed either before or after the pack/unpack routines are executed.

Test Creation Strategies

The main goal of functional verification is to create test cases that create and inject different stimuli such that the entire test space of the DUT is traversed. Test case generation strategies can be classified into two broad categories:

- One or a few complex testbenches using randoms, covering the entire test space

- Many smaller and simpler testbenches, each focused on a small part of the test space, using directed or random stimulus.

*One random
testbench for the
entire test space*
With testbenches that generate stimulus using random generation, specify the test case through command arguments that allow you to set probability weights, value limits, and so on. This lets you explore much of the test space of a DUT with a well-constructed random testbench and create test cases by providing different runtime arguments.

*Many smaller
testbenches*
You can also create many discrete tests that explore all the functional axes of the design. In this strategy, each test focuses on a specific feature and uses its own testbench or generator class to test that feature or functional axis of the test space. In less complex designs, using this strategy is simpler, because there are not that many functional axes.

Take an up-down counter as an example. If the UP command is given, the counter increments, while the DOWN command decrements the value. One functional axis is the UP or DOWN command; the other is the current value of the counter.

An interesting corner case, then, is exploring the boundaries of the counter value axis. For example, for a counter programmed to saturate at 16, giving an UP command when the value is 15 should force it to roll over. For the same counter, giving a DOWN command when the value is 0 should take it to 15.

*Functional axes
of complex
designs are
harder to identify*
Because a counter is simple, the axes are easily identified and test cases are easy to create. However, in a more complex design such as the MAC, functional axes may be harder to identify.

*Test case
generation
efficiency is very
desirable in
complex designs*
Even more complicated designs, such as network switches and routers, can have literally thousands of functional axes and, by implication, billions—maybe trillions—of possible test cases. For these devices it is clearly desirable to be able to create test cases efficiently. When deciding how many testbenches and generator classes need to be created, you have to trade off the number of testbenches or generator classes against the complexity of each testbench or generator class. No one choice is best for all complex designs. There can be many simple testbenches or a just few more complex testbenches, perhaps even just one.

*Efficiency of
corner case test
creation is very
important*
Again, the most interesting test cases are the corner cases—tests that operate at the boundary of one or more functional axes. In the MAC, for example, using minimum- or maximum-size packets would explore the boundaries of the packet-size axis.

One of the best measures of a verification strategy is how efficiently and productively you can create corner cases. Typically, any new corner case requires new functionality in the stimulus generator, the transactor, and the monitor. There are many ways to add that functionality:

- Use text-based configuration files to issue parameters or commands to the testbench

- Use runtime arguments to pass parameters or commands to the testbench

- Dynamically turn off constraints to select the stimulus type

- Overload methods of abstract base classes in derived classes to provide new capabilities

- Extend classes to create many different derived classes, and use polymorphism to sweep through the functional axes of DUT features

The first two of these techniques are discussed below. The other two, overloading methods and extending classes, are discussed in the next chapter.

Using Text Files

Text files are typically used in directed tests, where you specify the stimulus to be created. For example, in the MAC testbench, the text file could contain parameters such as

- Number of packets to generate

- Distribution of unicast, multicast, and broadcast packets

- Distribution of various packet sizes

- Probability of a collision on transmit

- Probability of different types of receive errors

If parameters are supported in the text file, then the testbench needs to support those features and the ability to read and parse the file. For a completely random test these parameters could be randomly generated and used in the test.

All the parameters described so far are used to direct random tests. Some test conditions may be difficult to specify unless you have control of the involved functional axes of the DUT.

A well-constructed random testbench (in which you can control randomization along all interesting functional axes) can hit all the corner cases. In a testbench that does not have this control, you have two options:

- Modify or extend the classes/constraints to provide this control

- Create a new testbench to hit that corner case

For example, perhaps you want to create a condition in the MAC in which there are two minimum-size packets in the transmit FIFO and you want to force an underrun to abort the current transmission. To add this capability the generator needs to set distribution weights to a high value and the transactor needs to slow down the read/write throughput to/from the MAC. Since the former has already been covered, let's focus on the latter. The transactor can have this capability put in at he beginning or it could be added later on by extending the transactor class(es).

When extending transactor classes, if the wait between consecutive transactor accesses to the host and the distribution of minimum packet sizes are both made user-controllable, a random test can create this test case. If, however, you do not want to add this functionality to the basic random testbench, a new testbench has to be created. In one extreme case, you might create the test manually— the transactor directly reads in the manually created test stimulus and the generator is disabled. This is inefficient and generally not recommended. The other implementation is to modify the transactor and constrain the generator to create multiple consecutive minimum-size packets.

Using Plus Arguments

Plus arguments (plusargs) are arguments or parameters that can be specified in the command line at runtime in most Verilog simulators and passed from the simulator to the testbench. They are always preceded with a + sign. For example,

```
+packet_len=64      //make packet length 64B
+pkt_64_dist= 100 //64B packet distrib is 100%
```

The string following the + sign is the name of the argument. The value following the = sign is the value of the argument. If the plusarg is interpreted as a true or false argument (i.e., as a check for plusarg only), no value needs to be specified.

Vera provides a built-in function to get plusargs: get_plus_args( ). It takes the name of the plusarg as a string and returns a value to the user or can be used as an enable. The syntax of this function is

```
<return_value> = get_plus_arg (<ret_val_type>,
   "<plus_arg_name>");
```

where ret_val_type can be

CHECK	Returns 1 if plusarg is present; otherwise 0
HNUM	Returns a hex value
NUM	Returns an integer value
STR	Returns a string

For the above plusargs packet_len and pkt_64_dist, this code

```
integer length;
if (get_plus_arg (CHECK, "pkt_len"))
   length = get_plus_arg (NUM,"pkt_len");
else length = 12;
```

checks if plusarg pkt_len is present, and if it is, it reads the value and returns it as an integer. Otherwise, it sets the length to 12.

In this example, get_plus_args( ) returns the integer 64:

```
integer min_pkt_dist;
if (get_plus_arg (CHECK, "pkt_64_dist"))
   min_pkt_dist = get_plus_arg(NUM,"pkt_64_dist");
```

This checks for pkt_64_dist plusarg and, if set, gets the value and uses it to set the minimum packet distribution.

Plusargs are used like text files; the major difference is that you do not have to write the string processing code.

Summary

The Vera randomization features and built-in constraint solvers can be used to generate a wide range of interesting stimulus. The only drawback is if you want to dynamically modify the distribution ranges for a sequence of stimulus. For that, you should be prepared to write your own constraint solver.

Table 8-4 shows the Vera constructs used in randomization.

TABLE 8-4   Vera Randomization Constructs

Keyword	Description
rand, randc	Generates random values for data members of an object
constraint	Specifies one or more limits on a rand or randc variable in the object
dist	Controls distribution of a rand or randc data member of an object
in and !in	Specifies the set from which the rand or randc variable can be taken (in) or excluded (!in)
Dynamic Constraints	
constraint_mode	Turns a constraint on or off
randomize() pre-randomize() post_randomize() pre-pack post_pack pre_unpack post_unpack	Built-in object methods
pack	Packs data from an object into a user-specified array
unpack	Unpacks data from an array into an object

CHAPTER 9

Object Extension & Polymorphism in Vera

This chapter builds on the basics of object-oriented languages and discusses extension of classes, overloading of functions and constraints, and abstract base classes. It also covers the application of abstract base classes as well as the use of overloading in creating test cases and extending testbench functionality.

Introduction to Inheritance & Polymorphism

Frequently during the verification process, new test cases are identified that require enhancements to the testbench. Corner cases usually require inserting specific capabilities into the testbench. In procedural languages, this requires modifying the code and possibly changing the data structures, a process that can and usually does insert bugs into working code. Object-oriented languages provide a higher level of reusability by deriving, or extending, new subclasses from existing classes.

Derived classes inherit the properties and methods of their base class

The process of extending a base class to create new, derived classes is known as *extension*. When a class is extended to create a derived class, the derived class inherits the data members, properties, and methods of its parent class. This is known as *inheritance*.

Overview of polymorphism and overloading

Polymorphism generally means the ability to take on many shapes. In object-oriented languages, when a new class is derived, some of the methods of the base class have to be redefined by overriding them in the derived class. This process is known as *overloading*. When an object invokes an overloaded method, the object type (whether it's part of a base class or a derived class) determines which implementation of the method is be used. Typically, this is done dynamically, at runtime. Dynamic selection of methods is known as *polymorphism*.

Vera supports extension and polymorphism for its objects. A class can simply be extended, and inherits (and possibly also overloads) only the properties of its base class. Optionally, its methods can be dynamically selected at runtime. There are many rules and issues dealing with runtime selection of methods in both extension and polymorphism; these are covered in detail in the following sections.

Extension

When a class is extended to create a derived class, the derived class inherits the properties of its parent class. Extension lets you do the following:

- Modify the behavior of a class function. For example, a basic queue class has an add-to-queue function, which adds an element to the tail of the queue. A derived class can be created to replace the add-to-queue function with a new add-to-queue function that inserts an element in sorted order. Modifying function behavior in this way is called *function overloading*.

- Add functionality to an existing class. For example, given a basic queue class, you can derive an enhanced queue class that adds the ability to view each of the members of the queue.

- Add to data abstracted by the class. For instance, given a basic class called rectangle, a derived class can be created that allows you to set the inside color and the line color of rectangle.

Take the example of an object called polygon, with a base class called polygon. It has data members for area, number of sides, length of each side, and circumference. It also has methods for calculating the area and the circumference. From polygon, you can derive classes for quadrilaterals, pentagons, hexagons, and octagons. The quadrilateral derived class can be used to derive the square class and the rectangle class. In the inheritance hierarchy below the polygon class, each of the derived classes overrides the methods for area and circumference and can add a method to draw the shape. Figure 9-1 shows the extension hierarchy of the polygon.

FIGURE 9-1 Polygon Class Hierarchy

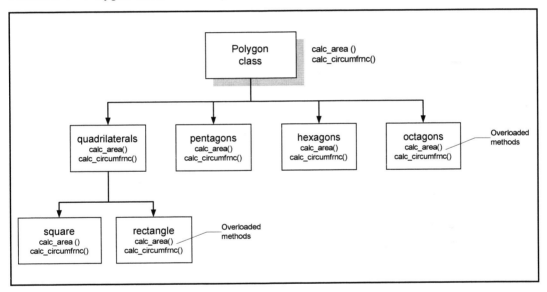

Similarly, if you develop a basic testbench, you can derive new classes from that base testbench and use these derived classes to test additional functionality without compromising the original tests.

Extending a Class in Vera

When a class inherits properties from another, the original class is known as the base class or superclass and the new class is called the derived class or subclass (these terms are used interchangeably from now on).

Take the example of the classes derived from the polygon base class. In the inheritance hierarchy of the polygon class, each of the derived classes inherits the methods and members of the base class and they override the base class methods for area and circumference. The derived classes also add a method for drawing the shape. The quadrilateral class is used to derive the square and rectangle classes. These classes inherit all the properties of the quadrilateral class and override the area and circumference calculation methods.

Basic Inheritance Rules

Vera has some rules for inheritance:

- A derived class inherits all the data members and methods of its base class.

- A derived class may add more data members or methods.

- All the inherited data members and methods are visible in the derived class.

- A derived class may overload any of the data members or methods of its base class.

- If a base class method is overloaded, it must use the same arguments as in the base class.

- A derived class can refer to base class members or methods (which have been overloaded in the derived class) by use of the super object reference. This mechanism can be used to refer only to the base class one level higher.

Vera supports extension of classes by using the *extends* construct, as in the syntax that follows:

```
class <class_name> extends <base_class_name> {
    <datatype> <member_name>;
    function <ret_type> <function_name> (parameter_list) {
        <statements>;
    }
    task <task_name> (<parameter_list>) {
        <statements>;
    }
}//end class definition
```

Consider a base class called base_count that adds two numbers (shown in
Figure 9-2):

FIGURE 9-2   Example base_count Class Hierarchy

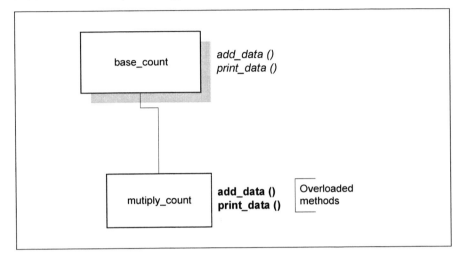

The code for base_count is

```
class base_count {
    integer first_data;
    integer second_data;
    task new (integer first, integer second) {
        first_data=first;
        second_data=second;
    }
    function integer add_data() {
        integer result;
        result=first_data+second_data;
        add_data=result;
    }
    task print_data() {
        printf("first=%0d\tsecond=%0d\n",first_data,second_data);
    }
}//end class base_count
```

In the following, base_count is extended to create a derived class
multiply_count which multiplies two numbers:

```
class multiply_count extends base_count {
    integer third_data;
    task new (integer first, integer second, integer third) {
        super.new (first,second);
        third_data=third;
    }
    function integer multiply_data() {
        integer result;
        result = first_data*second_data*third_data;
        multiply_data=result;
    }//end function
    task print_data() {
        printf("derived_class");
        printf("first=%0d\tsecond=%0d\tthird=%0d\n",
            first_data,second_data,third_data);
    }//end task
} //end class multiply_count
```

The multiply_count subclass has made several changes to base_count:

- Addition of a third data member, third_data

- Addition of a new function, multiply_data( )

- Overloading of the constructor new( )

- Overloading of print_data task with a different print_data( ) task

It also inherits the function add_data( ).

The overloaded print_data( ) task is changed from the original print_data( ) task. It prints the three data members, first_data, second_data, and third_data, whereas the old print_data printed only two data members, first_data and second_data.

The new function multiply_data( ) multiplies the three data members and returns the result.

While in our example there is no real need for a derived class (unless someone other than the original creator of the class is using shared code and needs to modify the original class), there are many real-world instances where a derived class can be valuable, such as

- Extending a base packet class to allow different packet types

- Extending a basic monitor to allow other functionality

- Extending a transactor class to add new features

- Extending a base generator class to generate different types of stimuli

- Code sharing among DV engineers, who can use libraries of classes and add functionality to them by extending the original classes

Implementation of Extended Classes in Vera

Derived class objects hold data members for the base class and derived class

In Chapter 7 you learned that when a base class object is declared, it contains a null handle, and when constructed, it is assigned a memory location and the handle becomes a reference for that memory location. Similarly, when a derived class object is declared, it too has a null handle, and when constructed, the handle references the memory location that holds the data members inherited from the base class as well as the newly added data members of the derived class.

Derived class objects have their own separate memory for data and methods

The methods section of the subclass is kept in a separate memory location from the data and contains both the derived and base class methods. Figure 9-3 shows a base class object and a derived class object. The derived class object has its own separate memory location where both the inherited and the extended data members are located, as well as a separate memory location for its methods.

FIGURE 9-3 Extended Class Memory Allocation

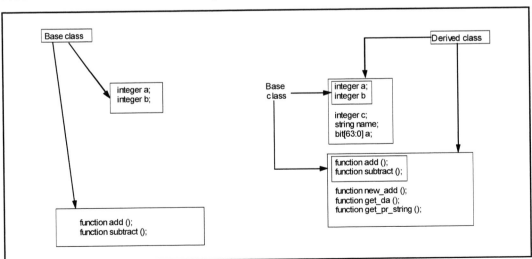

Assigning Derived Class Objects to Base Class Objects

A derived class not only inherits members and methods from its base class, but it is also treated as a valid object of its base class, so it can be assigned to a base class object. When assigning derived classes to base classes, there are two sets of rules:

- Rules dealing with assignment of derived classes to base classes

- Rules dealing with references to both overloaded and added (during extension) members of the assigned class.

Assignment Rules

The rules associated with assignment are

- A derived class object is a legal representative of its base class and may be assigned to a base class object.

- A base class object may be legally assigned to an object of a class that is higher in the same inheritance tree.

- In some cases, a base class object may be assigned to a derived class object. Use the built-in function cast_assign( ) to determine if an assignment is legal.

Referencing Methods & Members of the Assigned Class

These rules define how members of an assigned class, that is, a derived class object assigned to a base class object, are referenced:

- References through a base class object to a method overloaded in the derived class result in invocation of the base class method.

- References through a derived class object to an overloaded method result in access to the overloaded method.

- The extended members and methods of a derived class object (those added by the derived class) are not visible through the base class object.

- A derived class may reference the original (base class) versions of overloaded members or methods using the prefix super. For example, super.pr_data( ) in a derived class refers to the base class version of the pr_data method.

For example, consider the classes base_count and multiply_count discussed earlier. The code below declares objects for both base_count (mytop), and multiply_count (mynext). Both objects are constructed and then mynext is assigned to mytop. Finally mytop.print_data () is invoked.

```
program emcc_top_test {
    // start of top block
    // define global variables here if necessary
    base_count              mytop;
    multiply_count          mynext;

    // start of emcc_top_test
    mytop=new (5,10);
    mynext=new (7,14,21);
    mytop=mynext;
    mytop.print_data();
}// end emcc_top_test
```

The output of this program is

```
++----------------------------------------------------------------++
||              VERA VERIFICATION SYSTEM                          ||
|| Copyright (c) 1995, 1996, 1997, 1998, 1999 by Synopsys, Inc.   ||
||          All Rights Reserved                                   ||
||        VERA is a trademark of Synopsys, Inc.                   ||
|| CONFIDENTIAL AND PROPRIETARY INFORMATION OF SYNOPSYS, INC.     ||
++----------------------------------------------------------------++
Version: 4.4_Beta2.1
base_class:first=7 second=14
Vera: finish encountered at cycle    0
```

Take a look at the example in detail. Figure 9-4 illustrates the process.

FIGURE 9-4   Derived Object Assignment

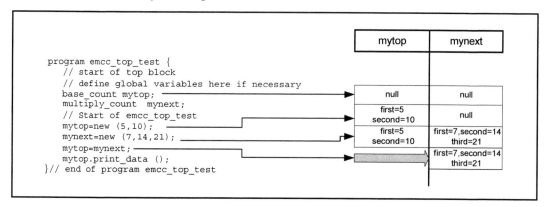

When the objects mytop and mynext are first declared, they do not reference objects, so they contain a null value.

When mytop=new(5,10) executes, memory is allocated for this object; the data members first and second are initialized to values of 5 and 10, respectively; and mytop now references this memory location.

When mynext=new(7,14,21) executes, first, second, and third are assigned values of 7, 14, and 21, respectively, and mynext now references the newly created memory location.

When mynext is assigned to mytop, and mytop.print_data( ) is invoked, it calls the print_data( ) method of mytop but prints the values of mynext. This is due to the overload properties of extended classes. These are described in the next section.

Overload Properties

Vera supports overloading of functions, data member types, and constraints. The most commonly used of these is function overloading, which is the topic of this section. Constraint overloading is addressed later in the chapter, starting on page 282.

Function Overloading

If a derived class overloads a function, all calls to that function from an object of the derived class result in the invocation of the overloaded function, not the base class function. In the previous example object mynext,

```
mynext.print_data();
```

executes the overloaded print_data( ) of the derived class multiply_count.

If a derived class object is assigned to a base class object, references to members of the base class using the base class object follow these rules:

- Task or function references use the base class task or function, regardless of whether they are overloaded in the derived class. For example,

```
mytop=mynext;
mytop.print_data();
```

invokes the base class print_data( ).

- New data members added in the derived class cannot be referenced with the base class object, only with the derived class object. For example,

```
mytop=mynext;
data=mytop.third_data;
```

results in an error, because third_data is not visible from mytop even after the assignment.

Using super to access functions in the base class

Use the "super" object reference to access, from a derived class object, a base class method that has been overloaded in the derived class. In our example, super.print_data( ) in a method in the mynext class invokes mytop.print_data( ). Note that super can go up only one hierarchical level, so you cannot use super.super.print_data( ) in a derived class of multiply_count.

While references to members and methods more than one level up the hierarchy can be done with methods that call super-methods (super.method_name), they should be avoided. Instead, consider redesigning the classes involved and their hierarchy.

Constructor Chaining

Vera implements chaining of constructors. If you have explicit initialization in your base class constructor(s), you don't need to re initialize the data members of the base class in the derived class, except to change the initialization values. All of the constructors in an inheritance hierarchy are called in order, beginning with the base class and ending at the class that invokes the constructor.

Figure 9-5 shows the inheritance tree for a sample set of classes.

FIGURE 9-5   Constructor Chaining

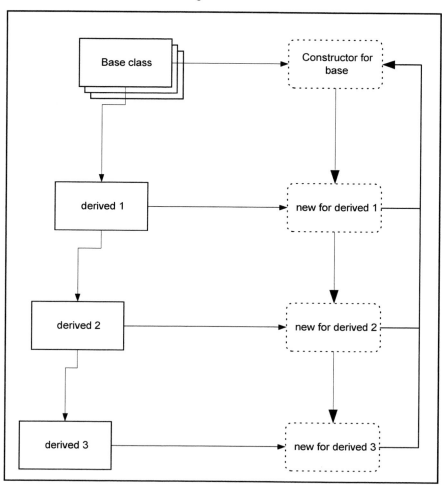

Each of these classes has a constructor. If the derived3 constructor is invoked, it first invokes the base class constructor and then walks down, invoking the derived1 constructor, then the derived2 constructor, and finally the derived3 constructor.

The following code example illustrates this:

```
#define OUTPUT_EDGE PHOLD
#define OUTPUT_SKEW #1
#define INPUT_EDGE PSAMPLE
#include <vera_defines.vrh>
#include "example.h"

// define interfaces, and verilog_node here if necessary
// declare external tasks/classes/functions here if necessary
// declare verilog_tasks here if necessary
// declare class typedefs here if necessary
class base {
    int a1;
    int b1;
    task new() {
        printf ("calling base constructor\n");
        a1=0;
        b1=10;
    }
}//base

class derived1 extends base {
    int c1;
    task new() {
        printf ("calling derived1 constructor\n");
        a1=1;
        b1=11;
        c1=111;
    }
}//derived1

class derived2 extends derived1 {
    task new() {
        printf ("calling derived2 constructor \n");
        a1=2;
        b1=12;
        c1=122;
    }
}//derived2

class derived3 extends derived2 {
    task new() {
        printf ("calling derived3 constructor \n");
        a1=3;
        b1=13;
```

```
        c1=133;
    }
}//derived3

program const_chaing {
    base    mybase;
    derived1 myderived1;
    derived2 myderived2;
    derived3 myderived3;

    myderived3= new;
} // end of program const_chaining
```

The output of this program is

```
++------------------------------------------------------------++
||            VERA VERIFICATION SYSTEM                         ||
||  Copyright (c) 1995, 1996, 1997, 1998, 1999 by Synopsys, Inc. ||
||          All Rights Reserved                               ||
||       VERA is a trademark of Synopsys, Inc.                ||
||    CONFIDENTIAL AND PROPRIETARY INFORMATION OF SYNOPSYS, INC. ||
++------------------------------------------------------------++
Version: 4.4_Beta2.1
calling base constructor
calling derived1 constructor
calling dervied2 constructor
calling dervied3 constructor
Vera: finish encountered at cycle   0
    total   mismatch: 0
            vca_error: 0
      fail(expected): 0
              drive: 0
             expect: 0
             sample: 0
               sync: 0
```

Passing Parameters to Base Class Constructors

If a base class constructor uses arguments, there are two options for providing them:

- Arguments can be provided when the derived class is declared.

```
class derived1 extends base (7,17) {
    //rest of class declaration
}
```

Vera calls the base class constructor with the supplied argument(s). However, this option is useful only if the argument values will not change.

- The derived class constructor can explicitly call the base class constructor as its first executable statement.

```
task new() {
   super.new (7,17);
   //other statements
}
```

Application of Inheritance

In general, inheritance is used for one of these purposes:

Code Reuse. If two or more classes have some things in common but also differ in other ways, the common elements can be put in a single class definition that these classes inherit. Since the common code is shared, it need only be implemented once. For example, if all CPU interfaces are similar, the common CPU interface elements can be shard in a class, but the class can be extended to add non-common elements or functionality.

Making Slight Modifications. Inheritance can also be used to modify classes that were not intended to be used as super classes. For example, let's say you have a class that reads data from the host interface of the MAC. Initially it does a read every clock when RxRdy is asserted, but later needs to be modified to add more delay between reads. That can be done by extending the base class and overloading the read method with a new one which adds delays between consecutive reads.

Applications in Testbenches

Adding functionality to testbenches

Classes can be extended to create additional functionality in the testbench. For example, the stimulus generator can be extended to create additional types of stimulus, and a monitor can be extended to check for different results. To take advantage of inheritance, code using base class objects may have to be modified to use the derived class. Inheritance is also helpful when you are using someone else's classes and just want to add functionality for your own testbench.

Supporting different modes of the ASIC

Most complex ASICs operate in one or more modes. Inheritance, along with polymorphism, can be used to implement tests for the capabilities of these chip modes. For example, let's say there is a single controller that implements both Ethernet and token ring. On way to handle that would be to have a generic base class, extend that class to add Ethernet packets, and have different extension to add token ring capabilities.

Another interesting use of inheritance is to have different classes for different features and then test each feature using extended base classes. For example, you could have base classes for generators, transactors, and monitors that test basic features, and add tests for new features and add new capabilities in the generator, driver, and monitors by extending the base classes.

Take the Ethernet packet class example. Ethernet packets come in three formats (Figure 9-6):

Ethernet format
IEEE 802.3 without VLANs
IEEE 802.3 with VLANs

FIGURE 9-6 Ethernet Frame Formats

Ethernet Bluebook Frame

Preamble (7 bytes)	SFD (1byte)	Destination address (6 bytes)	Source address (6 bytes)	Length (2 bytes)	Data (46-1500 bytes)	FCS (4 bytes)

802.3 Frame

Preamble (7 bytes)	SFD (1byte)	Destination address (6 bytes)	Source address (6 bytes)	Type (2 bytes)	Data (64- to 1518 bytes)	FCS (4 bytes)

802.3 VLAN ID

Preamble (7 bytes)	SFD (1byte)	Destination address (6 bytes)	Source address (6 bytes)	VLAN ID	Type (2 bytes)	Data (46 - 1500 bytes)	FCS (4 bytes)

One way to generate packets is to include a packet type in the packet and use that to create a type or length field and to decide whether to include the VLAN ID.

Including the VLAN ID is more difficult, however. The payload length can be increased by the size of the VLAN ID to compensate for the extra bytes needed. But in this case, the VLAN tag is just an extra byte in the payload and it is purely random, without any user control.

The other option is to use inheritance to deal with VLANs. Figure 9-7 shows the inheritance hierarchy for the packet class to support VLANs. The ieee format packet is derived from the base packet class. It inherits the properties, members, and methods of the base and overrides the base class packet size limit constraint. The ieee vlan packet class extends the ieee packet class, and overrides the packet fields to insert a VLAN field in the middle.

FIGURE 9-7   Extending Packet Classes

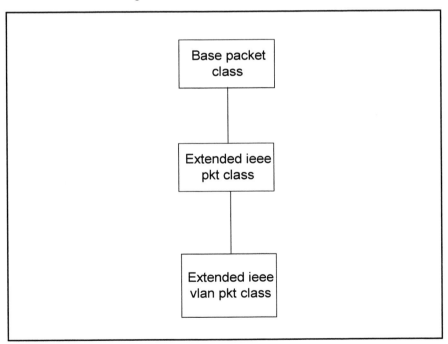

The following sample code shows this:

```
enum ptype = ieee, enet, ieee_vlan;
class ether_packet {
    packed          rand        bit[47:0]       dest_addr;
    packed          rand        bit[47:0]       src_addr;
    packed          rand        bit[15:0]       type_len;
    packed                      bit[7:0]        payld[];
    packed                      bit[31:0]       fcs;

    protected integer max_pkt_len;
    protected rand ptype pkt_type;

    constraint packet_size_limit {
        type_len >=64;
        type_len <=max_pkt_len;
    }
    constraint max_limit {
        max_pkt_len <= (pkt_type == ieee_vlan) ? 1522 : 1518;
    }

    task new();
    task gen_payld();
    protected task calc_fcs();
    task post_randomize() {
        calc_fcs();
    }
}//end class

class ether_pkt_ieee extends ether_pkt {
    //redefine type_len to type
    constraint packet_size_limit {
        type_len >= 1534;
    }
}//end class

class ether_pkt_ieee_vlan extends ether_pkt_ieee {
    packed          rand        bit[47:0]       dest_addr;
    packed          rand        bit[47:0]       src_addr;
    //add VLAN ID field
    packed          rand        bit[31:0]       VLAN_tag;
    packed          rand        bit[15:0]       type_len;
    packed                      bit[7:0]        payld [];
    packed                      bit[31:0]       fcs;
}//end class
```

You can use these extended classes by declaring and constructing objects of these types.

Polymorphism

Polymorphism allows base class functions to be overloaded in derived classes with runtime selection of the proper function. The word *polymorphism* is derived from *poly,* meaning many, and *morph,* meaning form. Polymorphism allows a class or a function to take many forms. Vera selects the appropriate form at runtime.

For example, imagine a function, draw, that draws a polygon, where the supported polygons are hexagon, pentagon, rectangle, and square. If you implemented a single draw function, it would contain many if-then-else or case statements to conditionally execute a code block for a specific shape. That makes the code very difficult to debug and maintain, even for its author.

Here is some pseudocode for figuring out the number of sides (note that this is just one of the many calculations involved in drawing a polygon):

```
if (type == hexagon)
    num_sides=6;
else if (type == rectangle)
    num_sides=4;
else if (type == square)
    num_sides=4;
else if (type = pentagon)
    num_sides=5;
```

In this example, it is still relatively simple to structure the calls, but in most testbenches, the structures are much more complex.

Polymorphism allows you to create separate forms of a particular function and bind each form to a specific object or data structure at runtime. This allows for code that is easily extensible and maintainable.

Vera supports polymorphism using virtual classes and virtual methods. These are discussed in the next section.

Virtual Classes

A virtual class object is a container used to bind to nonvirtual classes

Placing the prefix "virtual" in the class definition declares it as an abstract base class. An abstract base class is not constructed. Instead, its identifier is used as a container to reference the appropriate derived class and its properties and methods.

The Art of Verification with Vera

You can also declare methods (tasks and functions) within a virtual class as virtual. These methods are then dynamically bound to an appropriate derived class method at runtime.

The syntax is

```
virtual class <class_name> {
    <datatype> <data_identifiers>;
    <virtual> task <task_name> (<arg_list>);
    <virtual> function <return_datatype> (<arg_list>);
    task new() {
        <body of vera statements>;
    }
}
```

Figure 9-8 shows code for an example virtual class.

FIGURE 9-8 Example Abstract Base Class

```
virtual class abstract_base_class {
    integer test_val;
    virtual function bit my_func (bit [3:0] a, integer b, string n);
    virtual task my_task (bit [7:0] byte_a, integer my_num);
}

class my_derived extends abstract_base_class{
    integer new_val;
    task my_task (bit [7:0] byte_a, integer my_num) {
        ...
        ...
    }
    function bit my_func (bit [3:0] a, integer b, string n) {
        ...
        ...
    }
    task new () {
        ...
        ...
    }
}//end class myderived
class my_derived2 extends abstract_base_class{
    task my_task (bit [7:0] byte_a, integer my_num) {
        ...
        ...
    }
    function bit my_func (bit [3:0] a, integer b, string n) {
        ...
        ...
    }
    task new () {
        ...
        ...
    }
}//end class myderived
```

It illustrates the declaration of an abstract virtual base class and the extension of this class into two instantiable derived classes—myderived and myderived2. Both derived classes overload the two virtual methods declared in the abstract class. Figure 9-9 shows the class extension hierarchy.

FIGURE 9-9   Example Class Extension Hierarchy

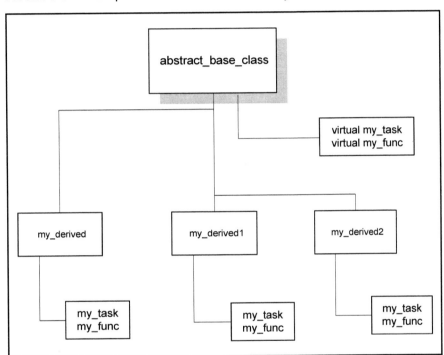

Instantiation & Assignment of Virtual Classes

Objects based on extended classes are declared in the following code example, which illustrates the binding of virtual methods to derived class methods:

```
abstract_base_class  my_ref;
my_derived  derived1;
my_derived2 derived2;

//from here on you can use my_ref
derived1 = new;

//my_ref now references derived1
my_ref=derived1;
```

```
//This invokes my_derived.my_task()
//but references to new_val can be done
//only through the derived class
derived2 = new;
my_ref=derived2;

//Now it invokes my_derived2 methods
my_ref.my_task (59,185);
my_ref.my_func (300,67,"2nd invocation of my_function");
```

FIGURE 9-10 Example Bindings of Virtual Tasks to Derived Class Methods

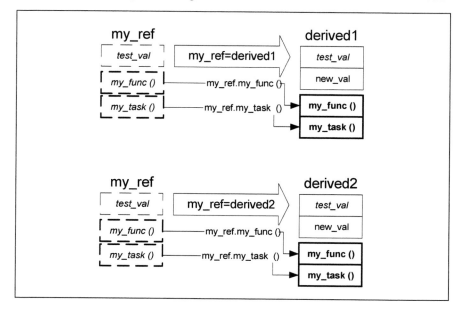

Binding to Methods

Binding to a method depends upon the derived class assigned to the abstract base class object

The derived class objects are first constructed (instantiated) and then assigned to the base_class object. From now on, all references to base_class object methods result in a call to the appropriate overloaded method in the assigned derived class.

Note that this is different from overloading in nonvirtual classes, where a reference to base class methods does not bind to the overloaded method of the assigned class.

The abstract_base_class is not constructed, but the derived classes are.

In the example, the my_derived object derived1 is assigned to my_ref. So a call to my_ref.my_func (15,88,"a value") invokes the my_func function from my_derived class. Similarly, the call to my_task invokes my_derived.my_task.

Later, the my_derived2 object derived2 is constructed and assigned to my_ref. Now a call to my_ref.my_func (300,67,"2nd invocation of my_function") invokes the my_func function of my_derived2 class. Similarly the call to my_task invokes my_derived2.my_task.

References to Data Members of Derived Classes

References to data members follow the same rules as in extension of nonvirtual classes. For example, consider the case where derived1 is assigned to my_ref. A reference to variable my_ref.test_val results in a reference to derived1.test_val. However, a reference to variable new_val cannot be made through the object my_ref. All references to new_val must be made using derived class objects e.g. derived1 or derived2. The methods of my_derived class can refer to new_val, even if they are invoked through my_ref of the base class object.

Virtual Methods

Vera supports virtual methods in abstract base classes and in normal classes. A virtual method provides a prototype for actual tasks or functions. The only restriction is that the derived class that overloads a virtual task or function must use exactly the same arguments and, in the case of functions, return types.

Vera automatically binds a method to a class object at invocation through a virtual method. For virtual methods, Vera searches down the hierarchy (away from the base class). The first nonvirtual method found is used. For real methods, Vera walks up the hierarchy. Note that this is opposite to the way binding in inheritance and the overloading of nonvirtual methods works.

Also note that the search begins at the current class. The current class is the class where the method is invoked. If the virtual method is invoked from another method, then the current class is the class of that method.

Virtual methods can be declared in either virtual classes or in nonvirtual classes. In virtual classes, the virtual method needs to declare only arguments, and if the virtual method is a function, a return type. For example,

```
virtual task find_node (bTree n);
virtual function bit is_node_valid (bTree node_tree);
```

In a regular (nonvirtual) class, when a virtual method is declared, it must provide the arguments, a return type (if appropriate), and a body. In the following code example, a virtual method, find_node( ), is declared in a nonvirtual class.

```
virtual task find_node (bTree n) {
    bTree node;
    //body of task find_node
    if (n.node_val > 100)
        node=parent;
    else if (n.node_value == 100)
        node=child_a;
    else if (n.nodevalue < 100)
        node=child_b;
}
```

In the absence of regular methods, Vera binds to virtual methods with a body

A regular class that contains a virtual method can be instantiated. The virtual method can be invoked from an object in this class, and executed if no other method can be found for binding. When Vera cannot find a non-virtual method to bind to, it uses the most recent virtual method with a body.

Example of Automatic Binding with Virtual Methods in Regular Classes

The example below shows a class for a binary tree data structure. The class bTree is a nonvirtual class containing a virtual method. The class bTree_search extends bTree and overloads the virtual method with a nonvirtual method. Figure 9-9 shows the hierarchy.

FIGURE 9-11   Example bTree Hierarchy

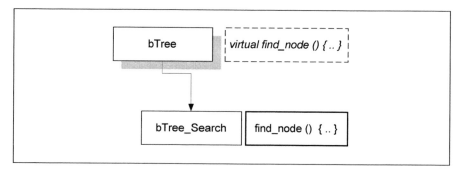

```
class bTree {
    integer         node_val;
    bTree           parent;
    bTree           child_a;
    bTree           child_b;
    task new() {
        ...
    }
    virtual task find_node (bTree n) {
        bTree node;
        //body of task find_node
    }
}//class bTree

class bTree_search extends bTree {
    task find_node (bTree n) {
        ...
    }
}//class bTree_search
```

The code below illustrates instantiation of the two classes declared above.

```
program test {
    bTree Tree;
    bTree_search search;
    bTree Test_tree;
    Test_tree=new();
    Tree = new();
    search = new();
    Tree=search;
    Tree.find_node ();
    ...
}
```

Automatic Binding to Virtual Methods

It is generally better to carry the virtual method down the hierarchy and overload it with a nonvirtual method only at the lowest level possible. The function can be overloaded below the level where the virtual tag is removed, but from then on, dynamic binding does not apply. Dynamic binding stops at the first nonvirtual declaration of the method in the hierarchy.

In the above example, when Tree.find_node( ) is invoked, Vera searches the bTree class and sees a virtual method for find_node. It then goes down the hierarchy to the next derived class, bTreeSearch. There it finds a real method, find_node( ), and uses it.

If, however, bTreeSearch keeps find_node as a virtual method but with a different body, and a new class, bTreeSearchInt, that is derived from bTreeSearch, overloads find_node with a real method, as shown below,

```
class bTreeSearchInt extends bTree {
    task find_node (bTree n) {
        ...
    }
}
```

then the hierarchy looks as shown in Figure 9-12.

FIGURE 9-12   Example bTree_Search Extended Hierarchy

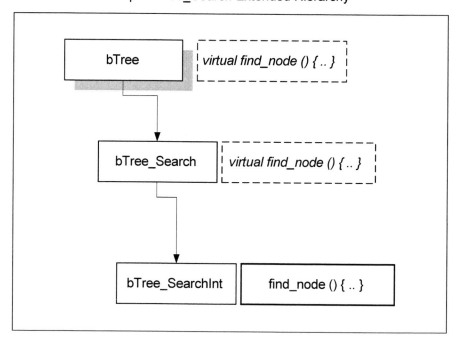

If a bTreeSearchInt object is assigned to an object of type bTreeSearch,

```
bTreeSearch         search_tree;
bTreeSearchInt      int_search_tree;
search_tree=new (...); int_search_tree=new (...);
search_tree=int_search_tree;
search_tree.find_task (n);
```

upon invocation Vera automatically binds to bTreeSearchInt.find_node( ).

If, however, bTreeSearch declares find_node( ) as a virtual method and an object of type bTreeSearch is assigned to an bTree object, as shown below:

```
bTreeSearch     search_tree;
bTree           tree;

search_tree=new (...);
tree=search_tree;

tree.find_task (n);
```

then tree.find_task (n) searches and binds to the virtual method find_node( ) declared in bTreeSearch.

In general, if a method has many forms and you need binding to occur automatically upon invocation from a base class, then virtual methods and abstract base classes are the preferred mechanism. If, however, you just need extension of the capability of the class and do not require automatic binding, then inheritance with derived classes is better.

Rules for Virtual Classes

The following list summarizes the rules governing virtual classes:

- A class declared as virtual cannot be constructed. It is just a container.

- A virtual class may contain virtual methods.

- A virtual class may contain nonvirtual methods.

- In virtual classes, only the virtual method prototype (declaration) needs to be declared.

Rules for Virtual Methods

The following summarizes the rules governing virtual methods:

- A virtual method may be declared in a virtual class or a nonvirtual class.

- A virtual method declared in a nonvirtual class must provide a body if the class and its subclasses are to be instantiable.

- A virtual method can be overloaded in a derived class. The new method must exactly match the virtual method prototype.

- A virtual method can be overloaded with another virtual method in the hierarchy.

Rules for Dynamic Binding

The following rules govern dynamic binding of virtual methods:

- The current class is the class of the object that invokes the method or the class of the method from which the method was invoked.

- If the method is not defined at the current class, Vera searches upward in the tree (in the direction of the base class).

- If the base class is reached without finding the method, the search failed.

- If the method is declared in the current class as virtual, Vera searches down the inheritance tree until the first nonvirtual method is found.

- If no nonvirtual method is found, Vera binds to the last virtual method with a body it found during the search.

Overloading Constraints

Another aspect of classes that is useful in testbenches, especially for random stimulus generation, is constraints. A class can be extended to add or overload only constraints. Here is a constraint addition example:

```
class test_gen {
    rand integer a;
    rand integer b;
    constraint a_limit {
        a >50;
    }
    task new () {
        ...
    }
```

```
    }

class tester extends test_gen {
    constraint b_limit {
        b < 30;
    }
}
```

The class tester extends test_gen but adds only a constraint for b. If necessary, class tester can also create a new a_limit, basically adding a new constraint. For example,

```
class tester extends test_gen {
    constraint a_limit {
        a < 49;
        a > 0;
    }
    constraint b_limit {
        b < 30;
    }
}
```

Now class tester not only adds constraint b_limit but also overrides (overloads) and replaces a_limit with a new constraint.

As the previous example shows, constraints can be overloaded in derived classes. A constraint can be overloaded if the derived class uses the same constraint name. Everything else can be changed inside the constraint block.

Looked at from a higher level, constraints control the value or range of values for some aspect of the stimulus. Typically, constraints can be classified as

- Hard constraints

- Soft constraints

Hard Constraints

Hard constraints typically implement some sort of invariant that should not be violated by the stimulus; if it is violated, the DUT will not function properly. For example, the minimum packet size in Ethernet is 64 bytes and the maximum packet size is 1,522 bytes. The Ethernet MAC will report an error if the minimum packet size or maximum packet size is violated.

Hard constraints may be declared as constants, but if you plan to do error testing, you might want to declare hard constraints as variables.

Soft Constraints

Soft constraints can be changed for each new test case. These can be further classified into boundary values or typical values.

Soft constraints are normally overloaded or declared as variables and used as parameters for other constraints. Ideally, they are modified dynamically or selected at runtime.

Creating Test Cases by Overloading Constraints & Methods

During verification, new test cases emerge requiring additions to existing classes. Test case creation can be done in many ways in Vera. Some of these have been described in Chapter 8. Here we are interested in the creation of test cases by overloading constraints or methods.

In test case creation there are two types of changes:

- Enhancements to a test case to do things that were not thought of at the time the class was implemented

- Specific changes to add corner cases

Enhancement can be added by modifying constraints or by extending or overloading methods. For example, in the Ethernet MAC case, you can change the maximum packet size constraint to generate too-long packets.

Corner cases, however, are sometimes more difficult to implement. Testing corner cases, by definition, requires the verification engineer to do one of the following:

- Create a specific sequence of events

- Cause a specific set of conditions, events and transactions in the RTL to happen simultaneously.

The former can be implemented by modifying the stimulus generator. The latter usually requires modifications to the transactors and the monitors.

These can be handled in one of two ways:

- Modify existing classes and methods. Even if this does not require changes to code that instantiates and assigns these classes, it may break existing test cases.

- Overloading methods and/or constraints. This is done by creating new derived classes that overload relevant methods and /or constraints. This does require changes to the code that instantiates and assigns these classes.

Overloading constraints is a better way to create sequences or enhance stimulus generation

Overloading constraints allows you to specify completely the new constraints or new distribution sequences, and thus gives you better control over the stimulus. The stimulus generator and transactor behavior can be precisely controlled. This method is usually better for creating specific sequence of events or for adding enhancements to implement things that were not thought of at the creation of the class(es).

The drawback, however, is that each test case takes some time to develop, because new code is required, and test case generation efficiency is reduced. Therefore, this method (overloading methods and constraints) should be used with care.

Try to define all methods as virtual in the abstract class

Note that you can use abstract base classes and then define derived classes based on these abstract classes. Try to define all possible methods as virtual in the abstract base classes, since this allows use of polymorphism for generating newer test cases.

Take the MAC stimulus generation classes:

```
virtual class packet {...}
class ether_packet extends packet {...}
class ieee_pkt extends packet {...}
class ieee_vlan_pkt extends packet {...}
```

Use virtual methods with bodies at each derived class

Having one level of hierarchy is good if only random basic tests are needed. For corner cases, however, some methods in the derived classes may need to be overloaded. In order to use polymorphism, it might make sense to have derived classes of the abstract class use virtual methods with a body. This allows polymorphism at every level.

FIGURE 9-13 Packet Class Hierarchy

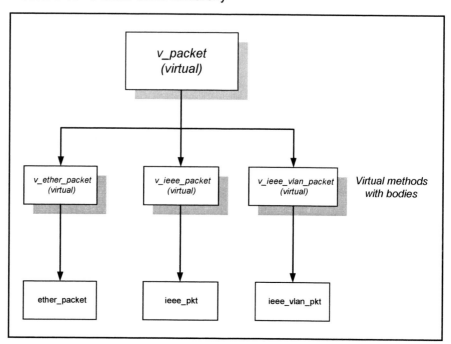

The code below shows extension of the abstract base class. Figure 9-13 above shows the hierarchy implemented in this code.

```
virtual class v_packet {...}
class ether_packet extends packet {...}
class ieee_pkt extends packet {...}
class ieee_vlan_pkt extends packet {...}
class ether_packet_x extends v_ether_packet {...}
class ieee_pkt_x extends v_ieee_packet {...}
class ieee_vlan_pkt_x extends v_ieee_vlan_packet {...}
```

You can now create a new test case by using a second derived class, which overloads a virtual method of the first derived class to change functionality of the method to create a desired outcome.

For example, to force a CRC error on a receive packet, you could create a bit in a single class to programmatically override the crc_calc routine and force a CRC error during generation. However, that requires modification of the class data and methods.

Another option is to make use of polymorphism, by extending ether_packet again to ether_pkt_crc_err:

```
//This class creates packets with CRC errors
class ether_pkt_crc_err extends ether_packet_x {...}
```

Then instantiate an ether_pkt_crc_err object and assign it to a packet object. Now the new test case can be used by invoking the CRC routine from the base class that will bind to the new CRC routine.

Guidelines for Using Inheritance & Polymorphism

Inheritance and polymorphism can be easy to implement. However, styles that make sense in traditional programming may not make sense in design verification. The following sections discuss some guidelines for using inheritance and polymorphism.

When to extend a class

• Use extension either to add functionality to a shared class or when you need dynamic binding of methods.

If a class is being shared in a group and changing the functionality of the class might affect the work of others, then simply extending the class and using the derived class is best. If, however, the class is not being shared, how to modify it depends on the amount of functionality being added.

If the change involves just one or two lines of code, you probably don't need a derived class. If, on the other hand, the changes are significant, consider extending the class. Note that if you do rely on extensive reuse, bugs in shared code propagate across all testbenches. Thus there is a trade-off between productivity and the risk of propagating bugs.

Limit upward references

• Do not reference methods more than one level up in the hierarchy. The need for this can be avoided by good class design.

Use constructor chaining to Initialize extended objects

• Always use constructor chaining to initialize base class data members. This protects you in case the initialization for a class higher up in the hierarchy is changed. Those changes now are automatically reflected in the extended class.

When to declare virtual classes

• If the methods of a single class have many nested if-then-else or case constructs, consider building two or more classes starting with an abstract base class. Again, if only one or two if-then-else statements are needed, you probably don't need an abstract base class. If there are so many if-then-else or case statements that the code is unreadable, you definitely need virtual classes.

Declare methods at each level of the class hierarchy

- If you use virtual classes, make sure you declare the virtual method at each level of hierarchy, even if the virtual method is not needed at a particular level. This lets you override a method anywhere in the hierarchy without worrying about "holes."

Carry virtual methods down to the lowest level of hierarchy

- Do not declare a method as nonvirtual unless a nonabstract method is needed. This again allows you to carry polymorphism down to the lowest level of hierarchy.

Keep levels of hierarchy small

- Keep the derived class hierarchy to less than six levels, and preferably three levels or less. It is rare to need more than six levels of hierarchy. Deep hierarchies create confusion in runtime binding and also make the class structure harder to understand.

Use consistent naming schemes

- Use a consistent naming scheme for abstract classes, base classes, and extended classes. For example,

    Base classes can be named in UPPERCASE (e.g., BASE_PACKET).

    Abstract base classes can use a "v_" prefix (e.g., V_PACKET).

    Extend classes can use an "_ext" suffix (e.g., ether_packet_ext).

Conclusion

Polymorphism and inheritance are powerful features that can extend the functionality of a testbench without compromising existing test cases.

Polymorphism can support different modes as well as create corner case tests, which require precise control over the stimulus. Inheritance can be used to extend functionality, share common class libraries, and create tests for new features.

A testbench should be designed to support polymorphism up-front by declaration of abstract base classes for almost all stimulus generation and transactor classes.

Although polymorphism and inheritance can offer specific corner case testing, using them is not the most efficient mechanism for generating a large number of test cases to cover the basic features. For that, the testbench should support taking user input, in the form of either plusargs or text files.

CHAPTER 10

Generating Stimulus

This chapter presents a sample stimulus generator for the Ethernet MAC. It builds upon the MAC test plan discussed in Chapter 3 and illustrates some of the concepts discussed in Chapter 8.

The stimulus generator code shown is not production-ready; some of the methods required have not been implemented and placeholders have been used instead. Also not all aspects of the code have been fully tested in the verification environment. The generator illustrates some of the stimulus generation concepts used in design verification and in Vera.

The stimulus generator for the MAC generates packets and network events such as collisions, carrier sense, and MII error. The generated packets are passed to the transactor, which writes them to the MAC and then passes them to the monitor. The generated events are passed directly to both the transactor and the monitor.

On the host side, the stimulus generator generates packets, as well as events such as underrun and overrun. On the MII side it generates packets, packet error events, and network events.

Figure 10-1 shows two instances of the generator, one on the host side and one on the MII side. Each instance runs concurrently and independently.

FIGURE 10-1   Testbench Block Diagram

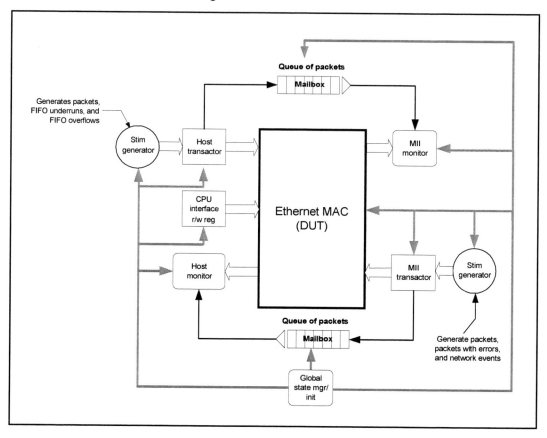

Generation Policies

The MAC testbench has three types of test cases, used in the following order:

- Random tests

- Corner cases

- Directed tests (controlled streams of packets and events)

Random Tests

In these tests, the generator randomly generates packets and events. The requirements for the Ethernet MAC test cases were discussed in Chapter 3. These requirements impact packet generation and error/event generation.

Packet Randomization

Packets can be randomized along the following parameters:

- Packet length

- Packet type (IEEE versus original Ethernet)

- Random destination address or current MAC address (for the MII side)

- Random selection of cast for the MAC destination address for MAC Rx packets generated on the MII side

- Random source address, or they can use MAC address (for the host side)

- Payload data

Random generation of packets is based on distribution weights for each of the packet parameters. Each weight has defaults that can be changed with plusargs, contained within a simulation or regression script for reproducibility. Regression strategies are discussed in Chapter 14.

Error & Event Randomization

The following errors and events are generated randomly:

- Generate packets with errors. These are needed on the MII side to test the MAC receive logic. The generator should create these error packet events:

  Too short packets
  Too long packets
  Alignment errors
  CRC errors in packets

- Generate collisions and carrier sense. Half-duplex transmission of packets requires that the MAC transmits properly even when it receives collisions during transmission. This requires the testbench to randomly generate these network events.

- Generate MII errors. Proper packet reception in the case of MII errors is done by randomly asserting the mii_err signal of the MAC.

- Rx FIFO overflow. An interesting case of packet reception is when the Rx FIFO is full and another packet is received by the MAC. In this case, the MAC is supposed to drop the new incoming packet and properly transfer the packet(s) in the Rx FIFO to the host.

- Tx FIFO underrun. An interesting case of packet transmission is creating a transmit underrun by letting the Tx FIFO run empty during transmission. In this case, the MAC should complete transmission of the current packet and report the underrun. The underrun should not affect transmission of any future packets.

- Maximum retries exceeded. A special case of transmission is when the MAC is forced to drop the packet if the number of retries exceeds the maximum specified. For this case, the generator needs to generate a very high frequency of collisions.

The generation of each of these events is based on a default distribution and a global event enable. The global event enable is used to prevent the generator from generating any of the events listed above. This allows the testbench to verify the basic functionality of the MAC before testing these features. The distribution weights of these events can be changed with plusargs. The global event enable can be turned on with a plusarg.

Corner Cases

The MAC has many corner cases. Some of the interesting ones are related to network events combined with various packet sizes. These events were discussed in the previous section and can be covered by existing randoms. However, by definition, corner cases are hard to identify and not all may be identified upfront at the time the test bench is created. Those that are identified after the initial testbench is created, require modification of the testbench. These corner-case tests need to be written explicitly and added to the testbench.

For these new tests, the user can either modify existing classes or create new derived classes. If the changes are very minor, they can be made directly to existing classes. However, this approach should be used with caution since it can break existing tests.

For tests requiring major changes the user can derive new classes. To support this type of testbench extension, all generator classes are defined by base abstract classes at the top of the class hierarchy. The actual random generator classes are then derived from these base classes. This allows the testbench to make use of polymorphism and easily add new tests without breaking older tests or requiring extensive modifications to code that instantiates the base classes.

Streams

Another interesting test is a specific pattern of stimulus sequences that affects the DUT. This kind of test is more commonly used with CPUs, where only certain instructions are valid after a given instruction. However, it can also be used in MAC testing to create interesting traffic streams. For this you can either use the Vera stream generator, build your own graph classes to generate traffic, or use dynamic distribution schemes. (A sample dynamic distribution class is shown in Chapter 8.)

For example, a sequence of maximum size packets would stress the receive datapath logic of the MAC and maybe cause an overflow, while a sequence of minimum size packets would stress the control path logic of the MAC. So a stream of continuous maximum size packets, which could induce an overflow, followed by a stream of minimum size packets, would verify that the control logic path of the MAC can recover gracefully from overflows.

Instances of the Stimulus Generator

There are two instances of the stimulus generator—one for the host side and the other for the MII side. The host side generates packets and some FIFO events, such as overflow and underflow. The MII side generates packets, error packets, collisions, carrier sense and MII errors.

In MII packets, collisions, carrier sense and MII errors can happen simultaneously. Packet errors affect packet generation and are treated as a directive to the packet generator. These events are generated concurrently in separate threads.

The stimulus generator has two main components:

- A packet generator, which generates good packets as well as packets with errors

- An event generator, which spawns separate threads for collisions, carrier sense, FIFO events, and MII errors

Packet Generator

The packet generator takes user directives, in the form of plusargs, to direct packet generation. It has two modes:

- On the host side, it generates packets for transmission of varying size, cast, and type (IEEE versus original Ethernet) of packet.

- On the MII side, it generates basic packets and varies the destination address value to match or not match the MAC Ethernet address. It also varies the cast of the Rx packets to allow unicast, multicast, or broadcast addresses and it inserts errors in Rx packets if the event generator so indicates.

Event Generator

The event generator also has two modes:

- On the host side, it generates overflow and underflow directives to the host transactor.

- On the MII side, it generates network events and packet errors. Packet errors are used by the MII-side packet generator to generate Rx packets. The MII-side event generator can also generate directives to the MII-side transactor regarding the IPG time. Events are generated asynchronously with other events and Tx and Rx packet generation.

Figure 10-2 shows the components of the stimulus generator.

FIGURE 10-2 Stimulus Generator Components

FIGURE 10-2 Stimulus Generator Components

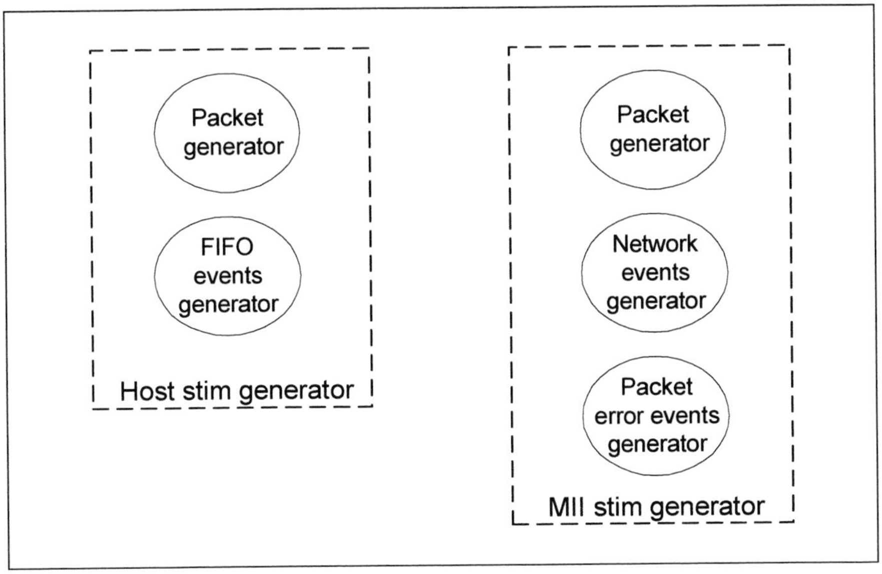

Interfaces to the Testbench

Both the host side and the MII side stimulus generators must interface to the transactors and the monitors within the testbench. This section details how messages and directives from each instance of the stimulus generator are passed to other components of the testbench.

Mailboxes are the primary means of message passing between components of the testbench in this example. Mailboxes were selected for their simplicity of implementation and the buffering they provide between threads.

Transactor Interface

Figure 10-3 shows the interface to the transactor on both sides of the MAC.

FIGURE 10-3   Generator Interface to the Transactor

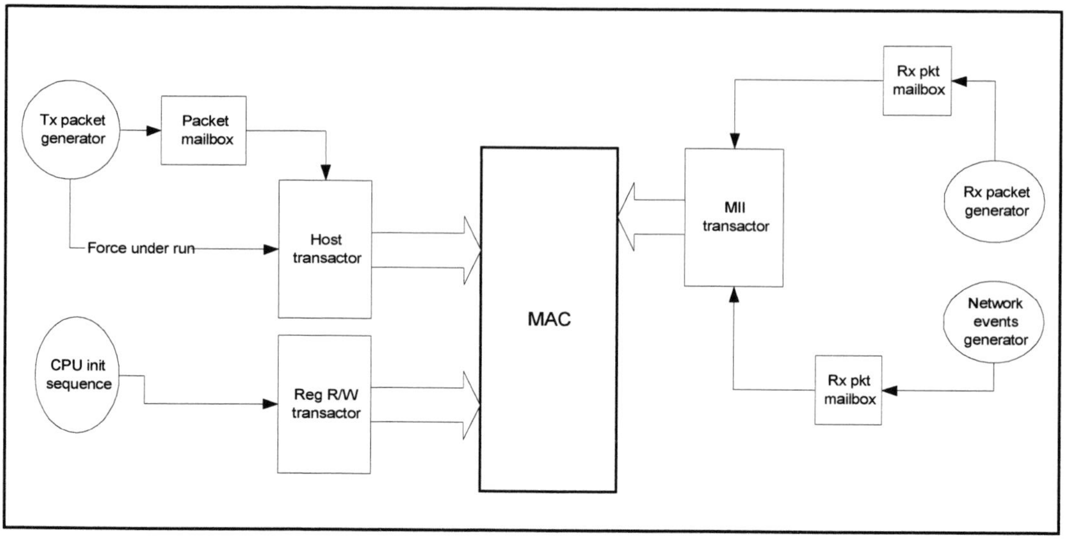

The host and MII generators each have a packet mailbox, which is used to write the packet to the corresponding transactor. Each generator writes packets into the mailbox, and the corresponding transactor reads packets out of it.

On the MII side, there is also a network events generator. The event generators randomly and asynchronously pick events, which are then sent via a mailbox to the transactor.

The MII event generator also generates directives such as violate IPG on receive packets. These are sent directly.

The host event generator generates directives such as force Rx overflow or underrun to the host transactor. These directives are passed using Vera variables.

All packets and events, except for underrun and overflow events, use a mailbox as an interface to the transactors.

Monitors Interface

Figure 10-4 shows the interface from the generators to the monitors and checkers.

FIGURE 10-4   Generator Interface to the Monitors

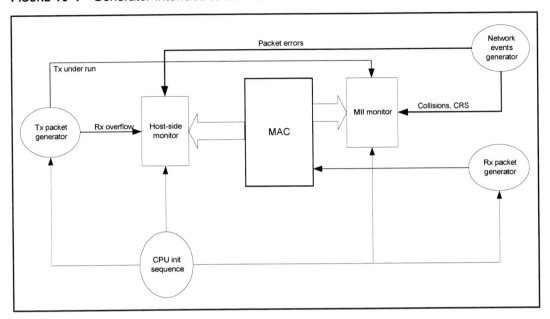

The host-side generator indicates to the MII-side monitor only that it is forcing packet underrun. To the host-side monitor, it indicates that an Rx overflow condition is set.

The MII-side generator provides the MII-side monitor with the network events it generates, such as collision and carrier sense. It informs the host-side monitor about such events as

- CRC errors

- IPG errors

- Packet size violations

- Alignment errors

Stimulus Generator Implementation

The stimulus generator is implemented as a class gen_stim, which is instantiated to create each instance of the generator.

Packet and event
generators are
instantiated
within the
gen_stim class

Packet generator objects and event generator objects are instantiated within the stimulus generator class. The gen_stim class has methods for generating packets and getting error events generated by the packet error generator. It also enables error generation in the err_mii_pkt object. Figure 10-5 shows the gen_stim class instance hierarchy.

FIGURE 10-5   gen_stim Class Inheritance Hierarchy

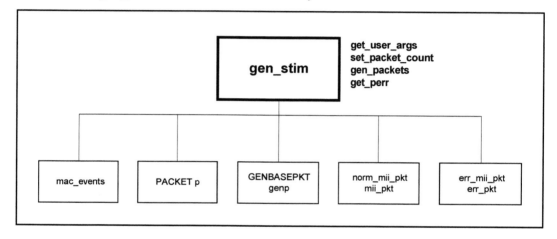

Getting User Directives

The stimulus generator gets user-supplied commands, via plusargs.

In testbenches there are two ways to get plusargs:

- Get all plusargs at startup and store them in a global plusarg object.

  This is difficult, because the global plusarg scanning routine needs to know all the plusargs to look for and what variables to store them in. You can't just look for wildcards and assign the value to appropriately named variables.

- Let each class or function that needs user input get the plusarg it needs.

  In this implementation, access to plusargs is left to the individual class or method. The benefit is that you don't have to set up a global parser for plusargs. The drawback is that the plusarg functionality is distributed and might get duplicated.

Each of these implementations works, but in this testbench, each class and method fetches its own plusargs and processes them locally. For regressions, the plusargs can be entered as options in the simulation or regression script configuration file. The script reads the plusargs from the configuration file and sets them on simulation command as plusargs.

Packet Generation Classes

The PACKET, GENBASEPKT, norm_mii_pkt and err_mii_pkt are packet generator classes and are described in detail in the section below, "Packet Generator Implementation". The mac_events class is the event generator class and is described in detail in the section "Event & Error Generator".

The gen_stim class constructor is passed a mode bit that indicates whether the instance is for the host side or the MII side. Using this information, the constructor enables the event generator.

The mode bit is also used by the gen_packets( ) task. The assignment of the derived class to the abstract class is based upon the mode bit. After that, generation is based upon the constraints set in the derived class.

The other two methods, get_user_args( ) and get_perr( ), get plusargs and packet_error requests, respectively.

The code for the gen_stim class is given below:

```
class gen_stim {
    mac_events   events_gen;
    PACKET p;
    GENPKTBASE   genp;
    norm_host_pkt host_pkt; //used for gen host packets
    norm_mii_pkt mii_pkt;   //used for gen mii_pkt
    err_mii_pkt err_pkt;    //used to gen err pkt for mii
    bit      enable_err;     //enables error gen
    bit      stim_gen_mode;  //host or mii mode
    int      packet_count;   //used to count packets
    int      gen_count;

    task new (int pkt_mbx, int ne_mbx, int pe_mbx, int oe_mbx,
              bit gen_mode, int pcnt) {
        packet_count = pcnt;
        gen_count =0;
        enable_err = 0;
        get_user_args();
        stim_gen_mode = gen_mode;
```

```
        if (enable_err & stim_gen_mode == MII)
            events_gen = new (ne_mbx, pe_mbx, oe_mbx, stim_gen_mode);

        fork
        {
            while (1) {
            get_perr (pe_mbx);
            @ (posedge CLOCK);
            }
        }
        {
            while (1) {
                gen_packets (pkt_mbx);
                @ (posedge CLOCK);
            }
        }//gen_packets
        join none
    }//new

    task get_user_args() {
        //packet count
        //forever
        //enable_error
        int pkt_cnt;

        if (getplusargs (CHECK, "EnErr+")) {
            enable_err = 1'b1;
        }
        else {
            enable_err = 1'b0;
        }

        if (getplusargs (CHECK, "pkt_cnt=")) {
            pkt_cnt = gpa (NUM,"pkt_cnt=");
            set_packet_count (pkt_cnt);
        }
    }//get_user_args

    task set_packet_count (int cnt) {
        packet_count = cnt;
    }
    task gen_packets (int xctmbx) {
        PACKET pkt;
        int i;

        while (packet_count >0) {
        if (stim_gen_mode == MII) {
            mii_pkt = new;
            err_pkt = new;
            if (enable_err) {
                genp=err_pkt;
                printf ("Using err_pkt \n");
            }
```

```
            else
            genp= mii_pkt;
        }//if
        else if (stim_gen_mode == HOST) {
            host_pkt = new;
            genp=host_pkt;
        }
        genp.gen_pkt();
        gen_count++;
        genp.pr_packet();
        pkt = genp;
        mailbox_put (xctmbx, pkt);
        packet_count --;
        }
        gen_count =0;
    }

    task get_perr (int perr_mbx) {
        int n;
        pkt_err_type pe;

        if (enable_err) {n=mailbox_get (WAIT,perr_mbx,pe,CHECK);
            err_pkt.en_err_pkts =1'b1;
            err_pkt.perr=pe;
            printf ("received pkt error command \n");
        }
    }
}//gen_stim
```

Packet Generator Implementation

Packet generator classes rely upon polymorphism and overloading of constraints to generate the proper packets. To allow for polymorphism, all generator classes start with a virtual base class at the top of the hierarchy.

For derived classes, the main generation issues are

- Cast, length, type

- IPG

- Generating the destination address on the MII side

- DA match/fail

Packet cast is important only for MII-side packets. For transmit packets, cast does not make a difference in the packet transmit logic. To set cast, set a pkt_cast variable, which is used by the gen_da( ) method of the MII packet classes to set the appropriate MSB(s) of the destination address. For example:

```
enum pkt_cast = unicast, multicast, broadcast;
pkt_cast ptype;
if (ptype == mcast) {
    {da[0],da[1]}=8'h01;
}
```

The destination address is important only in the receive logic of the MAC, where it has to match the MAC address to the packet's destination address and discard the packet if the two don't match. Therefore, in the MII packet generators, you want to add variables, constraints, and methods to help generate the destination address. To choose the packet type—for selection between IEEE 802.3 and original Ethernet packet format—the MII packet generator uses a pkt_type bit. Constraints are set to change the value of type_len based on the type.

Length is an important variable used to control packet size and generate alignment errors and too short and too large packets.

The length error conditions are randomly created by a separate thread running concurrently. If you have enabled errors, the err_mii_pkt generator is used.

Otherwise, the normal packet generators are used. This allows you to overload the length-related constraints in err_mii_pkt, which are dynamically set, based on the error type set by the packet error generator.

Packet Generator Requirements

From the above discussion, we can infer the requirements for the packet generator:

- Generate Ethernet or IEEE 802.3-format-compatible packets. VLANs are not supported in the current design but can easily be added.

- Vary packet size, including the ability to generate too short or too long packets.

- Vary packet cast randomly.

- In MII-side mode, vary the destination address to match or not match the MAC address.

- Create alignment errors, or CRC errors if required, in the MII-side mode.

- Run independently and generate a set number of packets (provided by plusargs or default), or continuously generate packets.

Class Hierarchy

Figure 10-6 shows the packet generator class hierarchy.

FIGURE 10-6   Packet Generator Class Hierarchy and Operations

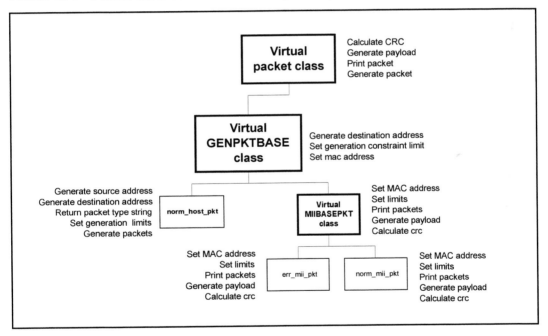

NOTE   *Naming convention: All base class names are in uppercase.*

The PACKET class is the abstract root class. It is needed so packets can be passed between transactors, monitors, and generators. It defines the basic packet and some virtual methods. The GENPKTBASE is the base abstract class used to generate packets. It is derived from the PACKET class and adds generation variables that set randomization constraints, and also adds the constraints themselves. The methods in this class are still virtual to allow polymorphism between the different packet generation classes and their methods.

norm_host_pkt is derived from the GENPKTBASE class and is used for host packet generation, packets that are transmitted by the MAC. norm_host_pkt adds the actual methods and constraints for randomization.

On the MII side is the MIIBASEPKT base class, and from it two classes are derived: norm_mii_pkt and err_mii_pkt.

It makes sense to create the base class first, since the methods and constraints for normal packet generation and error packet generation are different. Instead of having one very complex method, you have two simple methods.

For example, in normal host packets the destination address is generated randomly, whereas in MII packets the destination address can vary its cast or match/not match the MAC address in order to test the destination address match logic. Similarly, the packet length of normal packets is in the 64- to 1518-bytes range, while for error packets, the length constraints should violate that range.

Operations Supported

PACKET supported operations include

- Generate CRC. This method calculates the CRC for the packet.

- Generate payload. This method creates a random payload for the packet. The payld is generated by a method that also creates alignment errors. The payload is defined as an associative array of nibbles. Normally an even number of nibbles is generated. For alignment errors, an odd number of nibbles is generated.

- Print packet. This method prints the packet header for logging purposes.

- Generate packet. This operation randomizes the packet fields.

GENPKTBASE supported operations include

- Set generation constraint limits. This method allows the user to set or modify the limits used in the constraints.

- Set MAC address.

- Generate payload. A virtual method is used to bind to a derived class method to generate the payload.

- Generate packet. A virtual method is used to bind to a derived class method to generate the packet.

norm_host_pkt supported operations include

- Generate source address (for MII side). It set the source address in the packet to the MAC address.

- Return packet type string. Returns the type of packet as an ASCII string.

- Set generation limits. Sets values of variables used in constraints.

- Generate packets. Randomizes and creates the packet.

MIIPKTBASE supported operations include

- Set MAC address. Same as defined in GENPKTBASE.

- Set limits. Allows the user to set or modify the limit variables used in the constraints.

- Print packet. Prints the packet.

- Generate payload. Generates payload. Generates 2 x length nibbles.

- Calculate CRC. Calculates the CRC.

norm_mii_pkt supported operations include

- Set MAC address. Same as defined in GENPKTBASE.

- Set limits. Same as defined in MIIPKTBASE.

- Print packet. Prints packet headers.

- Generate payload. Generates payload. Generates 2 x length nibbles.

- Calculate CRC. Calculates the CRC.

- Generate destination address. Generates the destination address to match or not match the MAC address. Can also set the destination address to be multicast or broadcast to test the receive unit's acceptance of these types of packets.

- Generate packet. Used to randomize the data members of the class.

err_mii_pkt supported operations include

- Set MAC address.

- Set constraint limit variables.

- Print packet headers.

- Generate payload. This method can generate an odd number of nibbles to create alignment errors.

- Calculate CRCL. Generate CRC. Can also force the CRC to be bad to test CRC check logic in the receive path.

- Generate destination address. Generates the destination address as described in norm_mii_pkt.

PACKET Class

PACKET is the top-level class. It is defined as a virtual class and used by all testbench modules. Note that both the class and its methods are declared as virtual. This allows polymorphism in packets when necessary. The data members are defined to allow creation of Ethernet packets.

```
virtual class PACKET {
    //actual packet that will be sent into MAC
    rand    bit[47:0]   da;
    rand    bit[47:0]   sa;
    rand    bit[15:0]   type_len;
            bit[3:0]    payld[];
            bit[31:0]   crc;

    virtual task calc_crc();
```

```
        virtual task gen_payld();
        virtual task pr_packet();
        virtual task gen_pkt();
}
```

GENPKTBASE Class

GENPKTBASE is the base class from which all packet generator classes are derived. It is derived from the abstract PACKET class to allow transactors and monitors to use the same base objects.

It adds two enumerated type variables used to indicate the cast and type (IEEE or Ethernet) of the packet. It also adds constraint limiting variables and constraints for the packet length. The type_len field is supposed to be greater than 8800 for IEEE packets and less than 1518 for Ethernet packets.

```
//This is a base class for basic packet generation
class GENPKTBASE extends PACKET {
    rand  pkt_typeptype;
    rand  pkt_castpcast;
    protected  int        min_pkt_dist;
    protected  int        max_pkt_dist;
    protected  int        btw_pkt_dist;      //>64 < 1518B packet dist
    rand       int        pkt_len;           //generates pkt_len
    rand       bit[15:0]  type_value;        //ieee if pkt is ieee
    protected  hxword     mac_addr;
    //this bit indicates Host or MII mode
               bit        pkt_gen_mode;

    //force type value to be generated
    constraint type_value_limit {
        type_value > 8800;
    }
    //type_len is set for ieee type or orig enet length
    constraint type_len_limit {
        type_len == (ptype == ieee_no_vlan) ? type_value : pkt_len;
    }

    virtual task calc_crc() {
    }
    virtual task gen_payld() {
    }
    virtual task pr_packet() {
    }
    virtual task set_limits (int max_dist, int min_dist, int
    btw_dist){
    }
```

```
            virtual task set_mac_addr (hxword ma) {
            }
            virtual task gen_pkt() {
            }
    }//class GENBASEPKT
```

Event & Error Generator

The MAC testbench has three types of events:

- Errors induced by the host-side transactor

- MII packet errors

- Network events

There is a generator class for each of these event types.

In the host-side stimulus generator, you can activate the host events generator, spawned as a separate thread.

On the MII side, the stimulus generator can instantiate and activate the packet error generator and the network event generator. Each of these is spawned if you allow error generation. The network events are mostly related to half-duplex mode, so they can be controlled for instantiation only in half-duplex mode. In this example, even in full duplex mode, the MAC should behave properly if it sees collisions or carrier sense (CRS), so the network event generator is instantiated regardless of duplex mode.

The event generators run as separate threads. Each of these threads waits for a random time before generating an event. This allows a close approximation of the error behavior that occurs in a typical Ethernet network.

Generating Exceptions in Packets

The testbench has to support the following types of packet errors:

- Too short errors

- Too long errors

- Alignment errors

- CRC errors

The first three are packet length errors. The too short and too long errors are generated by creation of different constraints, hence the err_mii_pkt class. These packet errors can also be implemented in a single class by use of dynamic constraint modification. Using a derived class to generate the error packets, as is the case here, improves readability.

The alignment error is implemented by generation of an odd number of nibbles in the payload generator. The CRC error would be implemented by insertion of a modification in the CRC calculation if a real CRC routine were implemented.

The packet error generator randomly generates one of the four possible events. To make additional, more complex tests, you can generate packets with CRC, and too short errors to emulate collision fragments. This is left as an exercise for the reader.

When packet errors are generated, they are sent to a mailbox. There they are picked up by the MII packet generator and used to generate the next packet on the MII side.

Generating Network Events

The MAC can experience collisions, carrier sense, and MII errors. In a real system, these events can occur concurrently and simultaneously, so each is implemented as a separate thread that is spawned off at instantiation of the net_event object. The class defines three variables, one for each error. The error threads set or clear these variables randomly. Once every clock the send_event task checks these variables and sends them to an MII transactor mailbox.

Forcing Excessive Collisions

Each of these events has a user-modifiable probability. To force continuous collisions on a transmit packet, you can set the collision probability to 100 percent.

Host Events Generator

The MAC can see two conditions created on the host side:

- Rx overflow

- Tx underrun

Although overflow is experienced by packets arriving on the MII side, it is created when the host-side transactor does not read packets out of the Rx FIFO fast enough. A Tx underrun condition is created when the host-side transactor does not write to the Tx FIFO fast enough.

The host_events generator also runs as a separate thread under the event generator. It generates random events, which are sent via a mailbox to the host-side transactor.

Sample Code

The sample code that follows shows classes for packet generation as well as classes for event generation. It does not illustrate the actual CRC routines; instead, a placeholder is used. The purpose here is not to show a complete testbench, but to illustrate verification and Vera concepts.

Packet Generators

```
//These are errors that can be forced during packet creation.
extern bit en_err_pkts;

//This class generates standard Ethernet or IEEE 802.3 format packets
//no errors are supported.
//all packets are assumed to be generated on the host side which
//affects the gen-da task
class norm_host_pkt extends GENPKTBASE {
    //sets pkt_len which is used to gen payld
    constraint len_dist {
        pkt_len dist {64 := min_pkt_dist, 65:1517 := btw_pkt_dist,
                      1518 := max_pkt_dist};
    }
    task new() {
        min_pkt_dist=40;
        max_pkt_dist=40;
        btw_pkt_dist= 20;
```

```
    }
    task gen_payld() {
        int len;
        int i;
        len = 2*pkt_len;
        for (i=0; i <len; i++) {
            payld[i] = urandom();
        }
    }
    task calc_crc(){
        crc = 0;
    }

    function string ret_pkt_typ_s() {
        string s;
        if (ptype == ieee_no_vlan) {
            s = "ieee";
        }
        else if (ptype === eth_no_vlan)
            s = "ethertype";
        ret_pkt_typ_s =s;
    }

    task pr_packet() {
        printf ("Time:%0d ptpye=%s type_val=%d da=%0h sa=%0h type_len=%0d crc=%0h\n",
                gtl, ret_pkt_typ_s(), type_value,da,sa,type_len,crc);
    }
    task gen_sa() {
        sa=mac_addr;
    }
    task set_limit (int max_d, int min_d, int btw_d) {
        max_pkt_dist = max_d;
        btw_pkt_dist = btw_d;
        min_pkt_dist = min_d;
    }
    task set_mac_addr (hxword ma) {
        mac_addr = ma;
    }
    task post_randmize() {
        gen_sa();
        gen_payld();
        calc_crc();
    }
    task gen_pkt() {
        int status;
        status=2;
        printf ("time:%0d host packet Generated\n", gtl);
        status=this.randomize();
        if (status == 0)
            error ("randomize failed\n");
    }
}//class norm_host_pkt
```

```
class MIIPKTBASE extends GENPKTBASE {
    rand    bit     set_da_match;
            int     da_match_dist;
            int     no_match_dist;

    //sets pkt_len which is used to gen payld
    constraint len_dist {
        pkt_len dist {64:= min_pkt_dist, 65:1517 := btw_pkt_dist,
                        1518 := max_pkt_dist};
    }

    //this constraint sets probability of da_match
    constraint da_match_prob {
        set_da_match dist {1 :=da_match_dist, 0 := no_match_dist};
    }

    virtual task calc_crc() {
    }
    virtual task gen_payld() {
    }
    virtual task pr_packet() {
    }
    virtual task set_limits (int max_dist,int min_dist,int btw_dist){
    }
    virtual task set_mac_addr (hxword ma) {
    }
    virtual task gen_pkt() {
    }

    task new() {
        min_pkt_dist=40;
        max_pkt_dist=40;
        btw_pkt_dist= 20;
        da_match_dist = 100;
        no_match_dist = 0;
    }
}//mii_pkt

class norm_mii_pkt extends MIIPKTBASE {
    task new() {
        min_pkt_dist=40;
        max_pkt_dist=40;
        btw_pkt_dist= 20;
        da_match_dist = 100;
        no_match_dist = 0;
    }
    task gen_payld() {
        int len;
        int i;
        len = 2*pkt_len;
        for (i=0; i <len; i++) {
            payld[i] = urandom();
        }
```

```
    }
    task calc_crc(){
        crc = 0;
    }

    function string ret_pkt_typ_s() {
        string s;
        if (ptype == ieee_no_vlan) {
            s = "ieee";
        }
        else if (ptype === eth_no_vlan)
            s = "ethertype";
        ret_pkt_typ_s =s;
    }
    task pr_packet() {
        printf ("RxPKT: Time:%0d ptype=%s da=%0h sa=%0h type_len=%0d  crc=%0h\n",
                    gtl, ret_pkt_typ_s() ,da,sa,type_len,crc);
    }
    task gen_da() {
        if (set_da_match) {
            da=mac_addr;
        }
        else if (da == mac_addr)
            da = mac_addr + urandom();
        if (ptype == mcast) {
            {da[0].da[1]}=8'h01;
        }
        else if (ptyep == bcast)
            da = 48'hffffffff;
    }
    task set_limit (int max_d, int min_d, int btw_d) {
        max_pkt_dist = max_d;
        btw_pkt_dist = btw_d;
        min_pkt_dist = min_d;
    }
    task set_mac_address (hxword mac_a) {
        mac_addr= mac_a;
    }

    task gen_pkt() {
        printf ("time:%0d mii packet Generated\n", gtl);
        void=this.randomize();
    }
    task post_randomize() {
        gen_da();
        gen_payld();
        calc_crc();
    }
}//mii_pkt

//this class is used to generate error packets
class err_mii_pkt extends MIIPKTBASE {
    rand    int          max_len;
```

```
rand    int         min_len;
        bit         en_err_pkts;
        pkt_err_type    perr;

//error types can be : runt, too large , alignment, or crc error
//for alignment we add an extra nibble to payld in gen apyld
//for crc error we set the force crc error bit
//for runts or too long we create max_len and min_len and
//set pkt_len constraint appropriately
constraint packet_length_limit {
    pkt_len <= max_len;
    pkt_len >= min_len;
}

constraint min_len_limit {
    min_len == (((perr == runt)&& en_err_pkts)? (4) : 64);
}

constraint max_len_limit {
    max_len==( ((perr == too_large) & en_err_pkts) ? 2048 : 1518);
}

//this payld gen takes into account alignment error condition
task gen_payld() {
    int len;
    int i;
    len = 2*pkt_len;
    if (en_err_pkts && perr == align_err)
        len +=1;
    for (i=0; i <len; i++) {
        payld[i] = urandom();
    }
}//task gen payld

//this task looks at en_err_pkts and perr and
//if crc_err is set generates crc_error
task calc_crc() {
    crc =0;
}

function string ret_pkt_typ_s() {
    string s;
    if (ptype == ieee_no_vlan) {
        s = "ieee";
    }
    else if (ptype === eth_no_vlan)
        s = "ethertype";
    ret_pkt_typ_s =s;
}

task pr_packet() {
    printf ("Time:%0d ptype=%s da=%0h sa=%0h type_len=%0d crc=%0h\n",
            gtl,ret_pkt_typ_s() ,da,sa,type_len,crc);
```

```
    }
    task gen_da() {
        if (set_da_match) {
            da=mac_addr;
        }
        else if (da == mac_addr)
            da = mac_addr + random();
    }
    task set_limit (int max_d, int min_d, int btw_d) {
        max_pkt_dist = max_d;
        btw_pkt_dist = btw_d;
        min_pkt_dist = min_d;
    }
    task set_mac_address (hxword mac_a) {
        mac_addr= mac_a;
    }
    task gen_pkt() {
        printf ("Time:%0d error_mii packet generated\n",gtl);
        void=this.randomize();
    }
    task post_randomize() {
        gen_da();
        gen_payld();
        if (perr != crc_err)
            calc_crc();
    }
}//err_mii_pkt
```

Event Generation Classes

```
// define tasks/classes/functions here if necessary
enum net_events = idle,crs, collision, mii_err;
enum other_events = noevent, overflow, underrun;

class pkt_events {
    rand    pkt_err_type    pkt_err;
    rand    int             pkt_err_wait;
            int             no_pkt_err_prob;
            int             runt_prob;
            int             too_long_prob;
            int             align_err_prob;
            int             crc_err_prob;

    constraint wait_limit {
        pkt_err_wait > 0;
        pkt_err_wait <= 2000;
    }
    constraint pkt_err_dist {
        pkt_err dist {runt :=runt_prob, too_large := too_long_prob,
```

```
                    align_err := align_err_prob, crc_err := crc_err_prob };
    }

    task new (int mbxid) {
        pkt_err=runt;
        pkt_err_wait=128;
        gen_perr_events (mbxid);
    }

    task gen_perr_events (int perr_mbx) {
        pkt_err_type perr_type;
        fork {
            while (1) {
                repeat (pkt_err_wait) @ (posedge CLOCK);
                void=this.randomize();
                perr_type=pkt_err;
                printf ("Packet Error event generated \n");
                mailbox_put (perr_mbx,perr_type);
            }//while
        }
        join none
    }//gen_per_events

    task set_prob (int runt_p,int too_lg_p,int align_p,int crcerr_p) {
        runt_prob = runt_p;
        too_long_prob = too_lg_p;
        align_err_prob = align_p;
        crc_err_prob = crcerr_p;
    }
}//pkt_events

class net_event {
    rand  net_events   nevents;
    rand  int          net_event_wait;

    int  idle_prob;
    int  crs_prob;
    int  coll_prob;
    int  mii_err_prob;

    constraint wait_limit {
        net_event_wait > 0;
        net_event_wait <= 2000;
    }

    constraint net_event_dist {
        nevents dist {idle := idle_prob, crs := crs_prob,
                    collision := coll_prob, mii_err := mii_err_prob };
    }

    task new (int mbxid) {
        nevents = idle;
        net_event_wait = 64;
```

```
        set_prob (70,10,10,10);
        gen_net_events (mbxid);
    }

    task gen_net_events (int net_events_mbx_id) {
        net_events nete;
        fork {
            while (1) {
                repeat (net_event_wait) @(posedge CLOCK);
                void=this.randomize();
                printf ("net event generated \n");
                nete=nevents;
                mailbox_put (net_events_mbx_id, nete);
            }
        }
        join none
    }//gen_net_events

    task set_prob (int idlep, int crsp, int collp, int miip) {
        idle_prob = idlep;
        crs_prob = crsp;
        coll_prob = collp;
        mii_err_prob = miip;
    }
}//net_events

class host_events {
    rand    other_events    oth_events;
    rand    int             gen_interval;

    //randomization controls
    int    no_host_err_prob;
    int    host_overflw_prob;
    int    host_under_run_prob;

    task new (int hembx) {
        gen_interval = 512;
        gen_oth_events (hembx);
    }

    task gen_oth_events (int othmbx) {
        other_events oe;
        fork
        {
            while (1) {
                repeat (gen_interval) @(posedge CLOCK);
                void=this.randomize();
                oe=oth_events;
                mailbox_put (othmbx, oe);
            }
        }
        join none
    }
```

```
    task set_prob (int no_prob, int ovflw_p, int under_prob) {
        no_host_err_prob = no_prob;
        host_overflw_prob=ovflw_p;
        host_under_run_prob=under_prob;
    }
}//host_events

class mac_events {
    net_event       ne;
    pkt_events      pe;
    host_events     he;

    task new (int nembx, int pembx, int oembx, bit gen_mode) {
        if (gen_mode == MII) {
            ne= new (nembx);
            pe =new (pembx);
        }
        else
        he =new (oembx);
    }
}//mac_events
```

Main Program

The code below illustrates how the stimulus generator is instantiated and used. It shows two instances of the generator being declared and constructed, as well as creation of the mailboxes used to pass messages within the stimulus generator and to the rest of the testbench. The actual generators for packet and events are instantiated by the gen_stim class constructor, which in turn forks off the various threads needed to generate the packets and events.

```
#define OUTPUT_EDGE PHOLD
#define OUTPUT_SKEW #1
#define INPUT_EDGE PSAMPLE
#include <vera_defines.vrh>
#include "emcc.h"
enum pkt_err_type = no_err,runt, too_large, align_err, crc_err;
enum pkt_type =  ieee_no_vlan, eth_no_vlan;
enum pkt_cast =  unicast, multicast, broadcast;

// define interfaces, and verilog_node here if necessary
#include "emcc_top.if.vrh"

// declare external tasks/classes/functions here if necessary
#include "pkt_gen.vrh"
```

```
#include "stim_gen.vrh"
// declare verilog_tasks here if necessary

// declare class typedefs here if necessary

program emcc_top_test {
    // start of top block
    PACKET packet;
    gen_stim host_stim_gen;
    gen_stim mii_stim_gen;
    int  tx_pkt_mbx;
    int  rx_pkt_mbx;
    int  he_mbx;
    int  ne_mbx;
    int  pe_mbx;
    int  nul_mbx;

    bit en_err_pkts =0;

    tx_pkt_mbx = alloc (MAILBOX,0,1);
    rx_pkt_mbx = alloc (MAILBOX,0,1);
    he_mbx = alloc (MAILBOX,0,1);
    ne_mbx = alloc (MAILBOX,0,1);
    pe_mbx = alloc (MAILBOX,0,1);
    host_stim_gen= new (tx_pkt_mbx,nul_mbx, nul_mbx, he_mbx, HOST,5);
    mii_stim_gen = new (rx_pkt_mbx, ne_mbx, pe_mbx, nul_mbx,MII,8);

    repeat (100) @ (posedge CLOCK);
    // Start of emcc_top_test

} // end of program emcc_top_test
```

Init Conditions

The MAC initialization can be done via a text file, plusargs, or a combination of both. For example, the mode, full-duplex or half-duplex, can be set with plusargs. However, FIFO thresholds need to be specified, as do the transmit and receive enable and the interrupt configuration. These are set as defaults and can be overridden by user directives, which can be either in plusargs or a text file. In this implementation, the CPU transactor uses defaults overridden by plusargs.

Summary

This chapter has covered the basic stimulus generator for the MAC. It is by no means a complete generator. As the verification of the MAC progresses, you need to add many more capabilities to the testbench, by either extending or creating a derived class.

This stimulus generator provides the basic stimulus generation capabilities. Typically, at the end of verification the generator will have added significant code test cases not identified in the test plan. So it is very important to plan upfront how these new test cases will be added to the testbench.

CHAPTER 11

Building Transactors & Stubs

This chapter discusses transactors and their properties, shows how to identify transactor requirements, and presents an implementation of transactors for the MAC testbench.

Transactors

A transactor (also called a bus functional model) is a behavioral model that accepts input from a test or a stimulus generator and applies it to the design under test. The transactor usually accepts high level transactions as input and converts them to low level transfers. While applying stimulus, the transactor conforms to the protocol of the interface to which it is connected. A transactor can also sample the response of the device under test.

Figure 11-1 shows a high-level view of a transactor.

FIGURE 11-1   Transactor Concept

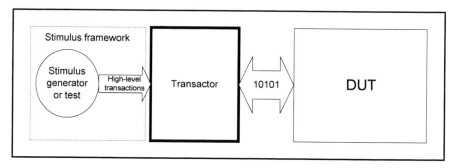

Automatic Transactors

An automatic transactor is behavioral stimulus code; it is special in that it is not driven by stimulus. Its main function is to complete handshaking with, or provide expected response to, the design to which it is connected.

FIGURE 11-2   Automatic Transactor Concept

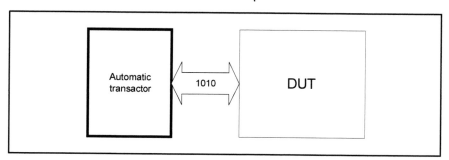

Identifying Transactor Requirements

Transactor requirements have two aspects:

- How they interface with the stimulus (the stimulus framework)

- How they interface with the design

Interfacing with the Stimulus Framework

This is usually the tough part of designing a transactor, for the following reason. Typically no interface is defined between the stimulus framework and the transactor because they are developed at the same time. So the interface must first be defined. The danger is that if you make the interface too simple or too restrictive, you might not be able to exercise the design completely and thus might miss corner cases. If the interface is too complex, it can make the stimulus framework too complicated, so directed tests will take a long time to develop. When developing a large testbench, the verification engineers working on the stimulus generator and the transactor need to have good communication, so that they do not end up making the interface too complicated.

A popular approach to determining transactor specifications is to look at the design interface and note, at a high abstraction level, which operations are performed. For each of those operations, create transactor routines.

For the MAC testbench the stimulus generator developed in the previous chapters will be used. Figure 11-3 shows an abstract view of the MAC testbench stimulus generator. The MAC transactor will communicate with stimulus generator via a mailbox.

FIGURE 11-3 MAC Stimulus Generator Abstract View

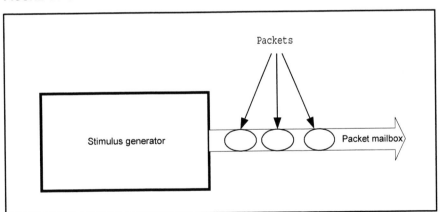

The MAC stimulus generator will provide a stream of good and erroneous packets (via a mailbox), which the transactor will then need to drive into the MAC design.

Interfacing with the Design

For the MAC testbench, stimulus is driven into the design from the MII side as well as from the host side. For this, you need at least two types of transactor: host and MII. Additionally, the host transactor needs to perform both register read and write operations and packet transfers. Since these operations are different in nature, you can partition the host transactor into two transactors, one for the Tx interface and another for the register file interface.

Figure 11-4 is a block diagram that shows how the various transactors connect to the MAC design. Implementation of the register file is not shown here.

FIGURE 11-4 MAC Transactor Block Diagram

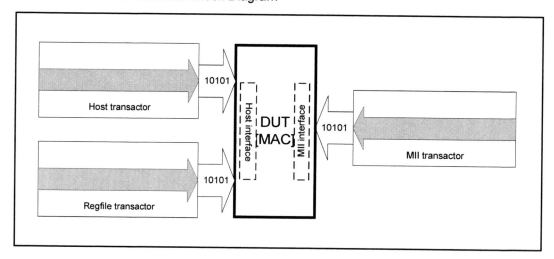

According to the design specifications of the MAC, various network errors and host events can affect data transfer to the MAC, so they need to be accounted for. These include

- Network collision while receiving

- Network collision while transmitting

- Host data underflow

- Host data overflow

- IPG variation on Rx MII side

This short list does not account for all possible test cases, but you can implement the transactor to be extensible and then add features as needed. The above list is a good starting point.

The Message Queue

One of the goals for a completed testbench is that it be self-checking. Response checking (which makes the testbench self-checking) is done via monitors. To do response checking, the monitors must have access to all transactions that take place.

So the transactors must register their activity in a log, which then lets the monitor determine whether a test passed or failed. To implement activity logging and to pass the logged information to the monitor, use a messaging queue.

The following shows a simple message queue that passes transactor information to the monitors.

```
#include <vera_defines.vrh>
// Create an enumerated type for the kind of messages sent
enum info_type   =
      /* there was fifo underrun     */   under_run,
      /* there was fifo overrun      */   over_run,
      /* crc error occurred          */   crc_error,
      /* xactor caused ipg violation */   ipg_violation,
      /* tells checker sim finished  */   done,
      /* initialized                 */   initialized,
      /* should receive a packet     */   transfer_ok;

// Base message class
class message_queue {
    string message;
    PACKET packet_sent;
    protected integer entries_in_hash = -1;
    protected info_type info[];

    task put(info_type new_message) {
        // take the message and add it to the hash
```

```
                entries_in_hash++;
                info[entries_in_hash] = new_message;
        }
        task display_message() {
            // print the message
            integer count;
            sprintf(message,"");
            if (entries_in_hash != -1) {
                for(count = 0; count <= entries_in_hash ; count++) {
                    sprintf(message,"%s %s ",message,info[count]);
                }
                sprintf(message,"Status of packet sent %s ",message);
                my_display(message);
            }
        }
    }
    function integer any_message() {
        // To check if there are any messages
        if (entries_in_hash < 0) {
            any_message = 0;
        }
        else {
            any_message = 1;
        }
    }
    // Function for checking to see if an event happened
    function integer check(info_type compare_message) {
        integer count;
        integer matched = 0;
        // Compare the event with all the events listed
        for(count = 0; count <= entries_in_hash ; count++) {
            if (info[count] == compare_message) {
                matched = 1;
            }
        }
        check = matched;
    }
}
```

Implementing the Requirements

The transactors of the MAC testbench have the following functional
requirements.

Host transactors must

- Drive good and erroneous packets into the design

- Emulate erratic host behavior by causing overflow and underflow conditions

- Perform register read and write operations

- Log all actions in the message queue

- Be extensible so they can incorporate missed requirements

MII transactors must

- Drive good and erroneous packets into the design

- Create network errors or collisions

- Log all actions in the message queue

- Be extensible so they can incorporate missed requirements

When designing transactors, start with the essentials and then extend

The first rule to follow when designing transactors is this: Start with the essentials, and then extend. There are several reasons why this is approach is desirable.

One is that it's best to develop only the functionality you need to implement, not functionality that might not be required later. The testbench and design are developed in parallel, so the initial design is capable of handling only simple transactions. A more complex testbench is therefore unnecessary at this stage. As the design matures, you can then enhance or extend your testbench to exercise more complex features of the design.

But if you implement sophisticated features you believe will someday be included in the design and those features are later eliminated, and all the time spent supporting those features is wasted.

This does not mean that you should turn a blind eye to corner cases and advanced features. You certainly should think about them and plan ahead, so you can support them if and when necessary. But it's generally not a good idea to implement advanced features in a testbench ahead of schedule.

In addition, there should be as small a delay as possible between the time a testbench feature is developed and the time it is debugged. If you develop more advanced features at the start, chances are you will not be able to test them. By the time the design finally catches up and bugs are identified in the testbench, a lot of time may have elapsed and you may have forgotten much about your code. In this case, debugging could take a lot longer than necessary.

MAC Transactor Architecture

Figure 11-5 shows a first attempt at the MII and host transactor implementations. Each transactor connects to an interface of the design and drives stimulus into it.

FIGURE 11-5   Packet Data Flow for the Basic Transactor: First Implementation Attempt

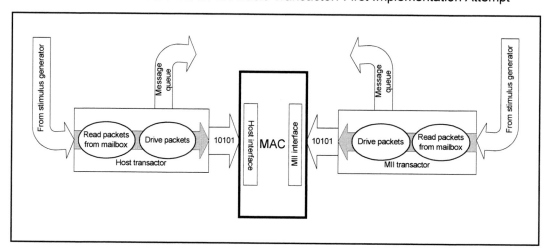

The initial task is to create virtual ports that provide a clean interface to the design. Virtual ports are discussed in detail in Chapter 5.

```
#include "mac_rtl.if.vrh"

port host_tx_port {
    transmit_enable;
    ready_to_transmit;
    transmit_data;
    transmit_byte_enable;
    transmit_select;
```

```
        transmit_sop;
        transmit_eop;
        clock;
}

port mii_rx_port {
        receive_data;
        receive_data_valid;
        receive_error;
        clock;
}

bind host_tx_port mac_host_tx_port {
        transmit_enable          mac_host_intf.TxEN;        // ->MAC
        ready_to_transmit        mac_host_intf.TxReady;     // <-MAC
        transmit_data            mac_host_intf.TxData;      // ->MAC
        transmit_byte_enable     mac_host_intf.TxBE;        // ->MAC
        transmit_select          mac_host_intf.TxSelect;    // ->MAC
        transmit_sop             mac_host_intf.TxSOP;       // ->MAC
        transmit_eop             mac_host_intf.TxEOP;       // ->MAC
        clock                    mac_host_intf.clk;
}

bind mii_rx_port mac_mii_rx_port {
        receive_data             mac_mii_rx_intf.RxD;       // ->MAC
        receive_data_valid       mac_mii_rx_intf.RxDV;      // ->MAC
        receive_error            mac_mii_rx_intf.RxErr;     // ->MAC
        clock                    mac_mii_rx_intf.RxClock;
}
```

Note that the functionality of these transactors contains many similarities. They both

- Connect to mailboxes and virtual ports to read generated stimulus

- Drive packets

- Record actions by putting messages in their respective message queues so that monitors can read them

- Are extensible

This is an ideal place to use the object-oriented features of Vera. Using objects will allow you to implement the features common to both transactors types in a base class and leave features unique to each transactor to be implemented in extended classes. Note that the virtual base class implements just the transactor framework; it cannot drive stimulus, and it can not be instantiated. The following is an implementation of the base transactor class.

```
#include <vera_defines.vrh>

// Base transactor class

virtual class transactor {
    integer semaphore_id;
    // Using a semaphore so multiple
    // instantiations of transactors do
    // not collide

    string  message;
    string  name;              // Name of the transactor instance
    integer stimulus_mailbox;  // Mailbox to read from
    integer message_queue_id;  // Message_queue to log to
    message_queue log_message;

    task new(string name, integer semaphore_id,
             integer message_queue_id) {
        this.name = name;
        this.semaphore_id = semaphore_id;
        this.message_queue_id = message_queue_id;
        display("Created a new instance of transactor");
        sprintf(message,"Semaphore_id is %0d",semaphore_id);
        display(message);
        sprintf(message,"Message_queue is %0d",message_queue_id);
        display(message);
    }

    // This routine is the scheduling workhorse of all transactors
    // It reads from the mailbox and calls drive_a_packet
    // If there are no packets to read, it exits
    task apply_stimulus(){
        integer mailbox_status = 0;
        PACKET packet_to_transmit;

        while (1) {
            // Get the semaphore, so from here on,
            // only one transactor actually executes
            display("Waiting to acquire semaphore");
            if (!semaphore_get(WAIT,semaphore_id,1)) {
                display("Couldn't acquire semaphore");
                return;
            }
            mailbox_status = mailbox_get(NO_WAIT, stimulus_mailbox,
                    packet_to_transmit);

            if (mailbox_status <= 0) {
                // There was nothing in the mailbox
                // So all packets have already been driven into the MAC
                sprintf(message,"Mailbox returned, it seems empty %0d",
                        mailbox_status);
                display(message);
```

```
            semaphore_put(semaphore_id,1);
            sprintf(message,"Semaphore released %0d",semaphore_id);
            display(message);
            this.log_message = new();
            this.log_message.put(done);
            this.log_message.display_message();
            mailbox_put(message_queue_id,this.log_message);
            return;
        }
        else {
            sprintf(message,"Read packet from mbx returned %0d",
                        mailbox_status);
                display(message);

                // Calls to drive_a_packet, which is always
                // transactor dependent
                drive_a_packet(packet_to_transmit);

                // Done driving so return the semaphore
                semaphore_put(semaphore_id,1);
                sprintf(message,"Semaphore released %0d",
                    semaphore_id);
                display(message);
        }
    }
}

// This will always be transactor dependent
virtual task drive_a_packet(PACKET packet);

// Task initialize
// Drive all interface signals to known good values
virtual task initialize();

// Print grep-able & informative messages
task display(string message) {
    string new_message;
    sprintf(new_message,"%s: %s", name, message);
    my_display(new_message);
}
}
```

For both transactors, the execution flow is as follows (Figure 11-6).

FIGURE 11-6   Execution Flow of the Transactors

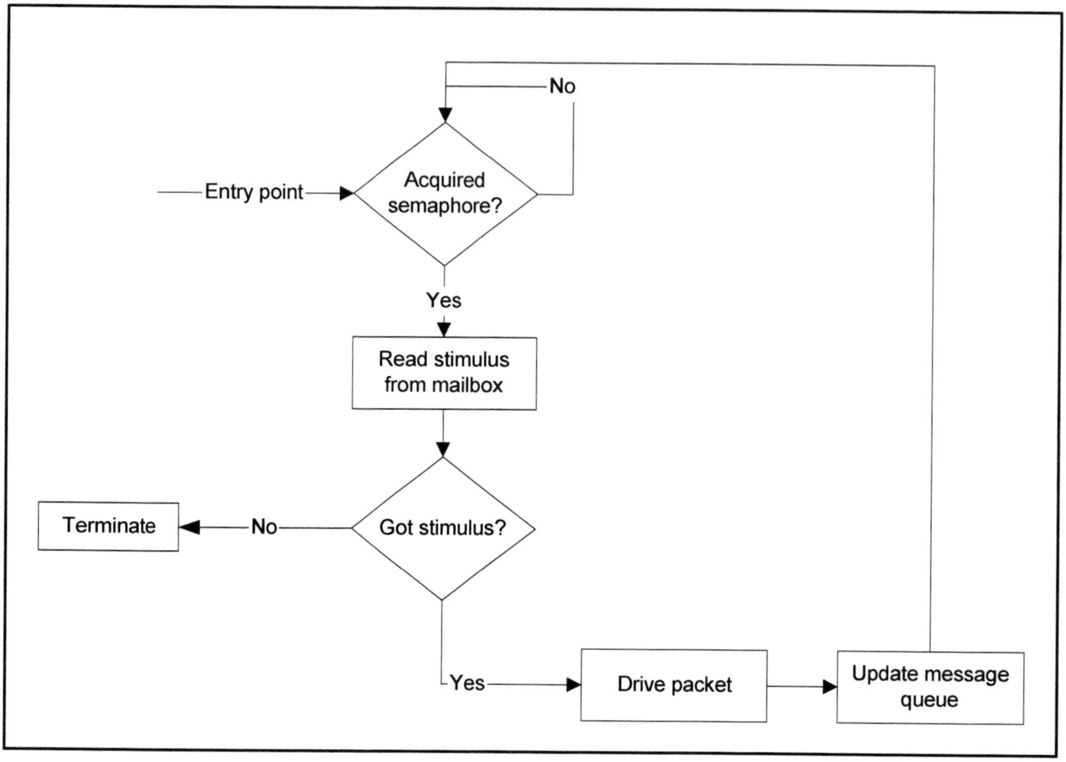

Note that the functionality in the base class implements functionality that is common to both transactors.

Note also the use of semaphores in the apply_stimulus( ) routine of the base class. This prevents drive conflicts when you use multiple instances of transactors or their extensions. All transactors connected to a common interface try to acquire the semaphore before they apply stimulus to the design, but only one transactor actually acquires the semaphore and drives the interface. The remaining transactors continue to wait until they too acquire the semaphore.

Once the transactor that acquired the semaphore is done driving the interface, it releases the semaphore. At that point, another transactor acquires the semaphore, and the cycle continues until there are no more packets to transfer.

The eventual result is a "round robin" type of scheme, as each transactor queues up a request to get the semaphore and the semaphores are granted in the order requested.

Extending the Base Transactor Class

The base class is next extended to incorporate the functionality specific to the host and MII transactors.

Host Transactor

The host transactor drives packets into the design through the host interface. For the host transactor, create a transactor_host class, which is an extension of the base transactor class. The implementation is as follows:

```
class transactor_host extends transactor {
    host_tx_port this_intf;   //Interface the transactor connects to

    task new (string name,
                host_tx_port port_to_connect_to,
                integer mailbox_to_connect_to,
                integer semaphore_id,
                integer message_queue_id) {
        super.new(name, semaphore_id, message_queue_id);
        display("Connected to host port");
        this_intf = port_to_connect_to;
        display("Connected to mailbox");
        stimulus_mailbox = mailbox_to_connect_to;
    }

    // Task initialize
    // Drive all interface signals to known good values
    task initialize() {
        // initialize interface
        // drive all signals to zero
        display("Initializing");
        @0 this_intf.$transmit_enable  = 1'b0;
        this_intf.$transmit_data     = 32'b0;
        this_intf.$transmit_select   = 1'b0;
        this_intf.$transmit_sop      = 1'b0;
        this_intf.$transmit_eop      = 1'b0;

        // wait for ready_to_transmit
        while (this_intf.$ready_to_transmit !== 1'b1) {
            repeat (1) @(posedge this_intf.$clock);
            display("Waiting for transmission readiness");
        }
```

```
            // Wait a little while longer for things to settle out
            repeat (20) @(posedge this_intf.$clock);

            // We are done with initialization
            display("Initialization Completed");

            // Update the message queue
            this.log_message = new();
            this.log_message.put(initialized);
            this.log_message.display_message();
            mailbox_put(message_queue_id,this.log_message);
        }

        task apply_stimulus() {
            super.apply_stimulus();
        }

        // Task drive_a_packet does one transfer on the host side
        // and takes care of various signal assertions.
        // This is the crux of this transactor.
        virtual task drive_a_packet (PACKET  packet) {
            // Variables for packing
            integer transfer_number = 0;
            integer nbits = 0;
            integer offset = 0;
            integer left   = 0;
            integer right  = 0;
            bit[31:0] data_stream[];

            // Pack the packet
            nbits=packet.pack(data_stream,offset,left,right);

            for (transfer_number = 0; transfer_number < offset;
                        transfer_number++) {
                if (transfer_number == 0) {
                    @1 this_intf.$transmit_select = 1'b1;
                    while (this_intf.$ready_to_transmit !== 1'b1) {
                        repeat(1) @ (posedge this_intf.$clock);
                        display("Waiting for transmission readiness");
                    }
                    @3 this_intf.$transmit_enable  = 1'b1;
                    while (this_intf.$ready_to_transmit !== 1'b1) {
                        repeat(1) @ (posedge this_intf.$clock);
                        display("Waiting for transmission readiness");
                    }
                    display("Asserting SOP");
                    @1 this_intf.$transmit_sop = 1'b1;
                    this_intf.$transmit_eop  = 1'b0;
                    this_intf.$transmit_data =
                                data_stream[transfer_number];
                }
                else if (transfer_number == (offset -1)) {
                    // Last transfer
```

```
        while (this_intf.$ready_to_transmit !== 1'b1) {
            repeat(1) @ (posedge this_intf.$clock);
            display("Waiting for transmission readiness");
        }
        // Assert EOP for 1 cycle
        display("Asserting EOP");
        @1 this_intf.$transmit_data =
                        data_stream[transfer_number];
        this_intf.$transmit_eop = 1'b1;
        @1 this_intf.$transmit_eop = 1'b0;
        // Update the message queue
        this.log_message = new();
        this.log_message.put(transfer_ok);
        this.log_message.display_message();
        this.log_message.packet_sent = packet;
        mailbox_put(message_queue_id,this.log_message);
    }
    else {
        while (this_intf.$ready_to_transmit !== 1'b1) {
            repeat(1) @ (posedge this_intf.$clock);
            display("Waiting for transmission readiness");
        }
        @1 this_intf.$transmit_sop   = 1'b0;
        this_intf.$transmit_data =
                        data_stream[transfer_number];
    }
    }
    }
}
```

MII Transactor

The MII transactor drives packets into the design through the MII interface. The MII packet format is a superset of the packet format the host transactor drives into the MAC, since it has two additional fields: the Preamble and the SFD (Start of Frame Delimiter). The values of the Preamble and SFD fields are predefined as follows

- Preamble –0xaaaaaaaaaaaaaaaa

- SFD – 0xab

Figure 11-7 illustrates the differences in the two packet formats.

FIGURE 11-7   Differences Between Host and MII Packet Formats

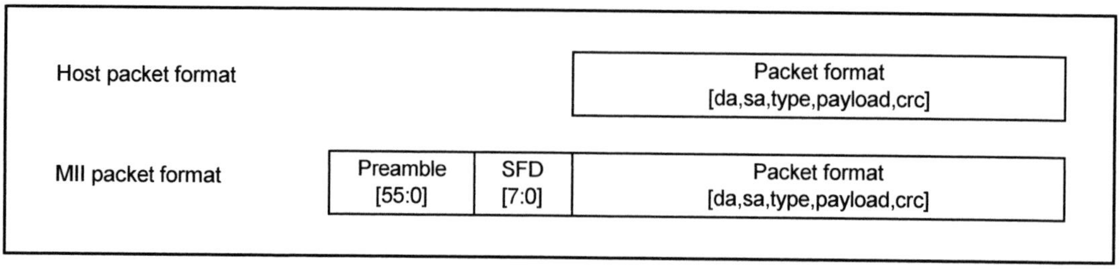

Host packet format			Packet format [da,sa,type,payload,crc]
MII packet format	Preamble [55:0]	SFD [7:0]	Packet format [da,sa,type,payload,crc]

A MII format is based on the host packet format, and defined by creating a new class, encapsulated_packet. The MII transactor drives packets of this class into the design. The implementation of the encapsulated_packet class is as follows:

```
class encapsulated_packet {
    // Fields of the MII packet format
    packed bit[55:0] preamble;    // preamble is not randomized
    packed bit[7:0]  sfd;         // sfd      is not randomized
    packed PACKET packet;
    task new() {
        preamble = {7{8'b10101010}};
        sfd = 8'b10101011;
    }
}
```

Interpacket Gap (IPG)

For the MAC to operate correctly, the interpacket delay (interpacket gap, or IPG) between two consecutive packets on the MII interface must be greater than the programmed IPG value. Packets arriving too frequently cause an IPG violation in the design. The MII transactor adheres to this policy. If the transactor causes an IPG violation by issuing packets too quickly, then it must inform the monitor it is connected to that an IPG violation has occurred. Implementing support for IPG involves creating a separate class, ipg_wait, as follows:

```
// Role of the ipg_wait class
// Creates a new ipg wait value for the mii_transactor
class ipg_wait {
    rand bit[9:0] wait_time_in_bits;  // integer cannot be randomized
    integer       wait_time;          // therefore declare it as
                                      // bit and then assign it to an integer
```

```
integer programmed_value = 50;      // this is the programmed IPG value
integer violation        = 20;      // weight of the violations

constraint ipg_dist {
    wait_time_in_bits dist {
        1 : (programmed_value -1) := violation,
        programmed_value: 1023 := (100 - violation)
    };
}
task new() {
    // new provides a fresh random wait value
    void = this.randomize();
    wait_time = wait_time_in_bits;
}
}
```

The MII transactor is implemented by the transactor_mii class, which, like the transactor_host class, is an extension of the base transactor class. The implementation is as follows:

```
class transactor_mii extends transactor {
    mii_rx_port this_intf; // The transactor connects to this interface

    task new   (string name,
            mii_rx_port port_to_connect_to,
            integer mailbox_to_connect_to,
            integer semaphore_id,
            integer message_queue_id) {
        super.new(name,semaphore_id,message_queue_id);
        display("Connected to mii port");
        this_intf = port_to_connect_to;
        display("Connected to mailbox");
        stimulus_mailbox = mailbox_to_connect_to;
    }

    // Task initialize
    // Drive all interface signals to known good values
    task initialize() {
        display("Initializing");
        display("Driving all interface signals to known good values");
        @1 this_intf.$receive_data        = 4'b1010;
        this_intf.$receive_data_valid     = 4'b0;
        this_intf.$receive_error          = 4'b0;
        display("Initialization Complete");
        // Update the message queue
        this.log_message = new();
        this.log_message.put(initialized);
        this.log_message.display_message();
        mailbox_put(message_queue_id,this.log_message);
    }
```

```
task apply_stimulus() {
    super.apply_stimulus();
}
task drive_a_packet(PACKET packet) {
    // Variables for packing
    integer transfer_number = 0;
    integer nbits   = 0;
    integer offset = 0;
    integer left    = 0;
    integer right   = 0;
    integer ipg_elapse_count = 0;
    ipg_wait ipg;
    bit[3:0] data_stream[];
    encapsulated_packet mii_packet;
    mii_packet = new();
    mii_packet.packet = packet;

    // Pack the packet
    nbits=mii_packet.pack(data_stream,offset,left,right);

    // wait for IPG
    ipg = new();
    sprintf(message,"Will wait %d cycles for IPG to elapse", ipg.wait_time);
    display(message);
    while (ipg_elapse_count < ipg.wait_time) {
        repeat(1) @(posedge this_intf.$clock);
        ipg_elapse_count++;
    }
    display("IPG elapsed");
    display("Sending payload");
    for (transfer_number = 0;transfer_number < offset; transfer_number++) {
        @1 this_intf.$receive_data = data_stream[transfer_number];
        this_intf.$receive_data_valid = 1'b1;
    }
    display("Packet sent");
    @1 this_intf.$receive_data_valid = 1'b0;

    // Update the message queue
    this.log_message = new();
    if (ipg.wait_time < ipg.programmed_value) {
        this.log_message.put(ipg_violation);
    }
    else {
        this.log_message.put(transfer_ok);
    }
    this.log_message.display_message();
    this.log_message.packet_sent = packet;
    mailbox_put(message_queue_id,this.log_message);
}
}.
```

The Main Program: mac_test

Now that you have the basic transactors, they can be used. The following code segment is a sample test that illustrates their usage:

```
program mac_test {
    // start of top block
    PACKET  packet;
    gen_stim host_stim_gen;
    gen_stim mii_stim_gen;
    int tx_pkt_mbx;
    int rx_pkt_mbx;
    int he_mbx;
    int ne_mbx;
    int pe_mbx;
    int nul_mbx;

    string message;
    bit en_err_pkts = 0;

    // These are the transactors
    transactor_host host_transactor0;
    transactor_mii  mii_transactor0;

    monitor_mii mii_monitor0;
    monitor_host host_monitor0;

    // Semaphore_id variables
    integer host_semaphore = 0;
    integer mii_semaphore  = 0;

    // Mailbox_id variables for the mailbox queues
    integer host_to_mii_msg_queue;
    integer mii_to_host_msg_queue;

    // this is the semaphore resource used by the host transactors
    host_semaphore =  alloc(SEMAPHORE,host_semaphore,1,1);
    if (host_semaphore == 0) {
        my_display("Semaphore failed");
    }

    // this is the semaphore resource used by the MII transactors
    mii_semaphore  =  alloc(SEMAPHORE,mii_semaphore,1,1);
    if (mii_semaphore == 0) {
        my_display("Semaphore failed");
    }

    tx_pkt_mbx = alloc (MAILBOX,0,1);
    rx_pkt_mbx = alloc (MAILBOX,0,1);
    he_mbx = alloc (MAILBOX,0,1);
    ne_mbx = alloc (MAILBOX,0,1);
```

```
pe_mbx = alloc (MAILBOX,0,1);
host_stim_gen= new (tx_pkt_mbx,nul_mbx, nul_mbx, he_mbx, HOST,28);
mii_stim_gen = new (rx_pkt_mbx,ne_mbx, pe_mbx, nul_mbx,MII,4);

// Allocation to the message queues
host_to_mii_msg_queue = alloc (MAILBOX,0,1);
mii_to_host_msg_queue = alloc (MAILBOX,0,1);

// instantiating the transactors
host_transactor0 = new ("host_transactor0",    // Name of the transactor
                mac_host_tx_port,      // Port it connects to
                tx_pkt_mbx,            // Mailbox it gets the stimulus from
                host_semaphore,        // Semaphore used to arbitrate grants
                host_to_mii_msg_queue);// Mailbox it logs transfers to


mii_transactor0 = new ("mii_transactor0",
                mac_mii_rx_port,
                rx_pkt_mbx,
                mii_semaphore,
                mii_to_host_msg_queue);

// Reset the chip
@1 mac_host_regfile_port.$reset = 1'b1;
mac_host_regfile_port.$chip_enable   = 1'b1;
@10 mac_host_regfile_port.$reset = 1'b0;
@2  mac_host_regfile_port.$chip_enable   = 1'b1;

// initialize all transactors
host_transactor0.initialize();
mii_transactor0.initialize();

// Apply global reset and chip enable
fork
{
    host_transactor0.apply_stimulus();
    host_transactor0.display("done");
}
{
    mii_transactor0.apply_stimulus();
    mii_transactor0.display("done");
}
join all
} // end of program
```

Extending the Functionality of the Transactors

You can now enhance the functionality of transactors as needed. To do this, you can either incorporate advanced features by extending the basic classes or by modifying the existing transactors.

Enhancing transactor functionality through class extension means you don't touch code that is already working. In addition, implementing some enhancements might require some complicated algorithms, which might make the basic transactor too complex, and thus bug prone.

Note that if a bug is discovered in the base transactor would have to be fixed it in extended transactors as well if you copied code from the base transactors to create the extensions. For this reason, it's always better to use inheritance instead of copying code.

For the MAC example, to add the ability to create FIFO overruns on the host interface, create a class transactor_host_overrun class that extends host_transactor class. You can then instantiate the extended transactor. The class hierarchy with the extended transactor is shown in Figure 11-8.

FIGURE 11-8   Transactor Class Hierarchy

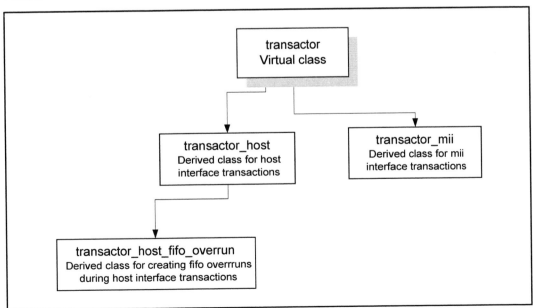

Creating the Extended Class

The framework of the extended class is as follows:

```
// This class specializes in creating FIFO overruns
// at the host interface
class transactor_host_fifo_overrun extends transactor_host {
    task new (string name,
                host_sending_side port_to_connect_to,
                integer mailbox_to_connect_to,
                integer semaphore_id,
                integer message_queue_id) {
        super.new (name,
                port_to_connect_to,
                mailbox_to_connect_to,
                semaphore_id,
                message_queue_id);
    }

    // Task initialize
    // Drive all interface signals to known good values
    task initialize() {
        // initialize interface
        super.initialize();
    }

    task apply_stimulus() {
        super.apply_stimulus();
    }
    task drive_a_packet (PACKET packet) {
        // Variables for packing
        integer transfer_number = 0;
        integer nbits;
        integer offset = 0;
        integer left    = 0;
        integer right   = 0;
        bit[31:0] data_stream[];
        display("Creating FIFO Overrun");
        nbits=packet.pack(data_stream,offset,left,right);
        ... // Implement the FIFO overrun code here.
    }
}
```

The declaration of drive_packet( ) in the transactor_host class must be virtual to make the dynamic method resolution pick the drive_packet( ) routine from the extended class.

Note how the functionality implemented in existing classes is used and only what needs enhancing is overridden.

Instantiating the Extended Class

To instantiate the extended class in a test program, create an instance of the extended class. Then for each instance created, fork off a process.

```
program mac_test {
    // start of top block
    PACKET  packet;
    gen_stim host_stim_gen;
    gen_stim mii_stim_gen;
    int tx_pkt_mbx;
    int rx_pkt_mbx;
    int he_mbx;
    int ne_mbx;
    int pe_mbx;
    int nul_mbx;
    string message;
    bit en_err_pkts = 0;

    // These are the transactors
    transactor_host host_transactor0;
    transactor_host_fifo_overrun  host_transactor1; // our extended transactor
    transactor_mii  mii_transactor0;

    monitor_mii mii_monitor0;
    monitor_host host_monitor0;

    // Semaphore_id variables
    integer host_semaphore = 0;
    integer mii_semaphore  = 0;

    // Mailbox_id variables for the mailbox queues
    integer host_to_mii_msg_queue;
    integer mii_to_host_msg_queue;

    // this is the semaphore resource used by the host transactors
    host_semaphore =  alloc(SEMAPHORE,host_semaphore,1,1);
    if (host_semaphore == 0) {
        my_display("Semaphore failed");
    }

    // this is the semaphore resource used by the MII transactors
    mii_semaphore  =  alloc(SEMAPHORE,mii_semaphore,1,1);
    if (mii_semaphore == 0) {
        my_display("Semaphore failed");
    }
```

```
// Stimulus generator code
tx_pkt_mbx = alloc (MAILBOX,0,1);
rx_pkt_mbx = alloc (MAILBOX,0,1);
he_mbx = alloc (MAILBOX,0,1);
ne_mbx = alloc (MAILBOX,0,1);
pe_mbx = alloc (MAILBOX,0,1);
host_stim_gen= new (tx_pkt_mbx,nul_mbx, nul_mbx, he_mbx, HOST,28);
mii_stim_gen = new (rx_pkt_mbx,ne_mbx, pe_mbx, nul_mbx,MII,4);
// End stimulus generator code

// Allocation to the message queues
host_to_mii_msg_queue = alloc (MAILBOX,0,1);
mii_to_host_msg_queue = alloc (MAILBOX,0,1);

// instantiating the transactors
host_transactor0 = new ("host_transactor0",    // Name of the transactor
              mac_host_tx_port,       // Port it connects to
              tx_pkt_mbx,             // Mailbox it gets the stimulus from
              host_semaphore,         // Semaphore used to arbitrate grants
              host_to_mii_msg_queue); // Mailbox it logs transfers to

host_transactor1 = new ("host_transactor1",
              mac_host_tx_port,
              tx_pkt_mbx,
              host_semaphore,
              host_to_mii_msg_queue);

mii_transactor0 = new ("mii_transactor0",
              mac_mii_rx_port,
              rx_pkt_mbx,
              mii_semaphore,
              mii_to_host_msg_queue);

// Reset the chip
@1 mac_host_regfile_port.$reset = 1'b1;
mac_host_regfile_port.$chip_enable = 1'b1;
@10 mac_host_regfile_port.$reset = 1'b0;
@2  mac_host_regfile_port.$chip_enable = 1'b1;

// initialize all transactors
host_transactor0.initialize();
host_transactor1.initialize();    // initialize the extended transactor
mii_transactor0.initialize();

// Apply global reset and chip enable
fork
{
    fork
    {
        host_transactor0.apply_stimulus();
    }
    {
```

```
            host_transactor1.apply_stimulus(); //drive stimulus
        }
        join all
        host_transactor0.display("done");
    }
    {
        mii_transactor0.apply_stimulus();
        mii_transactor0.display("done");
    }
    join all
}  // end of program
```

Using this technique, you can further extend classes and instantiate as many objects as you like with very little effort.

Conclusion

So far you have seen simple transactors whose functionality you can continue to improve. It is a good start to a verification effort, but clearly it has some weaknesses. For example, the round-robin semaphore-grant scheme used for multiple transactors can be replaced with a scheme that randomly distributes grants. Errors are not injected into the Preamble and SFD field of the stimulus packets. These issues can be dealt with as the testbench evolves.

Developing good and extensible transactors is fundamental to the success of a design, so it is important to plan ahead instead of rushing into implementations.

The flow for designing transactors should be as follows:

- Identify requirements.

- Create a base class that holds common data containers.

- Extend it to incorporate basic functionality.

- Further extend the extended classes to incorporate corner cases.

Use of the above methodology automatically allows for extensive code reuse in transactor development, and the resulting code is easier to maintain.

CHAPTER 12

Result Checking

This chapter discusses result checking, and its key components. It shows what it takes to devise an automated result checking strategy. It discusses basic test types and then introduces failure detection techniques, such as golden files, reference models, and monitors follows.

The chapter also discusses how to implement result checking strategy in a testbench. Finally, a result checking strategy for the example MAC testbench is developed and then implemented.

Glossary of Terms

The following terms are used in this chapter.

TABLE 12-1 Terms used in Result Checking

Term	Meaning
Response	The output of the DUT as a result of the injection of stimulus.
Environment	The testbench, including all components needed to create the stimulus, drive the stimulus, and analyze the response of the DUT.
Modeling	Mimicking some as aspects of the DUT functionality.

TABLE 12-1   Terms used in Result Checking (Continued)

Term	Meaning
Monitoring	Taking the DUT response and converting it to a higher abstraction level.
Checking	Evaluating the response to determine if the behavior was as expected.
Test	The collection of stimulus generation, stimulus injection, and response analysis components of the testbench.
Monitor	The component of the testbench whose prime function is to perform monitoring.
Reference model	The component of the testbench that imitates the behavior of the DUT or one of its features.
Checker	The component of the testbench whose main function is to perform checking.

It usually does not make sense to implement monitors checkers and models as individual blocks. So it is the norm to encounter testbench components that perform more then one function. For example a component may perform:

- Lots of monitoring

- Very little modeling

- Little bit of checking

Well what should such a component be called? A checker or a monitor or a model? According to the prevailing convention it is called a monitor because most of the functionality implemented in this component relates to monitoring.

What Is Result Checking?

Whenever a design is exercised by stimulus, it is important to make sure that its behavior conforms to the specifications of the architecture. If it does not do so, then a functional bug has been encountered and the design needs to be fixed. If the design did not conform to the architecture specification, the test used to exercise the design is flagged as failing.

In verification, exercising all aspects of the design is only half the task. The other half is figuring out if the design passed the tests. Not knowing whether the design passed the test defeats the purpose of verification.

So result checking can be defined as the technique for determining the outcome of a simulation, whether it passed or failed. It does not have to be performed in any specific area of the simulation environment; it can be done anywhere and everywhere. It is up to the environment developer as to how and where result checking is implemented. In a typical large-scale environment, result checking is performed at various places, as shown in Figure 12-1.

FIGURE 12-1   Abstract View of an Environment With Result Checking

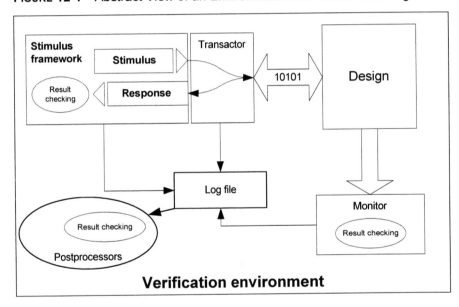

Performing Result Checking

To do result checking, we need to know how the design behaved and also if it behaved as expected. Design behavior is extracted from the simulation through the monitoring schemes implemented throughout the testbench.

Comparison with behavioral expectations can be done in one of two ways:

- Comparison checking

- Algorithmic checking

Either choice is appropriate, depending on the design.

Comparison Checking

In comparison checking, the correct behavior is somehow provided, either with the stimulus or generated dynamically, and compared to the actual behavior. If there is a mismatch then the test is flagged as failing. If the comparison passes then the test is flagged as passing.

Algorithmic Checking

In algorithmic checking, an algorithmic is run on the on the monitored response, and based on the result of that check, the test is flagged as passing or failing. The algorithm implements a conformance test that understands (i.e. models) an aspect of the design and makes sure that the DUT conforms to that specification.

An algorithmic check is a lot like a comparison check, except that the checker does not rely on external expected results and instead figures out the expected response automatically. So an algorithmic checker is like a reference model and a comparison checker bundled together. Since its primary function is to do result checking, however, it is considered a checker.

Requirements for Result Checking

The fundamental requirement for result check is the availability of both expected response of the DUT and actual response of the DUT. Once both are available, result checking can be performed.

The actual response of the DUT is never available before the simulation. So result checking cannot be performed before simulation.

The expected response can be:

- Provided with the test

- Computed before simulation

- Calculated dynamically at runtime

- Computed after simulation

When & Where Is Result Checking Performed?

Result checking can be conducted either at simulation runtime (dynamic) or through post processing (static).

Typically (not always) it is easier to develop a static result checking scheme, because this consists of just file parsing and string manipulation. However, this comes with the overhead generating and maintaining large log files, which can have an adverse effect on simulation performance. (Disk I/O is a slow process). Dynamic result checking is usually more complex, requires a lot of debugging, and comes with it own set of computation overhead.

Result checking is by nature a distributed task. Since some checks may be independent of all the others, it is usually not necessary to develop one giant result-checking component for the testbench. In fact, it makes more sense to develop many small result-checking components that operate independently, and implement them in strategic places in the environment. This allows each component to be implemented as needed, at runtime or after simulation.

Result Checking Strategies

The real challenge of result checking is figuring out the correct behavior of the DUT, the expected response. This is a difficult task. There most common techniques for doing this are

- Using predicted results

- Using comparisons (model-based results checking)

- Analyzing responses (algorithmic results checking)

These techniques are discussed in this section.

Checking with Predicted Expected Results

This is the most basic of techniques. In most cases, tests are manually written to test a specific feature of the design. The test writer has a good understanding of the design and by looking at the design specification can predict the response, which is then hard-coded into the test. If the actual response of the DUT does not match the expected response, the test is considered as failing.

Such tests take a lot of time to develop, as they are written manually, and the chance of making mistakes is high. Thus these tests usually require several debugging iterations. For large complex designs it is not feasible to have a verification strategy that is totally reliant on manual tests.

It is possible to generate random tests which have the expected response encoded in the test, but that relies on some sort of a model to generate expected results and thus falls under the category of comparison checking.

Result Checking through Comparison

Result checking through comparison, also known as comparison checking, is the process of comparing results of two simulations and noting differences. There are two prevalent comparison-based checking techniques: state-based and reference model-based.

States & Golden Files

Often a design is exercised with very complex stimulus patterns. By the time the test finishes, the machine is in a very complex state.

Instead of simulating a checking routine, which might be difficult to write and also take many simulation cycles, it makes more sense to compare the state of the machine against a machine state from a previous run of the same test. Additionally, simulating a checking routine can alter the state of the machine, such as during analysis of the cache line states in a CPU after certain instructions have been executed. If you simulate a cache-checking routine on the CPU model, the mere execution of the checking routine will affect the state of the caches and you will modify (and thus lose) the state you were trying to examine. However, by writing out the current state of the cache to a file and then comparing the log file against a saved state from a previous run of the same test, you sidestep the pitfall of state contamination. If mismatches are detected during state comparison, the test is tagged as failing.

Known good states (from previous runs) are considered "golden states." Golden state comparisons come in handy when you are dealing with the following kinds of test cases:

- Machine state checking tests, such as a reset test, where the intermediate or final state of the design is compared against the state file from a previous run

- Backward-compatibility tests

- Tests where checking is complex, such as a cache coherency test, where executing a checking algorithm can take excessive simulation cycles

Golden files, files that contain golden states, can contain information at various levels of detail. The designer of the environment can decide how much information is stored in the file. The file can store every flip-flop state or just the states of architecturally important components.

Information should be written out to golden files in an organized format. For example, instead of dumping out all the 1s and 0s from a memory module, the information should be organized in an address/data format. Thus, if the memory organization changes (perhaps because of a change made to the address decoding logic), the golden files are not affected. Additionally, the debugging of state comparison mismatches becomes very easy.

The following is an example of a state file for a very simple CPU. It shows register contents and modified lines in the mail memory:

```
// simple_test: golden file generated 05/01/2001
// at end of simulation
Reg0 = 0x00000
Reg1 = 0x00000
Reg2 = 0x00000
Reg3 = 0x00000
Reg4 = 0x10132
Reg5 = 0x11032
Reg6 = 0xbfef1
Reg7 = 0x00000

Pc = 0x12240

Address 0x0000 = 4000000000000000
Address 0x0020 = 00000008d0000000
```

```
Address 0x0040 = 000007500000e000
Address 0x0060 = 0abc649def000000
Address 0x0080 = 0000000000040000
Address 0x00a0 = 0000000000003000
```

Drawbacks of Golden File Comparison

Comparison against a golden state is useful, but the strategy has drawbacks. It is good for catching bugs that have been introduced since the last golden state was generated. But if the last golden state had errors, perhaps because of a prior design bug or a stimulus error, or if the design specification changed in a way that affects the architecture, golden file comparisons are not helpful.

Additionally, golden file are unavailable for new tests. To overcome these limitations, we turn to reference models.

Reference Models

A reference model is a behavioral representation of the design, typically implemented at a higher level of abstraction than RTL. Because reference models are not synthesized, they can be written algorithmically, which improves their simulation performance. They can be implemented in any language.

For a CPU, you can have a program, written in C, that models the architectural registers and the memory and executes assembly code. That is the reference model.

The advantage of using reference models is that they can generate golden files. You can run the same tests you would run on the actual design on the reference model and generate new golden files.

A result checking strategy might be to run the test through the reference model and then run the same test through the design and compare the results of the two runs, flagging any mismatches as failures. This prevents you from depending on golden files from old simulation runs, because you can generate golden files on the fly. Figure 12-2 illustrates this.

FIGURE 12-2   Reference Model Generating a Golden File

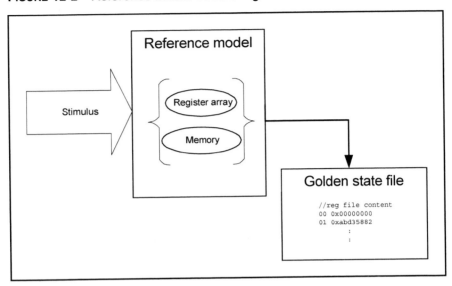

Cycle-Accurate Reference Models. Simple architectural reference models aren't sufficient when dealing with designs that implement architectures providing room for a lot of implementation-dependent features. Such designs are very common in the networking arena. For instance, in the MAC example, the design drops packets under stressful conditions. This is a property that is difficult to emulate in a simple reference model. If you want to model such features of the design, you must start modeling the pipelines and the FIFO. This leads to designing cycle-accurate reference models, which behave just like the design being implemented, clock cycle to clock cycle. That implies they are very detailed and complex, are prone to their own bugs (which hopefully are different from the ones in the design), and take a lot of resources to maintain.

Additionally, the reference model must now model the design and any other entities present in the simulation (transactors and other designs). This involves some overhead, as all the peripheral devices need to be modeled as well. To reduce this overhead, reference models are sometimes designed with simulation hooks that allow them to replace the actual design in the simulation, so that they simulate just like the design, and use the peripheral models already used in the simulation environment. All these capabilities can mean a lot of work, but using them is sometimes the only way of verifying a design—for example, modeling performance counters in an out-of-order machine, or modeling the packet dropping policy in a switch fabric.

Shadow Models. The advantage of using reference models instead of golden files from previous simulations is clear; you do not have to rely on ancient simulation results, because reference models can generate golden files on the fly.

Comparison with a golden state (which is probably the final state of simulation) is usually not enough, since an error might have occurred sometime during the simulation and later gone away. Such cases could be missed if comparisons are only performed on the final state, but they would be caught if comparisons were performed on all the intermediate states (between reset and end of simulation) through which the design transitions.

Errors present for only a short while in a simulation are known as transient errors. Monitors (discussed shortly) should catch transient errors, but due to lack of coverage provided by monitors, transient errors can remain undetected. Transient errors, although short-lived, are nevertheless errors, and they must be caught and fixed. Otherwise, they may reemerge and break the design under a different set of conditions.

But writing out every intermediate state to a golden file can cause severe simulation performance degradation, especially for a large design, because a lot of data has to be written to disk.

To get around this drawback, the design and the reference models are often simulated concurrently in step. All stimulus provided to the design is also provided to the reference. A state comparison is made on every transaction boundary using a monitor (more on this in the next section), and any mismatches are reported as errors. Models running in lockstep with the design are known as *shadow models*. This technique has the following advantages:

- Because state comparisons are done at runtime, there are no huge state files to deal with.

- Because state information is not written to a file, simulation performance typically improves.

- Because the reference model uses the same environment as the design, it eliminates the work of reproducing the whole simulation environment for the reference model.

FIGURE 12-3 Shadow Model Concept

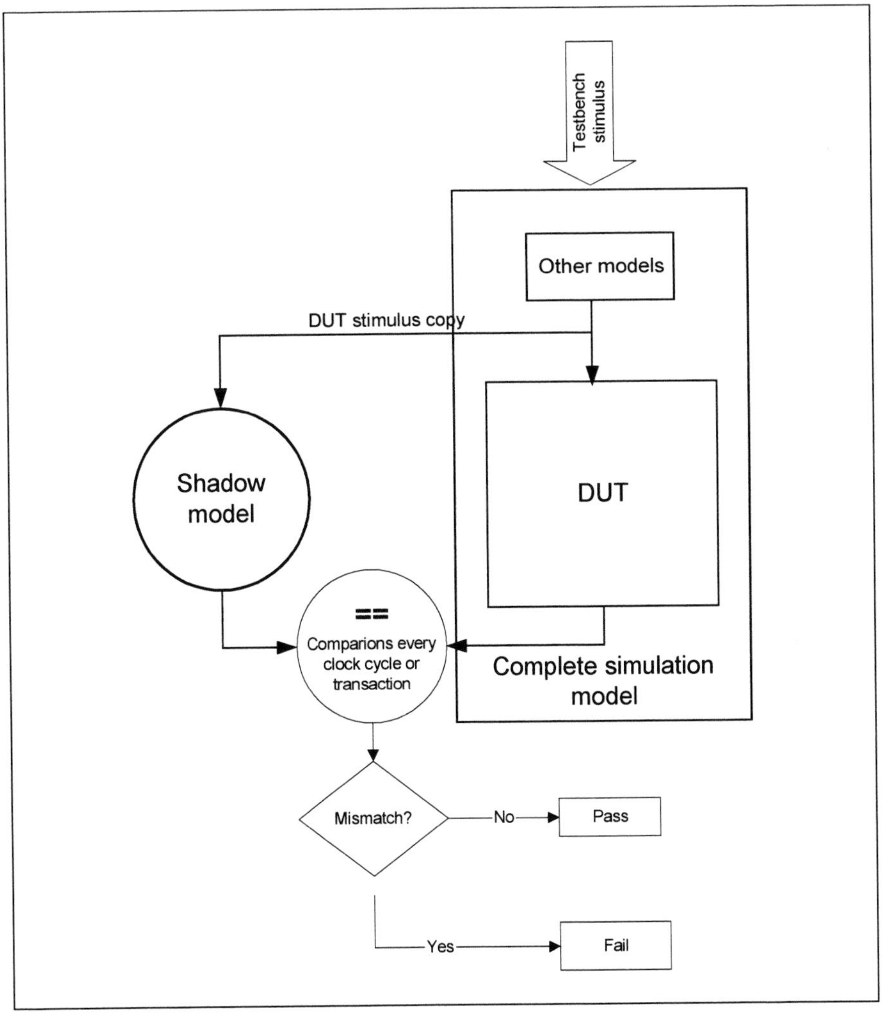

Tradeoffs When Designing a Reference Model

Designing or writing a reference model involves tradeoffs, which typically affect the level of detail modeled in the reference model.

Before developing a reference model, you should identify the elements that contain the globally visible states of the architecture necessary to make a representation of the architecture complete. Only such identified elements need to be modeled in a reference model.

For instance, in the case of a CPU, you need to model only the program counters, register file, and main memory to represent the design. The architecture specifies the number of user-programmable registers. Any implementation of the design should have those registers. Caches are merely optimization techniques implemented in a design, so they wouldn't necessarily be implemented. On the other hand, the reference model should model all the features on which the comparison is performed. For instance, if just the memory data is checked, then just the basic memory needs to be modeled. However, if cache states and coherency are checked, then the caches too must be modeled.

In the MAC example, implementation of a simple reference model would require just modeling a FIFO. Packets would come in, be queued into a FIFO, and be read out. In a sense, this is precisely what that message queue models.But dropped packets must also be accounted for. In such case, the packet drop policy of the MAC architecture would have to be understood and accounted for.

Comparison Checking with Monitors & Checkers

The state-to-state comparison strategy is not impervious to bugs, because it relies on the assumption that nothing can go wrong between states. It is like testing an automobile to see if it gets you from point A to point B. Testing doesn't check to see if the vehicle's tires wobble at high speeds. The car testing team should monitor the car and make sure no part of the car exhibits undesired behavior, such as wobbling, and the car should be instrumented so that the engineers can monitor the behavior of all parts of the vehicle while it is being put through its paces.

Designs do not necessarily misbehave only when they are being stressed; they might perform unexpectedly at other times as well. So it is important to monitor all parts of the design at all times. Instrumenting the design with monitors does this. Typically, code implementing a behavioral check is called a *monitor,* and its function is to observe and report design behavior (especially violations).

This may seem like what a reference model does, so how is a monitor different? A reference model merely maintains a copy of the memory element of the design, but it doesn't perform comparisons between the DUT and the reference model to report failures. The comparison code that checks for consistency between the design and the reference model is the part of the monitor that detects mismatches and flags failures. A monitor is therefore a superset of a reference model.

NOTE   *Though this code should really called a checker, it is not, since it is common to implement monitors such that no checking is done at runtime, and instead, information is written to a log file. This logged information is parsed post-simulation by an algorithmic checker. As a result, engineers often refer to any runtime checking or monitoring code as a monitor and only postprocessing checkers are called checkers.*

In environments in which no reference models are available, monitors maintain private copies of data (like mini reference models) and perform comparisons between DUT responses and their own copies of the data.

In addition to performing comparisons with a reference model, monitors can look for other violations, such as handshake protocol violations.

The overall task of a monitor is to flag detected errors. It can achieve that by using techniques such as detecting mismatches and protocol violations.

Monitors work very well with directed tests, because they are meant to monitor the design as it is being stressed. But their real value comes when they are used in conjunction with random tests. In such environments, monitors are the primary means of catching bugs. The complete environment becomes almost bulletproof when you add shadow models that perform state-to-state comparison.

Writing a monitor is not a simple task, and if you don't take care while designing one, it can quickly turn into a mess (chances are you will find more bugs in the monitor than in the design). A fundamental part of designing a monitor is to determine its scope. It is not necessary to implement all the checks in the same monitor.

The process of defining the scope of a monitor is as follows:

- Make a list of possible violations.

- Identify the abstraction level at which each of the possible violations will be detectable.

- Implement one or more monitors at each abstraction level.

Covering the Test Space

In addition to detecting errors, monitors help make sure the complete test space is covered. For instance, some corner cases are difficult to write directed tests for. A monitor can be designed to watch for the particular condition and report any occurrence of the condition when the design encounters it during simulation. This saves the verification engineer the task of writing a directed test for that particular case. This is often referred to as scoreboard testing. A more detailed discussion on covering the test space will presented in the following chapters.

Algorithmic Checking & Postprocessing

Instead of implementing runtime checks in monitors, you can dump informative messages to the simulation log file and analyze it for errors. This technique is called postprocessing.

Postprocessing checks are usually easy to implement, because the postprocessing script has all the information (from all the cycles) available to it (provided all the information was written out to the log file). Unlike runtime error detection schemes, where you have to be careful not to cause too much simulation overhead, postprocessing checks are relatively easy to develop and deploy, and their debugging does not require you to rerun simulations. The challenge for postprocessing checks is writing just the right amount of information to the log file.

The language of choice for implementing postprocessing checks is Perl. It is a powerful language, because it

- Is easy to program in

- Has very easy string manipulation

- Has concise and powerful regular expressions and pattern matching

- Supports advanced programming structures such as hashes and arrays

- Does automatic garbage collection

- Supports object-oriented programming

Because postprocessing relies on log file parsing, it is important that the log files contain relevant data (see the section "Printing Debug Information, Errors & Exit Status" that follows).

Drawbacks of
postprocessing

Theoretically, it is possible to avoid runtime checking altogether and do only postprocessing, but such an approach has severe drawbacks.

Because postprocessing can never be better than the information dumped to the log file and because 100 percent coverage implies analyzing 100 percent of the design, you would have to dump all the design nodes to the log file every cycle before you could hope to achieve 100 percent coverage. The log files would be huge, and the process of dumping information to them would make simulation performance unacceptably poor.

The second problem for postprocessing is that the tests must be complete before errors can be identified, even if errors are encountered at the beginning of the simulation. Simulation of these post-error cycles creates a computation overhead that could have been avoided if a runtime error checking methodology had been deployed.

However, this does not mean that everything must be done at runtime. If you try to do everything at runtime, there will be too much simulation overhead, because the monitors and checkers will use all of the compute resources of the simulating machine.

Runtime Checking Versus Postprocessing

Postprocessing is preferred for

- Algorithmically complex checks that require either a lot of computation time or a lot of debugging

- Algorithms that are dependent on an extensive state transition history over a long simulation time, such as performance monitoring or verification of stochastic processes

- Checks dependent on aggregation of information across multiple simulation runs

- Checks run on huge simulation models that simulate at a slow rate

For anything else, perform runtime checking.

Printing Debug Information, Errors & Exit Status

When dealing with complex designs, it important to print out simulation information that can be helpful in debugging. You can always look at waveform dumps to analyze exactly what is going on, but dumping waveforms is a time-consuming process and difficult if the only additional information is a message stating, "Test failed".

Vera provides several routines for dumping debug and exit status information in addition to printf( ).

For dealing with errors, Vera has its own set of built-in error tasks. It is not necessary to use all of them, but two are very helpful:

```
task error("<text_and_arg_formats>",<arg_list>)
```

The error( ) task is useful for flagging simulation errors. The usage is similar to that of the printf( ) task, except that the simulation can optionally be terminated when an error( ) task is invoked.

```
task exit(<status>)
```

The exit( ) task terminates the simulation with an integer status value.

These tasks, when used in conjunction with printf( ), provide most of the functionality needed to get useful information into a log file.

One powerful technique is to define custom information logging tasks based on these tasks. It is important to observe the following when implementing custom information reporting routines or, for that matter, whenever you're logging information:

- The print message should clearly identify the routine or class instance that prints the message.

- The message should contain the simulation time cycle time (if any).

- Logged messages should be assigned a severity level, indicating whether the message is information, error, or warning.

- Use switches to disable print messages selectively.

Developing a Result Checking Strategy

The basic considerations for developing a result checking strategy are as follows.

Identify the source of expected results. This is the foundation of result checking. Chances are a reference model or an algorithmic check will have to be developed. This is where most of the development time will be spent. Identify the limitation of the reference model, this will allow you to identify other monitors which will need to be developed.

If directed tests are used, implement a reference model that can run both stand-alone and in sync with the DUT. This will speed up the development of manually written tests, since the test will not have to be run through the a DUT simulation for each debug iteration.

Model only the architecturally important features. See if the model can be implemented at an even high level of abstraction. For example, the reference model implemented for the MAC testbench is really just a packet queue. Try to do runtime comparison if disk space is limited, otherwise, refer to the trade-off section for runtime checking vs. post processing.

Result Checking Strategy for the MAC Testbench

At a very high level of abstraction, the MAC design seems like two FIFOs. There are two separate data paths:

- Host interface to MII interface data path through which transmitted packets propagate

- MII interface to host interface data path through received packets propagate

Transactors for driving packets into the design from each interface have already been developed. Now we need to figure out a result checking strategy. Since the tests do not have expected responses, result checking must be done in monitors. But these monitor would have to know what the correct response of the design should be. This information will be provided by the message queue, which will serve as a very basic reference model.

Two monitors need to be developed, one for the host and another for the MII interface. When these monitors receive packets, they compare the received packet with the packet in the message queue. If the comparison passes, the design behaved correctly.

In some cases, for example, packet exceptions, erroneous packet are driven into the design. These must also be accounted for by the monitors. Packet exceptions result in one of two scenarios—the packet may be dropped, or the packet may propagate through the design and be modified or further corrupted by the design. In both cases, the monitor will encounter a mismatch. But before it is flagged as an error, the monitor must examine the additional fields in the message received from the queue to determine if a packet exception had been encountered.

Lastly, in case of CRC errors in the host-to-MII data path, the errors will be corrected by the design and there would naturally be a mismatch between the received packet and the expected packet from the message queue. In this case, the monitor must reverify the integrity of the packet to ensure that the CRC was generated correctly by the design.

Example MAC Testbench Overview

Monitors for the MAC analyzes the DUT response and determines if the DUT is functioning correctly. The monitor object is instantiated twice, once on the MII (network) side and once on the host side. Both monitors run concurrently. Each monitor simultaneously receives information from a transactor and the DUT. The transactor tells monitor about packet sent and notes any special conditions encountered while the stimulus was being applied to the design by writing this information into a message queue. The monitor reads these messages from the mailbox. Figure 12-4 shows a high-level block diagram for the MAC testbench including monitors.

FIGURE 12-4 Transactor Monitor Interconnects

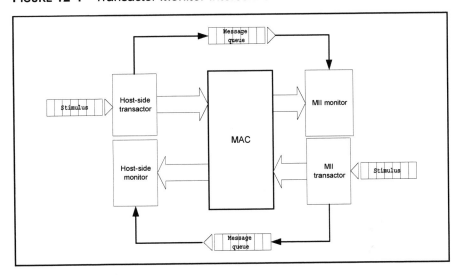

In this implementation of the testbench, most of the errors are detected through mismatches between the information received via the message queue and the response received by the design. Essentially, the message queue plays the role of a very simple reference model. The monitors dequeue a message from their message queue every time they receive a packet from the design and compare the message with the design response. If the packet was supposed to be dropped, the message queue contains that information and a miscomparison is not flagged as a failure.

MAC Monitor Implementation

The execution flow for the two monitors is the same. They read messages from the message queue while they analyze the DUT response. It makes sense to implement the execution flow in a base class and use derived classes to implement host and MII monitor specifics.

Requirements

Each monitor needs to do the following:

- Read messages from the message queue mailbox, so they can be compared with the design responses.

- Receive corrupted and uncorrupted packets from the DUT, since the design allows the propagation of corrupted packets, in some cases.

- Handle and compare various types of packet formats (IEEE/VLAN), since such packets are driven into the design and the design can handle them.

- Deal with dropped packets, since the design can drop packets in cases like FIFO overflow and corrupt packets.

Class Hierarchy

Figure 12-5 shows the class hierarchy for the monitors.

FIGURE 12-5   Class Hierarchy for the Monitor Classes

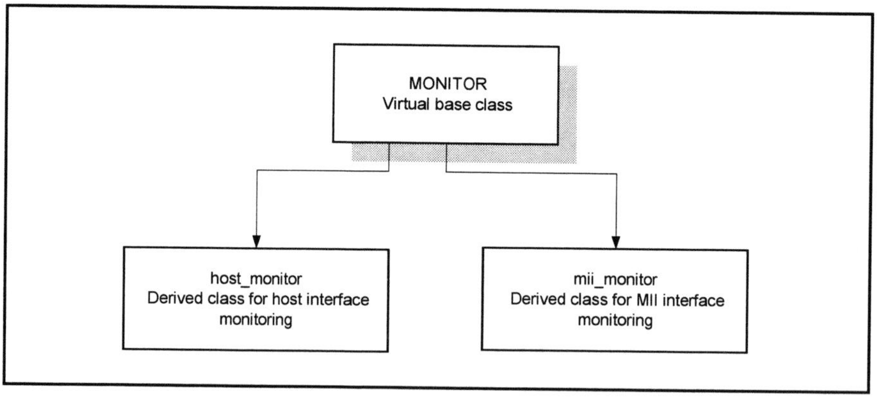

The MONITOR class is the abstract root class. Functionality common to both monitors, such as execution flow, should be implemented here.

The host_monitor class is derived from the MONITOR class. It analyzes packets received on the host interface (originally sent by the MII transactor).

On the MII side is the mii_monitor class, also derived from the MONITOR class. The monitor analyzes packets received on the MII interface (originally sent by the host transactor).

Deriving mii_monitor and host_monitor classes makes sense, since methods for receiving packets and analyzing the response from the two interfaces are very different. By using class extension in this case, you create two simple methods instead of one complex method.

Operations Supported in the Monitor Classes

The following is a list of implemented classes, along with the functionality implemented in each.

The MONITOR class performs these functions:

- Initializes the monitors

- Performs information printing

- Decides when to finish result checking

The host_monitor class performs these functions:

- Receives packets at the host interface, sent by the MII transactor

- Analyzes DUT response by sampling the response and comparing it to expected response

The mii_monitor class performs these functions:

- Receives packets at the MII interface, sent by the host transactor

- Analyzes DUT response by sampling the response and comparing it to expected response

- Monitors inter-packet gap violations

Base Monitor Class

MONITOR is the top-level class. It is defined as a virtual class. The MONITOR class implements the high-level execution flow of the monitor. Note that some methods are declared as virtual. This allows for polymorphism in the monitor methods. The following Vera code implements the MONITOR class.

```
// These are the states of the various threads used
enum monitor_threads =  init_state, busy_state, done_state;

// Base MONITOR class
virtual class MONITOR {
    PACKET packet_received;
    // The mailbox the monitor receives mesages from
    integer message_mailbox;

    string message;
    message_queue message_from_sender;

    // Name of the monitor instance
    string name;
    task new(string name, integer message_mailbox) {
        this.name = name;
        this.message_mailbox = message_mailbox;
        display("Created a new instance of monitor");
        sprintf(message, "Connected to Message queue %0d",
                    message_mailbox);
        display(message);
    }
    virtual function integer analyze_response();
    // Print grep-able & informative messages
    task display(string message) {
        string new_message;
        sprintf(new_message, "%s: %s", name, message);
        my_display(new_message);
    }
    // This routine is the scheduling workhorse of all monitors
    task start_monitoring() {
        integer mailbox_status = 0;
        integer status_monitor = 0;
        // start monitoring
        display("Polling Mailbox");
        // Blocking dequeue
        mailbox_status = mailbox_get(WAIT, message_mailbox,
                    message_from_sender);
        if (message_from_sender.check(initialized)) {
            display("Monitor Initialized");
        }
        else {
```

```
                  // Saw something unexpected, thus exit monitoring
                  error("Saw something else existing");
                  message_from_sender.display_message();
                  return;
            }
            // Start the real monitoring
            while (status_monitor == 0) {
                  status_monitor =  analyze_response();
            }
      }
```

There are four routines implemented in the base monitor class

- new( )—Creates a new instance of the monitor

- start_monitoring( )—Initializes the monitor and synchronizes it with the paired transactor

- display( )—Calls my_display( ), which can be either a simple printf statement or a more elaborate print routine. This implementation is left to the user.

- analyze_response( )—A virtual declaration of analyze_response, which is overridden by the derived classes. The function analyze_response( ) is always monitor-specific, and the primary routine implemented by all the derived classes. This routine does all the response analysis, message queue de-queueing, and packet comparisons.

Monitor Initialization & Termination

Upon initialization, the transactor sends an "initialized" message to its paired monitor; when the monitor receives the "initialized" packet, it resets. This allows monitors to synchronize with their paired transactors and avoid premature response analysis when the design is still being initialized.

At the end of a test the monitors receive a "done" packet from their paired transactors. This means that the test has ended and stimulus is no longer being driven into the design; thus it is ok to terminate.

MAC Packet Monitoring Issues

For the derived classes, the main monitoring issues are

- Packet type-based comparison

- IPG violation detection

- Destination address mismatch

- Dropped packets

For packet comparisons, you can implement a compare_packets( ) routine and add it to the PACKET class.

```
virtual function integer compare_packets(PACKET packet_to_compare) {
    integer error_count = 0;
    integer hash_entries = 0;
    if (da !== packet_to_compare.da) {
        printf("Da mismatched\n");
        printf("Expected %h\n", da);
        printf("Saw %h\n", packet_to_compare.da);
        error_count++;
    }
    if (sa !== packet_to_compare.sa) {
        printf("Sa mismatched\n");
        printf("Expected %h\n", sa);
        printf("Saw %h\n", packet_to_compare.sa);
        error_count++;
    }
    if (type_len !== packet_to_compare.type_len) {
        printf("Type_len mismatched\n");
        printf("Expected %h\n", type_len);
        printf("Saw %h\n", packet_to_compare.type_len);
        error_count++;
    }
    for (hash_entries = 0; hash_entries <payld_len;
    hash_entries++) {
        if (payld[hash_entries] !== packet_to_compare.payld[hash_entries]) {
            printf("Payload mismatched\n");
            printf("Expected %h\n", payld[hash_entries]);
            printf("Saw %h\n", packet_to_compare.payld[hash_entries]);
            error_count++;
        }
    }
    if (crc != packet_to_compare.crc) {
        printf("Crc mismatched\n");
        printf("Expected %h\n", crc);
        printf("Saw %h\n", packet_to_compare.crc);
        error_count++;
    }
```

```
      printf("Ending Packet comparison\n");
      compare_packets = error_count;
   }
}
```

Because all generated packets of the same type have the same fields, this routine suffices for all packet comparisons. But if additional packet types, with different formats, are derived from the PACKET class, the routine as shown will not work. Hence the routine is declared as virtual, since for these cases, you need to add compare_packets( ) routines to new classes.

Because monitors do not know what type of packet propagated through the MAC, they do not know which methods to invoke. To solve this problem, they assume that the packet received from the DUT is of the same type as packet received from the message queue. They use the messages received from the transactors to figure out how to unpack the packet sampled from the DUT, compare the sampled packet to packet from the message queue, and perform any other operation on the packet. They do this by making a copy of the packet read out of the mailbox and then unpacking the data received from the MAC into the copied packet.

The destination address is important only in the receive logic of the MAC, which has to match the MAC address to the packet destination address and discard the packet if the two don't match. Therefore, in the host monitor you need to account for any packets dropped because of a destination address mismatch and flag an error if a packet is received with a destination address that does not match the destination address value programmed into the MAC.

Accounting for dropped packets is the greatest challenge for the monitor. In the case of dropped packets, the monitor compares the packet received from the MAC with the packet received from the message queue. If a packet has been dropped, the comparison results in a mismatch. At this point, the monitor checks if the message received from the message queue contains information on events that can cause the MAC to drop packets. If so, the packet was dropped legally and there is no error; otherwise, the packet was dropped illegally and an error should be flagged.

Dealing with Exceptions in Packets

The testbench has support for the following types of intentionally injected packet errors:

- Packet too short errors

- Packet too long errors

- Alignment errors

- CRC errors

These packet corruption errors are created by the stimulus generator. For each, the monitor still expects the packet to propagate through the design. It then performs a packet comparison. If the comparison fails, it invokes a revalidate_packet( ) routine, which tells the monitor if the packet received from the message queue was corrupted to begin with. If it was a deliberately corrupted packet, the mismatch is acceptable; if not, an error is flagged. The implementation of the revalidate_packet( ) routine is left as an exercise. (The easiest way is to reverify the length and the CRC of the packet received from the message queue.)

Dealing with Network Events

The MAC can experience collisions, carrier sense, and MII errors. Each of these events can occur concurrently in a real system. The monitor polls the event mailbox to see if any of them has occurred. If so, the monitor expects the design to go through an abort retransmission. The monitor can also receive this information from the transactor via the message queue, though this method doesn't inform the monitor about network events.

Network events are processed as follows. The MII stimulus generator updates network event information at every clock cycle and puts that information in a mailbox. The MII transactor polls this mailbox in a separate thread and when it sees that in the current cycle it must cause a network event, it does so on the MII interface. At the same time, the MII transactor writes a message into the message queue that informs the host monitor that a network event has occurred. Then the MII transactor sends the packet during whose transmission this network event occurred.

If the network event occurs while no packet is being written into the design, the MII transactor still causes the event on the corresponding interface, but does not write information into the message, as no packet was affected.

Additionally, in the MII_monitor, packet reception is terminated if one is in progress, and message_queue is de-queued. This means that the monitor skips a comparison, as the packet received is no longer guaranteed to be a good packet. Dealing with network event is not implemented in the example shown and is left as an exercise.

Monitor Response Analysis Flow

Figure 12-6 shows the execution flow for each monitor.

FIGURE 12-6 Execution Flow for Each Monitor

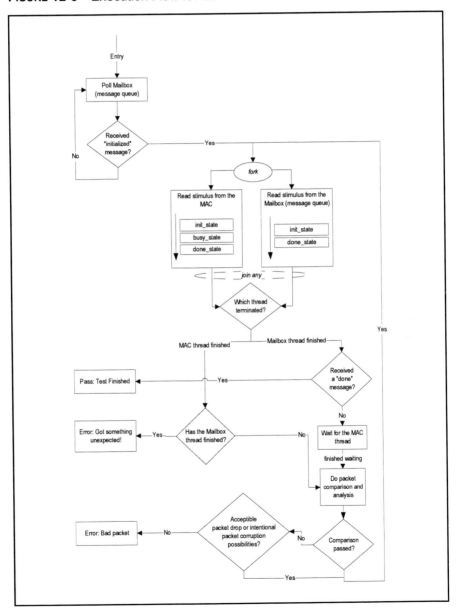

Host Monitor

The following code shows the implementation of the host interface monitor for the MAC testbench.

```
class monitor_host extends MONITOR {
    integer mailbox_status = 0;
    host_rx_port this_intf;

    task new(string name,
            integer message_mailbox,
            host_rx_port port_to_connect_to) {
        super.new(name, message_mailbox);
        this_intf = port_to_connect_to;
    }

    function integer  analyze_response() {
        bit[31:0] data_from_port[];
        integer index = 0;
        integer left =0;
        integer right = 0;
        integer offset = 0;
        integer nbits = 0;
        bit[7:0] packet_sent_da;
        integer timeout_counter = 50000;
        static integer last_packet_dropped = 0;
        monitor_threads packet_reception_thread;
        monitor_threads mailbox_reading_thread;
        // do the packet reception ...
        fork
        {
            packet_reception_thread = init_state;
            display("Waiting for activity on the interface");
            // Wait for rx_ready
            this_intf.$receive_select = 1'b1;
            while (this_intf.$receive_ready !== 1'b1) {
                display("Waiting to receive data");
                @(posedge this_intf.$clock);
                timeout_counter--;
                if (timeout_counter == 0)
                    error("Timed out because of inactivity");
            }

            packet_reception_thread = busy_state;

            if (this_intf.$receive_sop === 1'b1) {
                data_from_port[index++] = this_intf.$receive_data;
                @(posedge this_intf.$clock);
            }
            while (this_intf.$receive_eop !== 1'b1) {
                data_from_port[index++] = this_intf.$receive_data;
                @(posedge this_intf.$clock);
```

```
        timeout_counter--;
        if (timeout_counter == 0)
            error("Timed out because of inactivity");
    }

    // When EOP goes high data is still
    // valid, so read out the last 32 bits.
    data_from_port[index++] = this_intf.$receive_data;

    // Received the packet that needed to be received
    // Now deassert the receive_select signal
    this_intf.$receive_select = 1'b0;
    display("Done receiving data on the interface");
    packet_reception_thread = done_state;
}
{
    // Read from the message queue the packet
    // to be received at the interface
    mailbox_reading_thread = init_state;
    display("Polling message_queue");
    mailbox_status = mailbox_get(WAIT,
                    message_mailbox,
                    message_from_sender);
    display("Read a message from the queue");
    mailbox_reading_thread = done_state;
}
join any

// Figure out which threads are alive
if (mailbox_reading_thread == done_state) {
    // Waiting for reception
    if (message_from_sender.check(done)) {
        // Done monitoring
        display("Terminating, as no more packets expected");
        terminate;  // Terminate packet reception thread
        analyze_response = 1;
        return;
    }
    if (packet_reception_thread == init_state) {
        // We dropped the packet !
        terminate;  // Terminate packet reception thread
        // Add silent drop conditions here
        // Was there a da mismatch ?
        packet_received = message_from_sender.packet_sent;
        packet_sent_da = packet_received.da;
        if (compare_da(packet_sent_da)) {
            // There was a da mismatch
            // So Packet drop is acceptible
            analyze_response = 0;
            return;
        }
        else if (message_from_sender.check(ipg_violation)) {
            analyze_response = 0;
```

```
                    return;
                }
                else {
                    error("Unexpected packet drop");
                    analyze_response = 1;
                    return;
                }
            }
            if (packet_reception_thread == busy_state) {
                // Monitor is in the process of reception,
                // wait for it to complete
                while (packet_reception_thread == busy_state) {
                    @(posedge this_intf.$clock);
                }// Wait a clock cycle
            }
        }
    }
    else if (packet_reception_thread == done_state &&
             mailbox_reading_thread == init_state) {
        // We got something unexpected
        terminate;
        error("Unexpected Packet seen at the host interface");
    }


    // Copy the packet, so we can later unpack on top of it.
    // This will allow us the unpack the response
    // with the correct unpack method
    packet_received = new message_from_sender.packet_sent;

    // really the da from packet_sent
    packet_sent_da = packet_received.da;

    // Always corrupt the packet copied so
    // in case there is nothing to unpack
    // (which means a dropped packet), it will be detected
    packet_received.crc = 1'bx;

    void = packet_received.unpack(
                data_from_port,offset,left,right);

    if (!compare_da(packet_received.da)) {
        // The da of the packet should have
        // the programmed da of the MAC
        // else it is an error, because the MAC
        // does not receive packets
        // whose da does not match the programmed value
        error("Incorrect packet should have been dropped\n");
        analyze_response = 1;
        return;
    }
    else {
        if (packet_received.compare_packets
                (message_from_sender.packet_sent)) {
            // compare_packet routine will display the mismatches
```

```
        // ok, Something incorrect was received  maybe because
        // the packet was dropped check the message if the
        // packet was supposed to be dropped

        // Add legal drop conditions here
        // implementation not shown
        if (!compare_da(packet_sent_da)) {
            // OK the da of the packet sent was not
            // the same as the programmed value
            // so it was dropped
            analyze_response = 0;
            return;
        }
        else if (message_from_sender.check(ipg_violation)) {
            // The transactor had caused an IPG violation
            // so the it is a legal drop condition
            analyze_response = 0;
            return;
        }
        // No da mismatch and IPG vilation
        // check to see if it was a corrupt
        // packet to start with
        packet_received = message_from_sender.packet_sent;

        if (packet_received.revalidate_packet()) {
            // Packet was valid and the design corrupted it
            error("Packet mismatch\n");
            analyze_response = 1;
            return;
        }
        else {
            // Packet was corrupt to start with.
            // This is an acceptable drop condition
            analyze_response = 0;
            return;
        }
    }
    else {
        // Looks like all went well
        display("Packet received successfully");
        analyze_response = 0;
        return;
    }
  }
 }
}
```

MII Monitor

The following code shows the implementation of the MII interface monitor for the MAC testbench.

```
class monitor_mii extends MONITOR {
    integer mailbox_status = 0;
    mii_tx_port this_intf;

    task new(string name,
            integer message_mailbox,
            mii_tx_port port_to_connect_to) {
        //Use the method from the base class
        super.new(name, message_mailbox);
        this_intf = port_to_connect_to;
    }

    function integer analyze_response() {
        bit[3:0] data_from_port[];
        integer index = 0;
        integer left =0;
        integer right = 0;
        integer offset = 0;
        integer nbits = 0;
        integer elapsed_ipg = 0;
        integer timeout_counter = 50000;
        encapsulated_packet mii_packet;
        ipg_wait   ipg;
        static integer possible_retry = 0;
        monitor_threads packet_reception_thread;
        monitor_threads mailbox_reading_thread;
        mii_packet = new();
        // Do the packet reception ...
        ipg = new();
        fork
        {
            packet_reception_thread = init_state;
            display("Waiting for activity on the interface");
            while (this_intf.$transmit_data_valid !== 1'b1) {
                @(posedge this_intf.$clock);
                elapsed_ipg++;   // Count IPG
                suspend_thread();
                timeout_counter--;
                if (timeout_counter == 0)
                    error("Timed out because of inactivity");
            }
            packet_reception_thread = busy_state;
            display("Receiving data on the interface");
            while ((this_intf.$transmit_data_valid  === 1'b1) {
                data_from_port[index++]=this_intf.$transmit_data;
                @(posedge this_intf.$clock);
                timeout_counter--;
                if (timeout_counter == 0)
                    error("Timed out because of inactivity");
            } // done with stimulus reception
            display("Done receiving data on the interface");
            packet_reception_thread = done_state;
```

```
}
{
    // Let's read from the message queue,
    // the packet are we supposed to receive
    mailbox_reading_thread = init_state;

    // possible_retry can be used to make sure
    // we do not loose the packet in the message queue
    // in case of a retry during transmission
    // retry case is not shown here
    if (possible_retry == 0) {
        display("Polling message_queue");
        mailbox_status = mailbox_get(WAIT, message_mailbox,
                message_from_sender);
        // Unpack the packet using the
        // packet_expected methods
        display("Read a message from the queue");
    }
    mailbox_reading_thread = done_state;
}
join any

// Figure out which threads are alive
if (mailbox_reading_thread == done_state) {
    // We are waiting for reception
    if (message_from_sender.check(done)) {
        // We are done monitoring
        display("Terminating as no more packets are expected");
        terminate;   // Terminate packet reception thread
        analyze_response = 1;
        return;
    }
    if (packet_reception_thread == init_state) {
        // We silently dropped the packet !
        terminate;   // Terminate packet reception thread
        // Add silent drop conditions here
        // Was there a FIFO over run ?
        if (message_from_sender.check(over_run)) {
            // There was a FIFO over run.
            // So Packet drop is acceptible
            analyze_response = 0;
            return;
        }
        else {
            error("Unexpected packet drop");
            analyze_response = 1;
            return;
        }
    }
    if (packet_reception_thread == busy_state) {
        // We are in the process of reception.
        // Wait for the reception to complete
        while (packet_reception_thread == busy_state) {
```

The Art of Verification with Vera

```
                    @(posedge this_intf.$clock);
                }// Wait a clock cycle
        }
    }
    else if (packet_reception_thread == done_state &&
            mailbox_reading_thread == init_state) {
        // We got something unexpected
        terminate;
        error("Unexpected Packet seen at the host interface");
    }

    // copy the packet, so we can later unpack on top of it
    // this will allow us the unpack the stimulus
    // with the correct unpack method
    packet_received = new message_from_sender.packet_sent;
    mii_packet.packet = packet_received;

    // always corrupt the packet copied so
    // incase there is nothing to unpack
    // (which means a dropped packet), it will be detected
    packet_received.crc = 1'bx;

    // Now  we have the right methods available, so unpack
    void = mii_packet.unpack(data_from_port,offset,left,right);

    //
    // Packet comparison starts here
    //

    // First look for IPG violations
    if (elapsed_ipg < ipg.programmed_value) {
        // An IPG violation occured so terminate
        sprintf(message,
                "Detected an IPG violation",
                "programmed %d seen %d",
                ipg.programmed_value,
                elapsed_ipg);
        display(message);
        analyze_response = 1;
        return;
    }
    // No IPG violations, good!

    // Start packet comparion
    if (packet_received.compare_packets(
            message_from_sender.packet_sent) {
        // We have a packet mismatch.
        // Mismatch has been displayed by the
        // compare_packet routine

        // Why do we have a mismatch ?
        // Was there a FIFO over run ?
        if (message_from_sender.check(over_run)) {
```

```
                        // There was a FIFO over run.
                        // So Packet drop is acceptible
                        analyze_response = 0;
                        return;
                    }
                    // There was no FIFO over run.

                    // Was it a bad packet to start with?
                    packet_received = message_from_sender.packet_sent;
                    if (packet_received.revalidate_packet()) {
                        // It was a good packet, but the DUT corrupted it
                        // Definately an Error
                        error("Packet mismatch\n");
                        analyze_response = 1;
                        return;
                    }
                    else {
                        // It was a bad packet, so mismatches are acceptible
                        analyze_response = 0;
                        return;
                    }
                }
                else {
                    // Packet comparison was clean
                    display("Packet received successfully");
                    analyze_response = 0;
                    return;
                }
            }
        }
}
```

Instantiating the Monitors

The following code segment show how to instantiate (and thus use) the monitors developed in previous sections.

```
program mac_test {
    // start of top block
    PACKET  packet;
    gen_stim host_stim_gen;
    gen_stim mii_stim_gen;
    int tx_pkt_mbx;
    int rx_pkt_mbx;
    int he_mbx;
    int ne_mbx;
    int pe_mbx;
    int nul_mbx;

    string message;
```

```
bit en_err_pkts = 0;

// These are the variables used by the transactor
transactor_host host_transactor0;
transactor_host_fifo_overrun  host_transactor1;

transactor_mii  mii_transactor0;

monitor_mii mii_monitor0;
monitor_host host_monitor0;

// Semaphore_id variables
integer host_semaphore = 0;
integer mii_semaphore  = 0;

// Mailbox_id variables for the mailbox queues
integer host_to_mii_msg_queue;
integer mii_to_host_msg_queue;

// this is the semaphore resource used by the host transactors
host_semaphore =  alloc(SEMAPHORE,host_semaphore,1,1);
if (host_semaphore == 0) {
    my_display("Semaphore failed");
}

// this is the semaphore resource used by the MII transactors
mii_semaphore  =  alloc(SEMAPHORE,mii_semaphore,1,1);
if (mii_semaphore == 0) {
    my_display("Semaphore failed");
}

tx_pkt_mbx = alloc (MAILBOX,0,1);
rx_pkt_mbx = alloc (MAILBOX,0,1);
he_mbx = alloc (MAILBOX,0,1);
ne_mbx = alloc (MAILBOX,0,1);
pe_mbx = alloc (MAILBOX,0,1);
host_stim_gen= new (tx_pkt_mbx,
                nul_mbx, nul_mbx, he_mbx, HOST,28);
mii_stim_gen = new (rx_pkt_mbx,ne_mbx, pe_mbx, nul_mbx,MII,4);

// Allocation to the message queues
host_to_mii_msg_queue = alloc (MAILBOX,0,1);
mii_to_host_msg_queue = alloc (MAILBOX,0,1);

// instantiating the transactors
host_transactor0 = new ("host_transactor0", // Transactor name
        mac_host_tx_port,          // Port it connects to
        tx_pkt_mbx,                // Mailbox it gets the stimulus from
        host_semaphore,            // Semaphore used to arbitrate grants
        host_to_mii_msg_queue);    // Mailbox it logs transfers to

mii_transactor0 = new ("mii_transactor0",
        mac_mii_rx_port,
```

```
            rx_pkt_mbx,
            mii_semaphore,
            mii_to_host_msg_queue);

    // Instantiations of the monitors
    mii_monitor0 = new ("mii_monitor0",
            host_to_mii_msg_queue,
            mac_mii_tx_port);

    host_monitor0 = new ("host_monitor0",
            mii_to_host_msg_queue,
            mac_host_rx_port);

    // Reset the chip
    @1 mac_host_regfile_port.$reset = 1'b1;
    mac_host_regfile_port.$chip_enable   = 1'b1;
    @10 mac_host_regfile_port.$reset = 1'b0;
    @2  mac_host_regfile_port.$chip_enable   = 1'b1;

    // initialize all transactors
    host_transactor0.initialize();
    mii_transactor0.initialize();


    // Apply global reset and chip enable
    fork
    {
        host_transactor0.apply_stimulus();
        host_transactor0.display("done");
    }
    {
        mii_transactor0.apply_stimulus();
        mii_transactor0.display("done");
    }
    {
        mii_monitor0.start_monitoring();
    }
    {
        host_monitor0.start_monitoring();
    }
    join all

}   // end of program
```

Summary

In this chapter we discussed basic result checking techniques: golden files, reference models, and monitors. After that, a strategy to implement result checking in the MAC testbench was formulated, based on some of the result checking techniques initially discussed. Then we showed how to develop monitors for the MAC testbench. Each component of the monitor was discussed in detail, with an emphasis on code reuse.

The monitor example is a simple one, and more capabilities (like dealing with network exception) can be added later, by either extension or creation of derived classes. However, the example shows the basic framework of the monitor, clearly partitioning different aspects of the monitors, and thus is a good starting point.

CHAPTER 13

How Do I Know I Am Done?

The toughest question a verification engineer needs to answer is: How do I know I'm done? From a design flow perspective, this question can be rephrased as follows: How do I know we are ready to manufacture the first chip and test it in the engineering lab?

With nonrecurring engineering costs crossing a half-million dollars per chip per spin, and the turnaround time for each spin exceeding six weeks, these questions should not be taken lightly. When the large check is written, the entire team should be confident that the chip is going to work and that large sums of money are not being used to purchase malfunctioning chips. Furthermore, with ever-shrinking development cycles, it's imperative to minimize the number of chip spins.

So, how do you know you're done? Unfortunately, you can never answer this question conclusively. With today's complicated SoC designs, it is impossible to guarantee that you have subjected your design to every condition it could see once it has been fabricated and put into operation. The main goal of verification is to expose the design to as many unique conditions as possible within the allocated development cycle. Even with the best of intentions, the verification engineer can miss some troublesome conditions that result in bugs in the fabricated chip.

Fortunately, there are reasonable metrics that verification engineers can use to decide whether the design is ready to be tested in a lab. These metrics can be grouped under three main categories:

- The bug rate, which measures how rapidly bugs are found

- Coverage, which measures how much of the design has been verified

- Regressions, which periodically check previously verified functionality

Each of these topics is discussed below.

Bug Rate

Verification phases

The verification process has three phases:

- Bringing up the testbench and DUT

- Verifying basic test cases

- Verifying corner cases

In the first phase, the testbench resets the design and applies the most basic stimulus possible. For example, an Ethernet MAC bring-up environment begins by resetting the design and injecting a single packet on the host side. Next, the environment resets the chip and injects a single packet on the Ethernet side. Although a single packet flowing through the MAC is the simplest functionality for the MAC, passing these tests represents a major milestone for the MAC design and verification process.

Once the design has passed simple test cases in the bring-up environment, the basic test cases are attempted. For a full-duplex Ethernet MAC, for example, these tests involve continuous bidirectional traffic. Packet sizes are minimized, maximized, randomized, and set to any other value or mix of values deemed interesting.

The final phase of verification is the corner case testing. During this phase, the most complex test cases are applied. In the Ethernet MAC, for example, cases in which the MAC forces packet drop are explored—such cases include FIFO overflows and the occurrence of errors when the FIFO has two or more packets present. Because these test cases are the hardest to write and the bugs they find are the hardest to debug, this phase tends to be the longest of the three.

Tracking Bugs

Throughout the three verification phases, bugs should be carefully tracked so that a plot of bugs versus time can be constructed. Figure 13-1 shows the bug curve for a typical verification process. The portion of the bug curve generally associated with each verification phase is shown.

FIGURE 13-1   Bug Curve

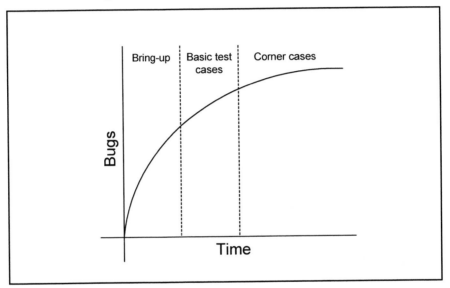

The bug curve asymptotically approaches a horizontal line

In the bring-up phase, bugs are found quickly because the basic functionality of the design is the easiest part to verify. For example, reset bugs are easy to find because they usually cause incorrect behavior with any input stimulus.

As the easy bugs are fixed, verification moves into the basic test cases phase and more complicated bugs are found. Because these bugs take longer to uncover and there are fewer of them, the bug rate decreases.

As verification continues into the corner cases phase, bugs get harder and harder to find and the bug rate continues to dip. Eventually, when verification is almost complete, the bug rate becomes zero. When the bug rate has been zero for a reasonable amount of time, the verification process might be considered complete.

Verification is not complete unless the bug rate is zero; however, a level bug curve does not necessarily mean the design is 100 percent functionally correct. New bugs cannot be found if new functionality is not being tested. It is possible, and probably likely, that another bug lurks somewhere in the design, waiting for the proper test case to reveal it.

Coverage

Generally, coverage refers to the portion of a design that has been successfully tested. Because there are many ways to look at the feature set of a design, there are many types of coverage. The most common types of coverage are

- Test plan coverage

- Code coverage

- Functional coverage

All three types of coverage are discussed below.

Test Plan Coverage

As its name implies, test plan coverage measures the number of passed tests specified in the test plan. Verification is not complete until 100 percent test plan coverage has been achieved. Less than 100 percent test plan coverage implies that identified test cases have either not been run or have not passed.

The operation of untested functionality can never be guaranteed. The underlying philosophy of the verification team should be: "If it isn't tested, it isn't working." Although this advice may seem overly pessimistic, the assumption that the easy functionality works has bitten countless verification teams.

As discussed in Chapter 2, there are three primary methods for generating a test plan, and a complete test plan utilizes all three methods. Using all three methods is not only important in test case generation, but it is also important in deciding when testing is complete. If test cases are missing, you get premature attainment of 100 percent test coverage. Remember, testing is only as comprehensive as the test plan.

Test cases applied to RTL may not be complete Of course, it is possible that even though the test plan is comprehensive, the test cases themselves, when applied to RTL, are not. In other words, the applied tests might not fully implement the test plan by taking into account every possible combination of events or sequences of events. Only the test case writer can eliminate this possibility, but with complex designs, it is impossible to guarantee that all required test cases have been applied.

Code Coverage

Code coverage helps uncover the absence of test cases in both the test plan and applied test cases. It automatically instruments the design under test to measure the amount of the code the tests exercise, and it generates reports. Code coverage does not know whether the design behaved correctly in response to a test case; it knows only which portions of the design were stimulated by the test case.

Code coverage is measured in many ways. The common methods are

- Block coverage

- Path coverage

- Expression coverage

- State transition coverage

The following sections present descriptions of these methods, the general advantages and disadvantages of code coverage, and a recommended usage of code coverage.

Block Coverage

Block coverage measures the coverage of Verilog blocks. In general, a Verilog block is anything that opens with a begin statement and closes with an end statement, or anything that can be expanded into multiple statements by the inclusion of begin/end delimiters.

For example, the following always block is a single block:

```
always @(posedge CLOCK) begin
    x = 1'b0;
    y = a & b;
end
```

Blocks can be nested in blocks. For example, the following always block is really three blocks. The first is the always block itself. The second is the block executed when the if statement is true, and the third is the block executed when the if statement is false. Note that the third block is a single program statement.

```
always @(posedge CLOCK) begin
    if (my_var) begin
        x[0] = b & c;
        x[1] = b ^ c;
    end
    else
        x[1:0] = 2'b0;
end
```

Many constructs have multiple blocks. For example, each case item within a case statement is a block.

In general, assign statements are not considered blocks. They are not allowed within always blocks, or in blocks other than the begin/end delimiters of a module. Although assign statements are not covered by block coverage, they are covered by expression coverage.

Block coverage usually reveals state coverage

Because state machines are typically coded as case statements, with each case item being a unique state, state machine state coverage is usually revealed by block coverage. Some code coverage tools, however, have state machine extraction, so that state coverage can be tracked separately, regardless of how the state machine is coded.

Block coverage usefulness depends on coding style

The usefulness of block coverage is extremely dependent on block coding styles. If assign statements are the primary code statement and synchronous logic is always written as always @(posedge CLOCK), block coverage does not reveal interesting data. Assign statements are not measured, and as long as CLOCK is toggling, every block will be covered.

However, if other statements, such as if statements and case statements, are used, block coverage can reveal whether features have been left untested. In the code segment above, for example, block coverage would reveal whether my_var has been in one state or both. However, it would not reveal whether all possible combinations of the inputs of the blocks, b and c, have happened; it would only reveal whether both sides of the if statement have executed.

Complete block coverage

Because block coverage is the coarsest-grained coverage measurement, a design is not fully verified unless it has complete block coverage. If block coverage is not 100 percent, either large pieces of the design have been missed in verification or the design has unreachable blocks. Unreachable blocks can be removed, which not only helps bring block coverage to 100 percent but also saves real estate on the fabricated chip. Of course, if the unreachable blocks exist for debugging purposes, the blocks shouldn't be removed, and they can be excluded from the calculation of block coverage.

Path Coverage

Path coverage is an extension of block coverage. It monitors the progression of execution through blocks that implement decision trees. For example, the code presented above has two paths, one through the always block and the positive block of the if statement, and another through the always block and the negative block of the if statement.

If there are nested conditional statements within blocks, path coverage determines all possible paths through the logic and measures the coverage of those paths in the simulations run.

Advantages and limitations of path coverage

Path coverage goes one step beyond block coverage in identifying whether features have been tried. Sometimes, independent paths through logic describe multiple features. Therefore, the path coverage report is a useful addition to the block coverage report.

Like block coverage, path coverage is extremely dependent on block coding styles. It does not find paths through assign statements, and paths present for debugging purposes need to be excluded from the coverage report. Finally, large blocks with many conditional statements can create path explosion.

Expression Coverage

As you saw in Chapter 4, expressions are combinations of variables, numbers, and operators that have a numerical result.

Expression coverage measures the combinations of input variables to which expressions have been exposed. For example, in a simple two-input AND statement, expression coverage measures whether the two inputs have been in all four possible combinations.

More complicated expressions are broken down into their components. For example, an AND-OR tree is first broken into its top-level OR expressions. The AND expressions that make up the top-level OR expressions are then analyzed for their individual expressions. This process repeats until the leaf AND, OR, and XOR operations are found. These leaf operations can have multiple inputs, but they are always basic AND, OR, or XOR terms.

The code deconstruction below shows how an AND-OR expression is broken down into simple operations that are measured individually. Data is collected for the progressive deconstructions that are shown on every line. Some code coverage tools have options that specify for how many levels reduction data should be collected, and some collect data only for the top-level expression or for the full deconstruction.

```
x = (((a && b) || c)  || (d && e && f));// top level of expression
    (    expr1   )  || (   expr2   )  // 2 input OR
    ((expr3 ) || c)                    // 2 input OR
    (a && b)                           // leaf 2 input AND
                       (d && e && f)  // leaf 3 input AND
```

Advantages and limitations of expression coverage

Expression coverage is independent of coding style because expressions are found in most statements. The right-hand side of an assign statement is an expression, as is the conditional statement in an if statement and a case statement.

Expression coverage is the most useful code coverage described in this book so far for determining whether all features have been tested. Most features, though not all, can be found in a design by examination of the expressions. For example, the generation of x above is described by the function of its input values a, b, c, d, e, and f expressed above. If the input variables are generated in an expression, they too will have expression data collected.

Complex expressions, or even relatively simple arithmetic operations, can lead to expression coverage explosion, especially if expression coverage is collected at all levels of expression deconstruction. For this reason, it can be very hard to achieve 100 percent expression coverage.

Unfortunately, code coverage tools collect data for all expressions separately. Sometimes the features of the design are expressed by the combination of two or more expressions. In these cases, expression coverage misses features that should be covered. However, expression coverage is much more complete than block or path coverage.

State Transition Coverage

State transition coverage, also called state machine arc coverage, first extracts the state machines from the RTL. Because state machines have many coding styles, some code coverage tools do a good job of state machine extraction while others need to be aided by directives embedded in the code.

Once the state machines are found, their possible states are discovered and the specified state transitions or arcs are extracted. Sometimes, the static extraction of state machines helps find bugs because the bubble diagrams produced by the coverage tool reveal extra or missing arcs. The tool then collects the state transitions seen in simulation, revealing the absence of transitions, which implies missing test cases.

Advantages and limitations of state transition coverage

State transition coverage is an excellent tool for discovering whether state machines have been fully explored. Quite commonly, state machines are the most complicated part of a design. Therefore, covering them fully is extremely important.

Most code coverage tools measure only the arcs of each individual state machine. Unfortunately, the interactions of state machines are even more complicated than the individual state machines, and those interactions cause the most obscure bugs.

Some tools have attempted to tackle this difficult issue, but the combinations of state machines explode exponentially, and most of the combinations are uninteresting because most state machines are unrelated to each other. Unfortunately, it is difficult for the code coverage tools to determine the relationships between state machines, so they either extract too much information or not enough. Either way, the resulting report isn't very useful. When most extracted data is uninteresting, the interesting nuggets get lost, but erring on the side of not providing enough information is worse.

Advantages & Limitations of Code Coverage

Unbiased measurement

The primary advantage of code coverage is that it provides an unbiased way to measure the amount of the design code exercised by the test cases. At worst, this automatic measurement reassures the verification team that the design has been covered. At best, this measurement shows the design and verification teams what has not been fully tested.

Provides insight

Besides showing how much of the design remains to be tested, the coverage report gives further insight into the test cases run. It is common for a coverage report to reveal that the design behaved differently than expected in response to a test case. This can happen for a couple of reasons: The test case didn't hit the case it was intended to, or the intended case didn't actually stimulate the expected logic. At this point, either a new test case must be written, or further insight into the design is gained. Either way, the coverage report is a big help to the verification team, because it helps ensure complete coverage and complete understanding of the design.

Unreachable logic exposed

Another advantage of code coverage is also a disadvantage: It exposes unreachable logic. If the logic is truly unreachable, no possible test case can hit it, and it can safely be assumed that the logic is a waste of real estate on the chip. However, sometimes unreachable code is not unreachable logic. It is common, purely for debugging purposes, to put into the design assertion statements that are never synthesized. If they are there simply for early detection of bugs, such as default statements in fully specified case statements, they should always be uncovered. These unreachable blocks are not a design or verification problem; rather, they are a useful tool for design and verification. The limitation with code coverage tools, then, is that the known unreachable portions of code need to be excluded. With aggressive use of debugging lines in the RTL, which is highly recommended, this elimination process can be tedious.

The problem can be even worse at the chip level, where some features may not be tested because they are fully explored at the unit level. Those untested features will show up as uncovered code, and they also need to be ignored. When the known untested areas are added to the debug-only uncovered areas, finding the interesting parts of the coverage report can be difficult. On the flip side, excluding them all from the coverage report takes a lot of time.

Simulation performance hit

Because code coverage instruments the design and collects its data during simulation, it slows down simulation significantly. Some tools incur large startup overhead, but then reduce the speed impact as simulation progresses. Even with these more advanced tools, the simulation overhead is significant, anywhere from 33 percent to 200 percent. This performance reduction is enough that code coverage tools should not be run with every simulation during the verification process. Rather, they should either be used once the verification team believes that it has covered the entire design, or periodically to measure the ongoing progress of the verification effort.

Code structures do not express all features

Code coverage measures only automatically extractable code structures. Not all design features are expressible in this manner. In a processor, for example, coverage of blocks, paths, state transitions, and expressions should reveal whether all instructions have been executed. Each individual instruction should have some amount of code attributable to it, whether it is in a block, an expression, or a state transition. However, code coverage cannot tell you whether all sequences of instructions have been executed, because the sequences do not necessarily have unique logic assigned to them.

Code coverage cannot find missing logic

Code coverage shows only that coverage of existing code is missing; it cannot show that the design is missing code. Only a test case with the correct stimulus to induce incorrect behavior in the design can find that logic is missing. Therefore, 100 percent code coverage is required for complete coverage, but that by itself does not insure complete design coverage.

Recommended Usage of Code Coverage

Use code coverage, but use other tools too

Code coverage is recommended for showing there are no holes in the verification, but it is not recommended as the sole gating criterion for chip fabrication. The following sections discuss other criteria that should be used in conjunction with code coverage when deciding if a chip is ready for fabrication.

Block-level code coverage is usually sufficient

If individual blocks are well tested at the unit level, code coverage at the unit level is sufficient. Because unit-level environments are more controllable, all features of a unit are easily tested at the unit level, but some features are not easily testable at the full-chip level. If features are not tested at the full-chip level, the full-chip coverage report will reveal plenty of uncovered RTL because of the known omissions, and these false negatives will obscure the true negatives. In such cases, unit-level coverage reports provide a better indication of the coverage of blocks.

If verification of all features is expected to take place at the chip level and not at the unit level, code coverage should be run at the chip level, not at the unit level. A good approach is to combine the coverage reports from the most complete environments available but not necessarily run code coverage everywhere.

Summary—Code Coverage

The types of code coverage are summarized in Table 13-1.

TABLE 13-1   Code Coverage Summary

Type of Code Coverage	Constructs Instrumented	Examples
Block	Begin/end blocks	The true and false clauses of if statements. Case items in case statements.
Path	Paths through decision trees	The paths through nested if statements or nested case statements.
Expression	Inputs of expressions	Inputs of AND, OR, and XOR expressions.
State transition	State machine state transitions	Sequential combinations of state machine states.

The benefits of code coverage include the following:

- It measures test case coverage in the existing logic.

- It shows whether test cases stimulate the logic in the expected manner.

The limitations of code coverage include the following:

- It cannot uncover missing logic.

- It cannot extract and measure every feature or combination of features in a design.

- It cannot determine whether a design behaves correctly.

Code coverage is a necessary tool for checking the existing verification, but it is not sufficient to prove comprehensive coverage.

Functional Coverage

As you have seen, code coverage has limitations. Because it is automatically extracted from the RTL, it may not be able to decipher whether all design features have been tried, since not all design features are automatically extractable from blocks, paths, expressions, or state transitions.

These harder-to-extract design features usually describe a stimulus sequence, transaction, or sequence of transactions. For example, in an Ethernet MAC, harder-to-extract transactions include packet reception and packet transmission, which can be subdivided into interesting transactions, such as their occurrences with different source and destination addresses, with different packet sizes, and with or without collisions.

The same transactions are present in an Ethernet switch, although the switch has an additional transaction, the forwarding decision. Again, the forwarding decision can be subdivided into many interesting transactions, including forwarding decisions made to destination addresses which may or may not already be mapped in the forwarding table.

Functional coverage picks up where code coverage ends and measures the coverage of these harder-to-extract design features. To implement functional coverage, the verification team writes tools that monitor the relevant portions of the design, and then the team analyzes the coverage of these design features.

For example, when verifying a processor pipeline, the interesting functional coverage is the sequences of instructions seen. If a particular sequence has not been seen, a missing data hazard and bypass case could have been overlooked. Therefore, the sequences of instructions are analyzed for missing combinations. In this example, an interesting aspect of the coverage is the number of consecutive instructions to analyze. The length of the interesting sequences can be determined by measuring the maximum depth of the instruction pipeline.

Functional coverage is a manual process

Unfortunately, code coverage tools do not automatically extract functional coverage. Some tools, such as the Vera coverage facility, automate the collection of functional coverage statistics as much as possible, but an engineer still has to specify how to detect the occurrence of the relevant design features.

Use code coverage tools first

Because functional coverage is a manual process, use code coverage tools first and augment those results with functional coverage analysis. When code coverage tools provide functional coverage, use that information. Then write functional coverage tools to fill the holes.

Wait until the verification team believes that verification is nearly complete or until code coverage reports show nearly complete coverage before beginning functional coverage. If test plan or code coverage reports show the basics are not covered, harder-to-extract design features definitely will not be covered. Furthermore, once code coverage is complete, it is easier to determine what design features need additional measurement.

Functional coverage enhances code coverage

Although functional coverage is a great tool for enhancing code coverage reports, it is still only as good as the analyzed design features and test cases used to stimulate those design features. Therefore, designs cannot be considered fully covered even if functional coverage and code coverage show they are fully covered. Even so, 100 percent functional coverage and 100 percent code coverage are important considerations in answering the "Am I done yet?" question.

Regressions

A regression is a suite of passed tests that is rerun on a periodic basis. When a regression shows that previously passed tests have failed, it either proves that previously working functionality has broken or that a test case has not been updated for a redefined feature. Either way, a failing regression shows that the combined design and verification environment has taken a step backward.

Failing regressions are common

As design and verification progress, failing regressions are common. Regressions fail because

- New functionality breaks existing features

- Bug fixes break related features

- Timing fixes break associated features

- Tests are not updated for changing design specifications

For these reasons, regressions are useful for monitoring the health of the combined design and verification environment.

The Regression List

Ideally, tests are added to the regression list as soon as they are finished. (A finished test is one that stimulates all intended functionality and passes.) Adding finished tests to the regression sooner provides earlier feedback about the stability of the design and also prevents the inadvertent omission of the test from the regression list. Just as verification is only as good as the test cases tried, the regression is only as good as the tests it includes.

Regression list documents the completion of the test plan

The regression list is not just useful for ensuring that the design stays functional; it is also useful for tracking the completion of tests and therefore for deciding when verification is complete. When all tests in the test plan have been passed in the regression, the test plan is complete and verification may be complete. Of course, a fully populated, passed regression is not a guarantee that verification is complete, because some tests might still be missing.

The Frequency of Regressions

Regressions should be run often so fixes can be made quickly

Regardless of why previously passing tests now fail, it is best to learn about design changes early so the bugs they cause can be fixed right away. If regressions are run often, any design change that causes a failure can be pinpointed as having been made between the previously passed regression and the newly failed regression.

It is easier to figure out what has gone wrong when the list of changes is small. Remember, tests are not added to the regression until they pass. Therefore, when designs fail regressions, they fail for unforeseen reasons. It can be difficult to debug these problems in an environment that includes many modifications to investigate; it helps to have a smaller list of suspects.

Automatic nightly regressions are best

Ideally, regressions are run automatically every night, starting relatively early in the verification process, so that daily design changes are automatically subjected to known good tests. This prevents surprises later. The design and verification teams will find out the next morning if a design change has caused an old test to fail, and it will still be fresh in the designer's mind why that change was necessary. It is easier to fix the new problem at this point than later, when the rationale behind the original change is a distant memory.

Automatic regressions are better than manual regressions, because they allow the verification team to focus on new tests while tools continue to run the old tests in the background. The design and verification teams need to look at regression results only in case of failure, and they can sleep easily, knowing that their daily changes are being checked by the nightly regressions.

Multiscoped Regressions

Unfortunately, all tests cannot be run every night. Because the full diagnostic suite for a complex SoC design is large, a complete set of tests can take days or longer to finish. To produce useful results every morning, the set of diagnostics should be split into multiple overlapping regression lists. There are many ways to split up multiscoped regressions, one of which produces a nightly regression list and a weekly regression list. This approach is described in the following paragraphs.

Nightly regressions

As the name implies, nightly regressions are run every night so the teams can get quick feedback. Tests that gather the most coverage in the shortest amount of time should be carefully selected for the nightly regression, so that the morning results are as complete as possible. Code coverage tools can be used to help assess the coverage of the chosen tests. The test plan coverage of the tests can also be used to generate the list of tests for the nightly regression.

The length of time available for nightly regressions is determined by the excess nightly CPU time. Regressions are not normally run during the day, because sufficient excess CPU time is rarely available then. However, if excess CPU time *is* available, there is no reason why the nightly regressions cannot be renamed daily regressions and run during the day, as well as overnight. Regardless of the available CPU time, the goal in nightly or daily regressions is to maximize the coverage obtained in the limited time available.

Weekly regressions

Weekly regressions are run every weekend. They contain diagnostics that garner the highest level of design coverage at that point in the verification process. This list can be made up of every passed test written, but redundancies, if present, can be excluded. After verification is complete, the weekly regression list achieves full coverage as measured by all methods: code coverage, functional coverage, and test plan coverage. In fact, the weekly regression list can be used to collect the coverage data with the code coverage tools. Therefore, the weekly regression list is used to measure the progress of the verification process.

If tests needed to gain full coverage take more than a weekend of spare CPU cycles, another level of granularity, such as monthly regressions, can be added. Weekly regressions then become a more complete check of all the changes made during the week, while the monthly regressions measure the completion of the verification process.

Constructing the nightly and weekly regression lists
Normally, the nightly regression list is constructed first. As tests are finished, they are added to the nightly regression list until the nightly regression takes too long to complete. At that point, the coverage of tests in the nightly regression is evaluated and redundant tests are moved to the weekly list. As more tests are finished, they are placed on one of the two regression lists. If adding new tests means that the nightly list now takes too long, other tests are removed from the nightly list to adjust its duration. Again, the goal is to maximize the coverage obtained during the nightly regression.

Regressibility

To be automatically regressible, a test needs to be self-checking and reproducible. Clearly, if tests are not self-checking, an automatic regression tool cannot be written to collect their pass/fail status, which means that automatic results cannot be generated. The reproducible component of tests really applies to tests outside of regressions as well; what good is a failed test if it cannot be rerun to verify a fix?

The Regression Script

The automatic regression tool, usually called the regression script, implements all the features discussed here and a few more. Specifically, it

- Takes a snapshot of the design and verification databases

- Builds all necessary simulation models

- Launches all tests

- Checks the results of all the tests

- Cleans up by removing unneeded files

Each of these processes is discussed below.

Taking a Snapshot of the Database

The regression script first asks the revision control system for a fresh, new snapshot of the design and verification databases. A discussion of revision control systems and their usage is beyond the scope of this book, but a snapshot of the database at a predetermined time is best. This allows the design and verification teams to know by when their daily changes must be checked in if they are to be included in that night's regressions. Generally, they shouldn't check in changes just before the snapshot time if they know the changes will break the regression.

Building Simulation Models

Second, if a simulator with separate compile and simulate phases is used, the regression script builds the simulation models required for the regressions. The script should be configured to know where and how to build these executables. Clearly, this task is easier if there is a standard way to build simulation models, but the script build commands can also be configured on a per-model basis. If many simulation models exist, building them in parallel can save time.

Launching Tests

Third, tests associated with each simulation model are launched according to the regression list. Again, the task is easier if there is a standard way to launch tests, but if necessary, the script can issue different simulation commands for each test or model. If plusargs are used to configure tests, their configurations are stored in the regression list so that they can be applied appropriately. If preprocessors and postprocessors are required for a test, they need to be started by the regression script as well.

Running tests in parallel

Because most regression time is spent running tests, the task duration can be shortened dramatically if tests are launched in parallel on multiple CPUs. The regression script can manage the parallel processes itself, or it can utilize any number of workload-sharing tools on the free or commercial market. A full discussion of workload sharing is beyond the scope of this book, but it is an important part of the regression environment and someone skilled in systems management should take responsibility for its implementation.

Determining Pass/Fail Status

Fourth, as tests finish, their log files are parsed to make the pass/fail determination. Any number of events can cause a design to fail a test, including

- Error messages in the log file

- Truncated or nonexistent log files, which can indicate that the simulation ended prematurely or the disk became full

- Bad return codes by simulation scripts, workload sharing tools, or the simulator

Standardizing error messages greatly helps the regression script generate a useful summary. Again, the regression script could be configured to understand every error message format used by the team, but in this case, it is difficult for the script to catch all errors. It is easier for the script if the team standardizes on a couple of error message formats.

Alternatively, the regression script can simply execute a user-written script, which is then trusted to do everything required to run a given test and determine whether the design passed or failed that test. The result code of the user-written script tells the regression script whether to pass or fail the design.

However the regression script makes the pass/fail determination, the decision process should be well debugged. Regressions are not useful if failures are not detected. When this happens, the team receive a false and dangerous sense of security, and a badly broken design might make it to production. Alternatively, if passing designs are marked as having failed, a lot of debugging time is wasted. Although extra debugging time is less of a problem than overlooking failing tests, the team definitely has better things to do with its time.

Tabulating Results

After all tests are finished, or while tests are finishing, the results are tabulated in a convenient location. E-mailing the results to the team is helpful, since no one has to remember to check the regression results.

Hopefully, the design passed all tests and the regression script computes the number of passed tests in its report. If the design failed some tests, the regression script tallies the failed tests and, if possible, tells why they failed. It also provides a pointer to the files used by or created by the failed tests so that further debugging can take place. With this information, failing tests can be rerun to verify subsequent fixes.

Cleaning Up

Finally, because the regression process generates many large files, the script does its best to clean up after itself. Nothing related to failed tests should be removed, but log files generated by passed tests and simulation executables that had no failed tests can be deleted. Other temporary files generated by the build or simulate process can also be removed.

Running Randoms During Regressions

The regression facility also has an advanced use: running randoms. The best implementation of both randoms and regressions involves running many self-checking tests in parallel. In fact, the test input parameters are the only major difference between running a regression as described above and running randoms. If randoms are being run, the input parameters, including the random seed, should be changed with every invocation of the tests. The regression script is easy to augment to incorporate this facility.

Regression Summary

Regressions are suites of passing tests rerun periodically to ensure that the design and verification environment remains functional. The environment can break for many reasons, including the addition of new bugs to previously tested functionality. It is best to receive feedback about broken environments quickly so that they can be fixed more easily, but engineers should spend time writing new tests rather than continuously running old ones. For these reasons, regressions are best run automatically every night. Unfortunately, tests for an SoC design would never finish in one night, so regressions are often split into nightly regressions and weekly regressions. The nightly regression list is picked carefully so the highest amount of coverage is obtained in the time available every night.

Summary

"How do I know I'm done?" is the hardest question to answer in verification. If the following events have happened, there is a good chance that verification is complete:

- The test plans have been revisited to ensure they are comprehensive.

- The test cases have implemented all the test cases in the test plan.

- The bug rate has been zero for a reasonable period of time.

- Code coverage shows complete block, path, expression, and state transition coverage.

- Functional coverage shows complete coverage of harder-to-extract design features.

- Regressions show that all test cases are passing.

All of the metrics above rely on the assumption that test cases are comprehensive. For this reason, the test cases should be revisited one more time, and if the engineers cannot find any more test cases to try, verification can move into the lab with fabricated chips.

CHAPTER 14

Debugging

When tests fail, how do you go about debugging the problem? Unfortunately, there is no simple answer, since the problem can be in numerous places: in the generators, the transactors, the monitors, or the DUT. For today's large SoC designs, each of these components requires hundreds or thousands of lines of complex code. Finding bugs in these large components is a daunting challenge and consumes a lot of time during the verification process.

Fortunately, in addition to preventive programming (discussed on page 411), there are a several standard techniques that can help identify the location of problems as quickly as possible. These include

- Checking the simulation basics and looking for common problems

- Using printf( ) and $display( ) logging

- Using HDL (hardware description language) waveform viewers to see the values of HDL signals during simulation

- Using the Vera Debugger to see the values of Vera variables and the order of execution of Vera code during the simulation

The flowchart in Figure 14-1 shows how these techniques can be used. They are discussed in detail starting on page 417.

FIGURE 14-1   Debugging Flowchart

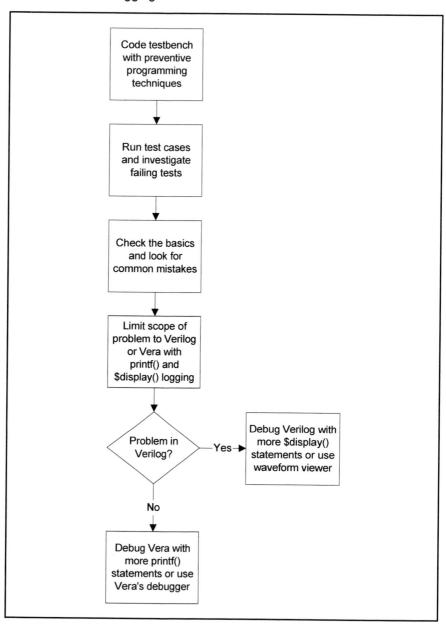

Preventive Programming

Obviously, the best way to debug a problem is to prevent it from happening in the first place. This isn't always possible, of course, but some coding styles and recommendations do help avoid bugs, or at least help you find bugs more quickly when they arise. These recommendations include

- Avoiding obfuscation
- Checking for invalid values
- Checking return codes
- Not relying on the order of execution of threads
- Trying complex computations in isolation first
- Using assertions liberally

These recommendations are discussed below.

Avoid Obfuscation

Obfuscated code can be defined as code whose intent cannot be discerned without significant effort. It is hard to debug obfuscated code because it is hard to determine what the code is doing and how it is trying to do it. If code is well documented, it is, by definition, not obfuscated.

Obfuscated code is the result of three practices:

- Using so many syntactic shortcuts that the intent of the code is hidden
- Using programming constructs for purposes for which they were not intended
- Creating large functions, tasks, or objects instead of modularizing them into smaller, easier-to-understand components

These are discussed below.

Obfuscation through Shortcuts

Syntactically, Vera is a clean language that does not lend itself to obfuscation through shortcuts. In contrast, pointers in C create ample opportunities for tricky shortcuts. Because Vera does not have C-style pointers, these possibilities are eliminated.

However, obfuscation through shortcuts is still possible in Vera. An example of this kind of obfuscation is the following:

```
result = ++q[index[++d]++];
```

Although this statement compiles and runs, predicting its behavior requires a detailed understanding of pre- and postincrement operators, operator precedence rules, and the order of execution of operators at the same precedence level. And though you may remember these rules while writing the code, it is unlikely that you will remember them well enough to decipher this statement some time later. It is also unlikely that other engineers looking at this code will understand it immediately. For both of these reasons, this code is obfuscated.

The intent of tricky code is always forgotten

Some engineers think they will always remember what their code is trying to do, regardless of how tricky they make it. In practice, though, the rule of thumb is as follows: The trickier the code, the higher the probability you will forget what it is doing. If you need to look at it a few years later, which is common, you will definitely have forgotten what it is doing, and debugging it will take far longer than necessary.

Obfuscation by Use of the Wrong Mechanism

When two or more Vera mechanisms have overlapping functionality, it's possible to choose the wrong mechanism. For example, events are meant for thread synchronization and ordering. As Chapter 6 showed, events can create a FIFO ordering of thread execution if the threads sync to an event with the HAND_SHAKE trigger type.

Semaphores can create the same result. A semaphore is allocated with a single key, and all threads wait for that key to be available. Because Vera grants access to semaphores in FIFO order, the threads execute in FIFO order.

Although both mechanisms get the job done, events are preferred because their purpose is, in fact, thread synchronization and ordering. This is what events were designed to do. When event code is debugged, it will be assumed, in this case correctly, that the goal of the code is synchronization. If that isn't enough of an indication for the debugging engineer, the code itself even states HAND_SHAKE.

Semaphores, on the other hand, are meant for a different purpose—arbitrating shared resources. In the case of thread ordering, the shared resource is the processor that executes the threads, but that's an unobvious use. In addition, the order in which threads gain access to the shared processor is not immediately obvious, since it is contained in the Vera implementation of semaphores and not explicit in the code itself. This creates two problems— first, that the intent of the code is obfuscated, since the debugging engineer could easily make the wrong assumption about what the semaphores are used for; and second, that the code itself would break if or when Vera changes the way semaphores are implemented.

Obfuscation through Nonmodular Code

It is difficult to comprehend functions, tasks, or objects when they try to accomplish too many things. Generally, it is easier both to understand and to maintain smaller, more modular code structures.

Therefore, if you find yourself confused about the functionality of large functions, tasks, or objects, eliminate their obfuscation by splitting them into multiple, independent constructs; in other words, modularize your code to make it more understandable.

Comment Your Code

If you insist on writing complicated or obfuscated code, comment it well so that the intent is known. Those comments will be huge time-savers when the inevitable debugging process commences.

In fact, keep in mind a more general form of this statement: Comment all of your code very well. If everything is well commented, nothing is obfuscated.

Check for Invalid Input Values

Make sure functions include checks for invalid input values. Although this may seem unnecessary, because you believe you will always call functions with valid values, invalid values do turn up. It is far easier to find out that a complex function was called with an invalid value than to have to figure out why its result is bad and backtrack through all of the code to its inputs.

For example, let's say that a single-port memory model contains the following inputs: an address, a chip select, a read or write selector, and the write data input bus. The memory model should make sure that the following conditions are always true:

- The chip select is never X.

- When the chip select is asserted, the read or write selector is not X.

- When the chip select is asserted, the address bus is not X.

- When the chip select is asserted, the address is within the allowable range.

- When the chip select is asserted and a write is selected, the input data bus is not X (if the designer of the block certifies that this condition should never arise).

Every condition except for the last one verifies that the behavior of the simulation matches the behavior of the synthesized logic. From the point of view of functional verification, Xs behave randomly as either 0s or 1s in synthesized logic, so they should be present only when ignored, which is verified by these conditions. The final condition is optional because designers sometimes write Xs into memory on purpose.

Check Return Codes

You should always check return codes that communicate the success or failure of a function. Sometimes the return codes tell you that you called a function with invalid inputs. At other times, return codes tell you that the function had a different problem. Either way, you want to know that the called function did not succeed, so that you won't rely on its results.

For example, when using mailbox_get( ) to retrieve an entry from a mailbox, a bad return code tells you that the specified mailbox ID does not exist or that no entry is available in the mailbox. Either way, you want to know that the mailbox did not dequeue an entry even though you expected it to. If you blindly use the entry you expected to get, an unknown value will be used instead, with unpredictable results.

Optionally check
return values
Sometimes you should check return values as well as success codes. Return values are the data results of an operation and do not necessarily include a function success or failure indication as described above; thus, they could be unpredictably invalid. Whenever invalid return values are possible, check them. It could save considerable debugging time later.

For example, associative arrays of bits or integers return X if the index accessed has not been written. If the associative array is expected to return a non-X value, checking the validity of the return value will prevent the invalid value from propagating through the testbench. The assoc_index( ) function can also be used to check the validity of an associative array index before it is used.

Do Not Rely on the Order of Thread Execution

Although the Vera thread scheduler is predictable in the current version of the program, you shouldn't rely on its predictability. For example, setting a variable in a producer thread and then expecting the variable to be valid right away in a consumer thread without explicit synchronization is asking for trouble. The situation is worse if the consumer thread modifies the variable and a third thread is expected to see the results right away, again without explicit synchronization.

Relying on the order of execution of threads may work, but it is a bad idea for three reasons. First, you are dealing with obfuscated code, because the assumption about the order of execution of threads is not specified in the code, but in the way Vera works. Second, future versions of the Vera scheduler might order the threads differently, which would break this code. Third, future code modifications might change the order of thread execution, which would also break your code.

This rule can be generalized as follows: Never rely on the order of execution of anything other than events, which specifically guarantee order.

For example, do not rely on the order in which threads receive access to semaphores. If you want threads to execute in a specific order, trigger events and sync to them in the order desired, or use the HAND_SHAKE trigger type to implement a FIFO ordering. Not only does this approach prevent obfuscated code, but it also will not break when Vera changes the order in which it schedules resources, or when you restructure code so that the unconstrained order of execution changes.

Try Complex Computations in Isolation First

You have already seen why design verification takes place at various levels in the design, such as at the block level and the chip level. The same arguments apply to complex verification environments. When a complex computation is programmed, it most likely has bugs. Make sure the computation works in isolation before placing it in a larger context.

For example, if your testbench includes a cyclic redundancy check (CRC) function, test the CRC function before including it in a larger testbench. It is much easier to test the CRC function in isolation, because the testbench constrains your ability to give the CRC function arbitrary input values, and it slows down the frequency of CRC computations. Furthermore, the larger environment contains other bug sources besides the CRC function. When you are debugging the larger environment, it is comforting to know that the CRC function works correctly and therefore can be assumed to be correct when the inevitable debugging of that environment commences.

Use Assertions Liberally

Recall that assertions are monitors that check for invariants, conditions that should be true regardless of the stimulus provided. They find bad behavior automatically, and also earlier than might otherwise be possible.

Because assertions eliminate a lot of debugging, you should use them whenever and wherever possible. Assertions are usually simple, so they are quick to program and have little impact on simulation speed. Because they can save huge amounts of debugging time, they are worth their small overhead.

For example, if a one-hot state machine has two state bits asserted, the design will be unpredictable. At the periphery of the design, something will eventually go wrong. If you first detect a problem at the periphery, you must first trace it back to the bad inputs to the one-hot state machine, and then continue tracing to its cause. Keep in mind that there can be long pipelines between the cause of the problem and the detection of the problem at the periphery. If an assertion tells you that the one-hot state machine is not one-hot, you can immediately eliminate part of the debugging trail.

The example task below checks, on every clock cycle, that a state vector of up to 32 bits has exactly 1 bit set. This task can be used to verify that all one-hot vectors in the environment are one-hot, including one-hot state vectors and one-hot arbitration grant signals.

```
task check_one_hot (bit[31:0] vect, integer num) {
    integer i, cnt;
    fork
    {
        while (1) {
            @(posedge CLOCK);
            cnt = 0;
            for (i=0; i<num; i++)
                cnt += vect[i];
            if (cnt !== 1)
                error ("State vector %h is not one hot!\n",
                       vect[num-1:0]);
        }
    } join none
}
```

DUT buses of up to 32 bits can be passed directly into check_one_hot( ) by referencing their interface and signal names. Signals within binds can also be passed in directly. For example,

```
check_one_hot (my_interface.four_bit_bus, 4);

check_out_hot (my_bind.$twenty_bit_bound_bus, 20);
```

The Debugging Process

If you have followed all of the debugging avoidance techniques and something still goes wrong, what do you do? This section examines the debugging process, which can be summarized as follows:

- Check the basics first.

- Generate debugging information to help limit the problem.

- If the problem appears to be in HDL, look at the HDL waves.

- If the problem appears to be in Vera code, use the Vera Debugger.

Check the Basics First

Although most of the basic problems will be flushed out early in the verification process, it is important to check all of them before digging deeper into the testbench, the DUT, and the algorithms they implement. The problems presented here are either improper configuration of the simulation environment or common Vera coding errors. In particular, check that

- The latest vshell is included in the simulation

- The Vera executable (the .vro) is up-to-date

- The correct .vro is loaded

- Interface signals and clocks are properly connected

- You have not made common Vera coding mistakes

The Latest vshell Should Be Included in the Simulation

Vera interfaces will not work unless the most recent vshell is included in the simulation because the vshell instantiates the Verilog/Vera communication described by Vera interfaces. If you are using a compiled simulator, make sure to recompile the simulation executable with the latest vshell. Similarly, make sure that interpreted simulators point to the correct vshell upon invocation.

Remember that the vshell does not change every time you change your Vera code. It changes whenever you change a global variable or an interface definition, but not when you change a virtual port or bind. Vera generates a new vshell automatically whenever it compiles Vera code into its .vro executable. Therefore, when you change a global variable or an interface definition, make sure to generate a new vshell by compiling your Vera code and then recompile your simulation executable, including the new vshell.

The .vro Should Be Up-to-Date

Although the vshell changes only when an interface is changed or a global variable is added, the Vera executable changes with every Vera code change. Make sure to recompile your Vera code before running your simulation. Otherwise, the simulation environment will not incorporate Vera code changes.

The Correct .vro Should Be Loaded

Make sure the correct Vera executable is loaded at simulation time. If you have different tests that compile into their own executables, you may be using the Vera multiple module support or you may be specifying a different executable with +vera_load= plusarg. Either way, make sure the simulation loads the correct executable by checking the file names and paths given to the runtime environment.

Signals and Their Clocks Should Be Connected

When signals are sampled from the DUT or driven into it, check that their interfaces are properly defined and that they are properly instantiated in the testbench through their ports and binds.

In the vshell, you can see which signals are connected, and if you look at the instantiated Verilog hierarchy, you can see if they are connected properly. Sometimes it is easiest just to generate a signal dump of the design and the vshell and visually check that the interface signals are connected properly. The signal dump also helps verify a related interface signal problem: signals stuck at a particular value.

Make sure to check the clocks associated with interface signals. They can be checked in exactly the same way as the other signals in the interface. In other words, the Verilog hierarchy or a signal dump of the vshell shows you where clocks are connected.

Also verify that the specified clocks are behaving as clocks. If an interface clock is not driven, it will never see clock edges, and synchronous signals bound to those clocks will hang, waiting for edges. Quite often the problem with hanging Vera code is interface clocks that remain at X or Z. Clocks remaining at a DC value of 0 or 1 also hang synchronous Vera signals.

Common Vera Coding Mistakes

Table 14-1 lists some of the common Vera coding mistakes. Before you spend time looking into a complex algorithm, make sure you didn't make one of these errors, all of which are easy to make and therefore extremely common.

TABLE 14-1   Common Vera Coding Mistakes

Common Mistake	Result or Example
Infinite loops, such as while(1) loops without a statement that blocks the execution of the thread	Simulation freezes.
"join any" constructs where an unexpected thread finishes first	Execution of the parent thread continues earlier than expected.
Improper use of equality or inequality operators, such as == vs. ===	Xs must match with === but are don't cares with ==.
Improper use of bitwise and logical operators	A[1:0] & B[1:0] is equivalent to {A[1] && B[1], A[0] && B[0]}, but A[1:0] && B[1:0] is equivalent to (A[1:0] > 0) && (B[1:0] > 0).
mailbox_get( ) that doesn't dequeue an entry and where the return code is not checked	An invalid mailbox entry is used.
Task and function name spaces that become interchanged because, when the task or function is invoked, a return value is obtained when it shouldn't be, or not obtained when it should be	Task is called instead of function, or vice versa.
Null values driven into the DUT when valid values are expected	The DUT behaves unpredictably.
Signal sample or drive timing that is mis-specified in the signal's interface definition	The signal is sampled or driven one cycle before or one cycle after expected.

Logging with printf() and $display()

Now that you know that the simulation basics are configured properly and that you have not made a common mistake, you need to obtain more information about the problem in order to isolate it. One of the easiest ways to obtain more information is to log the progress of the testbench via calls to printf( ).

Anything relevant to the problem should be added to a call to printf( ). For example, in an Ethernet switch, log the packets sent and the packets received. Log all the inputs into the generated packets. If decisions are made randomly, log the random distributions as well as the resulting decisions. All errors detected in the testbench should be logged as well.

Adding $display( ), the Verilog equivalent of printf( ), to the design also helps. For example, in an Ethernet switch, inputs to the forwarding engine and the reception of packets by the output block can be logged. All errors detected in the design should be logged as well.

Logging Time Stamps & Identifiers

No matter what portion of the design or testbench is being logged, it is almost always useful to include a time stamp with every log statement. Whenever the ordering of events is important, the time stamp identifies the ordering and pinpoints simultaneous events. Time stamps also help correlate the log file statements with events seen in waveform viewers and the Vera Debugger (both of which are discussed later in this chapter).

Identifiers are useful for log statements as well. They can identify the portions of the design that are relevant for the log statement; the function or task that generated the log statement; or a unique ID of the thread that generated the log statement. Regardless of what is being identified, the UNIX program grep can be used to search for that identifier, which helps tremendously when sorting through log files. In highly concurrent environments, for example, sorting statements by the thread that generated them can be necessary for debugging the thread that behaved incorrectly.

Multiple log files, instead of log statement identifiers, can be used to sort the debugging information. In this case, separate log files must be opened and maintained with fopen( ), fprintf( ), and fclose( ). It may be easier to use printf( ) with identifiers, because Vera automatically sends the output of printf( ) to both stdout and the default simulation log file. $display( ) automatically sends its output to stdout and the default simulation log file as well, so if you need debugging statements from both the Vera and Verilog worlds in one place, it is easier to use printf( ) and $display( ).

Logging Blocking Statements

In general, adding a printf( ) will not change the order of execution of threads, because a thread continues execution until a blocking statement is reached, and printf( ) by itself does not block the execution of a thread. However, it is possible to add signal samples to printf( ) that do block the execution of the thread until the sampling event named in the interface specification of the signal is reached.

For example, if the following printf( ) executes concurrently with the my_signal sampling event, the printf( ) finishes execution immediately. However, if the printf( ) executes at any other time, it waits for the my_signal sampling event before continuing execution.

```
printf ("my_signal is %h at time %d\n", my_interface.my_signal,
        get_time(LO);
```

If the signal sample in the printf( ) statement does block the execution of a thread, the threads execute in a different order than they would have without the addition of the printf( ). Moreover, because the blocking statement can be added in the middle of the thread, the assumption that the thread will execute uninterrupted until the next blocking statement ceases to be true; it executes until the new printf( ) is reached. Because this can change the behavior of concurrent threads, be careful when adding blocking statements to your logging statements.

Verbosity

Some intelligence needs to be used when figuring out what to log. If everything in the design is logged, it will be hard to find relevant information in the log file. Similarly, if not enough information is logged, required information may not be present.

One way around this problem is to use multiple verbosity levels. While logging, check a verbosity level and use that level to increase the logging detail. When a bug is found in a particular area, have everything possible in that area logged by setting the verbosity level to the most verbose mode. When an area is considered to be 100 percent correct, log at a lower verbosity level to capture only information that may be helpful for debugging other blocks.

Sometimes you may need to rerun a simulation with a higher verbosity level in order to log more detailed information. As long as designs are well tested before the verbosity level is lowered, this happens infrequently.

Verbosity level manipulation can occur in a postprocessor as well. In this situation, every log statement contains a verbosity flag. To view the log at different verbosity levels, you can either construct a simple viewer or extract the desired lines with grep. Either way, you do not need to rerun the simulation to change the viewed verbosity level.

The methods for changing verbosity levels, including those described above, are

- Runtime variable checks

- Compile-time preprocessor macro checks

- Logging with a verbosity flag and filtering with a postprocessing viewer

- Any combination of these methods

Custom Logging Task

Although printf( ) and $display( ) work very well for logging, a simple custom task can automate the repetitive aspects of logging. Such a task takes the string you want to be logged, an identifier, and a verbosity flag as inputs, automatically evaluates the verbosity flag, appends the current time stamp, the identifier, and the string to be logged, and then calls printf( ) or $display( ). Your testbench would call this custom task instead of printf( ) or $display( ) directly. Not only would this custom task standardize logging formats, but it would also make changing the standard logging format a simple matter of modifying one task. It also centralizes the code that controls verbosity levels. A sample custom logging task would look like the following:

```
task log (integer verbosity, (string id=default_log_id),
          string log_string) {
  string temp_string;
  if (verbosity <= verbosity_level) {
    sprintf (temp_string,"%s-%0d: %s\n",id, get_time(LO),log_string);
    printf ("%s", temp_string);
  }
}
```

The log( ) task can be made a global task as long as default_log_id and verbosity_level are made global variables.

If implemented as a class method, log( ) can provide even more automation. In this case, the default identifier, default_log_id, can be made a data member of the class and configured upon object instantiation. When log( ) is called from within the class, it automatically appends this instance specific identifier to the logged statement. Similarly, if verbosity_level is made a data member, each class can be configured with a different verbosity level.

Advantages & Limitations of Logging

There are many advantages to debugging by logging. First, logging slows down the simulation less than HDL signal dumping. Second, the logs can be formatted in any way that makes debugging faster. In other words, the information relevant to a transaction can be logged together, even if that information is accumulated from all over the testbench and the design. Third, the log files can be grepped, which makes it easier to follow transactions through the design than visually following the transactions over long periods of time in the signal waveforms.

Unfortunately, logging is a manual process, so you have to spend time figuring out what needs to be logged and deciding how to log it. This is usually not very difficult, although it does take time if a lot of information needs to be logged.

Example

As an example of how logging can help isolate the location of a bug, consider the reception of an unexpected packet in an Ethernet switch. A packet can be received unexpectedly if it was forwarded to the wrong port, if it was corrupted through the switch, or if the switch fabricated it.

To find out which error case occurred and thus where to begin the debugging process, first compare the unexpected packet to the packets found through all logging mechanisms.

If the packet is seen only by the output block and not by the input blocks, it was corrupted or fabricated. In this case, find the packet at the output block and trace it backward until its origin is found.

If the testbench injected the packet, then either the forwarding engine is broken or the testbench expected it on the wrong port. First check the testbench by analyzing the packet header and the state of the forwarding engine at the time the packet forwarding decision was made. If the testbench made the incorrect decision, fix it. Otherwise, follow the packet to the forwarding engine to see why the packet was misrouted.

Logging packets as they travel between blocks and all the state used to make forwarding decisions helps limit the focus in debugging to the area where the problem occurred.

HDL Waveform Viewers

HDL waveform viewers show the progression of all requested signals in the HDL hierarchy during the requested simulation times. They can show the progression of every signal in the entire HDL design during the entire simulation run, or a subset of the signals during specified simulation times.

Configuring signals and time frames for viewing is waveform-viewer-specific; see the documentation provided with your viewer for more details. Because they can quickly present the behavior of everything relevant to a DUT problem, waveform viewers are great for studying the behavior of DUT microarchitecture.

HDL waveform viewers have two methods of communicating with the HDL simulator to receive signal change information. The first is runtime communication. As HDL simulation progresses, the simulator sends change information to the viewer, and the viewer updates its display right away. The second method is through an intermediate file. The HDL simulator creates a waveform dump file, and the waveform viewer reads this file to create the display.

Use a waveform viewer when a DUT bug is suspected

If a DUT bug is suspected and a waveform viewer is not already enabled or the HDL signal dump does not already exist, enable your favorite viewer or enable the HDL dump and rerun the test case. If necessary, load the waveform dump into your favorite viewer and find the bug. The log files should give you a good starting place and time for tracking events in the design. Start where and when the first bad event was recognized or where and when related events occur. Keep tracking those events until the incorrect behavior is found.

A full discussion of the usage of waveform viewers is beyond the scope of this book, but note that although their interfaces vary quite a bit, they are usually intuitive to use. They contain a design hierarchy viewer that lets you add signals to the waveform window. Signals in the waveform window can be organized as you desire.

Source Code Integration

Some waveform viewers contain source code integration features. They have two windows, the familiar waveform window and an additional source code window. The source code window usually displays the source code hierarchically. It allows you to jump between signal drivers and loads simply by clicking on the signal names in the source code.

You can move signals into the waveform viewer window by dragging them from the source code window, and when a signal is dragged to the source code window from the waveform viewer window, the display in the source code window automatically moves to the driver of that signal. In addition, you can annotate the source code window with signal values at the time marked in the waveform window.

Although these enhancements sound quite simple, they are incredibly handy and save a lot of debugging time, because debugging is contained within a single, integrated environment.

Vera Globals Are in the vshell

Because Vera has limited waveform viewer integration, debugging complex interactions between the testbench and the design can be difficult. In general, you can see the design behavior in the waveform viewer and the testbench behavior in either the logs or the Vera Debugger.

However, you can see some Vera state in the waveform viewer. Any integer or register declared globally in the Vera program is automatically updated in the vshell. If the vshell is dumped, you can see the changes to the state of the global variables in the waveform viewer as well.

Clearly, the usefulness of seeing global variables in the waveform viewer is limited, because you usually want to see a variable declared inside an object. To see a lower-level variable in the Verilog waveform dump, you can declare a global variable of the proper type and size and update it anytime you change the variable you want to see. The Vera wait_var( ) function can be used to automate this process, as shown below.

```
// global variables can be seen in Verilog
// waveform viewers within the vshell
integer global_copy_of_var;
fork
{
    while (1) {
        // var_to_trace can be any integer or
        // bit variable in the program hierarchy,
        // although it is copied into an integer here.
        // Use object.another_object... notation where necessary.
        wait_var (var_to_trace);
        global_copy_of_var = var_to_trace;
    }
} join none
```

Although this is a lot of work for a limited benefit, it can be useful at times. Note that if you are using a compiled simulator, you need to recompile your simulation executable after Vera generates a new vshell with your newly declared global variable present.

Propagate Xs Whenever Possible

Although verification engineers cannot control the design style employed by DUT designers, they should recommend that the designers propagate Xs whenever possible because it speeds debugging and verification dramatically. When Xs are seen in a design in which correct behavior is expected, the Xs are telltale signs that a bug needs to be fixed. In an HDL waveform viewer, Xs are much easier to trace back to their origins than are incorrect 1s or 0s because they stand out in the waveform viewer. Additionally, some waveform viewers can trace the origin of Xs automatically.

Example

For example, consider a state machine with a one-hot state vector. If the outputs of the state machine are driven to X whenever the state vector is not one-hot, the Xs will be quickly detected and can be easily traced to the non-one-hot state vector in the state machine. However, if the outputs are not driven to X, they are driven to 0 or 1, which can mask the bug with the one-hot state vector. In the simulated case, the bug might be masked, but in another case, the bug might not be masked, causing incorrect behavior. As long as this second case is detected, the bug can be fixed, but recall that good verification is the art of accelerating the detection of bugs so they can be fixed sooner. Had those Xs shown up in the simulation the first time, the bug would have been fixed sooner.

Common places to propagate Xs

There are a few common places where Xs can be propagated, none of which affect synthesis:

- The default statement in case statements

- The output of memory models whenever an entry has not been initialized

- The output of memory models whenever the load enable is not asserted

If Xs result in bad behavior because of any of the above cases, there is a bug because the design has used bad data or control information. Quite commonly, the bug is simply that the design does not gate off the invalid information

Vera Debugger

Much as waveform viewers show the cycle-by-cycle progression of HDL simulation, the Vera source-level debugger shows the progression of Vera execution, code statement by code statement. The Vera Debugger is great for debugging the microarchitecture of Vera code.

As this chapter has discussed, it is possible to debug complex Vera code with print statements. However, the more complex the Vera environment, the more challenging debugging with print statements becomes. When to use print statements and when to use the Vera Debugger boils down to personal preference.

The Vera source-level debugger runs in parallel with simulation and presents the status of the Vera code by halting the simulation at user-specified breakpoints. A breakpoint can be set on any line of Vera code. If the breakpoint is associated with a multiply-instantiated code block, the breakpoint can be applied to all instances of the code block or only a single instance.

When the simulation is halted, the Debugger graphical user interface shows the current values of all requested variables and the status of all requested threads. The Debugger reveals which threads are blocked and why, which threads are scheduled for execution, which thread is currently running, and where execution will resume when the simulation is restarted.

While the simulation is stopped, you can add more breakpoints, add visibility into more variables and threads, modify the state of variables, or resume execution until the next breakpoint. Changing the values of variables allows for bug fix experimentation without altering the Vera code.

There are many methods for entering the Debugger the first time, including entering it at simulation time 0 with the +vera_debug_on_start plusarg or when a breakpoint statement in the Vera code is encountered. Once the Debugger is entered, you can add additional breakpoints and visibility into any desired variables and threads and resume the simulation. The Debugger then stops on the next breakpoint encountered.

Debugger Commands

Table 14-2 shows an overview of the commands supported by the Vera Debugger. Invoke commands by clicking on icons in the Debugger interface or by selecting the command from the pull-down menus. See the *VERA Graphical Debugger Guide* for more information.

TABLE 14-2   Debugger Commands

Command	Operation
Continue	Advances simulation to the next breakpoint or verification error
Stop Debugging	Closes the Debugger and terminates simulation
Break Debugging	Halts the Debugger
Run To Cursor	Advances simulation to the line of code at the current cursor location or to the next breakpoint
Break HDL Simulator	Halts the HDL simulator and presents the HDL simulator command line interface
Step (Any Context)	Advances simulation to the next executable Vera statement
Step Out	Advances simulation to the next breakpoint or to the end of the current context
Step Over (Same Context)	Advances simulation to the next breakpoint or to the next statement in the current context, skipping statements executed in other contexts
Step (Same Context)	Advances simulation to the next breakpoint or to the next statement in the current context, including statements in contexts called from or forked by the current context
Insert Breakpoint	Inserts an enabled breakpoint at the current cursor location
Delete Breakpoint	Deletes the breakpoint at the current cursor location
Enable Breakpoint	Enables the breakpoint at the current cursor location
Disable Breakpoint	Disables the breakpoint at the current cursor location
Insert Context Breakpoint	Inserts a context-sensitive enabled breakpoint at the current cursor location
Delete Context Breakpoint	Deletes the context-sensitive breakpoint at the current cursor location

TABLE 14-2   Debugger Commands (Continued)

Command	Operation
Enable Context Breakpoint	Enables the context-sensitive breakpoint at the current cursor location
Disable Context Breakpoint	Disables the context-sensitive breakpoint at the current cursor location
Delete All Breakpoints	Deletes all breakpoints
Enable All Breakpoints	Enables all breakpoints
Disable All Breakpoints	Disables all breakpoints
Add Break On Change	Halts simulation when the selected variable or expression changes value
Add Conditional Break	Halts simulation when the selected expression evaluates to True
Add Cycle Break	Halts simulation after a specified number of clock cycles of a specified clock
Add Watch	Adds the selected variable, expression, or object to the global watch window

The Debugger Screen

Figure 14-2 shows the Vera Debugger screen. Below the menu bar is a command bar where you can execute common commands by clicking on icons.

The project workspace window, below the command bar on the left, shows all contexts in the current environment and the currently active context. The project workspace window can also show the location and status of all breakpoints and the files used to implement the current environment.

The source window, below the command bar to the right, shows source code for the current Vera environment and the next line of code that will be executed when simulation resumes.

The global watch window, on the bottom left, shows variables, expressions, and objects from all contexts.

The local watch window, on the bottom in the middle, shows variables, expressions, and objects in the currently active context.

The datatype workspace window, on the bottom right, shows the status of semaphores, mailboxes, regions, and events.

The status bar at the bottom shows the current simulation time and cursor location.

FIGURE 14-2   Vera Debugger Screen

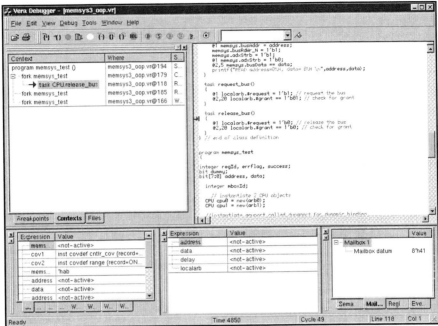

Debugger Strengths

When complex computations produce incorrect results, it is incredibly useful to see all the inputs to the computation and all the intermediate results generated before the final results emerge. With the strategic application of breakpoints, all of this data becomes visible in the Debugger.

In highly concurrent environments, it is useful to follow the execution of all threads to see how they depend on each other and therefore how they are misbehaving. For example, in the Debugger, it is easy to see the order in which threads receive access to a semaphore. If they utilize a resource or process data in an unexpected order, the resulting bugs become clear once the thread execution order is revealed.

Logging Versus HDL Waveforms Versus Vera Debugger

Although it is possible to debug every problem with logging, it is not necessarily efficient. Logging helps when tracking the macroarchitecture of a design and testbench, but it isn't necessarily efficient when tracking the microarchitecture of a design and testbench, since a large number of print statements is required and a large log file is generated.

As an alternative, HDL dumps give good visibility into the entire HDL design and ease the study of the microarchitecture of a design. Similarly, the Vera Debugger gives good visibility into the entire Vera testbench and eases study of the testbench microarchitecture.

Both HDL waveform viewers and the Vera Debugger have an additional advantage: their graphical user interface. Of course, there is overhead associated with graphical user interfaces. And while some people love graphical user interfaces, some people hate them.

Personal preference dictates the choice of logging versus viewing HDL waveforms and utilizing the Vera Debugger. Personal preference also dictates when to switch between these tools. If you like viewing text files or creating your own viewers, you should probably stay with logging. But if you spend too much time adding and maintaining log statements and verbosity levels, you may want to move to something else. If you like the interfaces provided by waveform viewers and the Vera Debugger, then you should probably start using them sooner rather than later in the process.

Simultaneous Waveform Viewing & Vera Debugging

Sometimes debugging cannot be isolated quickly to only the HDL environment or the Vera environment, and debugging requires simultaneous usage of both a waveform viewer and the Vera Debugger.

In this situation, a runtime waveform viewer might have advantages over a file-based waveform viewer, since the progression in the HDL and Vera worlds can be watched simultaneously. Furthermore, the values of Vera variables can be changed in the Vera Debugger and resulting modified signal drives can be seen right away. This process can continue with live updates in both the HDL and Vera worlds until the bug is discovered. Fortunately, this debugging setup is required infrequently, since printf( ) logging usually pinpoints a problem to either the HDL or Vera fairly easily.

Summary

Although debugging cannot be completely avoided, preventive programming can make it less frequent, and there are many techniques for easing the debugging process when it does occur.

When writing your testbench, make sure to check for common problems and make sure error messages are displayed when problems do arise. This shortens debugging time by pinpointing problems as early as possible.

When a problem does needs further study, first check the simulation basics. Make sure the latest testbench and vshell are included in the simulation and that the signals in your interfaces are properly connected. If the basics are not working correctly, nothing else will work properly.

When the basics check out, start collecting more information about the problem so that you can track it down. Logging, HDL waveform viewers, and the Vera Debugger are all tools that ease this process. Familiarize yourself with all three tools so that you can decide which you'd rather use for which types of bugs.

Index